Advance Praise for **Keeping the Promise**

"...This book addresses the crisis of democratic public education and public life in America. The authors focus on how dominant leadership models have failed schools and universities, and discuss the kind of democratic leadership needed in unsettling times in America [in order to] reclaim the notion of "the promise." In this case, the promise has to do with public education that levels the playing field rather than reproduces inequalities, that recognizes difference without "othering" it, and that establishes the condition for a democratic habitus. This book...provides a set of recommendations and analyses that [are essential] for those interested in progressive educational change, and in nurturing responsible, honest, and enlightened educational leadership in our schools and universities."

Carlos Alberto Torres, Professor, Social Sciences and Comparative Education;
Director, Paulo Freire Institute, University of California-Los Angeles

"It is not often recognized that school leadership was a central, explicit concern in the first graduate program in social foundations of education at Columbia Teachers College in the early 1940s. This book, more than any other I can think of, brings together social critique, democratic theory, and school leadership practice in ways that extend that original agenda. Each well-chosen chapter makes a valuable contribution to addressing the central questions posed by the editors: 'In an age when the democratic promise of public education is "at risk," what is the responsibility of educational leaders? To whom and for what are they responsible?' Every school leadership program in the nation should be addressing these tensions, and this volume is unique in its ability to help them do so."

Steve Tozer, Professor and Coordinator, Ed.D. Program
in Urban Educational Leadership, University of Illinois-Chicago

"...Up to this point, if I wanted my graduate students in educational leadership to learn about different conceptual and epistemological perspectives on education, I sent them to professors in curriculum and instruction. Now we have this outstanding collection of chapters, authored by scholars who cut across disciplinary boundaries, to help us rethink educational leadership in an age of accountability. Because notions of leadership should be of concern to all educators, regardless of position, this book should be required reading not only in every educational leadership program in the country, but in every education department. It moves beyond simplistic critiques of accountability and leadership, and deftly reveals the complexities of leadership in ways that will enrich students' conceptual thinking and push the bounds of their own research and practice."

Colleen Capper, Professor, Educational Leadership and Policy Analysis,
University of Wisconsin-Madison

Keeping the Promise

Studies in the
Postmodern Theory of Education

Joe L. Kincheloe and Shirley R. Steinberg
General Editors

Vol. 305

PETER LANG
New York • Washington, D.C./Baltimore • Bern
Frankfurt am Main • Berlin • Brussels • Vienna • Oxford

Keeping the Promise

Essays on Leadership, Democracy, and Education

Edited by
Dennis Carlson and C. P. Gause

PETER LANG
New York • Washington, D.C./Baltimore • Bern
Frankfurt am Main • Berlin • Brussels • Vienna • Oxford

Library of Congress Cataloging-in-Publication Data

Keeping the promise: essays on leadership, democracy, and education /
edited by Dennis Carlson, C.P. Gause.
p. cm. — (Counterpoints: studies in the postmodern theory
of education; v. 305)
Includes bibliographical references and index.
1. Educational leadership. 2. Postmodernism and education.
3. Democracy. I. Carlson, Dennis. II. Gause, C. P.
LB2805.K376 371.2—dc22 2006023355
ISBN 978-0-8204-8199-9 (paperback)
ISBN 978-0-8204-9729-7 (hardcover)
ISSN 1058-1634

Bibliographic information published by **Die Deutsche Bibliothek**.
Die Deutsche Bibliothek lists this publication in the "Deutsche
Nationalbibliografie"; detailed bibliographic data is available
on the Internet at http://dnb.ddb.de/.

Cover design by Lisa Barfield

The paper in this book meets the guidelines for permanence and durability
of the Committee on Production Guidelines for Book Longevity
of the Council of Library Resources.

Printed in the United States of America

Contents

Introduction

Dennis Carlson and Charles P. Gause

This volume aims to take a fresh look at educational leadership, and the qualities of democratic educational leadership, in an age when the democratic promise of public education is "at risk" of being abandoned, forgotten, and emptied of meaning. What is the responsibility of educational leaders in such a context? To whom and for what are they responsible? These are the questions that frame the chapters in this text. Although the contributing authors represent a diverse array of scholars working in the fields of educational administration, the cultural foundations of education, curriculum, and the cultural studies of education, all find "common ground" in a commitment to forms of educational leadership, and pedagogical leadership, that advance the democratic promise of public education at all levels—from elementary education through graduate programs in educational leadership. In its most radical terms this promise has been that public education can provide the basis for an informed, engaged citizenry, fully capable of their own self-governance, and armed with forms of critical consciousness that allow them to question the commonsense beliefs embedded in political speech and popular culture texts. Beyond this, the democratic promise of public education has been about "leveling the playing field" so that people are not held back, disadvantaged, or discriminated against by class, gender, race, sexual orientation, or other markers of difference and identity. This requires that public education be at the forefront in fighting entrenched systems of domination and oppression, and the institutional structures and commonsense beliefs that support them. Finally, and consistent with all this, the democratic promise of public education has been associated with what John Dewey called the "habits" of democratic public life. In essence, the argument is that democracy is more than a set of abstract principles of governmentality, that it is something we practice in our everyday lives, and thus something that becomes "habit" in the good sense. Public schools and colleges in this sense are "embryonic communities" of democratic public life, teaching young people the "habits" of respect for difference, freedom of expression, questioning and debate, working with others, and participating in the "making" of a democratic culture. Of course, any habits that become so taken for granted that doing things differently would be "unthinkable" would not be democratic. So the habits of everyday life in public schools and college need to be continuously made the topic of deliberate self-reflection and change.

If public education is, ideally, about keeping this promise of democratic public life, then to be an educational leader involves a promise as well, a promise or commitment to be guided by a promise or covenant. Nietzsche wrote that to "dare to make promises" is to commit ourselves to a course of action that we will pursue "in spite of all accidents, in spite of destiny itself" (1956, p. 191). Similarly, Hannah Arendt observed that "Without being bound to the fulfillment of promises we would be condemned to wander helplessly and without direction" (1998, p. 237). For Jacques Derrida, democratic leadership is the response to the "summons" of the promise, a summons to be responsible when "one can always not respond and refuse the summons" (Derrida, 2004, p. 83). To approach educational leadership in these ways is to move outside the realm of formal role obligations and bureaucratic authority and to reengage in the battle being waged over whose values, and what vision of the future, will prevail in a profoundly new and unsettling age. How will progressives respond to the crisis of democratic public education and public life in America? Or will they not respond to the summons and sink into a politics of cynicism and despair?

As we write, the answer to these questions is not clear. Nor is the future of public education. The hour may be late for the idea of public education as anything more than the "skilling" of future workers for various rungs in an increasingly inequitable labor force and socioeconomic order, or the "normalizing," disciplining, and surveillance of young people to make them docile subjects of power. Of course, public schools have never lived up to their democratic promise; so we must avoid nostalgia for the "good old days" or a "golden age" when public schools supposedly promoted social advancement for the poor and racial minorities and taught the habits of democratic civility to all. Since the institutionalization of mass public schooling in America in the early twentieth century, schools have served to reproduce class, race, gender, and other inequalities more than they have promoted equality of opportunity and respect for difference; and educational leaders been influenced more by industrial than democratic models of organization and control. But there is reason to believe that things are getting worse as the transformation of "public" education into for-profit and religious networks of schools is continuing unabated, as high stakes testing is driving more and more poor white, black, and

Latino youth out of school, as urban schools are transformed into panoptic institutions of surveillance and policing, and as the effects of economic restructuring and social dislocation impact adversely on the lives of young people.

In the face of all this, many progressive educators have rushed to the defense of public schools, and such a defense is needed. Public schools are still one step removed from direct free market competition, and from religious indoctrination. But we need to be careful that in defending public schools we do not tacitly endorse public schooling in its current forms. For it is not currently working very well to advance democratic promises, and to begin serving democratic interests it will need to be thoroughly re-imagined and reorganized. This, we believe, is the primary task of progressive educational leaders and public intellectuals today. Furthermore, the democratic re-imagination and reconstruction of public education cannot proceed outside the context of a broader political and culture movement for democratization in America. Such a movement must take on the loose coalition of interest groups that make up the current hegemony in America: elite corporate interests and free-market "neo-liberals," social conservatives, and the religious right. And to take back the state from this hegemonic power bloc progressives will need to forge a powerful new democratic discourse, a commonsense way of "thinking" education and educational renewal that makes sense to a broad spectrum of Americans and that links educational issues to issues of class, race, gender, and sexuality. We hope that this book contributes in some small way to such a response.

A progressive response begins, we believe, with the critique and deconstruction of dominant discourses, narratives, and images of educational leadership. For example, one of the controlling images of educational leadership in both professional discourse and popular culture representations is that of the administrator. Thus, to speak of an educational leader is to think of the educational administrator—most often either a school principal or a district superintendent. Some would say that the language of "educational leadership" is meant to be more inclusive and to replace the language of "educational administration," with its more bureaucratic and hierarchical orientation. This is indeed an encouraging sign, expressed in the recent re-naming of "old" departments of educational administration in schools of education as "new" departments of educational leadership. At the same time, the association between administration and leadership may actually be reinforced by such a re-naming if the new and the old departments are engaged in the same thing—the professional preparation of school administrators. If educational leadership is to take on democratic meaning, it will be through a more inclusive understanding of who leaders are and what constitutes leadership, an understanding that includes teachers and others—even students—as leaders. Of course, one of the reasons that the association between administration and leadership remains so strong is that the language of educational administration depoliticizes the exercise of bureaucratic authority. So long as leadership is represented and understood as merely a form of rational bureaucratic management of a system that uses objective assessment tools (standardized tests) to reward merit (by both students and teachers), then it is hard to see how public schools serve to reproduce class, race, and gender inequalities. So long as we continue to use a language of educational administration, we are encouraged to approach what goes on in public educational sites as a management problem, calling for managerial, technical "solutions." This does not mean that educational administrators cannot be democratic educational leaders. But it does mean that to be democratic educational leaders they must be subversive administrators. They assume responsibility for insuring that marginalized youth pass the tests they need to pass in order to have a chance to advance themselves in the dominant culture. But they also work with others to carve out some space for alternative practices that affirm students' cultures and identities, and they work for the day when they can assess students in ways that do not stack the deck so unfairly against some.

Dominant discourses of educational leadership have also taken for granted a leader-follower binary that has been undemocratic in its effects and needs to be deconstructed. According to this binary way of thinking, some people are born with leadership attributes, while others are born with follower-ship attributes. In a patriarchal culture, men are defined as having leadership attributes and women are defined as having follower-ship attributes, or the lack of leadership attributes. They are emotional, indecisive, weak, dependent, and so on. So it should not be surprising to find that gendered constructions of "leadership" have entered into the gender politics of schooling. Historically, men have been hired and promoted as administrators, and even more particularly white, middle class, heterosexual males. So long as leadership is represented in American popular culture, and in the professional discourse on educational leadership as a primarily white, male, middle class, heterosexual attribute, then "Others" will be relegated to the margins of power in education. Furthermore, the forms of discourse and practice associated with dominant leadership groups will be privileged in the school: specifically, linear, technical-rational, hierarchical, objectivist, and quantifiable forms. This suggests that in unpacking the leader-follower binary in education we inevitably confront many of the forces and structures of domination that currently stand in the way of democratic change.

Another taken-for-granted image or trope in dominant discourses of educational leadership has been that of "society" as an organism, a unified system in which various subsystems work together to meet the "needs" of the organism to survive, adapt to changes in its environment, and grow and develop. This functionalist systems theory became popular in the United States in the 1950s and has never really stopped being dominant in mainstream research in education. Educational leaders are thus managers of the educational subsystem, making sure that the "needs" of the society are met—for well skilled citizens and workers—and that the social system is able to adapt to changes in the environment in an incremental manner. The problems with this perspective are numerous, but in general they include a reification of social order, so that it is represented as one, unified "thing," an organism that speaks with one voice, expressive of one will. One must think only of the "needs" of the organization, or of the nation, as if organizations and nation's had voices and needs. The alternative to this functionalist systems theory of leadership is some variation on conflict theory, which frames the analysis of educational leadership throughout this volume. Conflict theory is based on the proposition that there is no unified system, with one set of interests and "needs." Instead, institutions are organized out of and around conflict between competing power blocs, alliances, and strategic coalitions of interests. This is consistent with the Gramscian notion of struggle between hegemonic and counter-hegemonic power blocs and worldviews. In such a struggle, one is never just an educational leader for a "system," but rather a hegemonic or counter-hegemonic leader. We either serve to advance the interests, agendas, and commonsense understandings of dominant groups and power blocs, or we advance the interests, agendas, and worldview of counter-hegemonic groups.

Beyond the critique of dominant discourses, representations, and practices of educational leadership, the essays in this volume speak to the attributes of a more democratic and liberatory leadership. Among these attributes is a commitment to a politics of hope without illusion. Contributing authors vary considerably as to how much hope they hold out, and the source of this hope. But one way or another, all of these chapters are works of hope, finding hope even when the battle is not going well—and in this point in public education it is not. This is where it is important to tell stories that are honest in the sense that they confront us with the real and significant forces that currently stand in the way of a meaningful democratization of public education and public life. Progressive stories, at their best, help individuals and groups deconstruct the beliefs and practices that keep them oppressed or disempowered and face the reality of their situation. Currently that reality is that transnational capitalism plays an ever-increasing role in establishing the discursive parameters for educational policy and practice, and public schools (particularly urban public schools) are being called upon to assume a heightened role in the surveillance, policing, and regulation of "problem youth." If the authors in this volume offer no illusions about the challenge progressive educational leaders face in reconstructing public education along more democratic and liberatory lines, they do help recover hope and a possibility in a cynical age, a hope rooted in a recognition that culture is contested and thus open rather than determined. They open up possibilities for critical reflection and strategic action at various sites, and they help develop linkages between various movements, alliances, and axes of struggle to bring progressives together around at least a strategic united front politics. To tell these kind of research stories is to neither overdetermine nor underdetermine what goes on in local educational sites. Instead, authors ask questions having to do with how we might advance democratic projects in public education within the dynamic of control and contestation in American education and culture.

The democratic educational leader that emerges through these various chapters bears much in common with both Gramsci's "organic intellectual" and Foucault's "specific intellectual." Educational leaders of this type do not speak in the name of the oppressed, but, as Foucault said, "alongside them, in solidarity with them, in part because others' oppression is often inseparable from their own" (1980, 126). Such leaders cross back and forth across the borders that separate insider and outside perspectives or standpoints. They are insiders to the extent that they identity with and represent groups that have been marginalized, silenced, or disempowered. Yet they maintain some critical distance from the commonsense beliefs and taken-for-granted attitudes of those they represent, a critical distance that allows them to help marginalized and disempowered peoples engage in critical self-reflection on what keeps them oppressed and how they might respond. The intellectual or educational leader thus plays a critical role in the development of what Gramsci called a "philosophy of praxis," a form of educational work aimed at the critical intellectual development of that group or movement with which the intellectual is aligned in solidarity. The disempowered cannot become empowered until they can organize themselves around a discourse of struggle and affirmation, and according to Gramsci, "there is no organization without intellectuals" (1971, p. 334). All of this raises important questions about how educational leaders understand their role and whether we might be better off defining the role of the educational leader first and foremost as an intellectual of a certain type, who helps people reflect on their conditions within the context of efforts to change those conditions.

Finally, many of the chapters in this volume serve to disrupt the theory-practice binary that has been so firmly entrenched in education for the past several decades. Democratic progressives, for a number of reasons, have most often ended up on the theory side of the divide. The language of democratic and liberatory education, ironically, still circulates more freely in the liberal arts academy than in the public schools, where one might expect to find it. It will do no good to blame one side or the other for this predicament. So long as public schools continue to be organized by the current hegemonic discourses of reform, progressives in the academy can play only a limited role working within public schools. In the academy, there is some limited space for a progressive counter-hegemonic discourse to form, although the university is now under many of the same pressures public schools have faced to adopt corporate models of accountability, standards, and outcome-based learning (Readings, 1996). So progressives must fight to maintain critical intellectual traditions in the academy even as they work to deconstruct the binary that traditionally has separated theory and practice, the academy and the public school, the progressive intellectual and the battles being waged in American public life. Only through such a praxis, we believe, can progressives offer a hope that is not romantic or naïve, a hope without illusion (Carlson, 2005). Paulo Freire observed that praxis offers a hope rooted in the incompletion of self and social reality. Such a hope may be "thwarted by injustice, exploitation, and oppression; [but] it is affirmed by people's yearning for freedom and justice" (Freire, 1970, p. 28). All of this means that the promise of democratic public education cannot be fully extinguished, and that although a good many forces (both ideological and material) stand in the way of the fuller democratization of American public education and public life, democratic educational leadership is still guided by the promise of what could be, and should be. This volume emerged out of this faith in the promise of democratic education in an age characterized by: global restructuring, new information technologies, free market ideologies, multiculturalism and diversity, and the dismantling of the liberal welfare state, among other developments.

In the late 1990s, the Department of Educational Leadership at Miami University, with the support of a grant from the Ohio Department of Higher Education, began the dialogue that ultimately led to this collection. The "Leadership, Culture, and Schooling Initiative," as it was called, brought together education faculty from throughout the United States for a series of summer retreats, conference symposia, and other activities over the course of five years (1999–2004). The editors were active participants in this Initiative-sponsored dialogue—Carlson as a professor in the Department of Educational Leadership, and Gause as a doctoral student in that department assigned to work with the Initiative. Gause subsequently became a faculty member in the Department of Educational Leadership and Cultural Foundations at the University of North Carolina Greensboro, which has played a leading role in advancing and extending the dialogue. Among the contributors to this volume are those who attended one of the summer retreats sponsored by the Initiative, along with others whose work is consistent with the general perspective on educational leadership advanced through the Initiative dialogue. As we see it, that dialogue is now an ongoing conversation linked to an incipient movement to bring critical, cultural lenses to the study and practice of educational leadership in ways that open up possibilities for democratic change. We hope this volume contributes in some small way to that conversation and movement. We would like to thank Daniel Chapman, at the University of North Carolina at Greensboro, for his important contributions in bringing this book to press.

References

Arendt, H. (1998). *The human condition*, second edition. Chicago: University of Chicago Press

Carlson, D. (2005). Hope without illusion: Telling the story of democratic educational renewal, *International Journal of Qualitative Studies in Education*, 18:, 21–45.

Derrida, J. (2004). *Eyes of the university*, J. Plug, Trans. Stanford, CA: Stanford University Press.

Foucault, M. (1980). *Power/knowledge: Selected interviews and other writings, 1972–1977*. C. Gordon, Ed. Brighton, UK: Harvester.

Freire, P. (1970). *Pedagogy of the oppressed*. New York: Seabury Press.

Gramsci, A. (1971). *Selections from the prison notebooks*. Q. Hoare and G. Smith, Eds. and Trans. New York: International Publishers.

Nietzsche, F. (1956). *The birth of tragedy and the genealogy of morals.* F. Golffing, Ed. and Trans. New York: Doubleday.

Readings, B. (1996). *The university in ruins.* Cambridge, MA: Harvard University Press.

Part One

The Cultural Context
of Educational Leadership

Are We Making Progress?
The Discursive Construction of Progress
in the Age of "No Child Left Behind"

Dennis Carlson

One of my favorite science fiction novels about progress is H. G. Wells's *Things to Come* (1935), which was made into a Hollywood movie in 1936. Wells offers us a vision of the future from the past, an early-twentieth-century representation of an imagined future in the year 2059. Humanity is about to make a giant leap to the moon in a rocket, which is a significant achievement. Wells suggests that the project to send men to the moon provided a pragmatic means of creating a new, highly stratified society, with a large working class and a smaller class of scientists, engineers, and managers who run the state and who lead a reluctant citizenry down the long road of progress carved out by modern science and engineering, in league with the leaders of modern industry. Right before the launch of the moon rocket there is a revolt among the workers, and they rush to storm the launching pad. One anonymous worker calls out: "What is all this progress? What is the good of progress?…We must measure and compute, we must collect and sort and count. We must sacrifice ourselves…What is it, this progress?" (p. 118). I think those are very good questions to ask now, and particularly about much-touted progress in the "war" on underachievement in schools serving those marginalized by race, class, ethnicity, and language. Whose interests are being served by all of this progress in raising standardized test scores? Is it even "real" progress, or just a manufactured progress, the result of an aggressive policy of "teaching to the test"? Who and what is being sacrificed in the process?

It was Dostoyevski, a half century before Wells, who warned that those who would lead people in the pursuit of progress often hold out the vision of some "crystal palace" that awaits us all if we just buckle under, work hard, and think positive—a crystal palace built by science and managed by social engineers. One trouble, according to Dostoyevski, is that the crystal palace is always something projected into the future. In the meantime, we are told we have to put up with a "chicken coop." Or we are told that the chicken coop we inhabit is really already a crystal palace. At any rate, people continue to live and work in chicken coops; and for all the talk of progress, the roofs keep letting in more rain each year. We are told again and again by education officials in the state and by their corporate "partners" in school reform that progress is being made in raising standards, in narrowing achievement gaps, in making teachers, principals, and school districts more accountable to the public, in aligning the curriculum with the test, and in other ways working toward the national goals set forth so boldly in "No Child Left Behind" (NCLB). Admittedly, policy makers and politicians are quick to point out, there are still some problems we have to "iron out" in achieving this goal, in re-building the nation's schools as crystal palaces in which no one is left behind and success is available to all. But with more quantitative research studies and more hard work on everyone's part, we're making progress. Indeed, President Bush's generic response to all questions about his administration's policies—whether educational or military—has been that we are "making progress," and just need to "stay the course." Somewhere down the road, we are told, if teachers and students work hard enough and people demand that schools be held accountable, the nation's public schools will be crystal palaces. In the meantime, urban educators and students are also told that they will have to continue to inhabit chicken coops, being content for now to visit some model crystal palace schools that have been reorganized to insure high standards, accountability, and "success for all." At times such as this I am inclined to think that if this be progress, and this is to be the crystal palace, then perhaps we can do without so much progress. Not that I am willing to abandon the language or the project of democratic progress entirely. Far from it. As a progressive, that would be more than a little contradictory. But progressives of the democratic sort will have to be careful to clearly distinguish their version of progress from the version that currently holds sway. They will need to engage in a battle over the meaning of progress, as part of a larger cultural battle over the meaning of democracy in America.

Words like "progress" and "democracy" have no essence, no fixed, given, stable, or unified meaning. From a post-structural perspective, the meaning of language is only to be found in the uses to which it is put historically, and the interests it serves. In one sense, all major power blocs and interest groups in American cultural politics are about making progress. They want to lead or guide American culture in a given direction toward a vision of a "good society," even if that good society is only to be a modified or revised version of a romanticized and mythologized past. This view of progress and leadership is post-structural in that it does not assume, as modernist discourse did, that progress has just one direction and teleology of development, or that the future will necessarily be "better" than the past—that is, freer, more equitable, and more just. If culture has no predetermined trajectory, and democratic progress is not guaranteed, the battle is over how people "think" progress, what kind of progress they "make," whose interests are served by differing discourses of progress, and what power relations are constituted through various discourses and practices of progress. While progress can and does take on diverse and even contradictory forms and directions, I will reserve the descriptive label "progressive" to refer to a leadership that is involved in advancing a radical democratic promise and vision. In education, this is the progressivism of John Dewey and of the social reconstructionist movement of the 1930s. In more recent forms it is a progressivism that emphasizes teacher empowerment and a culturally relevant curriculum, and the building of inclusive, diverse learning communities that affirm diversity and challenge inequalities of class, race, gender, sexual orientation, and other markers of difference and identity. Progressive educational leadership, in all of these forms, assumes responsibility for advancing a democratic promise, dream, and vision—through the opening up of possibilities for re-thinking and re-enacting democratic education and public life.

At the same time, much of the progressive project at this point, and of necessity I believe, has been focused on critiquing and deconstructing dominant discourses of progress in the nation's schools. For progressivism is locked in a battle with this hegemonic discourse on "making progress" in education, and both educators and broad segments of the public can begin to think outside the reigning narrative of progress, alternatives will simply be "un-thinkable," and thus un-speakable. Consequently, much of what I have to say in the following is aimed at deconstructing the hegemonic discourse on progress in American education, and more specifically progress in urban schools serving those most marginalized by class, race, ethnicity, and language. In this project, I want to indicate some of the ways educational leadership is constituted by discourses of progress, and by particular narratives, metaphors, and images of educational progress. Specifically, I want to map out a genealogy of educational progress in the recent past—since the early 1990s—leading up to the present. The hegemonic discourse on educational progress established through *A Nation at*

Risk (National Commission on Excellence and Education, 1983) in the early 1980s took on form and substance in the 1990s, which set the stage for the NCLB legislation and accountability machines that followed in the early years of the new century. The Nineties was a decade in which national policy in public education was shaped by a Democratic administration, but in a way that maintained continuity with the hegemonic reform discourse of the Eighties and even strengthened and extended that discourse. This dominant discourse of progress, with its roots in corporate and state interests and worldviews, has been only slightly different in its conservative and liberal forms. Liberals call for more money to make sure that no child is left behind, and moderates and conservatives call for less money and more cost-effective ways of "delivering" educational services and holding educators accountable to "the public." But both conservatives and liberals have advanced a common vision of progress for American public education tied to the interests and worldview of transnational capitalism and bureaucratic state elites.

In mapping out a genealogy of the idea of progress in recent American educational reform discourses, I am most indebted to the theoretical and conceptual scaffolding provided by Antonio Gramsci and Michel Foucault. Gramsci (1971) understood culture as a site of ongoing battle, organized along a number of overlapping fronts, between hegemonic and counter-hegemonic power blocs and commonsense discourses on progress. For Gramsci, the dominant discourse on progress is hegemonic in the sense that it sets the conditions of possibility for "legitimate" speaking and writing about what is wrong in society and what needs fixing. Cultural leadership is hegemony, the mobilization of discursive power to advance a commonsense agenda for change. To the extent that hegemony is fairly stable, it is at least partially because this commonsense perspective or worldview permeates and saturates the lived experiences of actors. In public schools, as Michael Apple has argued, this commonsense provides a framework to assist teachers and principals in organizing their everyday lives and relations together, and it enables them to believe they are "neutral participants in the neutral instrumentation of schooling" (2004, p. 201). At the same time, the economic and political interests served by the hegemonic commonsense are hidden or masked. Gramsci recognized that there is some good sense along with bad sense in hegemonic discourses, for they must win the consent of the governed and tap into cultural values that are widely held. For example, one might say that in the hegemonic discourse of NCLB, there is good sense in the provision that schools have to adopt policies to overcome socioeconomic, ethnic, and racial disparities in student achievement. Unfortunately, when this good sense is articulated within a broader hegemonic reform discourse that links it to more accountability and standardized testing, and when it ignores the impact of inequalities generated in the economic sphere, then its progressive potential is severely limited. As Apple observes, the current hegemonic discourse in education and public life "speaks to a populist impulse, but that impulse has been colonized by the Right in powerful ways" (2004, p. 201).

While the dominant or hegemonic discourse on progress in education has powerful interests behind it and appeals to commonsense beliefs, hegemonic discourses and power blocs are never stable or secure, and never without some oppositional discourse on progress. Indeed, one might say that hegemonic discourses always constitute themselves in the face of resistance and opposition, and that they are deployed to more effective control and manage this resistance and opposition. The language of accountability, standards, and excellence in education over the past several decades only makes sense as it is deployed against such resistance by students, teachers, principals, and school boards. This language of progress in education brings everyone in public schools under what Foucault called a "panoptic" and individualizing disciplinary power.

It also brings with it a set of tools or technologies to be used by local educational leaders to "make progress" in their schools—within a narrowly pragmatic, utilitarian, instrumental, objectivist, and prescriptive calculus. In *Discipline and Punish* (1977), Foucault identified disciplinary power as "the specific technique of power that regards individuals as both objects and as instruments of its exercise" (p. 40). Its instruments include, he argued: hierarchical observation, normalizing judgment, and the ritual of the examination. In the discourse and practice of systems management, we might say that hierarchical observation takes the form of complex management information systems and surveillance technologies designed to keep teachers and students under (in Foucault's words) "an intense, continuous supervision" (p. 174). As for "normalizing judgment," this includes the myriad techniques for evaluating, comparing, differentiating, and judging teachers and students according to supposed objective standards, and also those techniques used for correcting their presumed "defects" or "deficits" and awarding both privileges and punishments. Finally, there is the examination, which combines the microtechnologies of hierarchical observation and a normalizing judgment. Foucault is led to conclude that "the school became a sort of apparatus of uninterrupted examination" (p. 186). If the school historically has been organized and even spatially arranged as an examining institution, new behavioralist and systems management technologies are aimed at "making progress" in ways that could only be imagined in early times.

Felix Guattari (1984) has referred to these microtechnologies of progress as "machines," and in the postmodern age these machines, he argues, the micro-technologies employed in public institutions such as schools, increasingly are variations on the machines of transnational capitalism. He observes that "capitalism does not seek to exercise despotic power over all the wheels of society.... It is even crucial to its survival that it manages to arrange marginal freedoms, relative spaces for creativity" (1996, p. 235). What gives transnational capitalism its special power, according to Guattari, is its ability to re-order various heterogeneous activities and domains of cultural production, to main-tain control not through centralization of power, but through the decentraliza-tion of power to the point of production. Control is much more invested, consequently, in technical control—that is, in "machines." Schools may then be approached as sites where teachers and students use what Guattari calls "semiotization machines" to decode texts and produce certain objectified and quantifiable outcomes or truths (Carlson, 2003). What are some of these machines? They include policy documents and formalized procedures that specify how to prepare lesson and unit plans, what curriculum materials are to be used, and the "skills" students are to master through these curriculum materials; they include standardized tests and other evaluation technologies, as well as teacher observation and assessment rubrics, and they include procedures and machines for monitoring the classroom "production process," making interventions, labeling students, and so on. The cultural roots of the dominant machines of public education today are to be found in the hegemonic soil of transnational capitalism. The discourses of progress articulated by the repre-sentatives of elite economic interests, now on a global scale, have been, ac-cording to Guattari, about "de-territorializing" the machines of transnational capitalism and "re-territorializing" them by applying them to the reorganization of all public institutions. This has a good deal of relevance in interpreting the situation we face in public education, and in teacher education, and it is a chilling reminder that leaders in public education at all levels—from the elementary school to the university—are being called upon to align their work with the "machines" of NCLB.

I want to turn now to explore in more specificity some of the recent genealogical roots of these dominant discourses, practices, and technologies of progress in public education. This entails, first of all, a critical reading of several influential reports issued in the 1990s, by the Brookings Institute, a neoliberal think tank, as well as the National Education Commission on Time and Learning. Taken together, these reports point the way toward a narrowly pragmatic vision of urban schools that "work," even if they never ask: "works" for whom or for what? They tie progress to the elimination of time "wastage" in schools but never ask: what constitutes "wasted" time or "productive" time in the school day, and who decides? I then present a narrative of school reorganization in one urban elementary school consistent with this reform discourse. I argue that school reorganization models such as "Success for All" and the Baldrige Criteria may be understood as the latest "machines" of urban schooling. They are really a whole package of interrelated micromachines or technologies—all of the parts and tools needed by local administrators and teachers to "make progress" according to a predictable plan and timetable. In a concluding section I return again to the question of what might constitute democratic progressive counter-discourses or counter-narratives of progress, and how progressive educators can reclaim a politics of hope without illusion in the age of NCLB.

The Promise of Schools That "Work"

James O'Connor, in his influential book, *The Fiscal Crisis of the State* (1973), argued that the modern state, heavily indebted to elite economic interests, was torn between competing claims that it could not effectively resolve. On the one hand, the state had to provide essential social and health services and educate future workers and citizens—all of which capitalism depends upon to establish the conditions for higher worker productivity and increased profit margins. On the other hand, the state was under mounting pressure from elite economic interests not to draw too much money out of circulation to pay for public services and not to waste money on "unproductive" expenditures that do not directly produce profit. It was thus caught in a contradictory position. The fiscal crisis of the state, O'Connor argued, was also fueled by working-class cynicism and a middle-class tax revolt—something school districts faced every time they tried to pass a levy. In responding to the fiscal crisis of the state, policymakers adopted the pragmatic stance of pressuring public schools to become more "cost-effective." The way to make urban schools "work," from this perspective, was to begin with the "bottom line."

This is the tone set by the 1994 Brookings Institute report *Making Schools Work: Improving Performance and Controlling Costs* authored by Eric Hanushek and a team of economists at the Institute. The report begins with the assertion that "a fiscal crisis looms for America's schools." As student populations are on the rise, and as per-pupil spending is not keeping pace with this rise, the public is becoming more disappointed in their schools. Consequently, "taxpayers may well resist future expenditure increases with unprecedented insistence" in the years just ahead (Hanushek, p. xix). All of this means, the report concludes, that the efficient use of resources needs to receive more attention as an indicator of whether or not a school is "working." This is where teachers come in. A major recommendation of the report is that ways be found of lowering the labor costs in public education. The largest single component of the educational budget is teacher salaries, the report notes, so this is the logical place to cut costs. For this reason, calls for "smaller classes and commensurately more teachers" must be rejected, for they would raise labor costs dramatically when labor costs need to be cut further (p. 113). But how can labor costs be cut further? The report suggests that the best way to tackle labor costs in education is to introduce some version of a two-tier teaching system, with a relatively small group of teachers at the top, overseeing or working with a large group of para-professionals and teacher assistants. Class sizes could be increased since "studies show that reducing class size usually has no general effect on student performance" (p. 113). Larger classes, in turn, are to be made possible through more use of new computer technologies. The report notes: "Computers can replace teachers in certain tasks, such as drill-and-practice activities." Furthermore, "television and radio broadcasts, combined with correspondence materials, can provide high-quality education at relatively low costs" (p. 89). The clear implication here is that a "virtual school" could even be established, with students communicating with teachers via class websites and chat rooms and with instructional videos downloaded for personal viewing.

The other major recommendation of the report that speaks directly to teachers' work has to do with the concepts of "performance measurement" and "value added." In effect, this means evaluating and rewarding teachers (along with principals) according to how much they can raise student test scores over the course of a term or a year, given the group of students they are assigned. "Schools and teachers," the report recommends, "should be held responsible only for factors under their control and rewarded for what they contribute to the educational process, that is, the value they add to student performance" (p. 89). This translates into keeping meticulous and detailed records on student skill levels, and rewarding or punishing teachers according to an individual value added index. All of this requires, the report concludes, a sophisticated management information system (MIS) that is able to "identity the sources of poor performance" (p. 89). In many states and urban school districts across America, such systems have been constructed very rapidly over the past decade. For example, in Ohio, the Department of Education website recently included an article on "Improving Education with Business Intelligence" which noted that a parent could have one-click access to: how much each school district in the state spends per pupil each year, student attendance rates, enrollment figures, graduation rates, and proficiency test results. Another click gives the parent access to individual school data. The MIS is represented in the essay as a "tool" for parents that can be used in holding local school officials accountable, and as a tool school administrators can use to make important decisions and answer important questions, such as: "Why do students read better at this school? Why do they keep dropping out at that school?" Quick and easy access to MIS information promises to let us "get to the bottom" of such troubling questions. Within individual school districts MIS systems are now being used to compare individual teachers and administrators as well on a value-added criterion, and in some charter schools teacher pay is already directly linked to a value-added calculus.

All of this, the report concludes, will mean taking on the power of teacher unions, since they are presented as one of the major reasons urban schools are not "working" now. Among other things, the report argues that the union movement will need to endorse more performance incentives and merit pay systems and largely abandon the idea of tenure for teachers entering the system. According to the report, it is important that teachers already in the system who have been teaching for some time are not held to the same expectations as entering teachers, "to avoid alienating them and losing the enthusiastic participation that is crucial to success in incentive-based systems" (p. 118). New teachers are likely to be more receptive to these changes because they will not regard the new policies as "violations of past understandings or intrusions on their accustomed routine" (p. 7). This is another way of saying that if teachers do not get used to certain contract rights and the academic freedom and security afforded by tenure, they will not miss them. It also suggests a pragmatic strategy of winning the support of senior teachers currently in the system by exempting them, at least partially, from the new rules of the game. This also makes it easier for teacher union leadership to endorse merit pay systems.

The heading charted out in *Making Schools Work* was extended, and applied more particularly to schools serving socioeconomically disadvantaged students, in the 1998 Brookings Institute report *Fixing Urban Schools* (Hill and Celio, 1998). That report argued that the crisis of underachievement in urban schools could best be addressed by "an imposition of standards" that would "establish clear expectations about what students are to be taught and learn, setting high targets for student performance." The establishment of such standards would allow for the construction of an aligned system of tests, curricula, teacher training, and teaching materials which, in turn, "would attach real consequences to test results for schools, students, and individual teachers alike" (p. 6). What gets advocated here is an even more central role for state proficiency testing in determining every aspect of what goes on in urban schools. All of this will require, the report argues, relying more on "experts" to make important decisions in education, an expertise urban principals and teachers on their own supposedly lack, particularly in the realm of "devising improvement plans and assessing their own progress" (p. 76). As for school principals, their role is to exert "strong and authoritative leadership" in support of school plans for increased productivity and avoid anything that "compromises or diverts resources from the school plan" (p. 73). This smacks very much of a new version of scientific management in the public schools, tied (as scientific management was in the early twentieth century) to "the bottom line." What is new is that scientific management and the cult of efficiency in education now have far more sophisticated "machines" at their disposal—foremost among them standardized testing and MIS. The result is still the same, however. That is, the reduction of public education to the cost-effective production of economically utilitarian, standardized learning outcomes, and the treatment of principals, teachers, and students as workers subordinated to the "plan."

That management plan, the report indicates, might best be developed as part of a school reorganization model adopted and implemented in each school. This is what the report calls "design-based" reform, based on the presumption that when a school uses a defined and consistent approach to instruction, teachers, parents, and students "will fully understand what the school promises and what is required of them" (p. 7). While the report emphasizes the impor-tance of each school choosing its own reorganization model, it is quite clear that only models that reduce learning to standardized and objectified learning outcomes, and more particularly those standardized and objectified learning outcomes identified on state proficiency tests, stand much of a chance of competing for state funds to support reorganization. Furthermore, once teachers (often under pressure) vote to "buy into" a school reorganization model (to take "ownership," to use the language of reformers), they also buy into extra meetings and committees, more teacher and student assessment, and other extra responsibilities that would under normal conditions represent a violation of the teacher union contract. All of this imposition of control, much of it technical, is framed in the optimistic language of "making progress," and a technical rational language of "fixing" urban schools and making them "work" right—language which presumes that the problem with the nation's schools, including chronic underachievement among poor white, black, and La-tino/Latina youth, can be "fixed" in the same way that you can "fix" an engineering design flaw, or fix a clock so that it "works" again and doesn't lose time.

Time, and the belief that too much time is being "lost" or "wasted" in the classroom and in the school day, is a central trope that runs throughout these texts about "fixing" urban schools so that they "work" right. In education there is a long tradition of research based on the premise that the best way to raise student achievement levels is to increase "time on task." Time in this sense is made productive, and its organization and disciplined scheduling impact on teachers' work in a number of ways. Like the idea of the cost-effective school, the idea of the time-disciplined school also has a long history. E. P. Thompson, the British historian of the working class, in a now-classic essay on "time discipline and industrial capitalism," documented how schools for working class youth during the Industrial Revolution in England were designed to teach them time discipline, the kind of time discipline that prevailed in the factories (Thompson, 1993). In factories, all the machines were started up at the same time each morning, and they all stopped at the same time to allow workers breaks and to change shifts. Everything was dependent upon a minute-by-minute scheduling of production, including the synchronization of different chains of production so that everything came together at the right time. If workers were not at their stations on time, the entire production process often had to be shut down and then restarted. Yet workers of that time, raised according to a more cyclical and agrarian conception of time, were resistant to becoming slaves to the clock. Consequently, tardiness among workers was common, as was skipping entire days of work at a whim. Early schools thus at least partially were institutions designed to socialize young people into dominant regimes of time management and discipline, and this continues to be the case today.

But time management and time discipline in education extend far beyond this "hidden curriculum" of schooling. It impinges, as I have already said, into the realm of deciding how time in the school day can be more effectively managed to increase achievement levels. As Andy Hargreaves has observed, within a technical-rational discourse, "time...is an objective variable, an instrumental, organizational condition that can be managerially manipulated in order to foster the implementation of educational change" (1994, p. 96). In the 1990s, the most important and influential commission report to explicitly advance a time-disciplined reform agenda in public education was *Prisoners of Time*, the 1994 report of the National Education Commission on Time and Learning. That commission, established under the Bush administration in 1991, was composed of a select group of school board members, superintendents, and principals, along with representatives of The Business Roundtable and the Hudson Institute—both major neoliberal think tanks in education. According to the report, a major reason for the failure of school reforms to effectively raise achievement levels is that public schools are currently "prisoners" of an obsolete and outmoded conception of time tied to a fixed and rigidly scheduled school day of approximately six hours and a school year of approximately 180 days, more appropriate for an industrial than a post-industrial age. This helps explain the phenomenon of teachers, as time runs out on them, "cramming large portions of required material into a fraction of the time intended for it" (p. 8). The clock rules in the school, yet according to the report the typical school clock divides up time with little attention paid to what subject areas or curricular topics are of most worth—the so-called core academic subjects of math, science, social studies, and literacy that are assessed on state proficiency tests. In effect, the report suggests that existing time in the school day is not organized in a cost-effective manner. Finally, the report notes that all students are different, and some need longer to master the basic skills assessed on state tests. The existing schedule fails to acknowledge these different time needs of students.

Many progressives, I suspect, might agree with much of this assessment of the situation in public schools, that "time is learning's warden" and that public educators have allowed themselves to become prisoners of time. But the response suggested here is not consistent with the liberation of those who have been kept prisoners of time in public schools, including in particular teachers and students. Such a liberation would return control of time to teachers and students, within certain broad parameters. The response suggested here is rather consistent with a new managerial discourse. It calls for the replacement of an "outmoded" industrial conception of time with a more flexible, individualized, focused use of time as a resource in educational productivity, a use of time more consistent with post-industrial organizations and businesses. And just what does the new corporate discourse on time management imply for the restructuring of public schools, and particularly urban schools? For once again, these cost-effective reform discourses are having the greatest impact there.

The report's first recommendation is that schools eliminate the use of "academic time" (regular school hours time) for "non-academic" purposes during the regular school day. According to the report, non-academic purposes are all activities and classes not directly related to the "common core all students should master," which includes: English and language arts, mathematics, science, civics, history, geography, the arts, and foreign language. Everything else is to be relegated to the realm of the extra-curricular, something that can be offered through school clubs and activities after the regular school day. This includes: physical education, family life education, band and orchestra, yearbook and school newspaper classes, classes and programs for unwed teenage mothers, and driver's education. It also means the possible elimination of music, art, and physical education teachers (the so-called specials) at the elementary level. There certainly is some good sense to the idea that the school day should not be cluttered with a lot of classes and programs in which students are not learning much and in which the curriculum is not challenging. On the other hand, many of these "non-academic" classes play an important role in motivating young people, in helping them contribute to the community and engage in dialogue and common activity with other young people. Many of these "non-academic" classes are "safe spaces" where youth marginalized by class, race, and other markers of difference can engage in the kind of work that leads to self-affirming identities (Weis and Fine, 2003). So the piece-by-piece elimination of such spaces over the past decade is a serious cause for alarm, and one that impacts dramatically on urban schools.

What else constitutes "non-academic" purposes that need to be eliminated from the school day? According to the report, core academic learning is being sacrificed to make room for "education about personal safety, consumer affairs, AIDS, conservation and energy, family life, [and] driver's training" (*Prisoners of*

Time, p. 15). Now, this is an interesting grouping of topics, and to relegate them to the realm of the "non-academic," as if they were not central to the school's mission of teaching core academic subjects, is political. What gets valued as "academic" is instruction that is directly related to the skill needs of a "world class" work force that can compete with Japan and Germany, skill needs that supposedly can be and should be measured by more standardized testing on a more regular basis. Everything else gets jettisoned from the schedule. In response to such reform agendas, which are being pushed with increasing regularity by state officials these days, I think progressives will need to rupture or "trouble" the borders that separate the academic from the non-academic rather than erect them ever higher. Popular culture, for example, plays an increasingly central role in youth identity formation, and discussion or use of popular culture—such as hip hop culture and rap music—needs to be part of the curriculum. Yet, efforts to do so are currently stymied by reform efforts designed to erect more rigid borders between the academic and the non-academic.

A second major recommendation of *Prisoners of Time* has to do with expanding the role of the public school as a site for the supervision and surveillance of youth. The report observes that in many communities, particularly in "troubled" urban environments, children are growing up "without the family and community support" they need to do well in school. The crisis of childcare, the report says, "can no longer be ignored" (p. 34). Finally, schools in high-poverty urban communities are increasingly being called upon to work with police, child welfare professionals, and social workers to look after the "mental health" of students. This makes some sense from a progressive standpoint. Rather than assuming a less important role, public schools need to assume a more important role as community centers, as sites in which a wide array of services and activities are going on, year-round and all day. Schools needs to be much more "open" in this regard. But when this recommendation to expand the role of public schools in "troubled" urban neighborhoods is articulated within a conservative reform discourse, as it is in *Prisoners of Time*, it becomes part of a movement to bring urban youth under a more complete, totalizing, and individualizing surveillance, with public school leaders working closely with the local police department (see Carlson, 2005). Thus, in one urban middle school I worked with in Cincinnati, Ohio, in the mid-1990s, the juvenile court came to the school each Friday and held session, and police cars were routinely to be seen parked near the entrance to the school. The message was loud and clear: teachers and police are working together to keep marginalized urban youth under our collective gaze, so they don't get into "trouble." The trouble, of course, is that students may begin to view teachers and administrators in the same light they view police and begin to think of the school as a kind of prison.

Are We Making Progress?

Is the hegemonic discourse on progress in the "war" against chronic underachievement among urban youth "working"? Are we "making progress"? That depends on what we mean by "working" and "progress." Hegemonic discourses "work" to the extent that the public keeps believing in them. In that case, the dominant discourse on progress in urban schools has been working quite well or at least well enough. Much of the public still "buys" the ideas that test scores somehow are an objective assessment of achievement, and so long as test scores appear to be rising they seem unconcerned that our urban schools are chronically underfunded and more like "chicken coops" than "crystal palaces." But if we ask how much progress has actually been made in raising expectations and achievement levels for urban youth so that they have an equal opportunity to get ahead, then it is hard to mask the fact that we are not making progress or are making progress in the wrong direction. One of the reasons for not making progress has to do with what sociologists call "goal displacement," when a narrow, instrumental, pragmatic goal—in this case the goal of raising scores on standardized texts over a relatively short cycle of assessment, in the most cost-efficient way possible—becomes the "real" goal of an institution and may actually interfere with the official goal of, say, setting high expectations for all, or promoting critical thinking, or preparing young people to become active, productive members of society. Test scores may keep rising, and educational leaders may keep proclaiming that we are making progress in narrowing the achievement gap, but the gap remains elusively resistant to change.

A good example of "goal displacement" is provided by the so-called Houston Miracle. As governor of Texas, George W. Bush worked closely with corporate leadership in the state to overhaul the state's system of public instruction to bring schools into alignment with the latest approaches to cost-effective management in industry and the changing "needs" of the labor force. Houston was much touted as the exemplary model of this school reform based on a partnership between political and economic leadership in the state. It reported steadily rising passing rates on the new Texas Assessment of Academic

Skills (TAAS) test and seemed to be making remarkable strides in eliminating the achievement gap between white and minority children. When Bush became president, he brought with him to Washington as his new education secretary Houston's superintendent, Rod Paige. The "No Child Left Behind" law signed by President Bush in January 2002 gives public schools twelve years to match the progress made in Houston's schools in raising achievement levels and narrowing achievement gaps. Now we are beginning to learn more about how the Houston miracle was produced, or more accurately fabricated, as an ideological text.

A recent investigation of Houston schools by the *New York Times* revealed a "rampant undercounting of school dropouts," along with an over-reporting of how many high school graduates were college bound (Schemo and Fessenden, 2003, p. A1). Although 88 percent of Houston's student body is black and Latino/Latina, only a few hundred minority students leave high school "college ready," that is, having the college preparatory courses colleges are looking for in applicants. The investigation also revealed that gains on the state's high school proficiency exam were not transferable to other standardized exams of academic achievement. Finally, the *Times* investigation pointed to the fact that whereas the state has billed its high school proficiency exam as setting high standards for students, it was widely acknowledged in the state that it was a "minimum skills" test that was a ticket for minimum skills job. What this indicates is that the "Houston miracle" was only the illusion of progress. What real progress there was in raising test scores was produced through reforms that emphasize: frequent rounds of student assessment, remediation, and re-testing; a curriculum "aligned" with a particular standardized test; and assessment of teachers and principals on the basis of how effective they are in raising test scores. As most any urban school teacher can attest, if it's higher test scores they want, then it's higher test scores they'll get, even if it is through "drill 'em and test 'em" approaches that subvert meaningful learning. This is part of why there is a crisis of underachievement in urban schools to begin with (Carlson, 1992), and we must interrogate the discourse on progress that makes utterances about "miracles," such as that in Houston, possible. If this is the kind of progress we can expect in the age of NCLB, it is clear that progress has become part of the problem rather than the solution.

There is another reason, aside from goal displacement, that we need to critically interrogate about claims of progress in responding to the urban school crisis. This has to do with resistance and opposition, both individually and collectively, to the "machines" of urban school reform—by students to be sure, but also by teachers and even administrators. To suggest just how powerful this resistance can be, I want to turn to a discussion of two school reorganization models that have been influential in urban school districts—Success for All, and the Baldrige Criteria—and their implementation in one urban elementary school in a northern rust belt city. The school served a mixture of poor white, African American, and Latino/Latina students (87 percent of who were classified as coming from poverty backgrounds). I interviewed a senior teacher in this school, and reviewed staff development materials, to document the implementation of the two reorganization models and to assess teacher responses to reorganization. In the late 1990s, the state declared the school to be in "academic emergency," which meant that if test scores did not significantly rise and the achievement gap between black, Latino, and white students did not narrow, the school could be closed and teachers could lose their jobs.

In an effort to better "align" the curriculum with the state-mandated proficiency test in the fourth grade, which children had to pass in order to be promoted to the fifth grade and continue on toward the ninth grade proficiency test, the school's principal decided to apply to become a "Success for All" (SFA) school. This reorganization model, developed by the behavioral psychologist Robert Slavin, has been particularly popular in schools serving urban and rural poor children. It begins with a highly scripted curriculum, with a focus upon reading skills. Textbooks contain the exact words teachers are to say in introducing lessons, questioning students, and assessing learning outcomes. Every teacher in a given grade level is supposed to be on the "same page" at the same time and to move forward at a predetermined pace. Those students identified as skill deficient in particular areas are given special tutoring and remediation. In this elementary school, teachers agreed to do much of this tutoring before and after the regular school, for $15 dollars an hour. By the third year of SFA, teachers were getting fed up with what they called the "cookie cutter" approach to teaching advocated in SFA, and a group of the more senior teachers in the building marched into the principal's office one day to proclaim, "We're not little robots." Teachers were told to give the program more time, to see how it "worked." However, teachers were told that they might informally "be creative" in covering the skill-based curriculum and preparing students for this test. This defused some teacher resistance but only temporarily. At this point the "SFA police," as the teachers referred to the evaluation and support team from SFA, made one of their periodic visits. With little advance warning, the teachers agreed to do their best to "put on a dog and pony show" for the SFA consultants, but the visit did not go well. The SFA team wrote a follow-up report claiming that achievement test scores were not rising like they should in the school because the reorganization model was not being effectively implemented. Teachers were blamed in particular for not sticking to the scripted curriculum and schedule. As a result of this report, and after three years with the SFA model, SFA withdrew support from the school—in effect, excommunicating it from the SFA school network. In some desperation the principal began "shopping around" for another reorganization model that promised to raise test scores, and fast.

He found it in the Baldrige reorganization model. Sponsored by the Malcolm Baldrige Foundation, which was established to promote increased productivity and cost-effectiveness in American industry, the Baldrige school reorganization model and the "Baldrige Criteria for Performance Excellence" are now being supported with grant money through the U.S. Department of Education, in collaboration with the Bill Gates Foundation. In Baldrige schools, the official philosophy is that it is up to local school staff to decide how they will go about increasing "productivity," with the proviso, of course, that staff produce a steady stream of quantifiable output data on each student's skill levels, in each subject domain, on a short cycle of assessment. Teachers attend special workshops to learn how to write multiple-choice tests to assess students, along with workshops on how to use new computer programs and management information technologies that monitor and record student "progress." Students are given weekly computer printouts that detail exactly where they stand in each skill area, and class averages are plastered around the classroom walls as constant reminders to teachers and students of how they stand relative to goals for achievement.

As part of an action plan to raise achievement among those students identified as "at risk" of not passing the state proficiency test, teachers in this school accepted a plan put forward by the principal, in collaboration with the superintendent, to pull these "at risk" students out of regular classes and assign them all day to a special "drill 'em and test 'em" class with their own teacher, where they were to spend much of their time preparing for the test on computers. It might have been expected, but apparently was not, when this "action plan" was implemented, students assigned to it became informally defined as low-ability students, and more particularly as discipline-problem students, and this became a self-fulfilling prophecy. So achievement scores for these students did not rise dramatically as administrators had predicted. Furthermore, the teacher assigned to the room felt demoralized and on the verge of quitting. She had to deal with many of the worst discipline problems and did not feel that she was really teaching—only monitoring computer monitors and keeping students from getting into trouble. It was not long before many teachers in the building were beginning to vocalize their discontent about the Baldrige Criteria, as they had about SFA. Thus, when a consultant from the Baldrige Foundation visited the school, he received an "ear full." Teachers were quite blunt, asking, "Why are we doing this? Where is it going?" The consultant, needless to say, was not happy to see so many teachers with a "negative attitude," and within a short time of this visit, the school was dropped by the Baldrige Foundation, as it had been dropped by SFA. Again, test scores were not rising as expected, and once again, teachers and administrators were blamed for deviating from the plan.

The Baldrige Foundation website asks educators who might be interested in joining their network of schools: "Do you believe you have been making progress but want to accelerate or better focus your efforts? Try using our simple questionnaire, Are We Making Progress?" The questionnaire is designed to lead individuals through the "Baldrige Criteria": leadership, information and analysis, faculty and staff satisfaction, process management in the classroom, and results. To show how these criteria might be implemented in practice, potential clients, as well as existing clients, are encouraged to read *Malcolm and Me* (Maurer and Pedersen, 2004), about a hypothetical Baldrige Foundation school. The story begins with Bill applying for a teaching job and being interviewed by the superintendent, Dr. Johnson. The superintendent remarks that first and foremost, teachers in the district all agreed on one credo: "Our students are our customers and the product we deliver is to allow them to achieve to their highest potential" (p. 5). The language of "customer" and "product" is to be at the forefront of everyone's thinking in Baldrige Foundation schools. The student and his or her parents are customers, according to this discourse on reorganization, because they increasingly have the option of leaving and taking their "business" to a charter or voucher school. The other major concern expressed by Dr. Johnson in the interview had to do with the attitude he expected teachers to have. "If you want to work in this district," he tells Bill, "you have to come to believe as passionately as all of us in our mission, goals, and values" (p. 7). When Bill is subsequently hired to teach in a Baldrige Criteria middle school, he learns another important lesson. "The boss goes first." The "boss," otherwise known as the principal, must be the one who makes the plan work through her or his commitment to continuous improvement. Each year, the test scores are expected to rise until everyone in the school has passed the state-mandated exam, and the principal is ultimately held responsible for making this happen. But good principals need not be authoritarian bosses. They can provide help and support to teachers, and like Bill's principal, tell them "that she believed in him and believed in the ability of all her students to learn." This shift is away from a system of checking up on teachers, or even principals, to catch them "doing wrong," and toward a system of "helping them become better teachers and principals" (p. 21). In the happy ending to this narrative, Bill becomes a happy and effective teacher—happy because he knew what was expected of him and "had a firm grasp of what the district mission and values are" (p. 22), and effective because he trusted in the "map," the "educational design and delivery system" used in the school (p. 41).

Such optimistic and unrealistic narratives of progress are in marked contrast to the narratives of teachers and administrators working in "real" urban schools, as I have suggested. Hegemonic narratives of progress promote the simplistic belief that the problem of underachievement can be adequately addressed through better management machines, borrowed from industry, when in fact these machines contribute to the crisis of underachievement by demoralizing students, teachers, and administrators and by reducing learning to a set of behaviorally defined "functional literacy" skills and test-taking abilities. Along the way, teachers are being re-skilled as technicians and supervisors of a highly mapped out instructional process. As they say in Baldrige Criteria schools, "get out the map" and consult it frequently. But where is this map leading us? Are teachers likely to become enthusiastic supporters of a trip which is so thoroughly mapped out, and in which they are being called upon to sacrifice so much? These are the unanswered, even unaddressed, questions that haunt the dominant discourse on progress in urban schools.

Toward a New Discourse on Progress

In the mainstream discourse on progress in the "war" against underachievement, it is often said that reforms have come in waves. Thus, a first wave of reform is associated with top-down models of accountability designed to raise standards; a second wave is associated with site-based management and free market approaches to reform, and now a third wave is linked to school reorganization models that promise "success for all." Unintentional though it may be, the metaphor of reform as a wave washing over public schools conjures up images of a hurricane, or even tsunami, sweeping over a landscape and clearing everything in its path. In this case, urban schools, and the teachers, students, and administrators who live and work in urban schools, have been hardest hit. The sad truth is that so long as reform continues to be framed within the currently hegemonic discourses, it will not serve to advance democratic projects or empower urban teachers and their students. The sad truth is that progressive educational leaders will need to work hard to un-make much of the "progress" that has been made over the past several decades through wave after wave of neoliberal reform. They also will need to hold fast to what democratic progress has been made (in the way of affirmative action and a more multicultural curriculum, for example) and hold onto the collective memory of progressive struggle in America along a number of fronts. It is the idea and the promise of democratic public education rather than the dominant practice of public education that progressive educational leadership affirms (Dimitriadis and Carlson, 2003).

In forging a democratic discourse on progress in American education, the most immediate and pragmatic response among progressive educational leaders may well be a politics of individual and collective resistance to the "machines" of urban schooling, including "high stakes" testing. This is already beginning to happen in many states and has been associated with, among other things, organized refusals to take state-mandated proficiency tests. Teachers have an important role to play in such movements, as interested "insiders" aligned in solidarity with those students disempowered and effectively disenfranchised by high-stakes testing. As I have long argued, teachers represent a potentially powerful counter-hegemonic power bloc in democratic educational renewal, and there is much good, progressive work to be done in teachers' unions and professional organizations (Carlson, 1992). At some point, however, progressives also must move beyond critique and resistance toward the forging of a countermovement for progress in America, linked to a new commonsense discourse on the renewal of public education and public life.

The promise of democratic education and public life in America has been subverted over the past century and continues to be. But it nevertheless provides some scaffolding for constructing a new democratic discourse of educational renewal. That promise, projected upon a new cultural landscape, is about bringing people together across their differences in ways that do not erase difference but that engage them in a collective dialogue. It is about providing opportunities for individuals and groups to engage in the creative production of meaning and to contribute in diverse ways to public life. And it is also about empowering those who have been marginalized by class, race, gender, sexual orientation, and other markers of difference and identity so that they can develop their fuller potentials as human beings. For many of us who still believe in the radical democratic possibilities of the Enlightenment project, the most important thing that a counter-discourse must do is reawaken hope and challenge the dominant cynicism and vulgar pragmatism of the age. This hope, I believe, is still to be found in *praxis*, the unity of theory and self-reflective practice.

What progressive educational leaders can offer, then, is a hope without illusion, finding hope even when the battle is not going well—and at this point in public education it is not (Carlson, 2005). Progressive leaders must be honest in the sense that they confront teachers and other educators with the real and significant forces that currently stand in the way of meaningful democratization of public education and public life. Currently the reality is that transnational capitalism plays an ever-increasing role in establishing the discursive parameters for educational progress, and public schools (particularly urban schools) are being called upon to assume a heightened role in the surveillance, policing, and regulation of urban youth. If there can be no illusions about the challenge progressives face in reconstructing public education along more democratic and liberatory lines, progressive leaders can help recover hope that things could be different. They can open up possibilities for critical reflection and strategic action at various educational sites, and they can help develop linkages between various movements, alliances, and axes of struggle to bring people together around a strategic unified front politics.

To get beyond the current "stuck point" in progressive cultural politics, I believe post-structural perspectives can be particularly useful. Post-structuralism begins with the presumption that truth, since it is discursively produced and involved in constituting power relations, is never stable, secure, or unified, and never without its opposition. There always are oppositional discourses, practices, and spaces to be found within public schools and other sites in the public, although they might be quite marginalized and poorly linked. Furthermore, there are real limits to how far hegemonic discourses and microtechnologies can control practice. It is the role of the educational leader and public intellectual to help expand the potential of these oppositional spaces to link up and become transformative, to produce what Guattari (1984) called a "molecular revolution" that emerges out of many small, localized actions of resistance and re-imagination. This is the work of both Gramsci's "organic intellectual" and Foucault's "specific intellectual," the strategic work whose object is to expose certain taken-for-granted discourses that dominate and limit people, and build alliances and affiliations among various struggles against domination. Progressive educational leaders do not speak in the name of the oppressed, but, as Foucault says, "alongside them, in solidarity with them, in part because others' oppression is often inseparable from their own" (1980, p. 126). Progressive educational leaders work the boundaries between insider and outsider status, linking what is going on inside and outside of public schools and speaking in solidarity with those whose interests and voices have been silenced in dominant discursive constructions of progress in education. The intellectual thus plays a critical role in the development of what Gramsci called a "philosophy of praxis," a form of educational leadership aimed at the critical intellectual development of a group or movement with which the intellectual is aligned in solidarity (1971, p. 334). Such leaders maintain hope by returning again and again to the battle with a renewed conviction that the future is open rather than determined and that the democratic impulse in American education and culture has not been extinguished.

References

Apple, M. (2004). *Ideology and curriculum,* third edition. New York: RoutledgeFalmer.

Carlson, D. (1992). *Teachers and crisis: Urban school reform and teachers' work culture.* New York: Routledge.

———. (2003). Cosmopolitan progressivism: Democratic education in the age of globalization, *Journal of Curriculum Theorizing* (Winter): 7–31.

———. (2005). Hope without illusion: Telling the story of democratic educational renewal. *International Journal of Qualitative Studies in Education,* 18 (1): 21–45.

Dimitriadis, G., and Carlson, D. (2003). *Promise to keep: Cultural studies, democratic education, and public life.* New York: Routledge.

Dostoyevski, F. (1993). *Notes from underground.* Trans. R. Pevear and L. Volokhonsky. New York: Random House.

Foucault, M. (1977). *Discipline and punish: The birth of the prison.* Trans. A. Sheridan. New York: Vintage.

Foucault, M. (1980). *Power/knowledge: Selected interviews and other writings, 1972-1977.* New York: Pantheon.

Gramsci, A. (1971). *Selections from the prison notebooks.* New York: International Publishers.

Guattari, F. (1984). *Molecular revolution: Psychiatry and politics.* London: Penguin.

————. (1996). Capitalist systems, structures, and processes, in G. Genosko, ed. *The Guattari Reader.* Oxford, UK: Blackwell. pp. 233–247.

Hanushek, E. (1994). *Making schools work: Improving performance and controlling costs.* Washington, DC: Brookings Institution Press.

Hargreaves, A. (1994). *Changing teachers, changing times.* New York: Teachers College Press.

Hill, P., and Celio, M. (1998). *Fixing urban schools.* Washington, D.C.: Brookings Institution Press.

Maurer, R., and Pedersen, S. (2004). *Malcolm and me: How to use the Baldrige Criteria for Performance Excellence.* Lanham, Maryland: Scarecrow Education.

National Commission on Excellence and Education (1983). *A nation at risk.* Washington, DC: U.S. Government Printing Office.

National Education Commission on Time and Learning (1994). *Prisoners of time.* Washington, DC: U. S. Government Printing Office.

O'Connor, J. (1973). *The fiscal crisis of the state.* New York: St. Martin's Press.

Schemo, D., and Fessenden, F. (2003). Gains in Houston schools: How real are they?" *New York Times* (December 3), sec. A, p. 1, 27.

Thompson, E. P. (1993). *Time, work discipline, and industrial capitalism, in customs in common: Studies in traditional popular culture.* New York: The New Press, pp. 352–403.

Weis, L., and Fine, M. (2003). Extraordinary conversations in public schools, in G. Dimitriadis and D. Carlson, eds., *Promises to keep: Cultural studies, democratic education, and public life.* New York: Routledge, pp. 95–124.

Wells, H. G. (1935). *Things to come.* Boston: Gregg Press.

2

Schooling, Markets, Race, and an Audit Culture

Michael W. Apple

Changing Commonsense

In a number of volumes over the past decade, I have critically analyzed the wave after wave of educational reforms that have centered around neoliberal commitments to the market and a supposedly weak state, neoconservative emphases on stronger control over curricula and values, and "new managerial" proposals to install rigorous forms of accountability in schooling (Apple, 2000; Apple, 2006; Apple et al., 2003). The first set of reforms has not demonstrated much improvement in schooling and has marked a dangerous shift in our very idea of democracy from "thick" collective forms to "thin" consumer driven and overly individualistic forms. The second misconstrues and then basically ignores the intense debates over whose knowledge should be taught in schools and establishes a false consensus on what is supposedly common in U.S. culture (Apple, 1996; Apple, 2004; Binder, 2002; Levine, 1996). The third takes the position that "if it moves in classrooms it should be measured" and has caused some of the best practices that have been developed through concerted efforts in some of the most difficult settings to be threatened (Apple and Beane, 2007; Lipman, 2004; McNeil, 2000). Unfortunately, all too many of the actual effects of this assemblage of reforms have either been negligible or negative (Apple, 2006), or they have been largely rhetorical (Smith et al., 2004). This is unfortunate, especially given all of the work that well-intentioned educators have devoted to some of these efforts. But reality must be faced if we are to go beyond what is currently fashionable.

The odd combination of marketization on the one hand and centralization of control on the other is not only occurring in education; nor is it only going on in the United States. This is a worldwide phenomenon. And while there are very real, and often successful, efforts to counter it (see Apple et al., 2003;

Apple and Buras, 2006), this has not meant that the basic assumptions that lie behind neoliberal, neoconservative, and new managerial forms have not had a major impact on our institutions throughout society and even on our common-sense.

In many nations there have been attempts, often more than a little success-ful, to restructure state institutions (Jessop, 2003). Among the major aims of such restructuring were: to ensure that the state served business interests; to have the state's internal operations model those used in business; and to "take politics out of public institutions," that is to reduce the possibility that govern-ment institutions would be subject to political pressure from the electorate (Leys, 2003, p. 3). Chubb and Moe's (1990) arguments about vouchers mirror this latter point, for example.

This last point, removing politics from government institutions, is based on a less than accurate understanding not only of the state but of the market as well. While most economics textbooks may give the impression that markets are impersonal and impartial, they are instead highly political as well as inherently unstable. To this, other points need to be added. To guarantee their survival, firms must seek ways of breaking out of the boundaries that are set by state regulation. Increasingly, this has meant that the boundaries established to divide non-market parts of our lives must be extended so that these spheres can be opened to commodification and profit-making. As Leys reminds us, this is a crucially important issue. "It threatens the destruction of non-market spheres of life on which social solidarity and active democracy have always depended" (Leys, 2003, p. 4).

It is not an easy process to transform parts of our lives and institutions that were not totally integrated into market relations so that they are part of a market. To do this, at least four significant things must be worked on (Leys 2003, p. 4).

1. The services or goods that are to be focused upon must be reconfigured so that they can indeed be bought and sold.
2. People who received these things from the state must be convinced to want to buy them.
3. The working conditions and outlook of the employees who work in this sector must be transformed from a model based on collective understand-ings and providing service to "the public" on the one hand to working to produce profits for owners and investors subject to market discipline on the

other.

4. When business moves into what were previously non-market fields, as much as possible their risks must be underwritten by the state.

Under these kinds of pressure, standardized and competitive labor processes begin to dominate the lives of the newly marketized workers. But this is not all. A good deal of labor is shifted to the consumer. S/he now must do much of the work of getting information, sorting through the advertising and claims, and making sense of what is often a thoroughly confusing welter of data and "products." (See Van Dunk and Dickman, 2003 for how this works, and doesn't work, in voucher plans.) In the process as well, there is a very strong tendency for needs and values that were originally generated out of collective deliberations, struggles, and compromises, and which led to the creation of state services (Apple, 2000), to be marginalized and ultimately abandoned (Leys 2003, p. 4). Once again, in Leys's words, "The facts suggest that market-driven politics can lead to a remarkably rapid erosion of democratically determined collective values and institutions" (Leys, 2003, p. 4).

These arguments may seem abstract, but they speak to significant and concrete changes in our daily lives in and out of education. For more than two decades, we have witnessed coordinated and determined efforts not only to reconstruct a "liberal" market economy, but a "liberal" market society and culture. This distinction is important. In Habermas's words, the attempt is to have a "system" to totally colonize the "life-world" (Habermas, 1971). As many aspects of our lives as possible, including the state and civil society, must be merged into the economy and economic logics. Although there will always be counter-hegemonic tendencies (Jessop, 2003), our daily interactions—and even our dreams and desires—must ultimately be governed by market "realities" and relations. In this scenario—and it is increasingly not only a scenario, but a reality—a society and a culture is not to be based on trust and shared values. Rather, all aspects of that society are to be grounded in and face "the most extreme possible exposure to market forces, with internal markets, profit centers, audits, and 'bottom lines' penetrating the whole of life from hospitals to play-groups" (Leys, 2003, p. 35–36). As Margaret Thatcher once famously put it, "The task is not to just change the economy, but to change the soul."

Interestingly, because of the focus on measurable results and central control over important decisions, the federal government's power has actually been sharply enhanced. (Think of No Child Left Behind.) This has been accompanied by a loss of local democracy (and civil liberties as well). At the same time, the role of the state in dealing with the destructive rapaciousness produced by "economically rational" decisions has been sharply reduced (Leys, 2003, p. 42; see also Katz, 2001; and Shipler, 2004).

In attempting to understand this, in *Educating the "Right" Way* I argued that neoliberalism requires the constant production of evidence that you are doing things "efficiently" and in the "correct" way (Apple, 2006). This is going on at the same time as the state itself becomes increasingly subject to commercialization. This situation has given rise to what might best be called an *audit culture*. To get a sense of the widespread nature of such practices, it is useful here to quote from Leys, one of the most perceptive analysts of this growth:

> [There is a] proliferation of *auditing*, i.e., the use of business derived concepts of independent supervision to measure and evaluate performance by public agencies and public employees, from civil servants and school teachers to university [faculty] and doctors: environmental audit, value for money audit, management audit, forensic audit, data audit, intellectual property audit, medical audit, teaching audit and technology audit emerged and, to varying degrees of institutional stability and acceptance, very few people have been left untouched by these developments. (Leys, 2003, p. 70)

> The widespread nature of these evaluative and measurement pressures, and their ability to become parts of our commonsense, crowd out other conceptions of effectiveness and democracy. In place of a society of citizens with the democratic power to ensure effectiveness and proper use of collective resources, and relying in large measure on trust in the public sector, there emerged a society of "auditees," anxiously preparing for audits and inspections. A punitive culture of "league tables" developed (purporting to show the relative efficiency and inefficiency of universities or schools or hospitals). Inspection agencies were charged with "naming and shaming" "failing" individual teachers, schools, social work departments, and so on; private firms were invited to take over and run "failing" institutions. (Leys, 2003, p. 70)

The ultimate result of an auditing culture of this kind is not the promised decentralization that is bandied about rhetorically in most neoliberal self-understandings, but what seems to be a massive re-centralization and what is best seen as a process of de-democratization (Leys, 2003, p. 71). Making the state more "business friendly" and importing business models directly into the core functions of the state such as hospitals and education—in combination with a rigorous and unforgiving ideology of individual accountability (Leys, 2003, p. 73)—these are the hallmarks of life today. Once again, No Child Left Behind, high stakes testing, voucher plans, for-profit ventures such as Edison schools, and similar kinds of things are the footprints that these constantly escalating pressures have left on the terrain of education.

A key to all of this is the *de-valuing* of public goods and services. It takes long-term and creative ideological work, but people must be made to see anything that is public as "bad" and anything that is private as good. And anyone who works in these public institutions must be seen as inefficient and in need of a good dose of competition so that they work longer and harder (see Clarke and Newman, 1997). When the people who work in public institutions fight back and argue for more respectful treatment and for a greater realization that simplistic solutions do not deal with the complexities that they face every day in the real world of schools and communities, they are labeled as recalcitrant and selfish and as uncaring. Sometimes, as in the case of former U.S. Secretary of Education Page's public comments to what he thought was a sympathetic audience, they are even called "terrorists." And these "recalcitrant, selfish, and uncaring" employees—teachers, administrators, social workers, and almost all other public school employees—can then have their labor externally controlled and intensified by people who criticize them mercilessly, often as in the case of major corporations while these same businesses are shedding their own social responsibilities by paying little or no taxes.

I noted earlier that it is not just the labor of state employees that is radically altered; so too is the labor of "consumers." When services such as hospitals and schools are commodified, a good deal of the work that was formerly done by state employees is shifted onto those using the service. Examples of labor being shifted to the "consumer" include online banking, airline ticketing and check-in, supermarket self-checkouts, and similar things. Each of these is advertised as enhancing "choice" and each comes with a system of incentives and disincentives. Thus, one can get airline miles for checking in on one's computer. Or as some banks are now doing, there is an extra charge if you want to see a real live bank teller rather than using an ATM machine (which itself often now has an extra charge for using it).

The effects of such changes may be hidden but that does not make them any less real. Some of these are clearly economic: the closing of bank branches; the laying off of large numbers of workers; the intensification of the workload of the workers who remain. Some are hidden in their effects on consumers: exporting all of the work and the necessary commitment of time onto those people who are now purchasing the service; searching for information that was once given by the government; doing one's banking and airline work oneself;

bagging and checking out at supermarkets.[1]

This all may seem so trivial. But when each "trivial" instance is added up, the massiveness of the transformation in which labor is transferred to the consumer is striking. For it to be successful, our commonsense must be changed so that we see the world only as individual consumers, and we see ourselves as surrounded by a world in which everything is potentially a commodity for sale.

Mark Fowler, Ronald Reagan's chair of the Federal Communications Commission, once publicly stated that television is simply a toaster with pictures. A conservative media mogul in England seemed to agree, when he said that there is no difference between a television program and a cigarette lighter (Leys, 2003, p. 108). Both positions are based on an assumption that cultural form and content and the processes of distribution are indeed *commodities*. There are few more important mechanisms of cultural choice and distribution than schools. And under this kind of logic, one might say that schools are simply toasters with children. There is something deeply disturbing about this position.

Of course, many of us may be apt to see such things as relatively humorous or innocuous. Aren't market-based proposals for such things as schools and health care just another, but supposedly more efficient, way of making services available? But not only are these ideologically driven "reforms" *not* all that efficient (Apple, 2006), the process of privatization is strikingly different than public ownership and control. For example, in order to market something like education, it must first be transformed into a commodity, a "product." The product is then there to serve different ends. Thus, rather than schooling being aimed at creating democratic citizenship as its ultimate goal (although we should never romanticize an Edenic past when this was actually the case; schooling has always been a site of struggle over what its functions would actually be, with people of color being constructed as "not quite citizens." See Apple, [2000]), the entire process can slowly become aimed instead at the generation of profit for shareholders (Leys, 2003, p. 211–212). The fact that such things as the Edison Schools have not caught on as much as their investors had dreamed of means that the process of commodification is at least partly being rejected. For many people in all walks of life, the idea of "selling" our schools and our children is somehow disturbing, as the continuing controversy over Channel One, the for-profit television station now in 43 percent of all public and private middle and secondary schools in the United States, amply demonstrates (Apple, 2000). These intuitions demonstrate that in our everyday lives there remains a sense that there is something very wrong with our current and still too uncritical fascination with markets and audits.

David Marquand (2000) summarizes these points in the following way: \

> The public domain of citizenship and service should be safeguarded from incursions by the market domain of buying and selling...The goods of the public domain—health care, crime prevention, education—should not be treated as commodities or proxy commodities. The language of buyer and seller, producer and consumer, does not belong in the public domain; nor do the relationships which that language implies. Doctors and nurses do not "sell" medical services; students are not "customers" of their teachers; policemen and policewomen do not "produce" public order. The attempt to force these relationships into a market model undermines the service ethic, degrades the institutions that embody it and robs the notion of common citizenship of part of its meaning. (pp. 212–213)

In my mind, public institutions are the defining features of a caring and democratic society. The market relations that are sponsored by capitalism should exist to pay for these institutions, *not* the other way around. Thus, markets are to be subordinate to the aim of producing a fuller and thicker participatory democratic polity and daily life (see Skocpol, 2003). It should be clear by now that a cynical conception of democracy that is "on sale" to voters and manipulated and marketed by political and economic elites does not adequately provide for goods such as general education, objective information, media and new forms of communication that are universally accessible, well-maintained public libraries for all, public health, and universal health care. At best, markets provide these things in radically unequal ways (Katz, 2001), with class, gender, and especially race being extremely powerful markers of these inequalities. If that is the case—even if the definitions of the "public" were and often still are based on the construction of gendered and raced spaces (Fraser, 1989; Kelly, 1993)—the very idea of public institutions is under concerted attack. They need to be provided—and defended—collectively. Such things are anything but secondary. They are the defining characteristics of what it means to be a just society (Leys, 2003).

Unfortunately, the public has gotten increasingly used to the language of privatization, marketization, and constant evaluation. In many ways, it has become commonsense—and the critical intuitions that something may be wrong with all of this may slowly wither. Yet, in many nations where conditions are even worse, this has not necessarily happened (Apple et al. 2003). We can learn from these nations' experiences, and we can relearn what it means to reconstitute the civic in our lives (Skocpol, 2003). Education has a fundamental role to play in doing exactly that. But it can only do so if it is protected from those who see it as one more product to be consumed as we measure it.

Race and Markets

So far I have discussed the general tendencies surrounding the increasing marketization of everyday life and have argued that such tendencies will have deeply problematic effects. However, we need to be careful not to romanticize a past in which the state was supposedly responsive to all its citizens. As Charles Mills so powerfully argues, underlying our very idea of the modern liberal state and underlying the social commitments for which it supposedly stands is a *racial* contract (Mills, 1997; see also Omi and Winant, 1994). Further, as Gloria Ladson-Billings and others have claimed, in education as in so much else, "Race is always already present in every social configuring of our lives" (Ladson-Billings, 2004, p. 51). For these very reasons, it is imperative that we take a second look at the ways in which markets and audit cultures function—this time placing race at the center of our analysis, since different social positionings in society may give different meanings to neoliberal and neoconservative policies.

The criticisms of market relations and logics that I and others have made (see, e.g., Apple, 2006; Gillborn and Youdell, 2000; Marginson, 1997; Marginson and Considine, 2000; Whitty, Power, and Halpin 1998) are powerful. But these criticisms often carry a number of unacknowledged assumptions about race. The market has been much less responsive to particular groups than others. Indeed, the subject position of "consumer" has been much less available to African Americans and Latino/as than it has been for dominant groups. Thus, being actually *seen* as a "consumer," as someone who is a "rational economic actor," does have progressive tendencies within it when this position is compared to the histories of the ways people of color have been socially coded in the United States and elsewhere. When people of color actively take on this different coding, they are not simply being incorporated into dominant economic discourses and relations; they are also partly engaged in a form of counter-hegemonic action, one employing dominant economic discourses to subvert historically powerful racializing views that have had immense power in society (Apple and Pedroni, 2005; Pedroni, 2003). Let us examine this somewhat more closely.

At the outset, and as I show elsewhere, race has always been a key presence in the structures of feeling surrounding markets and choice plans in education. Many of the strongest proponents of vouchers and similar plans may claim that their positions are based on a belief in the efficiency of markets, on the fear of a secularization of the sacred, or on the dangers of losing the values and beliefs that give meaning to their lives. (These latter two fears are especially pronounced among the authoritarian populist religious conservatives who are among the strongest proponents of both vouchers and home schooling. See Apple, 2006, for more on this.). However, historically, neither the economic nor the moral elements of this critique can be totally set apart from their partial genesis in the struggles over racial segregation, over busing to achieve integration, and in the loss of a federal tax exemption by conservative—and usually white only—religious academies. In short, the fear of the "racial other" has played a significant role in this discursive construction of the "problem of the public school" (Apple, 2006).

Having said this, however, there is also increasing support for voucher and similar choice plans among "minority" groups. Given the fact that so much of the conservative tradition in the United States was explicitly shaped by racist and racializing discourses and practices,[2] and by a strongly anti-immigrant heritage as well, and given the fact that much of the current neoliberal and neoconservative attacks on the public sphere have had disproportionate effects on the gains of poor communities and on communities of color, the existence and growth of support among some members of dispossessed groups is more than a little striking.[3] A complex process of discursive and positional disarticulation and rearticulation is going on here, as dominant groups attempt to pull dispossessed collectivities under their own leadership and dispossessed groups themselves attempt to employ the social, economic, and cultural capital usually possessed by dominant groups to gain collective power for themselves. As we shall see, the label "conservative" cannot be employed easily in understanding the actions of all of the dispossessed groups who do ally themselves with conservative causes without at the same time reducing the complexity of the particular social fields of power on which they operate.

Perhaps the most interesting example of the processes of discursive and social disarticulation and rearticulation that one could find today involves the growing African American (at least among *some* elements of the African American community) support for neoliberal policies such as voucher plans (see, e.g., Moe, 2001). A key instance is the Black Alliance for Educational Options (BAEO), a group of African American parents and activists that is chaired by Howard Fuller, the former superintendent of Milwaukee public schools, one of the most racially segregated school systems in the United States. BAEO provides vocal support for voucher plans and similar neoliberal proposals. It has generated considerable support within Black communities throughout the nation, particularly within poor inner-city areas.

A sense of the language that underpins BAEO's commitment can be seen in the following quote:

> Our children are our most precious resource. It is our responsibility to love them, nurture them and protect them. It is also our responsibility to ensure that they are properly educated. Without a good education, they will [not] have a real chance to engage in the practice of freedom: the process of engaging in the fight to transform their world. (BAEO website)

Black Alliance for Educational Options's mission is clear.

> The Black Alliance for Educational Options is a national, nonpartisan member organization whose mission is to actively support parental choice to empower families and increase educational options for Black children. (BAEO website)

The use of language here is striking. The language of neoliberalism (choice, parental empowerment, accountability, individual freedom) is re-appropriated and sutured together with ideas of collective Black freedom and a deep concern for the community's children. This creates something of a 'hybrid' discourse that blends together meanings from multiple political sources and agendas. In some ways, this is similar to the long history of critical cultural analyses that demonstrate that people form bricolages in their daily lives and can employ language and commodities in ways undreamed of by the original producers of the language and products (see, e.g., Willis, 1990).

While this process of rearticulation and use is important to note, it is equally essential to recognize something that makes the creative bricolage in which BAEO is engaged somewhat more problematic. A very large portion of the group's funding comes directly from conservative sources such as the Bradley Foundation. The Bradley Foundation, a well-known sponsor of conservative causes, has not only been in the forefront of providing support for vouchers and privatization initiatives, but also is one of the groups that provided significant support for Herrnstein and Murray's book, *The Bell Curve* (1994), a volume that argued that African Americans were on average less intelligent than Whites and that this was genetic in nature.

Thus, it would be important to ask about the nature and effects of the connections being made between rightist ideological and financial sources and BAEO itself. It is not inconsequential that neoliberal and neoconservative foundations provide not only funding but media visibility for "minority" groups who support—even critically—their agendas. The genesis of such funding is not inconsequential. Does this mean that groups such as BAEO are simply being manipulated by neoliberal and neoconservative foundations and movements? An answer to this question is not easy, but even with my cautions stated above it is certainly not a simple "yes."

In public forums and in discussions that Tom Pedroni and I have had with some of leaders of BAEO, they have argued that they will use any funding sources available so that they can follow their own specific program of action. They would accept money from more liberal sources; but Bradley and other conservative foundations have come forward much more readily.[4] In the minds of the leaders of BAEO, the African American activists are in control, not the conservative foundations. Thus, for BAEO, they see themselves as strategically positioning themselves in order to get funding from conservative sources. What they do with this funding, such as their strong (and well advertised in the media) support for voucher plans (although this support too is contingent and sometimes depends on local power relations), is wholly their decision. For them, the space provided by educational markets can be reoccupied for Black cultural and/or nationalist politics and can be employed to stop what seems to them (more than a little accurately in my opinion) to be a war on Black children.

However, while I have a good deal of respect for a number of the leaders of BAEO, it is important to remember that they are not the only ones strategically organizing on this social field of power. Like BAEO, groups affiliated with, say, the Bradley Foundation also know *exactly* what they are doing and know very well how to employ the agendas of BAEO for their own purposes, purposes that in the long term often may run directly counter to the interests of the majority of those with less power at both the national and regional levels. Is it really in the long-term interests of people of color to be affiliated with the same groups who provided funding and support for books such as Herrnstein and Murray (1994) *The Bell Curve*? I think not, although once again we need to recognize the complexities involved here.

I am certain that this kind of question is constantly raised about the conservative stances taken by the people of color who have made alliances with, say, neoliberals and neoconservatives—and by the activists within BAEO itself. When members of groups who are consistently "othered" in this society strategically take on identities that support dominant groups, such questioning is natural and I believe essential. However, it is also crucial to remember that members of historically oppressed and marginalized groups have *always* had to act on a terrain that is not of their choosing, have always had to act strategically and creatively to gain some measure of support from dominant groups to advance their causes (Lewis, 1993, 2000). It is also the case that more recently national and local leaders of the Democratic Party in the United States have too often assumed that Black support is simply *there*, that it doesn't need to be worked for. Because of this, we may see the further development of "unusual alliances" over specific issues such as educational policies. When this is coupled with some of the tacit and/or overt support within some communities of color not only for voucher plans but for antigay, antiabortion, school prayer, and similar initiatives, the suturing together of some Black groups with larger conservative movements on particular issues is not totally surprising (see Dillard, 2001).

The existence and growing power of committed movements such as BAEO, though, does point out that we need to be careful about stereotyping groups who may publicly support neoliberal and neoconservative policies. Their perspectives need to be examined carefully and taken seriously, not simply dismissed as totally misguided, as people who have been duped into unthinking acceptance of a harmful set of ideologies. There are complicated strategic moves being made on an equally complex social field of power. I may—and do—strongly disagree with a number of the positions that groups such as BAEO take. However, to assume that they are simply puppets of conservative forces is not only to be too dismissive of their own attempts at social maneuvering, but I also believe that it may be tacitly racist as well.

Saying this doesn't mean that we need to weaken the arguments against audit cultures and the marketization and privatization of schooling and the larger society that I articulated earlier in this chapter. Voucher and tax credit plans (as I noted, the latter ultimately may actually be more dangerous) will still have some extremely problematic effects in the long term. One of the most important effects could be a *demobilization* of social movements within communities of color. Schools have played central roles in the creation of movements for justice. In essence, rather than being peripheral reflections of larger battles and dynamics, struggles over schooling—over what should be taught, over the relationship between schools and local communities, over the very ends and means of the institution itself—have provided a crucible for the *formation* of larger social movements toward equality (Hogan, 1982; Apple et al., 2003). These collective movements have transformed our definitions of rights, of who should have them, and of the role of the government in guaranteeing these rights. Absent organized, community-wide mobilizations, these transformations would not have occurred.

This is under threat currently. I have argued elsewhere that definitions of democracy based on possessive individualism, on the citizen as only a "consumer," are inherently grounded in a process of de-racing, declassing, and de-gendering (see Apple, 2006 and Ball, 1994). These are the very groups who have employed struggles over educational access and outcomes to form themselves as self-conscious actors. If it is the case, as I strongly believe it is, that it is the organized efforts of social movements that ultimately have led to the transformation of our educational system in more democratic directions (Apple, 2000)—and this has been especially the case for mobilizations by people who have been labeled as society's "others"— the long-term effects of neoliberal definitions of democracy may be truly tragic for communities of color (and working-class groups), not "only" in increasing inequalities in schools (see, e.g., Apple, 2006; Gillborn and Youdell, 2000; Lipman, 2004; McNeil, 2000), but in leading to a very real loss of the impetus for *collective* solutions to pressing social problems. If all problems are simply "solved" by individual choices on a market, then collective mobilizations tend to wither and perhaps even disappear. Given the crucial role played by organized movements surrounding education in the formation and growth of mobilizations among African Americans, Latino/as, and many other communities of color against the denial of their rights, this is not something to be welcomed (Apple and Buras 2006). If history is any guide here, the results will not be pleasant. Thus, although short-term support for neoliberal and neoconservative policies may seem strategically wise to some members of less powerful groups, and may in fact generate short-term mobilizations, I remain deeply worried about what will happen over time.[5] It is the long-term implications of individuating processes and ideologies, and their effects on the necessity of larger and constantly growing social mobilizations that aim toward substantive transformations within the public sphere, that need to be of concern as well.

Other points should be added here about what might be called the political economy of everyday life. I argued earlier that marketization and commodification, when accompanied by the shrinking of state responsibility, intensify the labor of the "consumer." This process relegates to the individual or the family all of the tasks of information gathering and evaluation. This often entails an extensive amount of work, especially for those communities and families with fewer economic resources, less technical skill, under-resourced or closed libraries and social service centers, and the emotional and physical burdens of simply providing for human needs in an unforgiving economy. Since, as Van Dunk and Dickman (2003) show, the major urban areas where marketizing tendencies such as vouchers are now in place are doing a very poor job of making information on schools, curricula, teaching, and so on, easily available to the public and especially to poor persons of color, this puts these "consumers" at a serious disadvantage.

Even with these difficulties, there is something much more complicated ideologically than meets the eye going on here. As I noted and as Pedroni and I have discussed at greater length (Apple and Pedroni, 2005; Pedroni, 2003), when persons of color take up the position of "rational economic actor," of consumer, this does have counter-hegemonic possibilities and does provide for opportunities for different social codings. However, while noting this—and it must be noted—possibilities are just that, possibilities. They require objective material conditions and resources in people's lived environments too in order for them to be acted upon. Such possibilities may not be easily acted upon under the conditions of neoliberal restructuring in the economy, in social and cultural services, health care, and in so much more in urban and rural communities populated by those who are seen as the constitutive outside in this society (see Katz, 2001).

Conclusion

I began this chapter with a critical overview of certain tendencies within our societies. I pointed to the steady growth of neoliberal restructurings of institutions and identities and to the hard and creative ideological work that such transformations require. In the process, I noted that commodification and audit cultures tend to reinforce each other and that these processes are played out on multiple terrains, with education being one of the most significant.

There has been exceptional work done on the ways in which class works in altered contexts such as these. For example, middle-class parents often have a store of cultural and social capital that enables them to employ such things as "choice" in education as part of complex conversion strategies that guarantee their own children's advantage (see, e.g., Ball, 2003; Gillborn and Youdell 2000; Power et al., 2003). There is also an emerging body of work on how this is related to gendered labor, particularly the work of mothers (see, e.g., Griffith and Smith, 2005). However, there has been less attention paid to the ways in which members of historically oppressed "minority" groups, particularly poor persons of color, *strategically* deal with issues of marketization, privatization, and "choice" in the United States.[6]

Part of my interest in this chapter is to provide a context for a serious discussion both of the meaning and the effects of such strategic actions on the parts of those who must act on a terrain in which historically grounded power relations and struggles take on even more complicated forms. They require a much more nuanced reading than our usual critical appraisals are apt to do. We must continue to engage in the critical work of detailing the ways in which conservative modernization is restructuring our lives and institutions. But this needs to be done with a thorough, and historically grounded, understanding of the need to broaden the "we" and, hence, to recognize the contradictory and multiple daily realities that govern these effects.

Notes

1. Of course, this is a differentiated experience. Supermarkets are less apt to even be found in inner city neighborhoods populated by poor persons of color.

2. "Progressive" traditions in the United States were not free of such racializing and racist logics. See, for example, Selden (1999).

3. That, say, a number of African American groups, ones that are making alliances with distinctly conservative movements, exist and are growing says something very important about the fascination with identity politics among many progressive scholars and activists in education and elsewhere. Too often writing on identity (wrongly) assumes that identity politics is a "good thing," that people inexorably move in progressive directions as they pursue what Nancy Fraser would call a politics of recognition. See Nancy Fraser (1997). Yet, any serious study of rightist movements demonstrates that identity politics is just as apt to take, say, angry and retrogressive forms—anti-gay, racist nativism, anti-women, and so on. For many such people, "we" are the new oppressed, with that "we" not including most people of color, feminists, "sexual deviants," immigrants, and so on. Yet, as I noted earlier, even people within these "despised"groups themselves may take on such retrogressive identities.

4. In this regard, Tom Pedroni's ongoing research on BAEO and similar groups is of considerable importance. See Pedroni (2003). See also, Apple and Pedroni (2005) and Apple and Buras (2006).

5. Dillard (2001). Angela Dillard is very fair in her assessment of what the implications of such support may be. She nicely shows the contradictions of the arguments and logic of the people she focuses upon. In doing so, she draws upon some of the more cogent analyses of the relationship between democracy and the maintenance of the public sphere on the one hand

and an expansive and rich understanding of what it means to be a citizen on the other. Readers of her discussion would also be well served to connect her arguments to the historical struggles over the very meanings of our concepts of democracy, freedom, and citizenship such as that found in Foner's (1998) illuminating book, but Dillard's discussion is substantive and useful.

6. There has been some discussion of the dangers of voucher plans by African American nationalist activists and scholars. See Bush (2004). On Black activism and the ways in which consumer struggles have led to positive effects both within dominant white controlled economic and political institutions and within Black mobilizations as well, see Sewell (2004).

References

Apple, M. W. (2006). *Educating the "Right" way: Markets, standards, God, and inequality.* New York: Routledge.

——— (2004). *Ideology and curriculum,* Third edition. New York: RoutledgeFalmer.

———. (2000). *Official knowledge,* Second edition. New York: Routledge.

———. (1996). *Cultural politics and education.* New York: Teachers College Press.

———, Aasen, P., Cho, M. S. K., Gandin, L., Oliver, A., Tavares, H., and Wong, T. H. (2003). *The state and the politics of knowledge.* New York: RoutledgeFalmer.

———, and Beane, J. A. (Eds.) (2007). *Democratic schools: Lessons for powerful education,* Second edition. Portsmouth, NH: Heinemann.

———, and Buras, K. L. (Eds.) (2006). *The subaltern speak: Curriculum, power, and educational struggles.* New York: Routledge.

———, and Pedroni, T. (2005). Conservative alliance building and African American support for vouchers. *Teachers College Record.* 107: 2068-2105.

Ball, S. (1994). *Education reform.* Buckingham: Open University Press.

———. (2003). *Class strategies and the education market.* London: RoutledgeFalmer.

Binder, A. (2002). *Contentious curricula.* Princeton, NJ: Princeton University Press.

Bush, L. (2004). Access, school choice, and independent black institutions: A historical perspective. *Journal of Black Studies,* 34: 386–401.

Chubb, J., and Moe, T. (1990). *Politics, markets, and American schools.* Washington, DC: Brookings Institution.

Clarke, J., and Newman, J. (1997). *The managerial state.* Thousand Oaks, CA: Sage.

Dillard, A. (2001). *Guess who's coming to dinner?* New York: New York University Press.

Foner, E. (1998). *The story of American freedom.* New York: Norton.

Fraser, N. (1997). *Justice interruptus.* New York: Routledge.

———. (1989). *Unruly practices.* Minneapolis: University of Minnesota Press.

Gillborn, D., and Youdell, D. (2000). *Rationing education.* Buckingham: Open University Press.

Griffith, A., and Smith, D. (2005). *Mothering for schooling.* New York: RoutledgeFalmer.

Habermas, J. (1971). *Knowledge and human interests.* Boston, MA: Beacon Press.

Herrnstein, R., and Murray, C. (1994). *The bell curve.* New York: The Free Press.

Hogan, D. (1982). Education and class formation. In M. W. Apple (Ed.), *Cultural and economic reproduction in education.* Boston, MA: Routledge and Kegan Paul.

Jessop, B. (2003). *The future of the capitalist state.* Cambridge: Polity Press.

Katz, M. (2001). *The price of citizenship.* New York: Metropolitan Books.

Kelly, R. D. G. (1993). We are not what we seem: Rethinking black working-class opposition in the Jim Crow south, *The Journal of American History,* 80: 75–112.

Ladson-Billings, G. (2004). Just what is critical race theory and what is it doing in a *nice* field like education? In G. Ladson-Billings and D. Gillborn (Eds.), *The RoutledgeFalmer Reader in Multicultural Education.* New York: RoutledgeFalmer, pp. 49–67.

Levine, L. (1996). *The opening of the American mind.* Boston: Beacon Press.

Lewis, D. L. (1993). *W. E .B. DuBois: Biography of a race, 1868–1919.* New York: Henry Holt.

———. (2000). *W. E .B. DuBois: The fight for equality and the American century.* New York: Henry Holt.

Leys, C. (2003). *Market-driven politics: Neoliberal democracy and the public interest.* New York: Verso.

Lipman, P. (2004). *High stakes education.* New York: RoutledgeFalmer.

Marginson, S. (1997). *Educating Australia.* Cambridge: Cambridge University Press.

———, and Considine, M. (2000). *The enterprise university.* Cambridge: Cambridge University Press.

Marquand, D. (2000). *The progressive dilemma.* London: Phoenix Books.

McNeil, L. (2000). *Contradictions of school reform.* New York: Routledge.

Mills, C. (1997). *The racial contract.* Ithaca, NY: Cornell University Press.

Moe, T. (2001). *Schools, vouchers, and the American public.* Washington, DC: the Brookings Institution.

Omi, M., and Winant, H. (1994). *Racial formation in the United States.* New York: Routledge.

Pedroni, T. (2003). *Strange bedfellows in the Milwaukee "parental choice" debate.* Unpublished PhD dissertation, University of Wisconsin, Madison.

Power, S., Edwards, T., Whitty, G., and Wigfall, V. (2003). *Education and the middle class.* Buckingham: Open University Press.

Selden, S. (1999). *Inheriting shame.* New York: Teachers College Press.

Sewell, S. K. (2004). The "not-buying" power of the Black community: urban boycotts and equal employment opportunity, 1960–1964. *The Journal of African American History,* 89: 135–151.

Shipler, D. (2004). *The working poor.* New York: Knopf.

Skocpol, T. (2003). *Diminished democracy.* Norman: University of Oklahoma Press.

Smith, M. L., Miller-Kahn, L., Heinecke, W., and Jarvis, P. (2004). *Political spectacle and the fate of American schools.* New York: RoutledgeFalmer.

Van Dunk, E., and Dickman, A. (2003). *School choice and the question of accountability.* New Haven, CT: Yale University Press.

Whitty, G., Power, S., and Halpin, D. (1998). *Devolution and choice in education.* Buckingham: Open University Press .

Weis, L., and Fine, M. (2003). Extraordinary conversations in public schools, in G. Dimitriadis and D. Carlson, eds., *Promises to keep: Cultural studies, democratic education, and public life.* New York: Routledge, pp. 95–124.

Willis, P. (1990). *Common culture.* Boulder: Westview.

3

Leadership, Culture, and Democracy: Rethinking Systems and Conflict in Schools

Richard A. Quantz

The air lies still across the coliseum. The murmurs and shuffling quiet as the black-robed figure of the Superintendent approaches the podium. Dr. Loner pauses for effect. Her gaze moves from her right to her left taking in the packed audience of the families and friends of today's graduates. Then she looks downward at the graduates themselves. A small smile grows upon her face. Spread before her are 14 rows of peaceful and hopeful young adults beautifully arrayed in 14 blue and white columns in a natural symmetry that represents all that is good about American education. With calm voice Dr. Loner addresses her audience, "Twelve years ago you began your schooling. It seems like an eternity to you, but to your parents it seems like yesterday. Whether an eternity or a mere moment, in that time, you have matured from small children to young adults. There have been many influences in your life from your parents to your siblings to your friends, but certainly some of those influences were found among your teachers and schoolmates. Part of who you are today grew in the education that you have pursued here. We are confident that your learning during these years is only the beginning of much more learning to come whether that future education is found in college or work." Dr. Loner's address continues for only a few minutes more and then, to polite applause, she returns to her seat on the dais. While the president of the senior class begins to speak, Mr. Gadhand, president of the school board, leans over and whispers to Dr. Loner, "When you look out at these fine young men and women---so proud and so pleased---you renew your faith in our future. You understand what all this hard work is about." Dr. Loner nods her head, takes in the orderliness of the coliseum once more, and releases a deep sigh of satisfaction.

 Far up in the visitors' seats a young woman observes the same venue, but she sees something dramatically different. Rising senior Sylvia Kleiner, here to watch her brother graduate, has trouble sitting still. She leans forward and then backward and various involuntary grunts let her parents and sister, Annie, know that something is bothering her.

 "What's the matter?" asks Annie.

 At first, Sylvia doesn't acknowledge the question, but then she swings her arm across her body in a dramatic gesture indicating the entire floor where the graduates are gathered. Annie looks at the floor but her puzzled face indicates that she had no idea what is upsetting her sister. "Can't you see it?" Sylvia exclaims in exasperation. "Those rows of white and blue!" Still no indication of understanding from Annie. "All the boys are in blue robes and the girls are in white robes! White! For purity! And the girls are carrying a rose!" The bitterness in her voice is barely controlled. "Here we are. Gathered to celebrate the transition of young people into adulthood and they are gendered! Marked by sex to take their different places in society! Guilty as charged at the beginning!" Annie just rolls her eyes and goes back to watching the commencement.

Introduction

Let me pause for a moment in the telling of this fictionalized rendition of a true story. I will shortly return to the anecdote, but before I do that I'd like to shift gears. For almost seven years, the Department of Educational Leadership at Miami University has been involved in an ongoing conversation around leadership and culture. About six years ago, through the Initiative on Leadership, Culture, and Schooling, our departmental conversation expanded to include voices from around the nation. The initiative has been an attempt to bring together into one conversation the voices of scholars who are based in the leadership discourses with those who are based in culture discourses such as curriculum and social foundations of education.

In this ongoing conversation we have found that we appear to share a social project: one with a commitment to social justice, a desire to expand the conceptualization of leadership, and the sense that the purpose of leadership was not to protect the status quo but to challenge it and, ultimately, to transform it. But we have also found that while we often use the same language, our words often mean different things. It should come as no surprise that while there were many areas of both agreement and disagreement, more often than not the biggest divisions appeared between those who drew on a leadership discourse versus those who drew on a culture discourse. On the surface, of course, why should we expect anything else? Except that those who were agreeing with each other and drew on a leadership discourse, did not necessarily draw on the same leadership discourse. And those who were agreeing with each other and drew on a culture discourse, did not necessarily draw on the same culture discourse. How is it that scholars whose work was based on the language of learning organizations or chaos theory or spiritual leadership would eventually end up agreeing with each other in opposition to a group of people whose cultural discourses were as varied as post-structuralism, cultural feminism, pragmatism, or critical theory. If we were to separate the two conversations so that leadership scholars and culture-based scholars were only speaking to each other, I'm convinced that we would end up with little agreement, happily entrenched in our common need as members of the academy to separate ourselves from each other. But when brought together in a conversation that crossed these disciplinary boundaries, we suddenly find that our apparently entrenched differences are less important than we thought. What is it that the leadership theories (as different from each other as they are) have in common? And what is it that the enormously different theories of culture share? In my own mind, the fundamental reason for this division ultimately and consistently could be found in the basic assumption about how to conceive of society. In other words, while scholars who use leadership discourses and scholars who use culture-based discourses might appear to be committed to a shared social *project*, each group assumes fundamentally different social *theories*. Because of our commitment to the daily practice of schooling, educational scholars have long been more invested in developing social projects than in refining social theories. We have been more inclined to leave the development of the basic theories to scholars in arts and sciences or in business. We have tended to adopt or adapt theories from these other fields and spend our time mostly focused on their implications for educational practice rather than to actively engage in the process of theory construction and critique itself. Of course the distinction between a social theory and a social project is itself a bit controversial, but I contend that while a social theory implicitly (or explicitly) implies a social project and a social project implicitly (or explicitly) assumes a social theory, the two are not precisely equivalent entities. A social theory attempts to explain how the sociocultural world works while a social project attempts to argue for how the sociocultural world *ought* to work.

What I believe that this seven-year experiment in cross-disciplinary conversation has taught is that those who utilize a leadership discourse typically assume some form of systems theory while those who use a culture-based discourse tend to assume some form of action or conflict theory. These social theories are not always, perhaps not even usually, explicit theories, but when you strip away the basic arguments, ultimately, we end up with one side assuming that society at large and schools in particular are systems while the others reject that assumption. With this division, we find ourselves at an impasse that interferes with our ability to successfully advance our common social project.

As one who is based in sociocultural action and conflict theories, this essay will attempt to clarify some implications of thinking about a leadership project that assumes a conflict theory rather than a systems theory. The anecdote with which I began this essay and which I weave throughout the rest of this argument will provide, I hope, a concrete example that will clarify the different point of view that a conflict social theory makes possible.

* * *

Rob pauses for a moment listening to the cracks and pings as the car begins to cool down. He takes in a deep breath of the fresh spring air from the open window and reflects on what has led him to this point. He pictures the first day of school that past fall when walking down the hallway with Sylvia they ran into the principal. "Hello, Dr. Williams," said Sylvia as she walked right up to him." Requiring boys to wear blue robes and girls to wear white robes at commencement is illegal. It violates Title IX. Therefore, if that practice continues, I want you to know now that I will not be willing to wear a white robe. Don't you think that we can start the new millennium off with a practice that does not restrict males and females to traditional stereotyped roles?"

Dr. Williams looked only temporarily taken aback and then he put his head back and had a good laugh. Rob can't remember Dr. Williams's exact words but does remember the patronizing attitude in that laugh and in the body language. Clearly Dr. Williams had not taken Sylvia's comment seriously.

"What was that all about?" Rob asked as the two continued walking down the hall. His question opened up a floodgate of outrage as Sylvia explained the problem of having such an obvious symbol of gender inequality as part of their ritual transition to adulthood.

Through the school year Sylvia never missed an opportunity to let Dr. Williams know of her concern and Dr. Williams always appeared genial and unoffended by these comments though he also never really seemed to take them seriously. That is until a month ago when Rob accompanied Sylvia to a meeting in Dr. William's office. While still maintaining a quiet and gentle tone to his voice, Dr. Williams explained to Sylvia that it was time for her to get over her problem with the colors of the gowns. He explained to her that if she didn't want to wear a white gown then she didn't have to attend commencement or she could sit in the audience, but she would not be allowed to march in with her class unless she was wearing a white gown. As Sylvia pressed her point that the practice violated Title IX, Rob was dismayed to hear Dr. Williams deepening and more edged voice explain what might happen if Sylvia continued to insist on wearing a different color than white. Among the possible consequences was expulsion from school and, therefore, not being allowed to graduate until the following December after making up the lost credits. And even arrest and being charged with a crime. Rob was startled by the harshness of the punishment. "Just for not wearing the right color gown?" he had asked himself. Up until that point he had been supportive of his friend's position, but had not himself been willing to do much more than try to persuade his friends, teachers, and parents that Sylvia had a good point. Why should we mark the ceremony that symbolizes our transition to adulthood with such obvious gendered distinctions? For the next couple of weeks Rob had struggled with what to do. Sylvia had made it clear that she was not backing down. She was willing to risk her diploma and her college scholarship and jail. What was he going to do?

Rob opens the car door and strides up to the front porch. Mr. Gadhand, the president of the school board, answers the doorbell himself. Rob says, "I wanted to make sure I gave this to you personally" and hands him a legal-sized envelope containing a letter explaining his support for Sylvia and her desire to eliminate the gender-biased practice of the two-colored gowns at commencement. The letter also explained that he is going to publicly express his support for this position by wearing a white gown at commencement. Rob's letter does more than just support Sylvia's position. It shifts the legal debate in wearing a robe of white or blue from a Title IX issue to a First-Amendment issue.

Systems Theories

To many people a school district is obviously a system. That is why we call them "school *systems*." Our language regularly constructs a systemic nature for our schools. We often complain about the way the "system" works. We have many millions of dollars aimed at "systemic reform." And we have "system-wide initiatives." Commonsense tells us to consider social organizations as social systems and school organizations are no exception.

But what is a system? While many different systems theories compete for their own understanding of a system, they do share some basic orientations. While in the last twenty years systems theories have shifted from structure to process, and from closed systems to open systems, to living systems, and from simple equilibrium theories to the more complex autopoietic theories, all contemporary systems theories conceive of a system as a bounded whole with interrelated components. And while they may not explicitly say so, they all also, according to Bailey (1994, p. 44) "assume an entropy value below maximum." In other words, systems have order. Much of the discussion in recent years revolves around exactly how to understand the boundedness of the whole, so that most systems theorists today prefer to think in terms of boundaries rather than borders seeing the former as more permeable than the latter. But such distinctions do not give up the idea that the system is a distinct thing, perhaps in interaction with its environment, perhaps even dependent on its surrounding context, but, nonetheless *an entity unto itself.*

Systems theory has been a part of social theory from the beginning and the number of different systems theories boggles credibility. The earliest elements of systems theory can be found in Herbert Spencer's organic analogy (Spencer, 1995/1881), but it was Vilfredo Pareto (Pareto and Livingston, 1963) who established the "system" as the backbone of the scientific study of society and who influenced Talcott Parsons's functionalist systems theory (Parsons, 1951) that came to dominate mid-twentieth-century social theory. These earlier systems theories adapted closed biological models and emphasized equilibrium, order, cooperation, and consensus. In recent years, systems theorists borrow more widely and emphasize change, randomness, complexity, and fluidity as the system adapts to new situations. As Bausch (2001, p. 2) suggests, these newer systems theories assume "ever-evolving processes of self-reproduction." New process-oriented systems theories continue to explode in numbers and include James Miller's Living Systems Theory (Miller, 1995), Peter Checkland's Soft Systems Theory (Checkland and Scholes, 1999), Kenneth Bailey's Social Entropy Theory (Bailey, 1994), Bertalanffy's General Systems Theory (Bertalanffy, 1973), Humberto Maturana and Francisco Varela's Autopoiesis Theory (Maturana and Varela, 1987), and Jeffrey Alexander's Neofunctionalist Systems Theory (Alexander, 1998), and a myriad of other theories going under such names as sociocybernetics, chaos theory, and learning organizations. And that only begins a listing. Perhaps the most influential contemporary theory would be Niklas Luhmann's Autopoietic Systems Theory (Luhmann, 1995). Luhmann's well-known, extensive and vigorous public debates with Jürgen Habermas may have influenced Habermas to re-formulate his Theory of Communicative Action in order to recognize a legitimate role for systems (but only when encapsulated within a conflict theory) (Habermas, 1984). Perhaps the one key feature of contemporary theories that marks them from the older ones is the assumption that systems are self-regulating and self-regenerating. The older systems theories assumed a stability that promotes stasis whereas the newer ones assume a stability that results from growth and adaptation. Where the older theories present equilibrium models, the newer ones offer evolutionary ones.

One of my frustrations with the conversation in educational leadership arises from the apparent lack of exposure to the underlying assumptions of systems theories that educational leadership theories assume. Perhaps this tendency arises because most educational leadership theories derive from the business literature which itself limits its discussions to systems thinking as opposed to systems theories. In many ways this focus on systems thinking rather than systems theories makes sense: educational administrators tend to be "can do" kinds of people who value Nike thinking ("just do it") rather than more reflective and cerebral approaches. But emphasizing systems thinking to the exclusion of systems theories may also lead to the inability to understand their own failure as leaders. Systems thinking may be thought of as applied versions of systems theories. Whereas systems theories present descriptive social theories, systems thinking might be thought of as prescriptive social projects. While systems theorists try to describe how social systems work, systems thinking advocates how systems *should* work. Much of the educational leadership literature does not build on the work of the systems theorists but on their interpreters, the systems thinkers who do not attempt to describe how leadership actually works within schools but how it ought to work. Of course, every descriptive theory should suggest certain logical prescriptions and every prescriptive project assumes a descriptive theory so the distinction between the two is not that they speak to different things as much as that they fail to speak out loud certain things. But to utilize systems thinking without understanding fully the underlying systems theories upon which they build leads to misunderstanding. On the other hand, if we actually understand the basic assumptions of the underlying descriptive social theory then we can understand better the strengths and weaknesses of the derivative prescriptive projects.

* * *

Dan Kleiner stands in Sylvia's doorway watching his daughter admire her blue gradua-tion gown in the mirror. "You realize," he says, "that despite all of the support you may have received from your classmates, you will be the only person at this commencement wearing the wrong color."

"You're wrong," she responds without turning. "Rob will wear a white gown."

"No guy is going to be caught dead wearing a white gown!" Dan exclaims.

Sylvia simply turns and looks at her father. Slowly Dan's face begins to change. Under-standing seeps into his eyes as he realizes what he has just said. For the first time since his daughter started this whole discussion nearly one year ago, he understands her point. He walks over and gives Sylvia a hug. Sylvia's phone rings, but she lets her answering machine get it.

"I thought you might like to know," says an unfamiliar voice, "that the school board just had an emergency meeting and they refused to change the requirement that boys wear blue and

girls wear white, but they also voted not to punish or bother in any way students who wear the wrong color."

Less than 24 hours later, Dan Kleiner sits in the stands wearing a blue and white ribbon on the lapel of his jacket. To his right all the members of his family are wearing the ribbons which are being distributed outside by adults and underclassmen to show support for those seniors who choose to wear the wrong color gown.

Dan sits in almost the exact spot that he had last year when his son had graduated. From this distance the coliseum floor looks almost exactly the same. The same people on the dais, the same banners on the backdrop, the same music being played by the same high school orchestra wearing the same uniforms. There is one small difference, however. The carefully ordered blue and white columns of graduates are disrupted in a few places where a white or a blue gown is distinctly out of place.

* * *

I believe two primary reasons exist for school administrators to think of schools as systems. One reason follows from school administrators' sincere belief that they work for the good of the whole. Like captains of ships, school administrators assume responsibility for the safe steerage of the whole entity. They cannot work for the interests of special parties but must, instead, work for the common good. Systems theories and systems thinking provide a language to understand the social situation in terms of the whole and to analyze its component parts to discover the places that seem to be interfering with the ability of the organization to achieve its common goals. They provide tools for the administrator to manage the flows so that the organization can achieve maximum success. Such tools provide a morally good reason for utilizing systems thinking and may explain why administrators so readily accept it. But other reasons also exist that make thinking of schools as systems so attractive to many administrators—covert reasons hidden from view, perhaps, even from the administrators themselves. And, perhaps, if these basically good people come to understand these other reasons, they will be horrified. But to clarify these other reasons, I need to briefly present an alternative understanding of the social.

Conflict Theories

Many who assume social organizations to be systems wonder how else we might conceive of them. "Of course, organizations are systems," they say, "Just look at them. They are bounded things with inter-related components. That's a system." But one of the most frequent criticisms of systems theories (and yet one of the least understood by its advocates) is that systems theories reify the system. To people like me, the confusion between thinking that an organization *is* a system and thinking about an organization as *like* a system is not a minor difference. For one suggests that the system exists in the world and operates in the world while the other suggests that the system is a linguistic construction that analysts can use to try and provide order to their own understanding of what they see in the world.[1] In other words, thinking of schools as systems is not a discovery of the way the world works but a metaphor for describing the way we think about how the world works. To the extent that schools are like systems, then the metaphor works, but to the extent that they are different from systems, then the metaphor misses. By using the metaphor of a system we are led to see certain things, but other things become harder to see. Understanding that an assumed theoretical position provides us with a linguistic pattern allows the analyst to search around for other theories that provide different linguistic organization and that might help direct our attention to different things and to interpret what we see happening in different ways.

Let me make it clear that I do not think that systems thinking is wrong. Far from it. I find much value in systems thinking. For much of my doctoral program, I had a double major. One of those majors was research and evaluation and the evaluation part of that major was entirely systems based. And part of the way in which I paid for my graduate education was as an evaluation consultant who worked with program administrators to apply systems thinking to their programs in an effort to help them gain a more ordered understanding of how their program was supposed to function and how it was actually functioning. And I believe that my consultations were of some value to the organizations with whom I worked. My argument is not with the use of systems as a model for understanding schools but with the reification of the metaphor of a system into the social organization itself. When we think the school organization *is a system*, instead of it being *like a system*, we limit our ability to understand our organization and, therefore, also limit our ability to consider remedies to our problems.

Are there other theoretical approaches available? Of course! One possible set of alternatives may be found in action theories. Action theories include Harold Blumer's symbolic interactionism (Blumer, 1969), Harold Garfinkel's ethnomethodology (Garfinkel, 1967), Peter Berger and Thomas Luckmann's phenomenological sociology (Berger and Luckmann, 1966), Anthony Giddens's structuration theory (Giddens, 1984), and Ulrich Beck's reflexive modernization

(Beck, 1992). Any one of these theories presents an alternative approach to thinking about organizations as other than systems. Each provides many possibilities for bringing new insights to our understanding of leadership and, yet, none is frequently utilized as a basis for analyzing and critiquing educational leadership.

Another set of possible theoretical alternatives may be found in the imperfectly named, but widely used term, conflict theory. Some of the most prominent of conflict theories include Marxist theories, certain neo-Weberian theories (such as Randall Collins's network theory (Collins, 2000) or Pierre Bourdieu's field theory (Bourdieu and Wacquant, 1992), the Frankfurt School's critical theory, many feminist theories such as the radical materialist feminism of Christine Delphy (Delphy and Leonard, 1984) or the feminist standpoint theory of Nancy Hartsock (1998), and numerous post-structural and postcolonial theories. Conflict theories tend not to use any metaphorical representation of society preferring instead to present society in terms of social actions. As Randall Collins (1975) might put it, social organizations are just the name we give to the little bubbles of reality that people create whenever they interact with others on a regular basis. Conflict theories may not share a common metaphor for organizations, but they share a belief that we can best describe the actions that we observe in organizations if we pay attention to how people divide themselves into groups that compete over manifestations of power. Conflict theories are not prescriptive social projects, but descriptive social theories. In other words, conflict theories do not necessarily argue that we should encourage conflict but only that conflict exists in human groupings and understanding those conflicts is one key to understanding what happens.

While conflict theories may not advance a particular metaphor for describing social entities, let me suggest that thinking of organizations as arenas may be a reasonable possibility. Rather than thinking of schools as a whole system, we can think about them as arenas—places where social groups gather and struggle over sociocultural issues such as the distribution of goods and services, the control over processes, and the legitimacy of identities and cultures. As such, schools are not to be thought of as a single whole that has a common goal. Individuals and their groups are not sub-components of a larger system who need to be organized into submerging their individual and group interests to that of some abstract whole but are individuals and groups who need to find themselves in a place where their identities and cultures are recognized as legitimate, and their unique visions are valued because if they do not, they will struggle against the institution that delegitimizes their interests.

From a conflict perspective, the common interests assumed by school administrators typically resemble the interests of the dominant elites more than that of the minority. When those who represent the interests of a minority try to speak and act for their interests, those in organizational power typically interpret such acts and statements as opposed to the common good of the whole system and, therefore, are defined as illegitimate. So we find that the special interests of administrators and policymakers and the community elites become the common good of the whole; whereas the special interests of the teachers, staff, students, and non-elite members of the community remain defined as merely special interests. Illegitimacy allows organizational sanctions to be applied which might include expulsion from the organization altogether. In other words, the assumption of systemic wholeness results in practices which claim to work in the common interest but which too often resemble the imposition of a hegemonic social order that represents the special interests of the dominant social groups. This is, of course, what happened in the fictionalized account of the true story that I relate in this chapter.

The school administration interpreted Sylvia's objection to the color of the gowns as illegitimate. Since legally the commencement is a school board function, students really have no legal right to influence its proceedings. And since the school board is believed to represent the common interests of the community, a challenge to the board's legally enacted policies or the administration's empowered implementation of these policies is taken to be not only illegitimate but a challenge to the common good. When students such as Sylvia and her friend, Rob, threaten to not follow the administration's chosen procedures, they are defined as refusing to submerge their own selfish interests to the interests of the whole. They are positioned as troublemakers and given the choice to either join in "for the good of the whole" or leave the organization. In other words, while many school administrators may have a morally good reason to think of the school as a system in which they assume the responsibility to act in the common interest, too often such a reason is no more than a political ploy that substitutes their own special interest for the common good. I suspect that while some administrators may understand this and act in a calculating manner, I also suspect that for many, perhaps the vast majority, the substitution of special interests of the elite for the general good of the whole is completely unreflective.

Think how differently leadership would look if instead of seeing a whole system with interlocking subgroups in a hierarchically arranged social order with a common interest, we understood that we were looking at an arena in which a myriad of shifting social groups were vying with each other over social goods. What is the job of a leader then? Who are the leaders? And how do we make sense of the fundamental problems that need to be addressed? And does our understanding of democracy change?

If the school is an arena of vying social groups rather than a system of interlocking parts, then what is the job of the school administrator as leader of the organization? For one thing, it requires the administrator to be more conscious of how apparently neutral policy enacted in the name of the common good may actually work for the special interests of the administration or other social elites. It would require that the administrator recognize that individuals who challenge the policies or practices of the administration may not be troublemakers seeking their own selfish interests but legitimate leaders representing the interests of an excluded minority. It would require the recognition that school administrators may not be the only leaders in the school, but that all kinds of people assume leadership roles as conflict situations arise between different competing groups. It would require the administrator to accept more the role of a mediator among competing interests rather than an advocate for the interests of the elites alone. Administrators might be more successful if they took the time to understand what the struggles are actually about rather than quickly assuming that counter-school behavior is the same thing as antieducational behavior. It would require that school administrators and policymakers and teachers and parents and elite community members develop a school where democratic associated living is practiced and, thereby, teaching the basics of democracy rather than the principle that those with the power rule and everyone else follows or pays the penalty.

Now please don't misunderstand me. I am not saying that systems thinkers would automatically dismiss students such as Sylvia and Rob. We could analyze the situation from a systems approach in order to try and eliminate the problem. We could draw stock-and-flow charts and create time-change graphs and identify single and double loops. In doing so we would identify some important things such as the realization that the system needs better feedback loops to represent the views of people like Sylvia. Perhaps a system which had allowed Sylvia to raise her point in public and see the extent to which she would be able to garner support within a democratic process would have deflected the situation. Given the obvious lack of support from other students and the community, perhaps having had the chance to raise the issue in public, have it debated, and have it shot down by her peers would have avoided the confrontation that developed. Of course, if Sylvia had been persuasive, it might also have required the school board to change its policy. A systems approach might help us see where the communication loops had failed and how we might restructure our system to help facilitate such information flow. But such language is technical language and reduces the issues to technical problems.

Is democracy well served by reducing fundamental conflicts to technical problems? After all, such technical thinking would be likely to improve our structured information flow. But understanding the school as an arena rather than a system would encourage us to see some things that the narrow, interest-based, and technical language of systems thinking has more difficulty in recognizing. Among other things it has trouble recognizing the larger social struggles that are being acted out. For example, Sylvia and Rob were not just acting as disgruntled individuals, but as members of large social movements in this country. Certainly one of those movements could be called feminism. One obvious way to understand this situation is as a conflict between patriarchy and feminism with the entrenched interests of patriarchy represented by the school district and the resistant interests of feminism represented by Sylvia and Rob.

Another one of the large social interests has been called "progressivism" (Hunter, 1991) which is in struggle with its opposition, "orthodoxy," and which underlies many of the political struggles that grab the headlines from abortion to drugs to welfare to vouchers to phonics to high-stakes testing and many, many more. According to Hunter, orthodoxy is a cultural frame that assumes that an eternal and external frame of reference exists for determining truth and right and that decisions should be based on applying those external standards to our decision making. In so doing, it is not so much a matter of us versus them, but of traditional right versus time-honored wrong. On the other hand, progressivism, according to Hunter, sees decisions of right and wrong, truth and untruth, not as matters that can be adjudicated by some eternal external standard, but by placing decisions into ever-changing contexts where right and wrong, truth and untruth are more fuzzy and changing. Using conflict theory it is easy to see that the administration's actions in the case of the blue and white robes were not working so much in the common interest, as in the interests of orthodoxy. By requiring girls to wear white and carry a rose and by requiring boys to wear blue and not carry a flower of any sort, the school board and their administrators were working to reinforce the idea of gender difference as something located in the basic physiology of the human being. Sylvia and Rob represent a progressive interest struggling to advance the ideas that gender is a socially constructed entity that only makes sense as we place it into its historical and cultural context. Of course, one could use systems theory and also recognize the underlying political interests at play. I am not arguing that it is not possible to do so using systems thinking, only that it is more difficult to do so and, therefore, less likely to be done.

From the conflict perspective, systems thinking is not really inaccurate as much as it is narrow and naïve. It is narrow for it defines the issue as technical and internal to the school itself and, therefore, the solution lies in accommodating or deflecting the disrupting force. At best the external is seen as context with input flows to individuals such as Sylvia. With systems thinking, it becomes too easy to define the problem as that of one or two individuals whose self-interests become selfish interests and can easily be discredited. But if we see the school as an arena, it becomes easier to recognize that these particular individuals are also leaders—leaders of a wider social movement working for those interests in this particular arena. Sylvia was not a malcontented aberration and troublemaker. She was a leader of a particular interest group. As leaders of a recognized and legitimate interest group, the organization needs to assign them legitimacy and find a way for them and for those whom they represent to feel that they belong in the organization rather than in opposition to it. It isn't a matter of using a majority-rule process to help identify so-called common interests as much as it is using a process that permits the multivoicedness of a diverse population who may not have much of a common vision at all.

The systems approach is not only narrow, but it is naïve for it is less likely to recognize the fundamental play of power within seemingly minor, apolitical issues. It is more likely to use the language of efficiency and objectivity to neutralize forces that challenge the status quo. Such technical language does not serve the common interest as claimed but the special interests of the dominant elites. Creating new feedback loops will not solve a problem that is fundamentally about the distribution of power. It will only provide better information to those elites to help them manage challenges to the present power distribution even more efficiently and, therefore, make the organization even less democratic.

In systems thinking, conflict is negative and must be averted where possible and defeated when it arises. In conflict theory, conflict is normal and, while maybe not always desirable, is sometimes, perhaps even frequently, desirable. The absence of conflict is more likely to indicate an oppressive hegemony than a democratic consensus. Democracy is not pleasant. It is stressful. Democracy is not holding hands and getting along. It is squaring off and getting along. In such situations, democratic leadership must concern itself less with creating cooling out mechanisms (Clark, 1960) that mitigate and soften resistance and more with mediating the natural and desirable conflicts within an organization. When administrators and teachers begin to recognize that their job is not to manage for technical efficiency but to mediate and organize various interests, then they begin to see the social life of their schools in a much different light. When they start to see students such as Sylvia and Rob as leaders who can help promote democratic processes rather than as troublemakers who challenge authority and, therefore, create the possibility of uncontrolled chaos, then they may begin to make decisions that work in the interests of education rather than of mere vocational training. For those of us interested in placing culture and democracy at the center of our understanding of leadership, using conflict theories to help us navigate through the shoals and shores of everyday life in schools is at least as necessary as using systems theories.

Notes

I would like to thank the faculty and students of the Department of Educational Leadership and Cultural Foundations at the University of North Carolina—Greensboro whose kind invitation to address them provided the impetus for an earlier version of this chapter.

1.   One can think of the system as a linguistic construction without assuming that the ordered and patterned interaction of people is merely discursive. While conflict theorists tend to agree with the first part, they disagree over the second. This is one of the distinctions between what are often referred to as modern and postmodern theories.

References

Alexander, J. C. (1998). *Neofunctionalism and after*. Malden, MA: Blackwell Publishers.

Bailey, K. D. (1994). *Sociology and the new systems theory toward a theoretical synthesis*. Albany: State University of New York Press.

Bausch, K. C. (2001). *The emerging consensus in social systems theory.* New York: Kluwer Academic/ Plenum Publishers.

Beck, U. (1992). *Risk society: Towards a new modernity.* Newbury Park, CA: Sage Publications.

Berger, P. L., and Luckmann, T. (1966). *The social construction of reality: A treatise in the sociology of knowledge.* Garden City, NY: Doubleday.

Bertalanffy, L. V. (1973). *General systems theory: Foundations, development, applications.* Harmondsworth: Penguin.

Blumer, H. (1969). *Symbolic interactionism: Perspective and method.* Englewood Cliffs, NJ: Prentice-Hall.

Bourdieu, P., and Wacquant, L. J. D. (1992). *An invitation to reflexive sociology.* Chicago: University of Chicago Press.

Checkland, P., and Scholes, J. (1999). *Soft systems methodology in action: A 30-year retrospective* (New edition). New York: Wiley.

Clark, B. (1960). The cooling out function in higher education. *American Journal of Sociology*, 65(6): 569–576.

Collins, R. (1975). *Conflict sociology: Toward an explanatory science.* New York: Academic Press.

———. (2000). *The sociology of philosophies: A global theory of intellectual change.* Cambridge, MA: Belknap Press.

Delphy, C., and Leonard, D. (1984). *Close to home: A materialist analysis of women's oppression.* Amherst: University of Massachusetts Press.

Garfinkel, H. (1967). *Studies in ethnomethodology.* Englewood Cliffs, NJ: Prentice-Hall.

Giddens, A. (1984). The constitution of society: Outline of the theory of structuration. Berkeley: University of California Press.

Habermas, J. (1984). *The theory of communicative action*, T. McCarthy, Trans. Boston, MA: Beacon Press.

Hartsock, N. C. M. (1998). *The feminist standpoint revisited and other essays.* Boulder, CO: Westview Press.

Hunter, J. D. (1991). *Culture wars: The struggle to define America.* New York: Basic Books.

Luhmann, N. (1995). *Social systems.* Stanford, CA: Stanford University Press.

Maturana, H. R., and Varela, F. J. (1987). *The tree of knowledge: The biological roots of human understanding.* Boston, MA: New Science Library.

Miller, J. G. (1995). *Living systems.* Niwot: Boulder: University of Colorado Press.

Pareto, V., and Livingston, A. (1963). *The mind and society: A treatise on general sociology.* New York: Dover.

Parsons, T. (1951). *The social system.* Glencoe, IL: Free Press.

Spencer, H. (1995/1851). *Social statistics: The conditions essential to human happiness specified, and the first of them developed.* New York: Robert Schalkenbach Foundation.

4

Some Historical Tensions about Sexuality and Gender in Schools

Jackie M. Blount

Introduction

Communities long have relied on schools to maintain normative sexuality and gender identity/presentation among their charges. This largely unspoken responsibility pervades nearly every aspect of schooling such as hiring practices, dress codes, social events including dances, sex-segregated extracurricular activities like athletics, and the curriculum. Its roots are so deeply embedded that the persons who inhabit schools on a daily basis simply tend to assume it always has existed.

For the most part, the acceptance of this sexuality and gender regulation has continued unabated, that is, until individuals or groups have challenged that authority. In recent decades, the movement for the rights of persons who are lesbian, gay, bisexual, transgender, or possess any of an increasing number of gender/sexuality transgressing identities—loosely organized under the some-times contentious label "queer"—has moved from hidden back rooms to the mainstream. Consequently, challenges to the sexuality/gender status quo have emerged in schools everywhere as students have joined the ranks of front-line queer activists.

This new realm of activism, however, has been met at each step of the way with a sometimes ferocious countermovement intended to subsume a growing panoply of gender and sexuality identities into a seemingly unitary model. This model encompasses only heterosexuality with clearly defined, distinct gender identities assigned by sex. Typically the right-wing countermovement has employed a range of strategies in the assault on identity proliferation. One is the use of language that evokes highly emotional reactions including fear and anger. Another vital strategy involves casting any discussions about gender and sexuality identities into strictly binary terms, essentially eliminating gradations and nuances.[1] Of course, this strategy must, by its nature, ignore the inherent complexities that exist in phenomena as deeply embedded as gender and sexuality.

As students and faculty in schools have challenged unitary models of sexuality/gender, conservative reaction has followed fairly predictably. The resulting skirmishes often turn into heated controversies as inflamed emotional language and strictly polarized logic reduce any chance for meaningful dialogue. Administrators typically respond by attempting to mitigate feared image problems in their communities by imposing hastily formed policies. When this happens, the hierarchy of social privilege shifts—additionally rewarding some while harming others. In the end, opportunities for meaningful democratic practice in schools are lost as discussion gets squelched and persons with nonconforming sexuality/gender effectively are erased from the process.

This cycle need not be perpetuated, though. School administrators who are courageous enough to demonstrate democratic leadership can open discussion about conforming and nonconforming sexuality/gender identities. They can work collectively with students who challenge gender/sexuality norms, rather than fearing them and imposing policies that effectively make them disappear. And they can help deconstruct the polarizing, emotion-laden language that often frames such confrontations.

Such effort on the part of school administrators requires courage, however. Long entrenched community pressures and norms, not to mention those of our society as a whole, make it much easier for those charged with administering schools to resort to strictly enforced rules that perpetuate conventionality. Adding to the difficulty of opening discussion around sexuality/gender is the fact that school administrators—and many school workers and board members, for that matter—assume that the present strictures on sexuality/gender in schools always have existed, or certainly have existed for a long time. This assumption precludes critical examination of how current conditions have come to be the way they are. Finally, school administrators may not realize that, demographically, they themselves fall into a long-standing pattern of principals, superintendents, and the like who have been hired as models of gender/sexuality conformity, or who, at the least, seem as though they would uphold such norms. Such explicit understandings seem necessary before critical, open discussion of issues concerning sexuality/gender norms in schools can unfold with integrity.

In this chapter, I offer one humble invitation to these understandings. I begin with a brief historical examination of how we have created and perpetuated unequal gender/sexual identities in public schools in the United States. I outline some of the ways that gender norms have been structured into school employment and, by implication, the implicit curriculum. I describe how, in the wake of the suffrage movement, concern about gender nonconformity became intertwined with a new and growing fear of homosexuality, a fear that burst fully into the open after World War II and found full expression in school personnel practices around the country. I discuss how schools then became the central focus of political- and religious-right activists during the 1970s and 1980s as they learned that the gay liberation movement's most vulnerable area, at least in the public mind, concerned the presence of gay and lesbian teachers in schools. Finally, I examine some of the ways that school administrators who are themselves sexuality/gender nonconforming, or who wish to be allies to those who are, face social and structural obstacles in their quest to establish fully democratic communities in their schools.

Sexuality/Gender Norms and School Work

From the mid- to late-1800s, the matter of who worked in schools and districts boiled down to a combination of economic utility and the preservation of gender norms. The rapid spread of common schooling around the country at mid-century produced an urgent demand for large numbers of teachers. Men, especially college-educated ones, had performed the bulk of school teaching before this time. However, the low pay that usually accompanied the work and the brutal, rugged conditions that often prevailed in rural schools made teaching unappealing to most men who enjoyed better opportunities elsewhere. Once early women teachers had demonstrated that they could acquire sufficient education to teach, withstand the rigors of rustic, underdeveloped community life, and manage the discipline of their motley students, school boards began hiring them. Because they typically demanded one-half to one-third the salaries of men, women teachers represented an exceptional bargain. Accordingly, the proportion of women teachers steadily increased so that by the 1870s, the men who had survived the Civil War chose to avoid the work that, in the minds of many, had become feminized. In 1900, women accounted for seventy percent of all teachers, a number that reached its zenith in 1920 when women held an astonishing eighty-six percent of all teaching positions.[2] The demographic feminization of teaching therefore had become so obvious during this time that any reference to a teacher likely evoked the image of a woman, not a man.

During the mid- to late-1800s when women began teaching in significant numbers, simultaneously school administrative positions appeared in districts around the country. Ostensibly, school boards added these positions, at first filled exclusively by men, to handle increased school-related chores such as providing firewood, inspecting school buildings, and examining teachers—though such early administrators sometimes scarcely possessed as much education or professional training as the female teachers they scrutinized. As Strober and Tyack have argued, gender seemed to be structured into schoolwork at this critical juncture when women became teachers and men, managers.[3]

As I have argued in other work, school administrators also may have been added as a way of keeping women's newfound economic and professional independence from going too far. After all, through teaching, middle-class women were able to live on their own for the first time in a manner that garnered some degree of professional and social respect. Before this, women generally were limited to living with their families, husbands, or some household willing to take them in. When critics worried that large numbers of independent women might choose to continue teaching and thus avoid marriage and motherhood, advocates such as Catharine Beecher offered the assurance that these concerns were unfounded because teaching *prepared* women for expected matrimonial and maternal commitments. When others expressed concern that married women teachers might suffer conflicts in whom they owed primary allegiance, either their husbands or their principals/superintendents, Beecher again voiced a simple and appealing solution. School teaching should remain the province of single women.[4] When schools hired female teachers, then, they overwhelmingly tended to choose single women. Over the second half of the nineteenth century, teaching essentially shifted from work done mainly by men to that done by unmarried women, a rather profound transformation in gender/sexuality norms.

During the late 1800s and early 1900s, the number of superintendencies also increased throughout the states and territories as school district expansion barely kept pace with dynamic population growth, particularly in urban areas. The men hired for these administrative positions usually commanded salaries several times higher than those of the teachers they supervised. In part, this is because men simply received higher salaries than women. Also, though, school boards generally expected the superintendents they hired to have families to support, which consequently justified higher salaries. Without question, this expectation of marriage for male school administrators ran counter to the requirement of unmarried status for women teachers.

I also have outlined in *Destined to Rule the Schools* that the relatively few men who decided to remain in schoolwork by the early twentieth century increasingly felt the pull to leave the classroom and instead to aim for the superintendent's office. Teaching not only had become demographically feminized work, but also it had come to be regarded as work that demeaned the masculinity of men. Maintaining a respectable, middle-class masculinity typically involved working alongside other men, not women. It meant exerting authority over others, not taking orders. It involved independence in thought and action, not scrupulous attention to following guidelines or enduring constant scrutiny. On the other hand, the superintendency, as configured, presented a safe place for men to preserve their sense of conventional, middle-class masculinity at least to the degree that teaching eroded it.[5]

By the early 1900s, then, gender and sexuality clearly factored into the structure of schoolwork in several ways. Single women performed the great bulk of all classroom teaching. Many urban school districts even went so far as to adopt policies formally banning married women teachers.[6] The work itself had shifted so that it required obedience and other characteristics expected of females. Conversely, school administration, particularly the superintendency, clearly had become the desired realm for men in schoolwork. In 1910, men accounted for ninety-one percent of all superintendents, for example.[7] School boards expected the men who held these positions to be married or marriageable. Furthermore, boards increasingly looked for "virile" men who evidenced physical vigor and "executive" qualities such as decisiveness, independence, and the ability to command social situations. The gender and sexuality strictures that had developed for classroom teaching reflected a sort of compromise between economic utility (school districts sought an inexpensive and abundant supply of teachers) and a need to preserve women's acceptable "place" in society (keeping them under the supervision of men to prevent them from becoming too independent). For administrators, though, gender and sexuality strictures developed mainly to preserve the sense of masculinity of the men who remained in what had come to be regarded as "feminized" work.

Not only did the sexuality/gender redefinition of school teaching and administration serve purely economic purposes while at the same time preserving norms, but also arguably it cast school workers somewhat in the role of models for students. To the extent that single women teachers modeled chastity or sublimated their maternal instincts into classroom duties rather than raising their own children; they were thought to serve as useful examples for their female students. Similarly, the presence of male administrators demonstrated to youth the means by which males were to govern females in domestic units. In a rather indirect, though powerful manner, the matter of whom school boards hired for teaching and administering became part of the implicit curriculum.

The state of affairs where women taught and men managed in schools generally persisted through World War II, but strains gradually developed. First, as districts and states enacted compulsory attendance laws—and then enforced them—schools continued expanding in number and size. Many boys resisted school attendance, though, and tended to drop out in significantly greater numbers than did girls. As this alarming trend came to light, experts rushed to provide explanations.[8] For instance, the male teachers in the New York City schools argued that women teachers exerted a feminizing influence on boys, a problem that they argued required greatly increased hiring of male teachers. Of course, such a recruiting effort would have required pay increases for men.[9]

Second, the success of the women's suffrage movement engendered a backlash movement that effectively eroded some of the social and economic gains women recently had won. Theodore Roosevelt contributed to this backlash with his famously expressed concern about "race suicide" among college-educated, middle- and owning-class white women who either refused to marry or did not bear as many children as in the past.[10] Spinster teachers became prime targets of such concerns because they were relatively well educated for the time; were socially, if not economically, middle class; and usually could not marry if they wanted to keep their jobs. Besides, women teachers accounted for many of the leaders and grass-roots workers of the suffrage movement, a role that fixed them squarely in the cross-hairs of women's movement antagonists.[11]

Third, awareness of persons with nonconforming sexuality and/or gender grew in the public mind. European sexologists published research describing "homosexuals," "inverts," "intersexuals," and the like in exhaustive detail, though much of such work tended to pathologize them. Publishers in the United States, eventually released translations of this work along with that of Freud. Though audiences for these volumes tended to be small and scholarly, discussion surrounding them eventually filtered into broader arenas. Also, communities of sexuality/gender nonconforming persons formed in urban areas, where they were increasingly visible—and prone to harassment by police, not to mention newspaper reportage. Artists, writers, and movie-makers began featuring characters with explicitly nonconforming sexuality/gender, that is, until Hollywood production codes imposed in the early 1930s drove such characters into hiding, with carefully coded language and symbolism making their existence clear to those who wanted to see them.[12]

Generally, then, public awareness of "homosexuality" increased during these years. Along with this awareness came a popular perception that some-how, gender nonconformity and same-sex desire went hand in hand. The commonly held view was that manifestation of one implied the existence of the other. For example, women who crossed lines of gender propriety came to be viewed as deviant in some manner, possibly even lesbian. The large ranks of unmarried women teachers as a class eventually were regarded as somehow suspect. School districts, however, continued to enjoy economic and other benefits from the continued employment of spinster teachers—that is until after World War II when returning veterans desperately needed employment and growing numbers of married women wanted to remain in the work force rather than relinquish their jobs. With the abundant availability of these newer pools of teaching candidates, and with a strong desire to shed the taint associated with employing so many single women/spinster/potentially lesbian teachers, school districts quickly dropped their marriage bans after World War II and began hiring married women teachers in great numbers, much greater even than their representation in the general labor force.[13]

A quiet, though growing awareness and suspicion of homosexuality became outright fear during the early Cold War years. Senator Joe McCarthy's much-publicized hunt for communists in government shifted focus to finding and purging homosexuals, a somewhat easier target. Soon, school officials around the country joined in the effort. They scrutinized their payrolls for suspected homosexuals who supposedly might recruit students "to freshen their ranks." In 1950, one popular magazine published perhaps the first major article warning parents to be on the look out for homosexual teachers. The piece frantically asserted, "Behind a wall erected by apathy, ignorance, and a reluctance to face facts, a sinister threat to American youth is fast developing." Teachers must be scrutinized carefully because, "[W]e lose sight of the fact that the homosexual is an inveterate seducer of the young of both sexes, and that he presents a social problem because he is not content with being degenerate himself; he must have degenerate companions, and is ever seeking younger victims." The author of this piece captured something of a growing, though unsupported, fear that homosexuality spread like a contagious disease, and furthermore that homosexuals must recruit aggressively among youth.[14]

Soon local and even state school officials joined in the hunt for homosexual school workers. Perhaps inspired by the screening for homosexuals instituted by the military during World War II, local school officials watched men for signs of effeminacy, which was thought to connote a propensity for same-sex intimacy.[15] School officials scrutinized women as well, particularly their clothing, grooming habits, social activities, and the presence (or lack) of a wedding or engagement ring. California passed post-war legislation mandating the notification of school officials whenever police snared teachers in homosexual sting operations. Resulting arrests inevitably meant that such teachers lost their jobs regardless of the veracity of the charges.[16] In Idaho, undercover investigators employed McCarthy-like tactics to identify men, including teachers, who supposedly ran a "homosexual ring" that preyed on boys.[17] And a special legislative commission established in Florida during the late 1950s to investigate the activities of communists and civil rights workers—but which failed to get traction in these efforts—turned its attention instead to purging the state's teaching ranks of homosexuals.[18] These and other widely reported efforts contributed to a climate where school workers feared betraying any cross-gender characteristics that might hint at homosexuality. As one teacher expressed it, "The suspicion is it."[19]

For the most part, school workers endured these purges quietly, having little legal recourse and even less open support. Matters changed in the aftermath of the Stonewall rebellion of 1969, however. This much-heralded event, in which patrons of a gay bar rioted for three days in response to the usual police harassment, came to symbolize the birth of a visible, grass-roots gay liberation movement. Self-identified gay, lesbian, and bisexual teachers joined activist organizations and then by the mid-1970s, founded associations specifically for L/G/B and eventually transgender (T) school workers. Lesbian and gay school workers then marched in gay pride parades, filed employment discrimination lawsuits, and otherwise sought to claim their identities openly while retaining their jobs.[20]

The larger gay liberation movement quickly gathered momentum as cities around the country organized their first gay pride parades. Some municipalities also enacted nondiscrimination ordinances that protected individuals from housing and employment discrimination on account of sexual orientation. This growing, flamboyant, and at times delightfully provocative movement no doubt made many people uncomfortable. Critics, looking for ways to attack the movement, quickly found its politically most vulnerable spot: lesbians and gay men who work with youth. Sensational headlines from the past lingered in memory two decades later with the consequence that many continued to perceive gay men and lesbians as inveterate child-seducers. A Gallup poll conducted in 1977 found that although the majority of those surveyed believed homosexuals should be protected from employment discrimination generally, this belief did not extend to educators. Instead, 65 percent objected to the presence of homosexual elementary teachers.[21]

In a most dramatic fashion, Anita Bryant capitalized on this fearful perception when in 1977 she campaigned to overturn the new Dade County, Florida civil rights ordinance that included "affectional or sexual orientation" among classes of persons protected from employment and housing discrimination. Gay liberation activists, confident of their growing national momentum, failed to take Bryant seriously at first. To them she seemed like a woman with "an obsolete singing career, followed by years of pushing orange juice on national television." Certainly her "image was not one to strike fear into the heart."[22] Nonetheless, she inspired emphatic support from the Christian-right when she explained her fundamental concerns with Miami's nondiscrimination ordinance: "First, public approval of admitted homosexual teachers could encourage more homosexuality by inducing pupils into looking upon it as an acceptable lifestyle. And second, a particularly deviant-minded teacher could sexually molest children."[23] Essentially, even though the ordinance protected persons of a broad range of occupations from employment discrimination based on sexual orientation, Bryant focused specifically on the issue of lesbian and gay teachers. Her "Save Our Children" campaign picked up significant financial support when she appeared on two then-popular, nationally syndicated Christian television shows, Jim Bakker's *PTL Club* and Pat Robertson's *700 Club*. In each case, viewers responded with more mail and contributions than for any previous episode of these shows.[24] On the day of the Miami vote, polls showed that the ordinance likely would remain in place. Ordinance supporters, generally confident of victory, failed to show up to vote. In contrast, Bryant's supporters swamped their precincts. Consequently, the ordinance went down by a 2 to 1 margin.

John Briggs, a California state legislator and friend of Bryant's, decided he wanted to build support for his own gubernatorial campaign by tapping into the same potent political base that Bryant had identified. In 1978 after a lengthy signature drive, he succeeded in introducing a state referendum, Proposition 6, inducing school districts to get rid of their lesbian and gay school workers and those who supported them. The referendum read:

> [T]he state finds a compelling interest in refusing to employ and in terminating the employment of a schoolteacher, a teacher's aide, a school administrator or a counselor, subject to reasonable restrictions and qualifications who engages in public homosexual activity and/or public homosexual conduct directed at, or likely to come to the attention of, schoolchildren or other school employees. This proscription is essential since such activity and conduct undermines that state's interest in preserving and perpetuating the conjugal family unit.[25]

Briggs's initiative drew intense national media attention. It also galvanized a massive grass-roots lesbian and gay rights movement that regarded this assault on one part of the movement, educators, as a symbolic attack on the whole. Many lesbian and gay teachers came out to work against the initiative even though in doing so, they risked losing their jobs should the initiative pass. Others worked quietly in the background. Coalitions of labor, persons of color, women, and other rights groups formed and pooled resources. Rosters of volunteers filled quickly, but usually only with first names because of the risks of exposure many feared. As the November ballot approached, polls showed public support shifting against Proposition 6, but campaign workers worried about a repeat of the Miami vote where a last-minute surge of conservative voters defeated lesbian and gay rights. Such fears dissipated, though, as the final tabulation revealed a decisive defeat for Briggs's handiwork.[26]

In the 1970s and 1980s, a number of different right-wing religious and political groups similarly attempted to limit the presence and visibility of LGBT persons in school work. For example, an Oklahoma law similar to the Briggs Initiative was struck down by the U.S. Court of Appeals after the Supreme Court deadlocked on the matter.[27] Second, during the early years of the AIDS pandemic, the public feared the presence in schools of anyone infected, or those with regular contact with anyone infected, even after the means of transmission had been clearly established. Communities clearly viewed gay male school workers with heightened suspicion during this time. Third, a bill introduced in the Missouri legislature attempted to classify homosexuality as a disease, and as such, to require a Division of Health registry listing the names of all homosexuals who worked with youth under 21 years old.[28] Without question, the frequently expressed views against lesbian and gay school workers involved two issues: (1) they were thought somehow to influence the sexuality/gender of the students with whom they worked, and (2) the recurring accusation that they wanted to molest youth persisted even in the face of mounting research indicating quite the opposite.[29]

Students on the Front Line

The front line in the battle for LGBT rights in schools shifted away from school workers and toward students in the late 1980s and early 1990s. As AIDS ravaged communities of gay men during these years, concern mounted that ignoring the existence of gay youth in the face of such a scourge amounted to condemning them to early deaths. The growing visibility of the LGBT rights movement also contributed to earlier awareness among youth of their own possible sexuality/gender nonconformity. Schools increasingly enrolled youth who claimed or were accused of queer identities and who then typically faced brutal emotional and physical abuse. Growing numbers of counselors and teachers learned about the profound self-loathing felt by some students who identified as lesbian or gay. To address this mounting need, the Delegate Assembly of the National Education Association (NEA) in 1988 passed a resolution supporting the idea that schools should offer LGBT youth counseling that helped them accept and adjust to their sexual orientation rather than compelling them to change.[30] The consequent support of the NEA assisted Virginia Uribe, a counselor in Los Angeles, to develop an innovative set of materials for working with LGBT youth in a program she founded, Project 10.[31]

Discussion about the welfare of LGBT youth received widespread media attention in 1991 when the U.S. Department of Health and Human Services released the Report of the Secretary's Task Force on Youth Suicide. This report, which had provoked strenuous internal resistance in Bush's presidency, declared at the start:

> A majority of suicide attempts by homosexuals occur during their youth, and gay youth are 2 to 3 times more likely to attempt suicide than other young people. They may comprise up to 30 percent of completed youth suicides annually.... Schools need to include information about homosexuality in their curriculum and protect gay youth from abuse by peers to ensure they receive an equal education. Helping professionals need to accept and support a homosexual orientation in youth. Social services need to be developed that are sensitive to and reflective of the needs of gay and lesbian youth.[32]

Journalists and activists on the left and right seized the opportunity that the release of this report presented. LGBT activists argued that in the interest of youth, acceptance and support for LGBT persons in schools were necessary. The shift in focus away from school workers and toward students probably felt like a relief to some activists who found that the public responded more favorably to the needs of youth than to those of adults who still seemed a bit suspicious to many. In contrast, critics on the political and religious right claimed that the statistics cited in the study exaggerated the phenomenon. They also charged that self-proclaimed LGBT youth needed counseling that steered them toward heterosexual and gender-conforming identities. Besides, any taxpayer funds used to support LGBT affirming counseling services or curricula, they argued, amounted to public support for values that ran directly counter to theirs.

Many students around the country who identified as LGBT or queer decided to take matters into their own hands as the 1990s wore on. Some started LGBT social groups in their communities and in schools. LGBT students in Massachusetts organized a state-wide lobby day in 1993 in which they successfully convinced state lawmakers to enact a law outlawing discrimination against them in schools.[33] Students around the country started gay/straight alliances in their high schools, an idea that spread with such breathtaking speed that by 2001, reportedly over 800 schools in forty-seven states had organized such groups.[34] Students often encountered deep resistance, as did Kelli Petersen who started a gay/straight alliance at her Salt Lake City high school. In reaction to Petersen's group, the Utah legislature passed a bill requiring school systems to forbid student clubs that "promote bigotry, encourage criminal conduct, or discuss issues of sexuality."[35] And finally, in a landmark ruling, Jamie Nabozny, a young man from Wisconsin, won a nearly $1 million judgment against administrators in his schools, who he argued did nothing to stop years of antigay verbal and physical abuse.[36]

In the final analysis, students have taken up the cause of winning rights for queer persons in schools. Over the 1980s through the present, the movement of queer issues from the shadows to the mainstream has brought awareness of the existence of sexuality/gender nonconformity so that individuals may recognize it in themselves at earlier ages than in the past. In part because some LGBT adults fear close association with youth on account of old, though unfounded, assumptions that persons with nonconforming sexuality/gender are, as a class, child predators, some queer teenagers have insisted on forming their own social support networks. No doubt, the Internet also has allowed queer youth to connect more fully with each other. One important strand of queer youth culture that has emerged is the insistence upon actively shaping individual and collective identities rather than having others foist labels, cultures, styles, and behaviors on them. LGBT students have, then, become centrally important in pushing schools toward including their voices and full participation on their terms.

School Workers and Democratic Communities in Schools

Leaders who wish to build democratic communities in their schools that include the full participation of queer youth must be mindful of several key challenges of this work. First, there must be acknowledgment that the persons chosen for school administrative positions historically have been gender/sexuality conforming—at least superficially. From the start, superintendencies and high school principalships typically have been filled by men. Data describing superintendent demographics in 2000, for example, reveal that men held 87 percent of all superintendencies. Of these men, 95 percent were married. This represents a dramatic difference from the marriage rate of men in the general population: 58 percent.[37] Job notices at mid-century reveal that school boards explicitly sought married candidates for their vacant superintendencies. Although such an overt requirement has been dropped, high marriage rates among male superintendents clearly have persisted. As I have argued in *Fit to Teach*, during the Cold War, the superintendency became a position that not only became closely identified with men, married men specifically, but also with what I have termed "hyper-masculine" men. School boards expressed with pride the athletic credentials of their superintendents, as well as other physical or behavioral attributes connoting virility or "manliness." This trend toward hyper-masculinization of the highest levels of school administrative work coincided with the expectation that administrators include among their duties the screening of personnel for suspected homosexuality. Once again, though the task of overtly screening personnel for evidence of gender/sexuality nonconformity certainly has diminished over the past few decades as districts and states have adopted nondiscrimination policies or laws protecting LGBT persons, the demographics of the superintendency have not changed accordingly.

Second, relatively few gender/sexuality nonconforming individuals currently hold school administrative positions such as principalships and superintendencies. In part, this is because school boards have not sought them—and very likely have actively avoided hiring them. As George Counts pointed out in his remarkable 1927 study, *The Social Composition of Boards of Education*, school board members tend to appoint persons demographically similar to themselves.[38] Because relatively few openly queer persons have been appointed or elected to school boards, the fact that few openly queer persons serve as school administrators should come as little surprise. Besides, superintendents in particular serve at the pleasure of their school boards. They have little recourse in the event that board members wish to terminate their contract on the basis of sexual/gender nonconformity. Boards also have the option of concealing their motives should a termination decision be based on perceived or real sexual/gender nonconformity. This is difficult to challenge, especially in states lacking nondiscrimination laws that include sexual/gender identity. Such school administrators might receive little or no support from their professional associations, which generally have avoided making protection of sexual/gender nonconforming members a priority. In short, there is little institutional support for sexual/gender nonconforming school administrators.

Third, school administrators, whether gender/sexuality nonconforming or not, face the threat of community resistance to policies or practices that acknowledge, include, or even support queer students and school workers. As Janice Irvine has detailed in *Talk about Sex*, her brilliant history of recent sex education battles in the United States, the religious- and political-right have mobilized powerful resistance not only to many sex education programs around the country but also to support of queer persons in schools. Arguably, they have built great strength by focusing on these topics, which they have turned into "hot-button" issues by controlling public speech about sex. In early battles concerning sex education, for instance, Irvine catalogs the successful rhetorical strategies used by the religious- and political-right: "anti-communist rhetoric, the dissemination of depravity narratives, sexual scapegoating, and a practice of strategic distortion."[39] In more recent battles they have employed similar tactics, but generally have depended heavily on using emotionally charged language and polarizing, binary logic. School administrators who have succeeded in diffusing tensions aroused when such divisive strategies have emerged have recast discussions in concrete terms while avoiding emotion-laden responses. They have conveyed the complexities and gray areas of the issues, refusing to fall prey to imposed binaries. They also have worked to build broad support for the larger issue of the welfare of *all* students and school workers.

Awareness of these obstacles and also of the history of sexuality/gender conformity in schools can help expand the possibility of creating truly democratic dialogue and decision making in schools. Through such awareness, school leaders can understand that gender/sexuality norms in schools have not always existed in their current form. Instead, they have emerged and shifted in response to particular economic conditions as well as to larger social notions of acceptable gender roles—which, arguably, are deeply connected with economic conditions as well. The establishment and perpetuation of gender/sexuality norms in schools have served some people well, but not others. A critical examination of whose needs have been served by these practices and whose have not can stimulate rich discussion that eventually might eliminate the expectation of gender/sexuality conformity in schools, a conformity that has systematically punished some in a most cruel and largely unquestioned manner. Instead, schools can be transformed into richly diverse communities alive with self-creation and mutual respect.

Notes

1. Janice Irvine has analyzed in great depth the rhetorical strategies employed by the Christian right during the past several decades in its crusades to reshape sex education and minimize the presence of persons with non-conforming sexuality/gender identities in schools. See *Talk about Sex: The Battles over Sex Education in the United States* (Berkeley: University of California Press, 2002).

2. *The Statistical History of the United States from Colonial Times to the Present* (Stamford, CT: Fairfield Publishers, Inc., 1965), 208.

3. Myra Strober and David Tyack, "Why Do Women Teach and Men Manage? A Report on Research on Schools," *Signs: Journal of Women in Culture and Society* 5(3) (1980): 494–503.

4. Catharine Beecher, "Petition to Congress," *Godey's Ladies Book* (1853), 176–177; and *The True Remedy for the Wrongs of Women* (Boston: Phillips, Sampson, 1851). I address the growing preference for single women teachers in *Destined to Rule the Schools: Women and the Superintendency, 1873–1995* (Albany, NY: SUNY Press, 1998), chapter 1.

5. See chapter 2 of *Destined to Rule the Schools*.

6. "Marriage as Related to Eligibility," *NEA Research Bulletin* (March 1942); and "Marriage as a Basis for Termination of Service," *NEA Research Bulletin* (May 1942).

7. *Destined to Rule the Schools*, 181.

8. For a thorough examination of the "boy problem," see the chapter by that title in Tyack and Hansot's 1992 classic, *Learning Together: A History of Coeducation in American Public Schools* (New York: Russell Sage Foundation).

9. "Appeal for Men Teachers," *New York Times*, October 4, 1911, col. 7, 12. This campaign to increase the hiring of male teachers— for which higher wages would be required—came in response to Grace Strachan's amazingly successful drive to win equal wages for male and female teachers. See Grace Strachan, *Equal Pay for Equal Work* (New York: B. F. Buck & Co., 1910), and Robert E. Doherty, "Tempest on the Hudson: The Struggle for 'Equal Pay for Equal Work' in the New York City Public Schools, 1907–1911," *History of Education Quarterly* 19(4) (1979): 413–434.

10. For examples of public work that voiced alarm about the declining birth rates among educated white women, see Charles Franklin Emerick, "College Women and Race Suicide," *Political Science Quarterly* 24(2) (1909): 269-183-269; and G. Stanley Hall and Theodate L. Smith, "Marriage and Fecundity of College Men and Women," *Pedagogical Seminary* 10(3) (1903): 275–314.

11. Patricia Smith Butcher, "Education for Equality: Women's Rights Periodicals and Women's Higher Education, 1849–1920," *History of Higher Education Annual* 6 (1986): 63–74. Susan B. Anthony and Carrie Chapman Catt are just two of the more notable suffrage leaders who had been teachers. Arguably, the suffrage movement depended heavily on teachers to organize it. One of the compelling reasons for this, as I've argued in *Destined to Rule the Schools* (chapter 3), is that women teachers and superintendents contended that they needed the vote to be able to have a voice in school matters. Many especially found it unacceptable that women could hold elected superintendencies in some mid/western states, but not vote.

12. I have discussed these changes extensively in *Fit to Teach: Same-Sex Desire, Gender, and School Work in the Twentieth Century* (Albany, NY: SUNY Press, 2005), chapter 4. For a more detailed treatment of queer characters in early U.S. films, see Vito Russo's classic, *The Celluloid Closet: Homosexuality in the Movies*, Revised edition (New York: Quality Paperback Book Club, 1995).

13. See *Fit to Teach*, especially table 4.1 and figure 4.1, 77.

14. Ralph H. Major, "New Moral Menace to Our Youth," *Coronet*, September 1950: 100–108.

15. For examples of how homosexuals were thought to be recognized, see Willard Waller, *The Sociology of Teaching* (New York: John Wiley & Sons, 1932), 147–149; and Major Baisden, *The Dynamics of Homosexuality* (Sacramento, CA: Allied Research Society, 1975), 12–13.

16. Karen Harbeck, *Gay and Lesbian Educators: Personal Freedoms, Public Constraints* (Malden, MA: Amethyst Press and Productions, 1997), 188–200. This groundbreaking book offers a compelling historical analysis and an extensive examination of case law as it reveals the experiences of lesbian and gay school workers.

17. John Gerassi, *The Boys of Boise: Furor, Vice, and Folly in an American City* (New York: Macmillan, 1966), especially 15–17.

18. Karen Graves currently is writing a significant book on this important episode in the history of lesbian/gay school workers. Also see Florida Legislative Investigation Committee, "Homosexuality and Citizenship in Florida" (1964), reprinted in *Government Versus Homosexuals*, edited by Leslie Parr (New York: Arno Press, 1975); and Harbeck, *Gay and Lesbian Educators*.

19. Quote from an interview conducted by Eric Marcus with an anonymous source. See Eric Marcus, *Making History: The Struggle for Gay and Lesbian Equal Rights, 1945–1990, An Oral History* (New York: HarperCollins, 1992), 72–73.

20. See chapter 6 of *Fit to Teach* for a more complete discussion of lesbian and gay associations of school workers. Some of the most active of these organizations existed in New York City (which published the excellent bulletin, *Gay Teachers Association Newsletter*), San Francisco/Bay Area, and Los Angeles. Karen Harbeck's *Gay and Lesbian Educators* is far and away the best source describing employment discrimination lawsuits filed during this time.

21. "65% in Poll Oppose Gays as Teachers," *Los Angeles Times*, July 17, 1977, sec. 1, p. 27.

22. "Bryant Rants … No Sunshine for Gays in Florida," *Lesbian Tide*, May/June 1977, 16–17.

23. "Anita's Circle," *Time*, May 2, 1977, 76.

24. Anita Bryant, *The Anita Bryant Story: The Survival of Our Nation's Families and the Threat of Militant Homosexuality* (Old Tappan, NJ: Fleming H. Revell Company, 1977), 13–15.

25. Pat Donohoe, "Initiative Measure to Be Submitted Directly to the Voters with Analysis," "Briggs" file, June Mazer Collection.

26. "How Sweet It Is!" *Lesbian Tide*, January/February 1979, 10–12.

27. "Students and Teachers Win Some, Lose Some," *The Advocate*, March 22, 1978, n. p.; Linda Greenhouse, "Vote Upholds Teachers on Homosexual Rights," *The New York Times*, March 27, 1985, n.p.; and *Board of Education of Oklahoma City* v. *National Gay Task Force*, No. 83-2030, Supreme Court of the United States, 470 U.S. 903.

28. "'Big Brother' Stirring in Missouri," *The Advocate*, March 13, 1974, 1.

29. John Merrow discussed the child-molestation bugaboo and the emerging body of research refuting it in "Gay Sex in the Schools," *Parents' Magazine* 52(9) (1977): 66, 100, 104, 106.

30. National Education Association, *Proceedings of the Sixty-Seventh Representative Assembly* (Washington, DC: National Education Association, July 4–7, 1988), 227–233.

31. Dell Richards, "Gay Teens in L.A. Helped by Model School Program," *Bay Area Reporter*, November 24, 1988, 14; and Craig Wilson, "Teacher Takes Homophobia to Task," *USA Today*, February 12, 1991, 4D.

32. Paul Gibson, "Gay Male and Lesbian Youth Suicide," *Report of the Secretary's Task Force on Youth Suicide*, Vol. 3 (Washington, DC: Department of Health and human Services, 1989), 110. Note: The initial four-volume work was not widely distributed. Reprinting of the chapter concerning LGBT youth suicide was held up for two years because of right-wing political resistance to the findings. The report only reached the media in 1991.

33. Karen Diegmueller, "Massachusetts Approves Bill Outlawing Bias Against Gay Students," *Education Week*, December 15, 1993.

34. Scott S. Greenberger, "Gay Alliance Taking Hold in Schools," *Boston Globe*, April 15, 2001, B5.

35. Karen Diegmueller, "Salt Lake City Prepares List of Banned Clubs," *Education Week*, May 1, 1996.

36. Ben Fulton, "It's a Bash," *Weekly Wire*, November 10, 1997, Http://weeklywire.com/ww/11-10-97/slc_story.html.

37. Thomas Glass, Lars Björk, and Cryss Brunner, *The Study of the American School Superintendency, 2000* (Arlington, VA: AASA, 2000), 15; *Bureau of the Census, Statistical Abstract of the U.S.* (Washington, DC: Author, 1999), Table 1418, 873. This census data also are available online at http:://www.census.gov/prod/99pubs/99statab/sec31.pdf.

38. George S. Counts, *The Social Composition of Boards of Education: A Study in the Social Control of Public Education* (Chicago: University of Chicago Press, 1927).

39. Irvine, *Talk about Sex*, 49.

5

Excavating Hope among the Ruins: Confronting Creeping Fascism in Our Midst

Valerie Scatamburlo-D'Annibale, Juha Suoranta, and Peter McLaren

The tradition of the oppressed teaches us that the "state of emergency" in which we live is not the exception but the rule. We must attain to a conception of history that is in keeping with this insight. Then we shall clearly realize that it is our task to bring about a real state of emergency, and this will improve our position in the struggle against Fascism. One reason why Fascism has a chance is that in the name of progress its opponents treat it as a historical norm. The current amazement that the things we are experiencing are "still" possible in the twentieth century is *not* philosophical. This amazement is not the beginning of knowledge—unless it is the knowledge that the view of history which gives rise to it is untenable.

—Benjamin, 1968, p. 257

On the threshold of World War II, Walter Benjamin was finishing what was to be his last piece of writing, an eloquently tuned collection of "fragments" about the concept of history. During the writing process he returned to the memory of Paul Klee's painting "Angelus Novus" (1920) which had once belonged to his cache of most prized possessions. He had acquired it in 1921, but was forced to sell it in order to pay his way out of Paris en route to the United States to escape the Nazis. Benjamin's trek across the Pyrenees proved to be too emotionally debilitating. On September 26, 1940, he took his own life at the Franco-Spanish border, in the town of Port Bou, with a lethal dose of morphine.

The fragment cited above was the eighth among Benjamin's "Theses on the Philosophy of History." In the ninth fragment he invoked Klee's aforementioned painting and remarked that the angel had his eyes wide open, and it was as if he was rapidly moving away from something that obviously terrified and annoyed him. He was staring toward the past, where he saw a single catastrophe which kept "piling wreckage upon wreckage." According to Benjamin, it appeared as though the angel would want "to stay and awaken the dead, and make whole what ha[d] been smashed," but a storm blowing from "Paradise" enveloped him—a violent storm which had caught his wings and prevented him from reaching them. The tempest blows the angel into the future to which his back is turned, and the debris before him "grows skyward" (Benjamin, 1968, pp. 257–258). In the context of the ninth thesis, Benjamin develops his conceptualization of historical life as an immense pile of ruinous rubbish which grows ever higher with the passage of time. And yet, among the fragments, there seems to lie the light of redemption, a ray of hope—but one which is to be found apparently only in the opposite direction—away from the current course of historical "progress."[1]

We cite Benjamin's eighth and ninth theses since they force us to look not only at the past, but at the present, and toward the future at a time when the catastrophe otherwise known as the Bush administration keeps piling up its wreckage the world over. Even a cursory glance at the contemporary social landscape seems to suggest that the "state of emergency" has intensified. Especially since September 11, 2001, the United States has been acting more and more like a nation-state pushed to the limits of imperial expansion, where fascism and war have become the preferred modus operandi. And now, as we have entered into the sixth year of George W. Bush's presidency, the never ending "war on terror" continues to rage. As we write, more than twenty-five hundred U.S. soldiers have lost their lives while over seventeen thousand have been maimed, psychologically traumatized or both in Iraq alone. Tens of thousands of Iraqis have been slaughtered, countless more mutilated—and the butchery has been legitimated as a regrettable but necessary price of "progress."

The cost of war has already exceeded $270 billion while almost thirty-six million Americans live below the poverty line—including 12.9 million children. Of course, the richest 1 percent of the American population—the "haves" and the "have mores" whom Bush has referred to as his "base"—continue to reap the benefits of his generous tax cut package which represents one of the most brazen redistributions of income to the wealthy that the nation has ever seen. Corporations and CEOs continue to make out like proverbial bandits. The vise-grip put on workers in terms of lower pay and poorly funded pension plans as well as artful tax dodging and creative accounting practices, have enabled several companies to reap enormous profits. In 2003 alone, forty-six large corporations paid no federal income taxes despite "earning a collective $30 billion in profits" and the CEOs of those forty-six companies that "skirted federal taxes (led by the pharmaceutical giant Pfizer) earned an average salary of $12.6 million"

(Talvi, 2005, p.10). Across the globe, 2.8 million people—almost half of the world's population struggle in desperation to live on less than two dollars (U.S.) a day. There are a billion people suffering from chronic hunger despite the fact that a mere fraction of what the United States currently spends on the military could end world hunger as we know it (Galeano, 2003, p.19).[2]

Contrary to the "official" proclamations emanating from the Bush administration's propaganda factory about the "benevolent" reasons for war (i.e., protecting the "homeland," liberating the Iraqi people, spreading "democracy" and "freedom" in the Middle East), these are the days of empire. While talk of imperialism once elicited shudders among the Washington establishment, it has been proudly and boldly reintroduced into the lexicon of the American government and media (Mahajan, 2003, p. 181). Indeed, today warmongers and corporate marauders openly talk about the need for a "strong empire to police an unruly world" (Roy, 2004a, p. 11) and Bush, who seems to think he is on a mission sanctioned by the Almighty, has gleefully assumed his role as Emperor. One might call his mission messianic militarism.[3]

Mahajan (2003, p.181) notes that it is already passé to say that the Bush administration's foreign policy is a new form of imperialism—a statement echoed recently by Arundhati Roy (2004a, p.11), who concedes that the "New Imperialism"—while a remodeled, streamlined version of what once was—is "already upon us." Of course, the history of American imperialism is a long and tortuous one but,

> [f]or the first time in history, a single empire with an arsenal of weapons that could obliterate the world in an afternoon has complete, unipolar, economic and military hegemony. It uses different weapons to break open different markets. There isn't a country on God's earth that is not caught in the cross-hairs of the American cruise missile and the IMF checkbook…Poor countries that are geopolitically of strategic value to Empire, or have a "market" of any size, or infrastructure that can be privatized, or, God forbid, natural resources of value—oil, gold, diamonds, cobalt, coal—must do as they're told or become military targets.

The message is clear—surrender to the might of the military-industrial-corporate machine or war, by any means necessary, will be waged. This drive toward global American empire or what conservative columnist Charles Krauthammer has called "the American hegemon" may not constitute a classic imperial mission for control of another territory. It may not be about establishing a set of colonies around the globe. But, it does reflect the use and projection of political and military power on behalf of a radical, pro-corporate, antigovernment, free-market fundamentalism that mainly benefits the global economic activities of the capitalist elite—all the while cloaked in the rhetorical garb of "progress" and "democracy."

And, of course, there is a domestic version of "Shock and Awe." It is represented by an agenda which, in addition to tax cuts for the wealthy, favors capital freed from government restraints, deregulation, privatization and cuts in public services, a systematic dismantling of labor rights and environmental protections, and a frontal assault on civil liberties. In the most fundamental sense, Bush and his right-wing minions are seeking nothing less than the total obliteration of the New Deal and any remaining vestiges of the social safety net. One need only review George W. Bush's recent budget to see this logic at work. The budget slashes or freezes domestic programs related to health care and education while boosting the Pentagon's financial coffers with a 7 percent increase to a whopping $439 billion. This figure is 45 percent greater than when Bush took office and the $439 billion "is only part of the increased largesse for the military-security complex; another $33 billion goes to the ill-managed homeland security agencies." Moreover, those amounts don't count the war itself—which requires another "$70 billion or more" (*The Nation*, March 6, 2006, p. 3). Concomitantly, at least 141 domestic programs have been placed on the chopping block. Education alone stands to lose $2.1 billion—from student loans to vocational training. As some commentators have noted, such tendencies are eerily reminiscent of earlier fascist regimes where the military took up huge portions of the budget while social welfare priorities were eliminated or marginalized (Britt, 2003, p. 2).

In fascist parlance, the federal government is presumably detrimental to individuals' rights to choose and to live freely as one desires (Eco, 1995). [44] So-called big government is seen as the enemy—at least when viewed in the context of its social component. This is part of the reason why the radical right is doing its utmost to demolish and undermine the government and especially its social and educational policies. Their desire is to defenestrate the federal government (with exceptions, of course, for "homeland security," spying, and military spending) and reduce its scale and powers dramatically—to shrink it, in the words of ultraconservative tax reform crusader Grover Norquist, to a size where it can be drowned in the bathtub. Of course, the devastating effects of this starve-the-government mentality were on tragic display in the aftermath of Hurricane Katrina. From the inept response of FEMA to the revelations about massive cuts to the Army Corps and projects designed to protect citizens from the ravages of floods and hurricanes, the abject failure of the Bush administration to provide aid to the most vulnerable was painfully evident.[5]

The wreckage continues to accumulate—from the blood-drenched streets of Baghdad to the images of desperate Americans clinging to rooftops and floating debris to the carnage wrought globally by "free market" policies. This sad state of affairs is a symptom of a "state of emergency" that has become the rule rather than the exception. What we have for all intents and purposes, is a fanatical right-wing administration that wants to permanently run the United States and that wants "a United States that permanently runs the world" (Schell, 2005, p. 9) on behalf of corporate interests and to the detriment of democracy everywhere.

At present it seems as if the angel of history's wings have been singed by the smoldering ruins and that his wish to wake up the dead—that is, to promote democratic social change by abolishing the harmful effects of illusory progress promoted by corrupt regimes—has receded into the dim recesses of an ever more distant memory. The wish has been overcome by a creeping fascism that has devoured our hopes and dreams. It has been undermined by those who promote political apathy, fear of the Other, social insecurity, and historical amnesia. It seems as if all the lessons of the past, the lessons of previous military and other catastrophes, and the lessons of past efforts to thwart dissent have all been forgotten, or never learned. But hopes and wishes for something better can never be completely extinguished particularly when linked to critical, spirited reflection and action. Enter revolutionary critical pedagogy. Among the core ideas of revolutionary critical pedagogy are the importance of intruding into realities which the security state has identified as "off limits" to all those but its own cabal of cognoscenti, to acquire the critical tools to analyze the historical past and present in order to promote a future of hope and possibility, to develop a language of analysis and critique that can help us discern the complexity of the current social fabric, including the capitalist totality in which it is embedded, to muster the civic courage to ask disturbing questions that might irritate dominant powers, and to seek the light of redemption that lies beyond the current course of history.

Revolutionary critical pedagogy is powered by the oxygen of revolutionary struggle: critique. It is animated, however, not merely by the intellectual practice of critique but by the desire to advance an alternative social vision of what the world should and could look like if freed from the mind-numbing ideologies propagated by the military-industrial-media complex. Never has a new vision of human sociality been more urgent in a world where the U.S. government seeks unchallenged supremacy over other nation-states via military means or by controlling the regulatory regime of supranational institutions such as the World Bank and the International Monetary Fund. Never before has an unrelenting critique been as needed to combat the domestic fascism being nurtured by an administration that worships at the philosophical altar of Leo Strauss and which views democracy as something that "must be prevented at all costs" (Shorris, 2004).

Creeping Fascism

If we survey the contemporary state of historical affairs in the United States in an honest and forthright manner, we cannot ignore the growing evidence of a fascist renaissance in our midst. While we are more than two generations removed from the repulsive horrors of Nazi Germany, it seems as though many of fascism's underlying principles are wafting through the air today. We also believe it is necessary to acknowledge that fascism represents one of the lasting undertows of Western culture in accordance with other forms of authoritarian thinking and acting—and this was evident long before the Bush administration revealed its fascist propensities. Indeed, the work of Erich Fromm, particularly in his classic book, *Escape from Freedom,* clearly illustrates how authoritarian forces have long shaped modern capitalist societies. The focus of his book was the paradoxical position in which people lived out their lives in the midst of evolving capitalism. For, as he states, capitalism enables unprecedented freedoms of individualism emerging from the original (Gemeinschaft-type) ties with other human beings and nature but also produces a sense of isolation, anxiety, and fear in light of (Gesellschaft-type) consumption-driven communities. Thus Fromm draws attention to the problem of freedom in its twofold meaning. He showed how freedom from the traditional bonds of premodern society made people more independent and self-reliant but, at the same time, especially in capitalist conditions, isolated them from each other and filled them with unprecedented doubts, fears, and anxieties.

While Fromm stressed the psychological side of freedom, he was firm in his claim that it could not be separated from the "material basis of human existence, from the economic, social and political structure of society" (Fromm, 1965 [orig., 1941], p. 298). Based on that premise, Fromm demonstrated how capitalist individual freedoms were largely delusive and illusionary and suggested that the realization of positive freedom was intimately "bound up with economic and social changes" (Ibid.). According to Fromm, the limits of freedom were always evident in capitalist society, and they were always tested as a result of various concrete material realities, including unemployment, alienated labor, social insecurity, and diminished possibilities for equality and a life free of oppression.

Fromm emphasized that a truly free and democratic life was only possible in a society in which such maladies had been overcome—one modeled, in Fromm's view, on a form of democratic socialism (p. 299). Without such a change, people were prone to particular forms of escape from freedom includ-ing submission to authority, destructiveness, and automaton conformity leading, at worst, to fascist-like conditions. The artificial and manufactured freedoms of bourgeois liberal capitalism isolated people from each other and to escape such a mentally and socially obstinate situation, there had to be something that could unite people, give them comfort, and a false sense of security. This could ultimately lead to fascist-like mindsets, to acquiescent submission to "strong leadership" or some overwhelming, larger than life ideology. Fromm's analyses are useful in identifying not only the undertows of historical traumas of "Western civilization," but also its current capitalist and imperialist practices. Fromm (pp. 300-301) notes that in fascist-like contexts, words are "misused in order to conceal the truth" and that the words "democracy, freedom, and individualism become objects of this abuse too."

At the current historical juncture, words like democracy and freedom have been taken into the service of that nebulous entity called "the West"—in other words, imperialism led by the United States. In addition to invoking the mantras of democracy and freedom to disguise imperialist desires, George W. Bush has repeatedly been referred to as a "strong leader"; the larger than life ideology currently operative is the "war on terror," and stoking fear has been employed as a political strategy.

The social and political production of fear has enabled the Emperor of U.S. Imperialism and his military apparatus to create secret detention centers in Europe where detainees can be tortured (or granted legal exceptions to the ban on torture), to cultivate new terror-detainee legislation (such as the Military Commissions Act of 2006) that could constitute an unconstitutional suspension of the writ of habeas corpus if the legislation retroactively strips the courts of jurisdiction to hear detainee cases, to participate in warrantless (in all senses—legal, political, ethical) wiretapping, to deploy government payroll "journalists" to prop up neo-con programs under the guise of objective reporting, to promote touchscreen voting machines, to nullify laws of which Bush doesn't approve with the use of 'signing statements'. The production of fear also works hand in hand with the production of patriotic sentiment through spectacles such as those associated with sports, providing an emotional canopy under which bristling generalities about "democracy" and "freedom" can work unmolested in neutering critical inquiry into the country's deeply embedded corruption and in diverting attention away from grand tragedies such as the war in Iraq and our subsequent collusion in acts of state terrorism.

Moreover, the Bush administration has repeatedly deployed a fear-mongering strategy that functions to impress upon people that grave enemies are lurking about, waiting to attack, and that they should seek shelter under the rubric of militarized, domestic power. Such tactics serve to frighten people in order to distract them from what is really happening to them. Bush (no doubt with help from his handlers) has mastered the art of scaring "the people" into submission. His most frequent used linguistic technique is the "negative framework" which represents a pessimistic image of the world. One observer claims that,

> Bush creates and maintains negative frameworks in his listeners' minds with a number of linguistic techniques borrowed from advertising and hypnosis to instill the image of a dark and evil world around us. Catastrophic words and phrases are repeatedly drilled into the listener's head until . . . it appears pointless to do anything other than cower. (Brooks, 2003, p. 21)

By instilling such fear in the populace, Bush has been able to advance a re-gressive domestic and social agenda and a disastrous foreign policy. Bush's domestic agenda parallels what he and his administration are now promoting in Iraq and globally—unfettered free market policies, privatization of virtually everything, and corporate rule in general. (And we musn't forget that the United States has 2,000 nuclear weapons on hair trigger alert and is developing earth-penetrating 'mini nuke' bunker buster bombs.)

In his "Eternal Fascism" (1995), Umberto Eco identified a series of traits that summed up the essence of "Ur-Fascism." These consisted of core ideolo-gies which never completely disappeared with the official defeat of Nazism, and which are now, arguably, looming at large in the global political arena. While Eco noted a certain degree of "fuzziness regarding the difference between various historical forms of fascism," he outlined a set of axioms that animated all forms of fascism. Laurence Britt (2003) has recently provided an "updated" examination of fascism's common threads. In what follows, we extrapolate from both Eco and Britt's analyses of fascist propensities that their presence should be cause for vigilance, concern, and critique among critical educators.

Christian Fundamentalism and the American Imperium

Both Britt and Eco note that one of the major characteristics of fascism involves the identification of "enemies" as a unifying cause around which a sense of collective identity can be forged since the only "ones who can provide an identity to the nation are its enemies" (Eco, 1995, p. 58). The identification of enemies/scapegoats as a rallying point is essentially designed to channel frustration and fear in controlled directions. This is often accomplished through the use of "relentless propaganda and disinformation" (Britt, 2003, p. 2) and by whipping up patriotic frenzy about the need to eliminate a perceived common threat.

Since "9/11," the all encompassing rubric of "terrorists" and "evil-doers" has served the Bush administration well as has the Manichean "you are with us or against us" rhetoric. And it was not just a matter of nations who allegedly "harbored" terrorists; any and all who defied Bush's call to war quickly became vilified as part of "them." When millions all over the globe protested against the U.S. invasion of Iraq, Bush dismissed them as "focus groups." Countries (including international allies) that did not support the administration's imperial misadventures were quickly labeled as anti-American, pro-terrorist, and their criticisms were characterized as evidence of weakness and an inability to confront "evil." And, many were also subject to national scorn. One need only look to the ridiculous lengths which some have gone to in demonizing France—from Bill O'Reilly's petulant "boycott France" initiatives to ex-Republican representative Bob Ney's (now indicted for his role in the Jack Abramoff imbroglio) preposterous charge to change the name of French fries to "freedom fries."

Recently, the "us and them" rhetoric has been taken a step further on the domestic front (cf. Goff, 2006). The "National Rally against Islamofascism Day," which took place at various sites across the United States in February 2006, was spearheaded by a group that calls itself the "United American Committee." The head of the organization stated that the purpose of the rally was to "unify all Americans behind a common goal" and against an enemy "that is seeking to destroy values we all hold dear." The group's website claims that Islam represents a war against "Western civilization" itself. Such assertions reaffirm those made by Clifford May who serves as president of the Foundation for the Defense of Democracies (FDD). May has likewise stated that the current American military aggression is not necessarily a war against terrorism or even against al Qaeda, but rather a war against Islamofascism that is aimed at "destroying" the Western world. It should be noted that May, served as Director of Communications for the Republican National Committee from 1997–2001 and is a signatory of the Project for the New American Century (PNAC)—the organization largely responsible for promulgating a unilateral American foreign policy.[6]

What is notable about such groups is their failure to admit that a form of Christian fascism envelops the administration and that it is every bit as frightening as the Islamofascism which they vehemently denounce. In this regard, it is hard not to invoke "Huey Long's famous idea that fascism would come to America clothed as anti-fascism" (cited in Meyerson and Robert, 2006). The unifying identity that is being promulgated by many on the right is one clearly rooted in Christian fundamentalism. Five days after "9/11," Bush referred to the war on terrorism as a "crusade" and in private conversations, he suggested that the terrorists despised Christianity (Woodward, 2002). After being reprimanded for his use of the term crusade, Bush has gone out of his way to praise Islam as a "religion of peace," has invited Muslim clerics to the White House for Ramadan dinners and has been careful to distinguish between Islam and terrorism—at least in front of the cameras. His rabid right-wing supporters, however, have taken every opportunity to denigrate Muslims and exploit and exacerbate what Eco refers to as the "natural *fear of difference*" (1995, p. 58). From Ann Coulter's vitriolic rant after 9/11 when she suggested that the United States should invade Muslim countries, slay their leaders and convert their inhabitants to Christianity to Jerry Falwell's assertion that Islam is an evil and wicked religion, far-right hate-mongers have fueled racist sentiment (Goff, 2006). In spewing their hysterical rhetoric, however, they failed to see how their own positions paralleled those of the "terrorists." Suddenly, we were immersed in the pathology of a "holy war"—one that was, however, defined by fundamentalists on both sides (Moyers, 2005a).

One could see this pathology embodied in the form of U.S. Army General William Boykin whom the Pentagon assigned to the task of tracking down and eliminating Osama bin Laden and other high-profile targets. Boykin, who had taken up with a group called the "Faith Force Multiplier" (a group whose members apply military principles to evangelism), had characterized the war on terrorism in apocalyptic terms as a "clash between Judeo-Christian values and Satan" (Cooper, 2003; Moyers, 2005a). According to Richard T. Cooper of the *Los Angeles Times*, Lt. Gen. William G. "Jerry" Boykin, the Deputy Undersecretary of Defense for Intelligence, is an "outspoken evangelical Christian" who has suggested that radical Islamists hate the United States because it is a "Christian nation," because its "roots are Judeo-Christian" and because the "enemy is a guy named Satan" (Cooper, 2003, p. A1). Boykin also claimed, from the pulpit of the Good Shepherd Community Church in Sandy, Oregon, that America's "spiritual enemy will only be defeated if we come against them in the name of Jesus." He added that the "battle that we're in is a spiritual battle. Satan wants to destroy this nation, he wants to destroy us as a nation, and he wants to destroy us as a Christian army" (Arkin, 2003). Not surprisingly, like so many "believers," Boykin has asserted that George W. Bush was "appointed by God" to lead the charge against evil wherever it lurks (Arkin, 2003).

Christian fundamentalists continue to perpetuate the myth of America as God's chosen nation and Bush as the messiah. And Bush himself has done nothing to stifle such grandiose proclamations. In fact, he has done quite the opposite as is evident from even the most sycophantic accounts of his presidency. Indeed, if one sifts through the likes of Bob Woodward's *Bush at War* and David Frum's *The Right Man*, as well as Bush's own public statements, what emerges is a picture of a President who is convinced that he is on a divine mission. As Chip Berlet has aptly noted:

> Bush is very much into the apocalyptic and messianic thinking of militant Christian evangelicals . . . He seems to buy into the worldview that there is a giant struggle between good and evil culminating in a final confrontation. People with that kind of a worldview often take risks that are inappropriate and scary because they see it as carrying out God's will. (Berlet, cited in *The Progressive*, 2003, p. 10)

This interweaving of religion and government is yet another characteristic of fascism identified by Britt and it is alarming at several levels. While the President is certainly free to practice whatever religion he chooses and while George W. Bush is certainly not the first leader to use religious rhetoric or to claim that the United States is under the wing of providence, his fundamentalist beliefs—especially as they relate to his foreign policy—are disturbingly dangerous. As Giroux (2005, p. xx) has argued, "Bush's much exalted religious fundamentalism does more than promote a contempt for critical thought and reinforce retrograde forms of homophobia and patriarchy; it also inspires an aggressive militarism, wrapped up in the language of a holy war."

Fitrakis (2004) has chillingly observed that the last time a Western nation had a leader so obsessed with the conviction that he was directed by God's leadership, he came in the form of Adolf Hitler. Far from being a "barbaric pagan or Godless totalitarian," Hitler believed that he was chosen by God to lead Germany to victory. Before launching his preemptive strikes throughout Europe, Hitler remarked: "I would like to thank Providence and the Almighty for choosing me of all people to be allowed to wage this battle for Germany" (cited in Fitrakis, 2004). He further remarked "I follow the path assigned to me by Providence with the instinctive sureness of a sleepwalker" (cited in Fitrakis, 2004). Fitrakis further notes some haunting similarities between Bush and Hitler on this issue. He is worth quoting at length:

> Hitler stated in February 1940, "But there is something I believe, and that is that there is a God . . . And this God again has blessed our efforts during the past 13 years." After the Iraqi invasion, Bush announced, "God told me to strike at al Qaeda and I struck them, and then he instructed me to strike at Saddam, which I did." Neither the similarity between Hitler and Bush's religious rhetoric nor the fact that the current president's grandfather was called "Hitler's Angel" by the *New York Tribune* for his financing of the Fuhrer's rise to power is lost on Europeans. Pat Robertson called Bush "a prophet" and Ralph Reed claimed, after the 9/11 attack, God picked the president because "he knew George Bush had the ability to lead in this compelling way." Hitler told the German people in March 1936, "Providence withdrew its protection and our people fell, fell as scarcely any people heretofore. In this deep misery, we again learn to pray . . . The mercy of the Lord slowly returns to us again. And in this hour we sink to our knees and beseech our almighty God that he may bless us, that He may give us strength to carry on the struggle for the freedom, the future, the honor, and the peace of our people. So help us God." At the beginning of Hitler's crusade on April 12, 1922, he spelled out his version of the warmongering Jesus: "My feeling as a Christian points me to my Lord and Savior as a fighter." Randall Balmer in *The Nation*, noted that "Bush's God is the eye-for-an-eye God of the Hebrew prophets and the Book of Revelation, the God of vengeance and retribution."

Many of Fitrakis's observations are reiterated by Stern (2005), who warns that we ignore a fundamental history lesson—that politics and religion don't mix as the rise of National Socialism proved—at our own peril.

Bush's extremism and religious fundamentalism should not come as a surprise to anyone remotely familiar with his clan's history of Nazi ties. George Herbert Walker, George W. Bush's maternal great-grandfather was one of

Hitler's most important backers who "funneled money to the rising young fascist through the Union Banking Corporation" (Fitrakis and Wasserman, 2003). And his great grandfather, Samuel Prescott Bush, founded and became the first president of the National Association of Manufacturers, a pro-fascist organization whose principal cause was defending industrial capitalism from the scourge of unions (Felien, 2005).[7] While Bush is certainly no Adolf Hitler based on the current historical record, the "preventative" and "preemptive" wars started by the current administration undoubtedly reflect the desire for global dominance that finds its most recent precedent in the history of the Third Reich. And, just as his great grandfather sought to defend industrial capitalism in the interests of the corporate elite, Bush is seeking to secure corporate rule in this age of globalized capital. As Sara Diamond (1995) states, the kind of right-wing Christianity which the Bush administration embraces and from which it garners so much loyalty "supports capitalism in all its forms and effects." Bill Moyers (2005a, p. 29) adds that the radical religious right are "foot soldiers in a political holy war financed by wealthy economic interests" while Phillips (2006, p. 22) notes that when it comes to matters of business, economics, and wealth, the tendency of the Christian right is "to oppose regulation and justify wealth and relative laissez-faire" and to tip its hat to corporations and those in upper-income brackets.

To see the roots of the agenda for American global dominion, one need only peruse the unsettling canon of the Project for the New American Century (PNAC). There, in plain sight, one finds the blueprint for the establishment of Pax Americana (i.e., America's version of a "peaceful" world). A report entitled "Rebuilding America's Defenses: Strategy, Forces and Resources for a New Century" penned in September 2000 by a cabal of far-right "intellectuals" was, in effect, wholeheartedly adopted as the Bush administration's foreign policy after September, 2001. Indeed, the tragic attacks of "9/11" provided the needed justification for adopting and implementing the plans (that had been years in the making) detailed in the document. Most of the plans delineated in the report were echoed in Bush's September 2002 National Security Strategy document (aka the Bush doctrine) with its emphasis on unilateral military action, preemptive strikes, and permanent U.S. military and economic domination of every region of the globe. As Foster (2006a, p. 12) has appositely noted, the Bush administration's declaration of a universal and protracted "global war on terrorism" doubles as a "justification for the expansion of U.S. imperial power." Foster goes on to state that,

U.S imperial geopolitics is ultimately aimed at creating a global space for capitalist development. It is about forming a world dedicated to capital accumulation on behalf of the U.S. ruling class—and to a lesser extent the interlinked ruling classes of the triad powers as a whole (North America, Europe, and Japan). . . The United States as the remaining superpower is today seeking final world domination. The "Project for the New American Century" stands for an attempt to create a U.S.-led global imperium geared to extracting as much surplus as possible from the countries of the periphery, while achieving a "breakout" strategy with respect to the main rivals (or potential rivals) to U.S. global supremacy. (2006a, pp. 14–15)

Foster's observations point to two related points of fascism outlined by Britt—the protection of corporate power and suppression of labor power. Britt (2003, p. 3) argues that in a fascist context large corporations are able to "operate in relative freedom" and to flout laws and regulations designed to protect workers. The United States had already been suffering from the toxic effects of corporate rule long before Bush was anointed President in 2000, however, under Bush's watch corporations have essentially been given free rein to pollute at will and to defy any regulatory constraints on their power. Scott (2006, p. 2) notes that the country is increasingly "suffocating from the deleterious effects of Big Money interests in virtually every arena—from public political processes to the privatization of much of what belongs to all of us." Moreover, there can be no doubt that workers have been under an especially brutal assault at the hands of the Bush administration. Indeed, John Sweeney once referred to Bush's administration as the "most anti-worker Administration in decades" (cited in Swanson, 2004). This has been made abundantly clear by Bush's refusal to support a significant increase in the minimum wage, his attacks on the rights of various categories of workers to organize, his wholehearted endorsement of outsourcing, and his vigorous backing of corporate-friendly free trade deals that weaken labor power and unions all over the world (cf. Rasmus, 2005). Bush's hostility toward labor predates "9/11" but since then, under the pretext of national security, his antiunion, antilabor positions have been elevated to new heights. He has blatantly used the fight against terrorism as an excuse to ban unions and roll "back the rights of workers across the board" (Bacon, 2003, p. 19). In a fascist milieu, organized labor is particularly targeted since it is seen as "the one power center that could challenge the political hegemony of the ruling elite and its corporate allies" (Britt, 2003, p. 3).

The Unpatriotic Professoriate

Core features of fascism also include the "cult of tradition" (Eco, 1995, p. 57) and the "disdain and suppression of intellectuals" (Britt, 2003, p. 3). The cult of tradition ignores that "traditions" themselves are social constructions and in doing so obscures their historical "constructedness." Instead, it refers to the glorious past as if history was eternal, carved in stone, and without contradictions. Therefore, in following and honoring petrified tradition there can be no learning, not to mention critical learning. General historical amnesia and political illiteracy, as well as mystification and mythologization of current world events, help the dominant to maintain their stranglehold on power while advancing a Manichaean worldview. In this sense, one can see how fascism generally entails a distrust of the intellectual world. For Nazis, universities were "nests of reds" and the "official Fascist intellectuals" were mainly engaged in attacking the "liberal intelligentsia for having betrayed traditional values" (Eco, 1995, p. 58).

These tendencies are clearly evident in contemporary American political and academic life. Dissident voices have invited the scorn of so-called patriots speaking on behalf of the American Imperium. As Beinin (2004, pp. 101–102) has aptly noted:

> Since the September 11 terrorist attacks…supporters of George W. Bush's Manichaean view of the world have mounted a sustained campaign to delegitimise critical thought…Universities and colleges have been a particular target of policing what may be thought and said…because they are among the few institutions where intelligent political discourse remains possible in the United States.

One of the first examples to plainly illustrate these propensities was a "report" issued by the American Council of Trustees and Alumni (ACTA) in November 2001 entitled *Defending Civilization: How Our Universities Are Failing America and What Can Be Done About It*. ACTA, formerly known as the National Alumni Forum, was founded by Second Lady and "culture war" veteran Lynne Cheney in 1994. Until recently, she served as a director to the organization.[8] ACTA's *Defending Civilization* was clearly intended to be one of the first salvos in the Right's reinvigorated war on liberal and left-leaning professors and in that quest the organization has shamelessly exploited the tragedy of "9/11" to advance its political agenda. One need only look to the front cover of the report which sports the famous photograph of three New York City firefighters hoisting an American flag amid the rubble of the World Trade Center to confirm that.

The report's authors, Jerry Martin and Anne Neal, claimed that while the vast majority of the citizenry (92 percent) had rallied behind President Bush's decision to go to war after the terrorist attacks, college and university faculty had not been as enthusiastic and hence were the "weak link" in America's response. Such language, in and of itself, parroted that used by the House Un-American activities Committee (HUAC) in its McCarthy-era witch hunts—in fact, HUAC used exactly "the same label for one of the scientists they pursued" (Chihara, 2001). For the most part, the report depicted the academy (and its presumably "liberal" faculty members) as a pacifist fifth wheel undermining the resolve of the nation and even scolded some professors for being "short on patriotism" (Martin and Neal, 2002, p. 1).

In its "original" form, the report borrowed a few pages from McCarthy's playbook and actually named names by citing 117 instances of so-called unpatriotic speech by university professors and administrators. Given that there are 3,600 colleges and universities in the United States that was hardly an astonishing figure. But even more interesting was the fact that nearly a third of the 117 examples came not from faculty but from students, various speakers at antiwar teach-ins and even protest placards (Scigliano, 2001). Others came from third hand sources as many of the so-called quotes in the report were cited from conservative websites and publications. Furthermore, many of the statements cited in the document were, arguably, rather innocuous including one that simply suggested that there was "a lot of skepticism about the administration's policy of going to war" and another which argued that "[We should] build bridges and relationships, not simply bombs and walls" (Martin and Neal, 2002, p. 14). If those weren't treasonous enough, a professor of religious studies from Pomona College was chastised for urging people to "learn to use courage for peace instead of war" (Ibid. p. 16).

After ACTA received some well-deserved criticism for its McCarthyite missive, it issued an edited version of the report—without the names. A revised and expanded version published in February 2002 also excluded the names of the presumed "offenders" but retained much of the inflammatory rhetoric. In a passage replete with the aforementioned characteristics (i.e., cult of tradition, a Manichaean worldview, etc.), the report accused professors of ignoring heroism and for failing to condemn the forces of evil:

Rarely did professors publicly mention heroism, rarely did they discuss the difference between good and evil, the nature of Western political order or the virtue of a free society. Indeed, the message of many in academe was clear: BLAME AMERICA FIRST...The events of September 11 underscored a deep divide between the mainstream public reaction and that of our intellectual elites...The American public had no difficulty calling evil by its rightful name. Why is it so hard for many faculty to do the same? (Martin and Neal, 2002, pp. 3–5)

Such sweeping generalizations mirrored the presidential bombast of George W. Bush who, in several post-9/11 speeches, referred to his government's position as the guardian of goodness and freedom that had to fight "evil" wherever it lurked. They also insinuated that any form of critical thought or dissent was clearly the province of debauched, traitorous, intellectuals. Hence, those academics who may have had difficulty in buttressing the simplistic logic of the Bush administration were characterized as acquiescent minions of terrorism. Of course, such accusations were ludicrous but any attempts to contextualize the events of 9/11 or to offer critical perspectives on a militarized policy response were regarded as unpatriotic. The message from ACTA was clear—fall in line behind Bush or else. Moreover, in singling out the "intellectual elite" of the nation, the report recited the same hackneyed formula that has been a mainstay of what Thomas Frank calls "backlash politics." Central to the jeremiads of backlash politicians, cultural conservatives, and right-wing rodomonts like Ann Coulter, Sean Hannity, Bill O'Reilly, and Michael Savage is an assault on the so-called liberal intelligentsia or elite that is hopelessly out of touch with "real" Americans—conservative, patriotic, God-loving and God-fearing citizens.

Presumably the intellectual elite are out of touch because they have succumbed to "academic trends" which valorize "moral relativism" and which "suggest that Western civilization is the primary source of the world's ills" (Martin and Neal, 2002, p. 5). Not surprisingly, the report revived much of the drivel churned out by cultural conservatives (including that of Lynne Cheney herself) in the early 1990s during the apex of the "culture wars" and repackaged it for a post-9/11 world. As a result, the twin bogeymen of Sixties radicalism and political correctness were summoned to explain the moral decay of higher education.

Until the 1960s, colleges typically required students to take survey courses in Western civilization. Since then, according to the report, those courses have been supplanted by a smorgasbord of often narrow and trendy classes and incoherent requirements that do not convey the great heritage of human civilization.

> Instead of ensuring that students understand the unique contributions of American and Western civilization—the civilizations under attack—universities are rushing to add courses on Islamic and Asian cultures and in the rush to add such courses, those institutions reinforce the mindset that it was America—and America's failure to understand Islam—that were to blame. (Martin and Neal, 2002, pp. 5–7)

The authors then directly quote none other than Lynne Cheney to further their arguments:

> To say that it is more important now [to study Islam] implies that the events of Sept. 11 were our fault, that it was our failure . . . that led to so many deaths and so much destruction," said the American Council of Trustees and Alumni's founding chairman Lynne V. Cheney in a speech on October 5. Instead, said Cheney, students need to "know the ideas and ideals on which our nation has been built . . . If there were one aspect of schooling from kindergarten through college to which I would give added emphasis today, it would be American history." (Martin and Neal, 2002, p. 7)

Space constraints prevent us from unpacking the aforementioned quotes in greater detail. Nonetheless, a few brief observations can be made. First and foremost, such comments imply (and not likely inadvertently) that U.S. policy is inherently just, that it must be obediently accepted, and that its leadership must never be doubted because the "homeland" is in perpetual danger of being wounded by irrational evildoers who hate "our" freedom and democracy. They also cast the entire issue in typical Manichaean fashion. As they have been prone to do in the past, cultural conservatives resort to simplistic formulations that pit the West versus the Rest, culture/civilization versus barbarism and the primitive contaminating forces of the "other." The sanctimonious indignation that typifies such a perspective rests on a defensiveness in which all "others" are seen as intent on ravaging "our" civilization and "way of life." In such accounts, the West (and America) is characterized as intellectually fecund and virtuous while the rest of the "non-Western" world is represented as intellectually sterile, disdainful of civility, and backward. And, of course, the uncritical West-is-best logic that animates such positions conveniently ignores the legacies of colonialism, imperialism, military aggression, and oppression which have characterized the enterprise of Western civilization. As Walter Benjamin so cogently reminded us, there is "no document of civilization which is not at the same time a document of barbarism" (1968, p. 256). Of course, such a dialectical grasp of history eludes the minds of Lynne Cheney and other culture war commandoes. Moreover, one could be tempted to ask Ms. Cheney and her ACTA colleagues why it is that the United States—presumably the greatest world defender of democracy—has, over the last five decades funded, advised, and sponsored the overthrow of democratically elected reformist governments that attempted to introduce egalitarian redistributive economic programs in countries such as Guatemala, Guyana, the Dominican Republic, Brazil, Chile, Uruguay, Syria, Indonesia (under Sukarno), Greece, Cyprus, Argentina, Bolivia, Haiti, and the Congo? (McLaren and Martin, 2005, p. 197)

For that matter, one may also ask why the United States government has participated in wars of attrition and attacks on "soft targets" such as "schools, farm cooperatives, health clinics, and whole villages in places such as Cuba, Angola, Mozambique, Ethiopia, Portugal, Nicaragua, Cambodia, East Timor, Western Sahara, Egypt, Lebanon, Peru, Iran, Syria, Jamaica, South Yemen, and the Fiji Islands" or why it has a record of direct military aggression through "invasions and assaults against Vietnam, Laos, the Dominican Republic, North Korea, Cambodia, Lebanon, Grenada, Panama, Libya, Iraq, Somalia, Yugoslavia, and Afghanistan?" (McLaren and Martin, 2005, p. 198). It is probably safe to assume that Cheney's version of American history would likely dispense with some of its more disconcerting details—including the prolonged and problematic U.S. intervention in the Middle East. It is precisely such history which Cheney and ACTA would like to suppress. Despite their stated objective of wanting students to be more informed about American history and Western civilization, what ACTA really wants is history to be taught in its most sanitized version.

Elsewhere in the report, on its website, and in its quarterly publication *Inside Academe*, ACTA has used the tragic events of "9/11" to reinvigorate the agenda of "cultural conservatism" and to apply the Bush Doctrine of "you are either with us or you are with the terrorists" to intellectual life. Through the use of hysterical and blatantly militaristic language, ACTA has called for a defense of the "homefront" and has suggested that "we" were attacked "not for our vices, but for our virtues" and for "our principles," which embody the "ideals of Western civilization and of free societies everywhere" and which draw the "hatred of those who despise a world based on liberty and the rule of law." [99] Such posturing draws on powerful expressions of nationalism—yet another characteristic of fascism identified by Eco (1995) and Britt (2003). Nationalism enfolds people and produces discourses that try to rally and unify the masses around a common theme or enemy; it celebrates the military and demonstrates a disdain of things foreign that often borders on xenophobia (Britt, 2003, p. 2). The nationalistic rhetoric of ACTA's documents imply that the war "we are waging is a war of moral humanity," and it valorizes obeying soldiers as heroes, as saviors of Western culture and "civilization saving it from a threat from the political underworld." The soldiers are "defending not only their own land, but also the whole moral world." These lines are not from any speech given by George W. Bush, Lynne Cheney, or ACTA spokespersons, but they might as well be since they adequately capture the sentiment of ACTA's pro-war rallying cries. The aforementioned lines are actually derived from an article entitled "The Veil Falls" penned by Joseph Goebbels shortly after the German offensive in the East in July 1941.

Cheney and her ilk have long fought for greater control over curriculum but they have been far less honest about it than their conservative predecessors like William F. Buckley. Buckley (the man often called the father of modern conservatism) published the polemic *God and Man at Yale: The Superstitions of "Academic Freedom"* in 1951. In that tract, he chastised the idea of academic freedom (for communists and liberals) and the independent academy. Buckley inveighed against the alleged "atheism" and secularism of professors, and suggested that universities should embrace one value system and seek to inculcate it in their students. The value system that Buckley advocated was one that would extol the virtues of capitalism and Christianity. To his credit, Buckley was always forthright about his pro-capitalist, pro-America, pro-Christianity agenda and his belief that academic freedom should be effectively denied to those who would disagree. Cheney and ACTA, on the other hand, cowardly resort to coded phrases like "Western civilization" and "freedom" to thinly disguise their agenda for cultural conservatism and their attempts to maliciously discredit those who refuse the brand of "patriotic correctness" that they are peddling. This becomes glaringly obvious toward the end of the report's prefatory remarks which, paradoxically, summon the ghosts of Hitler and Nazism:

> We learn from history what happens when a nation's intellectuals are unwilling to sustain its civilization. In 1933, the Oxford Student Union held a famous debate over whether it was moral for Britons to fight for king and country. After a wide-ranging discussion in which the leading intellectuals could find no distinction between British colonialism and world fascism, the Union resolved that England would "in no circumstances fight for king and country." As the *Wall Street Journal* reported: "Von Ribben-

trop sent back the good news to Germany's new chancellor, Hitler: The West will not fight for its own survival." (Martin and Neal, 2002, p. 7)

The authoritarian fervor epitomized in such remarks must be acknowledged for what it is—a blatant effort to equate critique with lending comfort to the "enemy." This statement, perhaps more than any other, captures the underlying essence of ACTA's report for it is nothing more than a cover for targeting certain forms of intellectual activity, censoring certain political viewpoints, and curtailing the free speech rights of those protesting the policies of the Bush administration. It also speaks volumes about ACTA's rigid demands for an intellectual culture of unquestioned obedience—one where critical faculties are lulled into slumber, one where anti-intellectualism and mind-numbing conformity reign supreme, one where loyalty to the Homeland's agenda is demanded at all costs.

The American Council of Trustees and Alumni is certainly not alone in its pursuit of ideological purity, nor is it the only organization that has revealed its affinity with the McCarthyite legacy that continues to cast a dark and menacing shadow over American political life. In fact, there is no shortage of examples. From Daniel Pipes' Middle East Forum which hosts the "Campus Watch" website which is essentially designed to harass liberal and progressive scholars and anyone remotely critical of America's pro-Israel foreign policy to David Horowitz's misnamed "Students for Academic Freedom" and his "Discover The Network" database that monitors liberal and left-leaning academics, the right has been launching an all-out offensive on academic freedom (at least for those professors who dare to challenge the Bush administrations) under the guise of a renewed "culture war." One of the more notable examples involved one of the authors of this essay (McLaren) whom the Bruin Alumni Association (a right wing organization headed by a former associate of Horowitz) labeled as number one on the "Dirty Thirty" list of the most dangerous professors at the University of California, Los Angeles. The "dirty thirty" scandal received international attention as a prime example of resurgent McCarthyism partly due to the fact that the Bruin Alumni Association offered a hundred dollars to any student who would secretly audiotape leftist professors on the UCLA campus. Of course, the real agenda of the right wing attack dogs assaulting the academy is about much more than "culture." Writing in 1991, Alexander Cockburn made an interesting observation about the "culture wars" and the controversy over "political correctness." He noted that although the attacks on the academy (characterized as a bastion of left-wing radicalism) were presumably being waged in the name of defending Western civilization, their real ideological intent was motivated by the need to fashion minds "sufficiently deadened to reason and history to allow the capitalist project to reproduce itself from generation to generation" (Cockburn, 1991, p. 691). His comments are even more apposite today for they sum up the true impetus for ACTA's initiatives—shaping minds and the academy in the service of corporate rule and American empire.

This becomes blatantly obvious if one follows the money. ACTA's major sources of funding (as are Horowitz's) are derived from a host of right-wing foundations including the Lynde and Harry Bradley Foundation, the Sarah Scaife Foundation, and the (now defunct) John M. Olin Foundation.[10] Central to the agenda of all of these foundations, for more than three decades, has been the promulgation of unfettered free-market ideology—not only at home but the world over. This impetus has become even more pronounced since 9/11 as the desire for American-led global corporate hegemony has intensified among neoconservatives. Far from being concerned with the moral fabric of the United States and Western civilization, the ultraconservatives behind these foundations are preoccupied with the profits that accrue from American global dominance. Theirs is an attempt to "promote empire abroad and corporate power at home" (Wolin, 2003, p. 13). They recognize, however, that the naked drive for power and dominance does not always play well in Peoria or in Thomas Frank's Kansas. So the more palatable patina of "cultural values" is employed to disguise their rapacious imperial ambitions and, what are essentially "economic ends" (Frank, 2004, p. 5). After all, the global "new world order" (i.e., American empire) which they covet necessitates the creation of a new moral order at home and culture often becomes the battlefield upon which the struggle for control over collective consciousness is waged. That is precisely the point of these foundations' support for organizations like ACTA and Students for Academic Freedom and nothing about it concerns democracy.

In fact, the interventions of culture warriors like Cheney, Horowitz, and others seek to eliminate the critical function of dissent and indeed critical thinking itself and replace it with an ideological conformity that is not only chilling but profoundly undemocratic. It is somewhat ironic that the authors of ACTA's report chose to raise the spectre of Hitler in their concluding remarks since it is *their* campaign against dissent that has a distinctive fascist ring to it. Hitler was able to establish policies of intolerance and suppression with robust public support by convincing the populace that such initiatives would result in a stronger, better Germany. His followers proudly proclaimed that a new, patriotic Germany would be born out of pain, fear, and danger while concomitantly warning that internal, menacing forces were working to undermine the nation from inside. Such posturing was part and parcel of the entire process of Nazification and specifically a campaign called "gleichschaltung"—which literally meant "getting in step." ACTA's calls to defend the homeland, Horowitz's efforts to publicly demonize dissidents, and other such tactics which brazenly exploit the fear and tragedy associated with "9/11" are jarringly evocative of "gleichschaltung."

Media Mendacity and Weapons of Mass Deception

Welcome Ladies and Gentlemen to…the arrival of friendly fascism. Regrettably, millions will die as before. But just think of the tremendous selection and savings you'll gain. Of course the loss of freedom and democracy are tragedies, I know, but consider the entertainment value contained within and to remind you, it is you, the people, who have mandated this course of our fate so please come with me…Look at the new face of power in America. This is your future you can never leave. Who said tyranny can't be fun. Friendly fascism is having so much fun, what else do you need? You'll learn to like what you must do. If you resist you are suppressed…We disconnect and start the war. We make life a commodity…Big business and big government distract us with entertainment. They manufacture our consent.

—Consolidated, from the LP *Friendly Fascism*, 1991

Robert McChesney has repeatedly noted that the mass media play an especially crucial role in democratic societies. In fact, he suggests that democracy itself requires that there be "an effective system of political communication, broadly construed, that informs and engages the citizens" and that draws "people meaningfully into the polity." As such, the manner by which the "media system is structured, controlled and subsidized is of central political importance" (McChesney, 1997, pp. 5–6). The fundamental principles of democracy depend, in many ways, upon the notion of a reasonably informed citizenry. Today, corporate domination of the media system poses serious challenges to a "functioning democracy and a healthy culture" (McChesney, 2004, p. 7). Indeed, four media giants—namely AOL-Time Warner, Viacom, Disney, and Rupert Murdoch's NewsGroup—control virtually everything we read, view, and listen to. McChesney is one among many media observers who have helped to draw attention to the incompatibility between corporate media and an ostensibly democratic society. Of course, the blame for the pitiful state of our democracy and the creeping fascism that we have identified cannot be laid solely at the doorsteps of corporate media organizations, but they have been a key factor in leading us down a dangerous path. As such, any attempt to delineate a program for educational leadership and democratic renewal cannot ignore the fundamental role played by media in shaping collective consciousness and public opinion. Nor can it ignore that the military-industrial-media complex, in this era of corporate-led globalization, essentially serves to propagate and enforce the views, values, and ideologies necessary to sustain it.

Britt (2003) argues that controlled mass media have played an important role in previous fascist governments. He writes:

> Under some of the regimes, the mass media were under strict direct control and could be relied upon never to stray from the party line. Other regimes exercised more subtle power to ensure media orthodoxy. Methods included the control of licensing and access to resources, economic pressures, appeals to patriotism, and implied threats. The leaders of the mass media were often politically compatible with the power elite. The result was usually success in keeping the general public unaware of the regimes' excesses. (p. 2)

Given the historical record, one could certainly argue that the American mainstream media tend to assume an obedient, if not, obsessive patriotic tone during times of international "conflict."[11] Yet the coverage of the Bush administration's war in Iraq (as it was in relation to Afghanistan) appears to be especially insidious in this regard. For the most part, the drive to war was largely devoid of historical context, lacked substantive debate, and most often served to buttress the Manichean worldview served up by the Commander-in-Chief. After the tragic events of September 11, the mainstream media became even more acquiescent to the Bush administration—this after their propensity for 'going soft' on Bush was already in plain view. Indeed, one need only go back to the days of G.W. Bush's first presidential campaign, the 2000 election debacle, and his subsequent appointment to the White House by the Supreme Court.[12]

While the media have recently begun to ask questions about the rationale initially provided by the Bush administration to justify their preemptive war in light of damning reports that have shed considerable doubt on most pre-war declarations, this does not and cannot excuse more than three years of cowardice and the media's collusion with an unconscionable level of administrative deception. This recent questioning cannot and should not absolve the media of their complicity in parroting the official line in the days, weeks, and months leading to the Iraq war—a line which was, at best, based on a combination of willfully gross exaggerations and brazen lies. In the buildup to the war on Iraq, the bulk of mainstream media coverage from headline news on television to the front pages of major newspapers, repeated the administration's "talking points' unquestioningly. During the almost surreal run-up to "Operation Iraqi Freedom," the American media—and particularly mainstream media networks—were transmogrified into hollow echo chambers that gleefully valorized U.S. military might and an unthinking patriotism.[13] With very few exceptions, the mainstream media have been used as propagandistic mouthpieces for Bush's "war on terror" and have greatly assisted in generating the kind of fear necessary to whip up patriotic fervor and populist support to military aggression. As Schechter has argued:

> There is an intimate link between the media, the war, and the Bush administration…Few administrations have been as adept at using polling, focus groups, "perception managers," spinners and I.O. or "information operations" specialists to sell slogans to further a "patriotically correct" climate. Orchestrating media coverage is one of their most well-honed skills, aided and abetted by professional PR firms, corporate consultants, and media outlets. (2003, p. 1)

From the Bush administration's lies about Iraq's weapons of mass destruction to Colin Powell's prop-filled and fallacious presentation to the UN Security Council; from the sanitized war coverage to the cheerleading of U.S. military might; from the staged rescue of Jessica Lynch to Bush's ridiculous "Mission Accomplished" propaganda stunt; from the failure to explore the explosive Downing Street memos to the unwillingness to address the government's use of illegal propaganda aimed at its own citizens, the mainstream media have been complicit in fueling the fascist renaissance we are now witnessing. And the culpability goes far beyond the obvious Bush sycophants at the Fox News Network which obviously serves as the propaganda arm for the Republican Party as so many have aptly demonstrated. Jan Nederveen Pieterse writes:

> In American media the ratio of pundits to reporters and opinion to information is roughly in the order of 10 to 1. Commentators and retired generals trump foreign reporting and produce 'embedded commentary' and in effect ideological drill based on recycling television images and comments in a pattern of incessant circular commentary. White House media hype is part of power narcissism and the mainstream media play their deferential part. The media perform a game of mirrors in which media are the content of media. The media interview media pundits whose business is spinning spin. Part of the American bubble is radio silence amid media noise—scandal after scandal but little follow-up; in Paul Krugman's words, a culture of cover-ups. Investigations are left to politically embedded commissions. One effect is systemic unreality—a preventive war in which there is nothing to prevent, an occupation cast as liberation, a coali-

tion of the willing that isn't really willing and not much of a coalition, Iraq reconstruction efforts that don't produce reconstruction, a $40 billion per annum intelligence effort that doesn't produce intelligence. A rollercoaster empire whose Kodak moments turn out to have been manufactured—the fall of Saddam's statue, the rescue of Private Lynch, the way Saddam was captured, the death of Pat Tillman. Throughout, the nation is tangled up in doublespeak and treats vaudeville as if it is high drama. (2006, pp. 995-996)

The issue also cuts much deeper and is part of a larger pattern/trend that has tilted most American media outlets even further to the right of the political spectrum. This has been enabled, in part, through various policies, most notably the Telecommunications Act of 1996 which allowed for greater concentration of media ownership. Additionally, the right-wing "flak" machine has also played a considerable role in these developments. For years, dating back to the early 1970s, conservative think tanks have promulgated the notion that the mainstream media are "liberal." This mantra, while far from reflecting media reality, has proven to be quite successful in its effect (cf. Alterman, 2003; Croteau, 1998; Husseini and Solomon, 1998; McChesney and Foster, 2003; McChesney, 2004; Parry 1998; and Scatamburlo, 1998).

The pro-business right well understood that changing media discourse was a crucial part of "mainstreaming" right-wing ideas and through a well-organized, well-financed, and fervent coterie of activists they essentially succeeded in doing so. McChesney and Foster (2003, pp. 12–13) note that the ability of the right-wing campaign in "popularizing the view that the news media have a liberal bias has been accomplished to some extent by constant repetition without any significant countervailing position." Additionally, the conservative campaign has meshed "comfortably with the commercial and political aspirations of media corporations" (McChesney and Foster, 2003, pp. 14–15). Such developments have clearly influenced the behavior of the mainstream media in recent years and have generally contributed to the uber-patriotism exhibited by most media outlets.

It may also help to explain how the U.S. media systematically enacted what amounted to media blackouts with respect to coverage of peace protests and public dissent occurring nationally and internationally during the run-up to the war on Iraq. While the mainstream media now occasionally give a nod to antiwar sentiment with the emergence of Cindy Sheehan as the face of the "movement," antiwar veterans of "Operation Iraqi Freedom" are accorded little if any attention. It is also the case that the media, particularly television and cable organizations, have failed to bring to light the true horrors of war.

Goldsborough has suggested that many Americans supported the Iraq war (although the tide has certainly shifted) because they didn't know what was really going on:

> For the most part, U.S. news organizations gave Americans the war they thought Americans wanted to see. Fake war. Thomas Kinkade war, prettified, romanticized, glorified war. Americans love blood and guts in their movies, but can't stomach the real stuff in their living rooms. (2003, p. 1)

Far more insidious and disturbing, however, than *what* the media reported or *how* they reported events in the build-up to, and subsequent, war in Iraq, is that which was virtually rendered invisible by the coverage. Herman and Chomsky (1988) have long contended that the media tend to line up with the government on fundamental matters—particularly those concerning foreign policy—not because of any conspiracy but largely because the media themselves are huge corporations that share the same economic and basic interests with the corporate elite that essentially controls the U.S. government.

In addition to Herman and Chomsky, Ben Bagdikian (2000; 2004) and a host of others have illustrated how media corporations share members of the board of directors with a variety of other large corporations including banks, investment companies, technology companies, and oil companies.[14] It is also imperative to note that the global media are, in many respects, the "new missionaries of corporate capitalism" since the commercial media system (dominated mainly by U.S.-based transnational corporations) works to advance the cause of global "free-market" ideologies and commercial values. As Moyers (2005b, p. viii) maintains, "media giants, operating on big-business principles" exalt "commercial values at the expense of democratic value." The multibillion dollar media conglomerates are global in scope and reach. In order to secure profits and new markets, they often rely on the governments of their own countries to protect their interests domestically and internationally. Many of those companies have a stake in the "new Iraq" for as Chatterjee (2003) has argued, Iraq is a "corporate gold mine." With the occupation of Iraq, U.S.-based media and telecommunications corporations are better positioned to dominate Middle East markets.[15]

But, much more than all of this is the fact that the American mainstream media have not really investigated the imperial ambitions of the Bush administration which has wholeheartedly put into practice the dictates of the "Project for a New American Century." This situation directly coincides with one of the central presuppositions of Herman and Chomsky's (1988) propaganda model—namely that the elite, agenda-setting media fulfill a propaganda function by essentially adhering to imperialist ideology and by legitimizing U.S. interventionist forays that generally pave the way for capitalist corporations to rob, exploit, and rape the natural resources and people of the developing world. In the case of the war on Iraq (and the "war on terror" in general), the media dutifully served as puppets in disseminating the carefully planned propaganda of the Pentagon and the official talking points of the White House. Far more egregious, however, was the role that the so-called news media played (and continues to play) in obfuscating from view the imperialist escapades of the U.S. government and the horror unleashed on the Iraqi people under the guise of the "war on terror."[16]

In a democracy, the media should, ideally, serve the interests of the people, providing them with the information needed to participate meaningfully in decision making. As Chomsky has noted, "where there is even a pretense of democracy, communications are at its heart." In the current media climate dominated as it is by a few huge transnational corporations, which stand to benefit from the increased spread of corporate globalization—by imperial means if necessary—democracy is ill served. On this topic, Moyers is worth quoting at considerable length:

> Giant megamedia conglomerates that our Founders could not possibly have envisioned are finding common cause with an imperial state in a betrothal certain to produce, not the sons and daughters of liberty, but the very kind of bastards that issued from the old arranged marriage of church and state. Consider where we are today. Never has there been an administration so disciplined in secrecy, so precisely in lockstep in keeping information from the people and—in defiance of the Constitution—from their representatives in Congress. Never has so powerful a media oligopoly...been so unabashed in reaching, like Caesar, for still more wealth and power. Never have hand and glove fitted together so comfortably to manipulate free political debate, sow contempt for the idea of government itself, and trivialize the people's need to know...[There is a] third powerful force—beyond governmental secrecy and megamedia conglomerates—that is shaping what Americans see, read, and hear. I am talking now about the quasi-official partisan press ideologically linked to an authoritarian administration that, in turn, is the ally and agent of the most powerful interests in the world. This convergence dominates the marketplace of political ideas today in a phenomenon unique in our history. You need not harbor the notion of a vast right-wing conspiracy to think this collusion more than pure coincidence. Conspiracy is unnecessary when ideology hungers for power and its many adherents swarm of their own accord to the same pot of honey. Stretching from the editorial pages of *The Wall Street Journal* to the faux news of Rupert Murdoch's

empire to the nattering nabobs of know-nothing talk radio to a legion of think tanks paid for and bought by conglomerates—the religious, partisan, and corporate right have raised a mighty megaphone for sectarian, economic, and political forces that aim to transform egalitarian and democratic ideals. (Moyers, 2005b, pp. ix–x)

Moyers's observations clearly illustrate that any attempt to resuscitate democratic principles, to excavate hope from the fascist ruins now littering the American political landscape must confront the role of the media.[17] Such a task, however, would have to entail more than teaching "critical media literacy" and educating students about how to deconstruct the images, messages, and texts which they are bombarded with on a daily basis. Rather, it would necessitate a critical investigation of the *political economy* of the mainstream media. Deconstructing media texts and representations is insufficient if the context in which they are produced is downplayed as is the case in many psychologized and liberally humanized, postmodernized version of "critical pedagogy." A revolutionary critical pedagogy recognizes that it is not enough to interrogate the menu of images offered up by the captains of the media industry—the key is to question the very menu being offered, to question why the parameters of discourse are so narrow, and how this all relates to the capitalist imperatives that structure the very organization of our media system. Artz elaborates:

These instances indicate the need to analyze the concrete relations and practices: How does communication occur and function? Who decides what and how? What tensions and contradictions exist and how are they resolved or intensified? What is the relationship between this communication or cultural practice and the rest of the social order—regulators, instigators, evaluators, spectators, facilitators, benefactors, and beneficiaries—and how does this communication practice reinforce, reproduce, challenge, or potentially transform those relations and why? For Marxism, communication has no fixed meaning, but it has actual material consequence as it occurs—both materially in the products, the institutions, the actions related to communication and symbolically in the language, rituals and meanings that are loosely strapped to those material practices. (2006, pp. 37-38)

Robert McChesney (2005, p. 11) echoes Artz's sentiments when he notes that, "if we want to correct the failures of media content, we have to change the system that breeds them." In this sense, it is incoherent to conceptualize a viable critical pedagogy, as do many of its current exponents, without a vigorous anticapitalist component.

Conclusion

In order to confront the tide of fundamentalist nationalism, the fascistic tendencies enveloping the United States and the global imperial march of the Bush administration, radical educators must be relentless in their critiques of neoliberalism which, as Harvey (2005, p. 66) reminds us, is "profoundly suspicious of democracy." We must resist the routine conflation of capitalism with democracy and democracy with the "free market" for as McChesney (1999, p. 11) cautions "neoliberalism is the immediate and foremost enemy of genuine participatory democracy, not just in the United States but across the planet." We must recognize that within the discourse of neoliberalism, the very notion of the "public good" is constantly devalued and, in some cases, even "eliminated as part of a wider rationale for a handful of private interests to control as much of social life as possible in order to maximize their personal profit" (Giroux, 2004, p. 46). Any discussion of, and any hope for, a reinvigorated democracy in our time must confront the neoliberal agenda and expose its antidemocratic tendencies. It must also be made clear that the globalization of capital has an equal opportunity clause permanently built into it in that it accommodates itself to all citizens in a way that makes it a truly universal social order as such, it is able to detotalize meaning, to constellate itself as 'truth-without-meaning' in so far as it transcends the limits of specific cultural/symbolic worlds. Understanding this will help students realize that capitalism—even outside of its European or North American center of imperialist gravity—poses an enormous threat to social and economic justice worldwide (Zizek, 2006).

Radical educators must also be courageous enough to challenge their students about the sordid underbelly of U.S. imperialism in its current and historical forms. A first step in this process may be to embrace what Zembylas and Boler (2002) have called a "pedagogy of discomfort." Such a pedagogy refers to the practice by which educators present to their students the often contradictory and highly emotional dimensions of nationalist rhetoric. It involves an investigation into the ways that public emotional expressions of grief and anger have been used, in the name of patriotism, by "ideological forces such as mass media to support a radical legislative redefinition of civil liberties" as well as military and foreign policies that constantly reconfigure the definitions of terrorism (Zembylas and Boler, 2002, p. 1). We agree with many of the intentions that animate Zembylas and Boler's formulation—particularly the claim that a "pedagogy of discomfort" would necessarily entail a "critical inquiry regarding American values and cherished beliefs," the "ways those are promoted abroad," and an examination of "why the US is the target of so much hostility around the world" (Zembylas and Boler, 2002, p. 3).

But we cannot comprehend how that might be possible without explicitly naming neoliberal capitalism and imperialism as Zembylas and Boler seem reluctant to do. In our estimation, a "pedagogy of discomfort" does not go far enough in confronting the stark realities of U.S.-led global capitalism and current configurations of American imperialism. In fact, the predatory role currently played by U.S. imperialism is all but absent in their exegesis as is an acknowledgement that the real source of terror for many people around the globe is the "market" as Galeano (2003) has argued. The globalization of capitalism has not in any sense been held accountable to democratic interests despite the best efforts of its cheerleaders (led by the United States) to hide its diabolical nature behind the non-sequitur claim that the free market promotes "democracy." The establishment view is all too quick to ignore the "empire of barbarism" being promulgated by the American government and aided and abetted by its military arsenal on behalf of a small corporate elite.

Moreover, we contend that it is not enough to encourage students to enter the zone of "ethical and moral differences" (Zembylas and Boler, 2002, p. 7) or to revel in what essentially amounts to the safe postmodern harbors of "ambiguity" and "indeterminism." It is not enough to engage in the ethical licentiousness and complacent relativism that no doubt flows from invitations to acknowledge that "others" may have different *interpretations* of the American government's actions abroad. These "others" do not merely have different interpretations of U.S.-led corporate globalization and militarism; they are living through the atrocities unleashed by it. Their views are not merely informed by a different worldview or ideological lens but rather are informed by the concrete experiential realities they encounter on a daily basis.

Despite the claims that a "pedagogy of discomfort" can be successfully linked with a sort of "critical cosmopolitanism," it remains all too *comfortable* in its underlying presuppositions. While students and educators securely ensconced in American universities, colleges, and schools may be afforded the luxury of exploring "within a post-structuralist and feminist tradition" how "emotions as discursive practices" constitute subjectivities (p. 4), and while they may have the privilege of engaging in a pedagogy of discomfort that is "fraught with emotional landmines" (p. 3), too many of the world's citizens cannot as a direct result of imperialism and militarism and their externalization as the constitutive 'obstacle' to democracy. The children of many war-torn countries face landmines that are not merely "emotional." Rather, the landmines they confront are real, material objects that rob humans of life and limb. The discomfort they feel is marked in blood, death and destruction. And, although the critical interventions of a "pedagogy of discomfort" may be useful in nurturing a "care for the self" away from the "normalizing power of the emotional discourses of patriotism" in the American context, it is rather difficult to imagine a Foucauldian-inspired "care of the self" being practiced by Iraqi students while depleted uranium poisons their environment, while bombs explode and corpses amass.

Our own approach—what Paula Allman (2001) has christened "revolutionary critical pedagogy"—seeks to up the radical ante for progressive education that, for the most part over the last decade or more, has been left rudderless amidst an undertow of domesticating currents. It attempts a bold critique of pedagogical practices that are easily co-opted to mainstream versions of bourgeois liberal humanism and feeble discourses of progressivism. It ups the ante by speaking out against the palpable growth of fascism in our midst (not to mention the 'superpower syndrome' with its reliance on concentrated military power by U.S. governing elites as a path to unipolar victory for strategic geopolitical interests); to challenge the neoconservative restoration we are witnessing with the Bush administration and its minions; to interrogate the symbolically overdetermined ideologies of right-wing evangelical Christians including their science fiction rapture theology and the pride they exhibit in taking anti-intellectual positions on just about anything related to the public good, and their willingness to bathe in the effulgence of talk-radio personalities who routinely engage in a mean-spirited and primitive patriotism that condemns political dissent as anti-American.

Revolutionary critical pedagogy needs to be fearless in confronting the myths of a benevolent American empire—those make-believe constructions that dull critical sensibilities and which promote a perpetual state of historical amnesia. It must remain resolute in naming the enemy—capitalism—a system whose benefits accrue to the few at the expense of many the world over; a system "that is at the heart of so much of humanity's suffering" and one which "praises greed, individualistic accumulation and selfishness, over sharing, compassion and the collective good" (Pruyn, 2005, p. xxii). It needs to be unwavering in its commitment to expose what Foster (2006[b]) refers to as naked imperialism and the current pursuit of American global dominance and uncompromising in its goal of fighting imperialism in the belly of the beast.

Facing up to acts of U.S. imperialism provides a crucial context for discussing world history in light of the globalization of capitalism and we in this country must share the burden of history. We cannot resort to the forms of historical sanitization preferred by the likes of Lynne Cheney; nor can we exempt our history from discussion and debate simply because it is *our* history. To share the burden of history we need to become critically self-reflexive about our political system, its economic, domestic, and foreign policies in light of the aforementioned context of globalized capital. And, we need to nurture that same sense of critical self-reflexivity in our students.

However, a revolutionary critical pedagogy recognizes the need to move beyond a narrow anti-U.S. imperialism stance, even as we acknowledge that "[a]t times the USA seems to exist in a time space all of its own—preoccupied with dramas of power and with its number one status in the world theater, as if in an endlessly prolonged Larry King Live Show" (Pieterse, 2006, p. 995). It acknowledges the urgency of establishing a principled stand against imperialism *in general* for as Foster reminds us, the growth of empire is not the exclusive province of the United States; rather it is the "systematic result of the entire history and logic of capitalism" (2006b, p. 13). George W. Bush is merely the most recent conductor of the political-economic locomotive otherwise known as neoliberal capitalism. As such, we must remember that despite the fact that "God's cowboy warrior"[18] (aka Bush Jr.) is perhaps one of the most dangerous presidents in U.S. history, the "machine he handles is far more dangerous than the man himself" (Roy, 2004b, p. 38).

At the same time, revolutionary critical pedagogy takes seriously the impassioned pleas of those like Arundhati Roy who implore us to remember that the battle to reclaim democracy must begin in America. She writes:

> [T]he only institution more powerful than the U.S. government is American civil society. The rest of us are subjects of slave nations. We are by no means powerless, but you have the power of proximity. You have access to the Imperial Place and the Emperor's chambers. Empire's conquests are being carried out in your name, and you have the right to refuse. (2004b, p. 67)

Now is a precipitous time for educators to help develop the kind of critical citizenry that is capable of responding to the challenge put to us by Roy. If we believe that democracy should be something more than the "Free World's whore," something more than "Empire's euphemism for neo-liberal capitalism" (Roy, 2004b, pp. 54, 56), we can no longer afford to remain indifferent to the horror and savagery unleashed by capitalism's barbaric machinations and we cannot ignore the contemporary role played by U.S. militarism in enforcing a neoliberal agenda that wreaks havoc with any semblance of democracy both at home and abroad. Let us listen to the voices which cry out for genuine freedom rather than free markets, peace rather than plunder. Let us be the democratic battering rams knocking down the walls of the imperial palace and let us excavate hope from among the ruins. Educational leadership in the twenty-first century demands nothing less.

Notes

1   For an elaboration on the theme of redemption in Benjamin's work, see Wolin, 1994.

2.   Some estimates suggest that global anti-hunger efforts could be fully funded for eleven years with the money which has already been spent on the Iraq war alone. See Fumo, 2006.

3.   See "Bush's Messiah Complex" in *The Progressive*, February, 2003, pp. 8–10.

4.   Of course, there are contradictions to this logic on the right—especially when it comes to a woman's right to choose.

5.   See for example, Sirota, 2005.

6.   PNAC is discussed below.

7.   In addition to helping re-arm the Nazis in the 1920s and 1930s, Samuel Prescott Bush also has the dubious historical distinction of hosting the Third International Congress of Eugenics on Long Island in 1931. One of the main purposes of that congress was to call for the forced sterilization of 14 million U.S. citizens.

8.   For more on ACTA and its McCarthyite practices, see Scatamburlo-D'Annibale, 2006.

9.   See *Inside Academe*, Fall 2001, vi (4) available at www.goacta.org.

10.   For a more detailed account of these conservative foundations, see Scatamburlo-D'Annibale, 2006.

11.   As Hedges (2003, p. 16) has noted: "In wartime the press is always part of the problem… When the nation goes to war, the press goes to war with it. The blather on CNN or Fox or MSNBC is part of a long and sad tradition."

12.   Douglas Kellner's (2001) *Grand Theft 2000: Media Spectacle and a Stolen Election* provides an excellent overview of the pro-Bush media bias that began to manifest itself during the presidential campaign. Others, including Susan Douglas (2000), have argued that the media essentially worked on a daily basis as a fifth column legitimizing Bush's candidacy. Large research studies including one conducted by the Pew Research Center and the Project for Excellence in Journalism found that media coverage during the 2000 race for the White House was heavily skewed, favorably, toward Bush while Gore received the worst of negative media coverage. See also Cohen, 2001; Kellner, 2003.

13. For a more detailed account of the mainstream media's complicity in promulgating the administration's deceit, see Scatamburlo-D'Annibale, 2005.

14. See www.mediachannel.org/ownership/chart/shtml for a breakdown of the Big Six media companies and www.fair.org/media-woes/interlocking-directorates.html for a telling list of the interlocking directorships of media and other large corporations.

15. We have already seen how corporations like MCI, formerly known as WorldCom, were awarded lucrative contracts (to the tune of $45 million) by the Pentagon to build a wireless phone network in Iraq—this despite the fact that WorldCom perpetrated one of the biggest accounting frauds in American business history and that it has never previously built such a network. We should also note that while both the Democratic and Republican parties have been the benefactors of WorldCom's financial largesse, its donations to Republican causes over the years have been massive.

16. To this we could add the complicity of telecommunications conglomerates (AT&T, Verizon, and Bell South) in undermining the civil liberties of millions of Americans through their cooperation with the government's domestic spying program.

17. When the Department of Homeland Security starts to fund "sentiment analysis" research into software that can monitor ideological dispositions towards the United States as reported in the global media, it is a signal that preparation for new "media wars" are in the making. Awarded to groups at Cornell, the University of Pittsburgh, and the University of Utah, such research grants are aimed at developing sentiment-analysis technologies for extracting and summarizing opinions from "human authored" documents and thereby "identifying common patterns from numerous sources of information which might be indicative of potential threats to the United States" (Braughman, 2006). Technically, such analysis is not to be used within the borders of the United States, but it would not be difficult to imagine the type of loopholes that could be manufactured in order to allow the government to target both mainstream and alternative media within the United States in order to silence domestic critics in a time of "permanent" war.

18. The phrase "God's cowboy warrior" is derived from McLaren and Jaramillo, 2005.

References

Allman, P. (2001). *Critical education against global capitalism: Karl Marx and revolutionary critical education.* Westport, CT: Bergin & Garvey.

Alterman, E. (2003, June 30). When it rains… . *The Nation*, 276(25): 10, 23.

Arkin, W. M. (2003, October 16). The Pentagon unleashes a holy warrior. *Los Angeles Times.* www.latimes.com/news/opinion/la-oe-arkin16oct16,1,6651326.story?coll=la-headlines-oped- manual.

Artz, L. (2006). On the material and the dialectic: Toward a class analysis of communication. In L. Artz, S. Macek, and D. L. Cloud, Eds. *Marxism and communication studies: The point is to change it.* New York: Peter lang, pp. 5-51.

Bacon, D. (2003). Screened out: How 'fighting terrorism' became a bludgeon in Bush's assault on labor. *The Nation*, 276(18): 19–20, 22.

Bagdikian, B. (2000). *The media monopoly, sixth edition.* Boston, MA: Beacon Press.

———. (2004). *The new media monopoly.* Boston, MA: Beacon Press.

Beinin, J. (2004). The new American McCarthyism: Policing thought about the Middle East. *Race & Class*, 46(1): 101–115.

Benjamin, W. (1968). *Illuminations.* New York: Schocken Books.

Braughman, J. (2006, October 9). "The global war on negative sentiment." *Swans Commentary.* http://www.swans.com/library/art12/jeb162.html

Britt, L. (2003). Fascism anyone? *Free Inquiry Magazine*, Spring 2003, 23(2). www.secularhumanism.org/index.php?section=library&page=britt_23_2

Brooks, R. (2003). A nation of victims. *The Nation*, 276(5): 20–22.

Chatterjee, P. (2003, May 22). Iraq: A corporate gold mine. *Alternet.org.* www.alternet.org.

Chihara, M. (2001, December 26). The silence on terrorism. *AlterNet.* www.alternet.org/story.html?StoryID=12145.

Cockburn, A. (1991, May 27). Bush and P.C.—A conspiracy so immense. *The Nation*, vol. 252: 685, 690-691, 704.

Cohen, J. (2001, March 25). Pitching softballs: Why are journalists going easy on Bush? *FAIR.* www.fair.org/articles/softball.html.

Cooper, R.T. (2003, October 16). General casts war in religious terms. *Los Angeles Times*, p. A1.

Consolidated. (1991). *Friendly fascism.* LP, Capitol Records.

Croteau, D. (1998). Challenging the "liberal media" claim. *Extra!* July/August: 4–9.

Diamond, S. (1995). The Christian Right seeks dominion: On the road to political power and theocracy. www.publiceye.org/eyes/sd-theo.html.

Douglas, S. (2000, December 25). Bush's fifth column. *In These Times.* 13.

Eco, U. (1995). Eternal Fascism: Fourteen ways of looking at a Blackshirt. *UTNE Reader*, Nov.–Dec. 1995: 57–59.

Felien, E. (2005). Bush: Covered in oil. *Southside Pride.* www.southsidepride.com/2005/articles/bush.html

Fitrakis, B. (2004). Again, why George W. Bush must be tried as a war criminal. www.freepress.org/columns/display/3/2004/873.

———., and Wasserman, H. (2003). Fourth Reich? The Bush-Rove-Schwarzenegger Nazi nexus. www.counterpunch.org/wasserman10062003.html

Foster, J.B. (2006a). The new geopolitics of empire. *Monthly Review*, 57(8):, pp. 1–18.

———. (2006b). *Naked imperialism: The U.S. pursuit of global dominance.* New York: Monthly Review Press.

Frank, T. (2004). *What's the matter with Kansas: How Conservatives won the heart of America.* New York: Metropolitan Books.

Fromm, E. (1965 [orig., 1941]). *Escape from freedom.* New York: Avon Books.

Frum, D. (2003). *The right man: The surprise presidency of George W. Bush.* New York: Random House.

Fumo, V. (2006, June 12). Fumo discusses the monetary cost of the war in Iraq: Remarks on the floor of the Senate. www.fumo.com/Floor_Speeches/P&RCost$6-12-06.htm

Galeano, E. (2003). Terror in disguise. *The Progressive*, February, 2003: 18–19.

Giroux, H. (2005). *Against the new authoritarianism: Politics after Abu Ghraib.* Winnipeg, Manitoba:

Arbeiter Ring Publishing.

————. (2004). *The terror of neoliberalism: Authoritarianism and the eclipse of democracy.* Boulder, CO: Paradigm Publishers.

Goebbels, J. (1941). The veil falls. www.calvin.edu/academic/cas/gpa/goeb15.htm.

Goff, Stan. (2006, October 14). American fascism is on the rise. *Alternet.org,* http://www.alternet.org/story/42884

Goldsborough, J. (2003, July 1). TV hid reality of Iraq War. *Daily Breeze.com;* www.signonla.com/content/opinion/nmgolds05.html.

Harvey, D. (2005). *A brief history of neoliberalism.* Oxford and New York: Oxford University Press.

Hedges, C. (2003, April 21). The press and the myths of war. *The Nation,* 276(15): 16–18.

Herman, E. and Chomsky, N. (1988). *Manufacturing consent: The political economy of the mass media.* New York: Pantheon Books.

Husseini, S. and Solomon, N. (1998). "The Right-Leaning Rolodex." *Extra!* July/August, p. 13.

Kellner, D. (2001). *Grand theft 2000: Media spectacle and a stolen election.* Lanham, MD: Rowman & Littlefield.

Kellner, D. (2003). *From 9/11 to terror war: The dangers of the Bush legacy.* Lanham, MD: Rowman & Littlefield.

Mahajan, R. (2003). *Full spectrum dominance: U.S. power in Iraq and beyond.* New York: Seven Stories Press.

Martin, J. L., and Neal, A. D. (2002). *Defending civilization: How our universities are failing America and what can be done about it.* Washington, DC: American Council of Trustees and Alumni.

McChesney, R. (1997). *Corporate media and the threat to democracy.* New York: Seven Stories Press.

————. (1999). Introduction. In N. Chomsky (Ed.), *Profit over people: Neoliberalism and global order.* New York: Seven Stories Press, pp. 7–16.

————. (2004). *The problem of the media: U.S. communication politics in the 21st century.* New York: Monthly Review Press.

————. (2005). The emerging struggle for a free press. In *The future of media: Resistance and reform in the 21st century.* Edited by R. McChesney, R. Newman, and B. Scott. New York: Seven Stories Press, pp.9–20.

McChesney, R., and Foster, J. B. (2003). The 'Left-Wing' media? *Monthly Review,* 55(2): 1–16.

McLaren, P., and Jaramillo, N. (2005). God's cowboy warrior: Christianity, globalization, and the false prophets of imperialism. In P. McLaren (Ed.), *Capitalists and conquerors: A critical pedagogy against empire.* Lanham, MD: Rowman & Littlefied, pp. 261–333.

McLaren, P., and Martin, G. (2005). The legend of the Bush gang: Imperialism, war, and propaganda. In P. McLaren (Ed.), *Capitalists and conquerors: A critical pedagogy against empire.* Lanham, MD: Rowman & Littlefield, pp.189–212.

Meyerson, G., and Robert, M. J. (2006, October 6). It could happen here. *Monthly Review,* www.monthlyreview.org/1006meyerson.htm

Moyers, B. (2005a). Reckoning with the God squad. *In These Times,* 29(21–22): 28–29.

————. (2005b). Foreword. *The future of media: Resistance and reform in the 21st century.* Edited by R. McChesney, R. Newman, and B. Scott. New York: Seven Stories Press, pp. vii-xxiii.

The Nation (2006). (Editorial) Less butter, more guns, March 6, 282(9): 3.

Parry, R. (1998). In search of the liberal media. *Extra!* July/August: 11–12.

Phillips, K. (2006). Theocons and theocrats. *The Nation,* May 1, 2006, 282(17): 18, 20–23.

Pieterse, Jan Nederveen. (2006). Beyond the American bubble: Does empire matter? *Third World Quarterly*, 27 (6): 987-1002.

The Progressive (2003). (Comment) Bush's messiah complex. February 2003, 67(2): 8–10.

Pruyn, M. (2005). Teaching Peter McLaren: The scholar and this volume. In *Teaching Peter McLaren: Paths of dissent*. Edited by M. Pruyn and L. Huerta-Charles. New York: Peter Lang, pp. xvii–xlv.

Rasmus, J. (2005). *The war at home: The corporate offensive from Ronald Reagan to George W. Bush*. San Ramon, California: Kyklos Productions.

Roy, A. (2004a). The new American century. *The Nation*, February 9, 278(3): 11–14.

———. (2004b). *An ordinary person's guide to empire*. Cambridge, MA: South End Press.

Scatamburlo-D'Annibale, V. (2005). In "Sync": Bush's war propaganda machine and the American mainstream media. In *Filtering the news: Essays of Herman and Chomsky's propaganda model*. Edited by J. Klaehn. Montreal, Canada: Black Rose Books, pp. 21–62.

Scatamburlo-D'Annibale, V. (2006). The new "P.C.": Patriotic correctness and the suppression of dissent on American campuses. In *Bound by power: Intended consequences*. Edited by J. Klaehn. Montreal, Canada: Black Rose Books, pp. 12–45.

Scatamburlo, V. (1998). *Soldiers of misfortune: The New Right's culture war and the politics of political correctness*. New York: Peter Lang.

Schechter, D. (2003, May 1). The link between the media, the war, and our right to know. *Mediachannel.org* www.mediachannel.org/views/dissector/moveon.shtml.

Schell, J. (2005). The fall of the one-party empire. *The Nation*, December 12, 281(20): 9.

Scigliano, E. (2001, December 31). Naming—and un-naming—names. *The Nation*. 273(22). www.thenation.com/doc.mhtml?i=20011231&s=scigliano.

Scott, G.A. (2006, April 12). The rise of Fascism in America. www.commondreams.org/cgi-bin/print.cgi?file=/view06/0412-32.htm.

Shorris, E. (2004). Ignoble liars: Leo Strauss, George Bush and the philosophy of mass deception. *Harper's Magazine*, 308(1849): 65-71.

Sirota, D. (2005). Welcome to New Orleans. *In These Times*, 29(21–22): 17–21, 36–37.

Stern, F. (2005). A fundamental history lesson: The rise of National Socialism proved politics and religion don't mix. *In These Times*, October 24, 29(21–22): 30–31.

Swanson, D. (2004, December 20). Media blackout on Bush's war against labor. www.counterpunch.org/swanson/2202004.html.

Talvi, S. (2005). Alls or nothings. *In These Times*, 29(21–22): 10.

Wolin, R. (1994). *Walter Benjamin: An aesthetic of redemption*. Berkeley, CA: University of California Press.

Wolin, S. (2003, May 19). Inverted totalitarianism: How the Bush regime is effecting the transformation to a fascist-like state. *The Nation*, 276(19): 13–15.

Woodward, B. (2002). *Bush at war*. New York: Simon & Schuster.

Zembylas, M. and Boler, M. (2002). On the spirit of patriotism: Challenges of a "pedagogy of discomfort." *Teachers College Record*. www.tcrecord.org/Content.asp?ContentID=11007.

Zizek, Slavoj. (2006). Schlagend, aber nicht Treffend! *Cultural Critique*, 33 (1): 185-211

6

Sissies, Faggots, Lezzies, and Dykes: Gender, Sexual Orientation, and a New Politics of Education?

Catherine A. Lugg

> To hear gay jokes and the words faggot and dyke—that's a common thing in the halls of every school, but it's completely ignored by the teachers…I mean these are people in authority—it just kind of reinforces that this is okay. And for those kids not out of the closet, who may not even recognize what it is, that's going to reinforce their self-hatred once they realize who they are (Herr, 1999, p. 247).
>
> – Elsie, African American lesbian and public high school student.

American researchers who study the politics of education have generally concerned themselves with the traditional schooling issues: resources and their allocation, interest group and ideological conflict, current educational changes (now described as "reform"), curricular content, staffing and a host of other nuts and bolts types of dilemmas and debates (Randall, Cooper, and Hite, 1999). Studies have generally employed frameworks ranging from the new institutionalism and rational choice theory (and whatever else is currently fashionable in the mainstream political science literature) to the older dissatisfaction theory.

However, *mainstream* politics of education and educational leadership researchers have paid far less attention to the deeper structural issues regarding socioeconomic class, race, ethnicity, sex, gender, sexual orientation, and religion and how they shape "who gets what, when and how" (Lasswell, 1958) in U.S. public education (Foster, 1999; Marshall, 1993; Marshall, 1999; Marshall and Anderson, 1995). This is not surprising because, historically, other areas of academic scholarship have also tended to ignore these issues. Across the disciplines and professional schools, mainstream researchers' ignorance of these contentious areas has been a cultural norm (Burke 2001; Novick, 1988).

Nevertheless, each of these deep structural features is intrinsic to the U.S. political culture. Therefore, they are repeatedly made manifest in various governmental forums including public schools. To be more direct, neither our Constitution nor our governmental institutions that are bound by Constitutional strictures are color blind—nor are they class-less, or gender neutral, and so forth (Gotanda, 1991; Necsu, 2000; Tushnet, 2001; Yoshino, 1998; 2002).[1] And so, public education as a *public good* has been and remains inequitably distributed along these social and *Constitutional* lines. These lines, however, can soften and harden depending upon the current political environment (Anyon, 1997; Bowles and Gintis, 1976; Capper, 1998; Hogan, 1992; Orfield and Yun, 1999).

Two of the most-prickly political issues involving U.S. public education have been gender and sexual orientation. Both have had historic saliency in shaping almost every aspect of public education from personnel policies to curriculum content to student conduct codes, extra-curricular activities and beyond (Blount, 1996; Britzman, 1995; Capper, 1999; Clifford, 1989; Epstein and Johnson, 1998; Harbeck, 1997; Kumashiro, 2001; Letts and Sears, 1999; Pinar, 1998; Sears and Williams 1997). For example, since the 1970s, numerous ballot initiatives and laws have attempted to ban queer people or those suspected of being queer—regardless of orientation—from working in public schools (Harbeck, 1997; Herman, 1997; Lugg, 1998; Stein, 2001). Furthermore, all manner of statewide and local political fights have erupted regarding possible "homosexual influences" lurking about in public schools (Diamond, 1998; Eskridge, 2000; Harbeck, 1997; Herman, 1997; Knauer, 2000; Lugg, 1998; Stein, 2001; Tenney, 1995). Moreover, a growing number of court decisions are defending both queer and non-queer children alike from physical violence and administrative callousness within public school settings along the lines of sex (gender) and orientation (Reese, 1997). Sadly, however, such gender-based violence reflects long-standing legal, political, and cultural norms of what "real" men and women *should be* and how they *should act* (Garland, 2001; Herr, 1999; Hutchinson, 1999; Pharr, 1988; Rehder, 2001; Stein, 2001; Terry, 1999).

This chapter seeks to chart a course through the contested areas of gender and sexual orientation in hopes of establishing a theoretical framework and an agenda for much needed future research. In building this study, I draw from two research traditions, particularly in the areas of history and law. My stance is that of a "critical" policy scholar. That is, I am drawing on Neo-Marxist Theory generally, and on QLT specifically (Case, 1995; Franke, 1995; Hutchinson, 1997, 1999, 2000, 2001; Valdes, 1995, 1998). Public schools are governmental entities ruled by laws, regulations, and policies. The people who teach, lead, study, play, and otherwise live within a public school's walls must conform to these dictates or face various legal sanctions including expulsion and job termination. These legal mandates are established through political processes that include court decisions at both the state and federal levels.[2] Therefore, legal theories can, in general, help analyze and explicate the basic structures that shape daily educational practices. In the areas of gender, sexual orientation, and a possible new politics of education, QLT can be particularly insightful.

The following section seeks to map the concepts of politics, gender, and sexual orientation and U.S. law. The chapter then moves to discussions of QLT and then presents a short, queer history of U.S. public education. Later, it explores the politics of gender and sexual orientation within contemporary politics of education. The study then offers some possible policy reforms employing a QLT analysis. The chapter concludes with a discussion of the implications that research and educational policy grounded on QLT might have for a new politics of education.

Politics, Gender, and Sexual Orientation and U.S. Law

I define politics very broadly—as a historical series of ever-shifting power relations, interactions, alliances, and conflicts between individual and collective actors. While politics can be formalized, that is, in a series of elections, budget referenda, laws, or court decisions, it can also be more informal, localized, and highly personalized, as in the case of micropolitics (Malen, 1994). These various contests can involve broad categories of status, recognition, legitimacy, and demonization, to the more mundane daily school routines of "who gets stuck with lunch duty." For purposes of this chapter, I am interested in how particular *legal* understandings of gender and sexual orientation shape nearly *every* aspect of public school life.

Defining gender is more problematic because the term is a rapidly shifting sociological and cultural construct. Over the past ten years, gender has been defined and redefined by philosophers, sociologists, queer theorists, feminists and others—all weighing in with their own meanings (e.g., Butler, 1990; Rudy, 2000; Yoshino, 2002). For purposes of this chapter, gender consists of a set of roles and behaviors that individuals are expected to follow as determined by societies and cultural, racial, ethnic, and religious groups of what it means to be "male" and "female." These understandings of gender have changed over time and vary from individual to individual (Blount, 1998; Chauncey, 1994; Kumashiro, 2001; Nagel, 2000; Somerville, 2000; Stein, 2001). Elaborate dress and behavioral codes have been constructed to reflect these shifting understandings, and sometimes, societies impose harsh political and legal sanctions on those who run afoul of such expectations (Blount, 1996, 1998; Case, 1995; Chauncey, 1994; Eskridge, 2000; Fajer, 1992; Franke, 1995; Nagel, 2000; Siegel, 2002; Somerville, 2000; Valdes, 1995; Yoshino, 2002). An important caveat with this definition is that "gender" may have little to do with an individual's actual biological sex or sexual orientation (Case, 1995; Eskridge, 2000; Franke, 1995; Miller, 1995; Somerville, 2000; Terry, 1999; Valdes, 1995; Yoshino, 2002). The distinction is thus: Gender is an ongoing, life-long series of evolving performances. Sex is chromosomal.

Yet by stating sex is chromosomal, I do not mean that it is dichotomous—which is the current U.S. *legal* understanding (Case, 1995, Franke, 1995; Greenberg, 1999, 2000; Nye, 1998; Valdes, 1995). According to medical research, there are common variations between XX (female) and XY (male) including XXX, XXY, XXXY, XYY, XYYY, XYYYY, and XO (in Greenberg, 1999). Additionally, some individuals who are legally "male" (XY) and "female," (XX) are born with ambiguous genitalia—that is, one cannot distinguish whether the infant is a boy or a girl by visual inspection.[3] Other individuals develop ambiguities as they mature (Greenberg, 1999; Potter and Summers, 2001). The collective term for such individuals is "intersexed," and intersexed people comprise anywhere from 1.7 individuals per 100, to 1 in 500 within the general population. There are literally millions of intersexed human beings across the globe (as cited by Beh and Diamond, 2000). Additionally, there are individuals who are transgendered, meaning that they do not identify with their sex or sex characteristics. Rather, their sense of "self" differs from their biology in profound and complex ways. A transgendered person who was born a male will identify as a female throughout most of, if not her entire, life. Likewise a transgendered person who was born female may identify as male. Those who elect to pursue sexual reassignment surgery are known as transsexual (Nye, 1998).[4]

Regardless of the *natural* variation in sex and sexual identity, U.S. law remains firmly fixed in a binary, polarized, and constructed view of sex (Case, 1995; Franke, 1995; Greenberg, 1999; Nye, 1998; Valdes, 1995). For example, in the midst of oral arguments before the Supreme Court, in *Oncale v. Sundowner Offshore Services, Inc* (1998), the following exchange took place regarding the language of Title VII:

CHIEF JUSTICE REHNQUIST: The statute doesn't say either women or men, it says "sex."

PETITIONER: It says "because of sex," your honor, correct, and I would interpret that to mean the two sexes: men and women.

CHIEF JUSTICE REHNQUIST: There are only two so far as we know of. (*Oncale v. Sundowner Offshore Services*, 1998)

Given the political and judicial proclivities of the current Bush administration that favors the appointment of "strict constructionists"[5] as federal jurists (Goldberg, 2002), these legal (and flawed) understandings of sex will probably remain in place for the foreseeable future.

Further muddying the conceptual waters regarding gender, sex, and sexual orientation is that much of the research on gender has conflated the term *gender* with both sex and sexual orientation (see Case, 1995; Franke, 1995; Somerville, 2000; Valdes, 1995). This is particularly acute in the area of law (Greenberg, 1999). Current Supreme Court Justice Ruth Bader Ginsburg is the author of the legal conflation of sex and gender (Case, 1995; Valdes, 1995). Ginsburg's rationale was, "for impressionable minds the word 'sex' may conjure up improper images" of what occurs in porno theaters. Therefore, she,

> stopped talking about sex discrimination years ago. . . . She explained that a secretary once told her, "I'm typing all these briefs and articles for you and the word sex, sex, sex, is on every page. Don't you know those nine men [on the Supreme Court], they hear that word and their first association is not the way you want them to be thinking? Why don't you use the word 'gender'? It is a grammatical term and it will ward off distracting associations." (Case, 1995, p. 10)

In much of the politics of education and educational leadership research gender has tended to mean research focused on biological women and girls (e.g., Foster, 1999) who are all assumed to be non-queer. Researchers have paid less attention to how individuals, who are considered females and males, and are queer and non-queer, perform according to their respective (and constructed) gender roles or social scripts within school settings (Blount, 1999, 1996; Clifford, 1989).

This situation is particularly acute in academic discussions of gender and male norms of educational leadership (Brunner, 1999b). In many instances, a simple and arguably facile dichotomy regarding possible differences in leadership styles is highlighted: men = power over; women = power through. Besides the obvious essentialist assumptions and overgeneralizations regarding ascribed biological sex and leadership, some authors skirt dangerously close to arguing that females engaged in educational leadership should be "lady-like" (Brunner, 1999a, 2000; Sherman and Repa, 1994).[6] I argue that a more precise term is *masculinist* (see Nagel, 2000) when discussing traditional male forms of educational leadership and leadership practices (Lugg, 1999). Women, in general, and effeminate men in particular (either queer or non-queer—see Case, 1995), might very well deviate somewhat from masculinist practices in their own gendered performances of leadership. Then again, depending on the individual, they may not (Bell and Chase, 1995).

Conflating sex and gender is problematic for practicing public school administrators who function in a highly legalistic environment. Legal researchers note that the United States and the individual states bar *sex* discrimination not *gender* discrimination (Case, 1995; Franke, 1995; Siegel, 2002: Valdes, 1995).[7] Hence, the law, as currently understood by practicing lawyers and judges has no mechanism to protect men from being fired if they act stereotypically female, although women have had legal recourse (Case, 1995). Such men are presumed to be homosexual—regardless of their actual orientation (Case, 1995; Franke, 1995; Terry, 1999).

I define sexual orientation as the sex of the person with whom one can most comfortably establish deep emotional connections—or sexual object choice (Somerville, 2000). In other words, with whom does the person "fall in love?" This capacity or proclivity for love (Valdes, 1995) may or may not have much to do with actual sexual behavior. Even celibate individuals have a basic sexual orientation although they do not engage in sexual acts (Terry, 1999; Valdes, 1995). Sexual orientation runs from heterosexual (an individual is attracted to people who are primarily the opposite sex from themselves) to homosexual (an individual is attracted to people who are primarily the same sex as themselves), to bisexual (an individual is attracted to both people of the opposite sex and the same sex).[8] In the United States, people who have followed a heterosexual orientation have received numerous social, legal, and fiscal rewards, while those who have *admitted* a homosexual or bisexual sexual orientation have been at risk for jailing, electroshock, beating, mutilation, state-imposed drugging, and/or death (Eskridge, 1994; 1997; 2000; Terry, 1999). For purposes of this chapter, I use the terms *queer*[9] to refer to people with a homosexual or bisexual orientation as well as those individuals who are intersexed, transgendered and transsexual. *Non-queer* refers to people with a primarily heterosexual orientation (Fajer, 1992; Rivera, 1999), and whose sex identity corresponds with their biology.

Historically, sexual orientation has often been confused with gender and sex (Case, 1995; Chauncey, 1994; D'Emilio, 1983; Franke, 1995; Knauer, 2000; Stein, 2001; Somerville, 2000; Terry, 1999; Valdes, 1995; Yoshino, 2002). The most common misnomer is the "wrong body thesis" which was popular in the late nineteenth and early twentieth centuries (Eskridge, 1997; Knauer, 2000; Terry, 1999). That is, men whose primary sexual orientation was toward other men were considered to be women trapped in male bodies, and women whose primary sexual orientation was toward other women were considered to be men trapped in women's bodies. This confusion still appears in the broader culture, and it can have its humorous moments. As legal scholar Marc A. Fajer (1992) relates:

> During an interview for a law teaching position, I had a conversation with a law school administrator who clearly was nervous about my inclusion of gay activities and gay-related works-in-progress on my resume. He expressed concern because, apparently, the media recently had attacked Yale University as being a "gay school," and he felt his law school could not afford that sort of publicity. I indicated that I had been publicly open about my sexual orientation for some time and might well publish gay-related scholarship fairly early in my career. I asked if he had any objections to hiring openly gay faculty. He said he did not; he was just concerned with "extremes." When I asked what that meant, he replied, "Well, I wouldn't want you showing up for class wearing a skirt and hose." In one of those rare moments in life when the correct response sprang to mind immediately, rather than a half-hour later, I replied, "I don't have the legs for it." (p. 514, internal citations omitted)

While queer individuals may very well engage in atypical gender behavior (or gender bending—see J. Edgar Hoover, Lugg, 2003), so do all manner of non-queer people (former NYC mayor Rudolph Giuliani has a well- publicized fondness for drag). Gendered behaviors may have little to do with a given individual's biological sex or sexual orientation. For purposes of this essay, sexual orientation is about emotional attachment; gender is about the perform-ance of identity, and sex is about biology—the legal definition. While these three categories may well interact at times and are legal constructions, they should not be considered predictive regarding an individual's behavior or identity (Case, 1995; Chauncey, 1994; Franke, 1995; Miller, 1995; Somerville, 2000; Valdes, 1995; Yoshino, 2002).

Queer Legal Theory

Queer Legal Theory emerged in the mid-1990s in response to larger political and legal events (Valdes, 1995). It is part of a larger movement within the U.S. legal academy of scholars who are concerned with issues of social justice. The following presents a brief, and somewhat incomplete, overview of QLT and its possible applications for U.S. public policy.

Queer Legal Theory springs from the intersection of several strains of progressive thought in legal theory including; Feminist Legal Theory, Critical Race Theory, Critical Legal Studies, and Gay and Lesbian Legal Theory (Valdes, 1995, 1997, 1998). It draws on Feminist Legal Theory's commitment to disestablishing patriarchy, Critical Race Theory's dedication to unmasking the deep racist structures within U.S. society and life, Critical Legal Theory's examination of how class structures are perpetuated and reinforced, and Gay and Lesbian Legal Theory's understanding of how heteronormativity (the notion that the entire world is non-queer, or that it should be) is reproduced, while queer identity and individuals are eliminated (Hutchinson, 1997, 1999, 2000; 2001; Valdes, 1995, 1997, 1998).

Yet, it moves beyond these theories in distinct and important ways. QLT rejects the tendency toward gender essentialism that unpins much of Feminist Legal Theory (Harris, 1990; Valdes, 1995), the heteronormativity reflected in early Critical Race Theory's analyses (Hutchinson, 1999, 2001), the over-reliance on class as the sole analytic variable in Critical Legal Theory (Valdes, 1995), and the inherently racist and classist assumptions reflected in Gay and Lesbian Legal Theory, and Gaylegal Theory in particular (Hutchinson, 1997, 1999, 2000; Valdes, 1995, 1998).[10] According to its leading theorist, Francisco Valdes:

> "Queer" as legal theory can and should help to signify inclusiveness and diversity. As culturally (and politically) reclaimed, the term's elasticity can and should accommodate all identities grouped into or within sexual minority categories, including the bisexual and the trans/bi-gendered. Using Queer cultural politics and studies as a substantive point of departure, Queer legal theory can be positioned as a race-inclusive enterprise, a class-inclusive enterprise, a sex-inclusive enterprise, and a gender-inclusive enterprise, as well as a sexual orientation-inclusive enterprise. Thus, Queer legal theory, perhaps even more so than Queer consciousness and Queer activism to date, must convey a sense of political resolution that this Project seeks to invoke: reflecting the gains and challenges of sexual minorities since the Stonewall Riots, Queer legal theory must connote an activist and egalitarian sense of resistance to all forms of subordination, and it also must denote a sense of unfinished purpose and mission. (1995, pp. 353–354. Internal citations omitted)

QLT is dedicated to eliminating those U.S. legal and social structures that privilege and enforce heterosexuality, patriarchy, white supremacy, and class advantage, with the legal and social liberation of sexual minorities—queers—as its principal focus (Valdes, 1995). Additionally, QLT challenges the crass majoritarianism (there are more of us than of you—so you lose) that too often is reflected in U.S. legislation, regulations and court decisions (Valdes, 1998).

Queer Legal Theory acknowledges many different ways "to be," and it is anti-essentialist in its theoretical outlook. Drawing on the burgeoning medical research on sex, sexual identity, and sexuality, and the explosion of research that considers gender as performance, QLT understands that orientation, identity, sex, and gender are highly variable. U.S. law, however, considers sex as the only proper jurisdictional category—both fixed and dichotomous (Valdes, 1995; 1998). According to QLT, there is no one way to be female or male, or queer, or for that matter, African American or White (Hutchinson, 1997, 1999, 2000, 2001; Valdes, 1995, 1997, 1998).

Two concepts of QLT that are key to understanding its anti-essentialist stance are *intersectionality* and *multidimensionality*. Intersectionality comes from the work of those Critical Race Theorists who examine the unique lives of women of color experiencing discrimination and violence. Many times, women of color experience discrimination because of their race and/or ethnicity, *and* because of their sex (Crenshaw, 1991). Yet, courts tend to recognize only the racism or the sexism in the discriminatory and/or violent acts, negating that the women involved experience discrimination and violence (and live) at the intersection of both race *and* sex (Hutchinson, 1999, 2000, 2001). Intersectionality theorists argue that to disentangle sex from race (or race from sex) becomes an act of essentialism. Intersectionality theorists also disavow the common assumption of more mainstream legal theorists, which include notions that there is one way to be raced (African American male),[11] one way to be sexed (white female) (see Hutchinson, 1999, 2000).

Multidimensionality moves beyond intersectionality by pushing the analysis to be more inclusive, considering class and orientation as well as sex/gender. According to Darren Hutchinson:

> Multidimensionality demands that we make explicit the racial and class (and other) assumptions that undergird our theories, realize these assumptions might (and likely do) limit the application of our theories, strive to discover the vast differences among individuals in oppressed social groups, and learn how these differences should (and do) affect theory and politics. Ultimately, I view multidimensionality as a discursive project

aimed at unveiling the complexity of subordination and identity and reshaping legal
theory to reflect and respond to this complexity. (Hutchinson, 1999, p. 64)

Multidimensionality acknowledges that to be "queer" can hold multiple
meanings and can be experienced quite differently, from person to person. It
also posits that individuals have multiple identities: one is not just "queer," one
also may be male, working class, and Asian. Similarly, people who are "non-
queer" also hold multiple identities, and some of these may be held in common
with queer people. Others aspects are distinct to a given non-queer individual's
own multi-layered position and life experiences (Hutchinson, 1999, 2000, 2001).
QLT adherents have used both intersectionality (Valdes, 1995) and multidimensionality (Hutchinson, 1997, 1999 2000, 2001; Valdes, 1998) as analytic tools.

Finally, QLT questions the cultural and legal demands that individual members of a given minority group, or members of multiple minority groups,
assimilate, covert, cover, or pass—or otherwise hide or distort one's identity—particularly queers (Rush, 1997; Yoshino, 1998, 2002).[12] "Passing" has
been a survival strategy for many oppressed people, at least for those who could
pass as white, male, Protestant, and/or non-queer. Hence, when the United
States was governed by strict racial apartheid, some light-skinned blacks passed
as "white" to gain access to jobs and decent housing (Rush, 1997; Yoshino,
1998, 2002). Likewise, some Jews and Catholics have been forced to pass as
Protestants. My late father-in-law repeatedly passed as Protestant to find work
as a carpenter in the Catholic-hating city of Columbia, South Carolina, during
the 1940s and 1950s. Oftentimes before being hired he would be queried as to
where he went to church—a test. He would always respond, "the first Christian
Church."

Queer Legal Theorists view such demands "to pass" as inherently discriminatory, undermining personal integrity and autonomy while eroding and
denying an individual's legal and political rights (Hutchinson, 1999; Valdes,
1995; Yoshino, 1998, 2002). Queer people, in particular, are repeatedly told they
must pass as non-queer to be hired, to visit their partners in the hospital,[13] to *not*
be bullied and harassed in school (see *Nabozny v. Podlesny*, 1996), and so forth. In
somewhat more enlightened situations, queers are told they must "cover" their
identities (Yoshino, 2002). They do not have to hide or deny their identity—they just can't talk about it. Mere mention is considered "flaunting." The
U.S. military's ban on queer personnel under the rubric of "Don't Ask, Don't
Tell," would be one example of covering. The final and most regressive form of
assimilationist bias would be "converting," where a queer person undergoes

some sort of "reparative" therapy, to change their identity from queer to non-queer. While converting is not as common for queers as it once was (Katz, 1992), queer children remain at risk for compulsory conversion (see Cruz, 1999; Goishi, 1997; Hicks, 1999).

Like other social justice oriented legal theories, QLT aims its theoretical analyses at legal and regulatory systems (like public schools), in hopes of disestablishing those structures and practices that oppress queer people. It is expressly future oriented in its approach (Valdes, 1995). One strategy for working toward a progressive future is to reexamine history and legal precedents for important clues as to how homophobic and heteronormative structures have been woven into governmental institutions. This chapter now turns toward a brief reexamination of the history of U.S. education.

A Short, Queer History of U.S. Public Education

After the Civil War, public education rapidly expanded throughout the United States. School districts preferred to hire single young women because they were assumed to be nonsexual, and given their subordinate status as women, they did not have to be paid a living wage (Blount, 1998; Clifford, 1989; Tyack and Hansot, 1982). Women could keep their positions as teachers so long as they remained unmarried. Upon marriage, they had the choice of either resigning or being fired by the school board (Clifford, 1989; Elsbree, 1939). With limited options regarding employment, increasing numbers of women decided to remain single, and they kept their teaching positions. The regulations regarding personal behavior placed on female teachers were nettlesome, and localities maintained broad understandings of "immorality" (Elsbree, 1939).[14] Teachers referred to the regulations collectively as "snoopervision"[15]; yet, the surveillance was a cost they paid to keep a teaching position (Clifford, 1989; Elsbree, 1939). By the 1920s, single women dominated the field of teaching (Blount, 1999; Rousmaniere, 1997).

Men who remained in the classroom were viewed with great suspicion (Blount, 1999; Chauncey, 1994; Clifford, 1989; Tyack and Hansot, 1982). It was an era when social roles and employment were fraught with stringent and highly differentiated gender expectations. To work in such a feminized field was simply *unmanly*, or in other words, an act of gender deviance (Blount, 1996; Clifford, 1989). Furthermore, the low number of male teachers led social commentators to grumble that the public schools were producing generations of effeminate (or "sissified") men (Blount 1996; Chauncey, 1994). One lasting effort to combat the feminized school environment was the addition of extra-curricular programs, including athletics, which would help boys to become "real" men. But the hoped-for growth in the number of male teachers failed to materialize.

Nevertheless, another professional avenue was opened for men. The expansion of public education to include high schools, coupled with the phenomenal growth in student population, demanded greater organizational coherence and efficiency from the public school system (Callahan, 1962). In the early twentieth century, the rise of educational administration became a career path for ambitious men (Blount, 1998; Tyack and Hansot, 1982). By consciously modeling their administrative practices after those of business*men* (Callahan, 1962)—while concurrently advocating that administrative candidates be properly schooled[16] and appointed by school boards instead of elected by the voting public—male educational administrators defined the new profession (Blount, 1998). Educational administration became by definition— *masculinist*—a career for married males with academic credentials.

The 1920s also brought issues of sexual orientation into the politics of education. The early twentieth century had seen the emergence of research on human sexuality. Sexuality researchers or sexologists noted that there appeared to be two primary types of human sexual expression: homosexuality and heterosexuality (D'Emilio, 1983; Katz, 1992; Smith-Rosenberg, 1989; Terry, 1999). Most of the early sexologists viewed homosexuality as an unhealthy and poor developmental outcome because such behavior violated *supposedly* natural gender norms and accepted notions of procreative sexual behavior (D'Emilio, 1983; Faderman, 1991; Law, 1988; Smith-Rosenberg, 1989; Terry, 1999). The early sexologists also thought that gender and sexual orientation were interactive—that is those individuals who displayed conventional gender behavior were considered to be heterosexual; those who did not were considered to be homosexual (D'Emilio, 1983; Chauncey, 1994; Smith-Rosenberg, 1989; Terry, 1999). Lawmakers seized on this new information and vastly expanded the sodomy laws' range and sweep to the point that to be queer was to be a criminal (see Eskridge, 1999; Terry, 1999).

One critical social expectation for all men and women was non-queer marriage (Chauncey, 1994; Faderman, 1991). In the popular press, as well as in the medical and scientific literature, heterosexual marriage was portrayed as emblematic of healthy psychological and physiological maturity (D'Emilio, 1983). Those individuals who remained single during their 20s were to be pitied;

past their 30s, they were to be viewed as possibly being pathological. For middle- and upper-class whites, in particular, non-queer marriage became the *only* socially acceptable form of adulthood (Chauncey, 1994).[17]

Additionally, the sexologists believed that a young person's orientation could be corrupted by pernicious or unfortunate influences. Researchers and social commentators repeatedly warned that the public schools might be harboring homosexuals. Unmarried staff members were portrayed as particularly menacing because generations of unsuspecting school children could be "contaminated" or seduced into the lifestyle (Knauer, 2000).[18] And so, public school personnel had a duty to ensure this contagion did not spread, or if it did, to take the proper corrective actions promptly (Conklin, 1927; Knauer, 2000). Educational administrators were to police both gender performance and sexual orientation, and they were granted great latitude in removing suspected queers (Lugg, 2003). Single female teachers became the objects of ridicule and scorn (Blount, 1998; Faderman, 1991). Female physical education teachers received particular scrutiny because of the lesbian stereotype and administrations were on the lookout for "muscle molls" (see Cahn, 1993). Yet, given the low labor costs of employing single women, they continued to be prized by economy-minded school boards (Clifford, 1989; Elsbree, 1939). Single male teachers, however, were beyond the socially acceptable pale.

World War II brought a great relaxing of the stringent gender expectations due to the critical labor and resource demands (D'Emilio, 1983; Scagliotti and Schiller, 1986). Yet, with the end of the war and the rise of McCarthyism in the late 1940s, suspected queers were subjected to a national witch-hunt. Fueling the hysteria was the repeated linkage of homosexuality with communism, hence the slur from the era "commie, pinko, queer" (D'Emilio, 1992, 1983; Harbeck, 1997). The publication of the first Kinsey report in 1948 on male sexuality and the second report in 1953 on female sexuality increased the paranoia regarding the "homosexual menace" (D'Emilio, 1992, 1983). Through numerous and meticulous interviews (Moore, 1947), Alfred Kinsey and his research team, found that heterosexual monogamy was *not* the overwhelming norm that it was supposed. Additionally, vast numbers of males and females had had same-sex erotic experiences, although the percentages for women were lower (D'Emilio, 1983). Kinsey's data indicated that sexual behavior was fluid and functioned on a continuum, as opposed to the commonly assumed and legal dichotomy of hetero- or homo-sexual behavior (Chauncey, 1994; D'Emilio, 1983; Halley,

1989). What was perhaps most shocking was Kinsey's contention that homosexual behavior was perfectly *natural* (Terry, 1999).

The interaction between Cold War hysteria, Kinsey's data, rampant homophobia and lurid and incendiary newspaper reporting proved to be a volatile mix (Alwood, 1996; Miller, 2002). Massive purges of suspected homosexuals swept through all branches of the federal government and the military (Faderman, 1991; Scagliotti and Schiller, 1986; Scientists' Committee on Loyalty Problems [SCLP], 1949). Taking the lead from the national government, states and municipalities also began actively hunting for "possible perverts" (D'Emilio, 1983; Eskridge, 1997; Harbeck, 1997). Gay men were repeated targets of police entrapment schemes executed by the newly established vice squads (D'Emilio, 1992; Eskridge, 1997; Marcus, 1992; Miller, 2002). Lesbian and gay bars were continually raided with patrons arrested for "disorderly conduct" if caught dancing or holding hands with a same-sex partner. Some individuals were arrested for "loitering" if they happened to be at the wrong place at the wrong time (D'Emilio, 1983; Eskridge, 1997). In most instances, those who were arrested faced further humiliation and possible violence because newspapers routinely printed names, addresses, and places of employment (Alwood, 1996; D'Emilio, 1983; Eskridge, 1997; Faderman, 1991; Sears, 1997; Miller, 2002).[19]

It was a time of great social and legal persecution, and public school educators were under intense scrutiny because maintaining a *demonstrably* non-queer educational force had become a matter of national security (Harbeck, 1997). In 1950, columnist Lee Mortimer of the *New York Daily Mirror* claimed that lesbians had formed cells in the public schools and were corrupting the unwitting into both Communism and lesbianism (D'Emilio, 1992, p. 60). Popular magazines carried stories such as "New Moral Menace to Our Youth," portraying homosexuality as a particular danger for young adults (Faderman, 1991, p. 145). Beginning in the 1950s, state legislatures *mandated* that educational administrators and school boards remove suspected queer personnel. Any *arrest* on a queer charge—not *conviction*—meant immediate job loss (Harbeck, 1997; Kepner, 1998). Mere suspicion of homosexuality was reason enough to fire both tenured and non-tenured staff on the grounds that they had violated the community morals standards and/or that they engaged in "moral turpitude" (Harbeck, 1997; Trebilcock, 2000). And if one was fired on a morals charge, licensure revocation was sure to follow. According to California teacher Billie Tallmij:

At that time there was a list of about twenty-one things that you could lose your teaching certificate for. The first one was to be a card-carrying Communist, and the second was to be a homosexual. ... The suspicion is it: You're convicted, hung, tied and quartered. And not only would not never teach in California, you would never teach again in public schools anywhere. (in Marcus, 1992, p. 73)

As in the 1920s, gender conformity was taken as a proxy for sexual orientation. Consequently, the greatest "proof" of one's solid non-queer status was heterosexual marriage. With the onset of the Baby Boom, school districts dropped their marriage bans in hopes of minimizing the looming teacher shortage (Blount, 1996). Among the general public, there was also great social pressure for adults to marry and to marry young (Scagliotti and Schiller, 1986; Miller, 2002). As Lillian Faderman notes:

Front marriages with gay men were not uncommon during the 1950s, not only for the sake of passing as heterosexual at work, but also in order to hide the truth from parents who could not bear their own failure in having raised a sexual non-conformist and who might have a daughter committed to a mental hospital for lesbianism. (1991, p. 148)

Those teachers, both male and now female, who wished to remain in the classroom would eventually *have* to marry to prove they had the proper moral fiber to work with children (Blount, 1996, 1998; Faderman, 1991).

For men, career opportunities expanded, particularly in the area of educational administration. With the Cold War freezing gender expectations into tightly differentiated social and job roles, the percentage of female superintendents went into free fall (see Blount, 1998, p. 5). But like their female counterparts, male teachers and administrators would also have to marry to be considered "employable," and male administrators, in particular, did so at rates higher than the general population (Blount, 1999). As Rose remembers:

Life was tough, especially if you were a man. ... You could never hold a job such as a teacher unless you had a wife and children. You simply weren't going to be accepted into the inner sanctum of the corporation or the schools. (Sears, 1997, p. 45)

For students attending public schools, it was a time of very little accurate knowledge regarding sexual orientation. They were in an environment of tightly monitored and regulated gender performance. Boards of education tightly circumscribed information on sexuality—if there was any to be had. The vast majority of U.S. public school districts would not even offer basic sexuality education courses until the late 1980s (Rhode, 1993/94). As a result, queer students had to figure things out on their own. David Burton recalls his school days from the 1950s:

> I knew I was gay from an early age, but I had absolutely no one to turn to for affirmation and nowhere to go for information—except the library. I knew all the terms and the prevailing theories, but I knew that I wasn't as the books described homosexuals to be. I also knew from the playground, locker room, and library that it was of no use to try to convince peers, family, church, and state of that.
>
> I could not defend myself against such overwhelming condemnation, so silence was my defense. My choices were to tell nothing and be dishonest with myself, or tell the truth and be condemned by others. (Bruton, 1994, pp. 177–178)

Merrill remembered that as a high school student, she was desperate for any information. As she recalls:

> I read the *Well of Loneliness.*[20] Of course, *The Ladder* [an early magazine for lesbians] had just gotten started. But that was not really accessible to us because we were just kids. Most of us didn't know how to get a copy of the magazine even if we would have the courage to do so. ... This kind of stuff was the height of radical. We were all so closeted and it was so illegal to be queer. You could be put in jail, put in mental hospitals! (in Sears, 1997, p. 27)

Given the climate of the era, students learned that to be queer was to be a sissy, a faggot, a lezzie, or a dyke—an object of derision and scorn (D'Emilio, 1983). Sadly, public schools were *legally bound* to reinforce the prejudice.

The early Cold War left its mark on the public schools in some remarkable ways. First, educational administration, which had become increasingly male and married, was by the 1950s, by definition, fiercely homophobic (Blount, 1998; Lugg, 2003). Public school administrators had to be *demonstrably* non-queer (Blount, 1996, 1999). The ideal was male, married, and masculinist. These non-queer credentials were further buffed if a prospective male administrator had coached a boys' athletic team (see Blount, 1998). Reinforcing the cultural and legal homophobic climate, administrators had a legal obligation to remove all suspected queers, as well as all other possible subversives (Lugg, 2003). Furthermore, they kept a close eye on both teachers and students. Second, while single women had long dominated public school teaching, the stringent gender expectations and rampant homophobia transformed teaching into a profession largely comprised of *married* women (Blount, 1998). Third, with the increased knowledge of sexuality, students were generally aware of homosexuality and bisexuality, if only on a most superficial and subconscious level. But given the Cold War hysteria and rampant homophobia, being queer was almost an insurmountable stigma (D'Emilio, 1983, 1992; Faderman, 1991; Katz, 1992; Miller, 2002).

Gender, Sexual Orientation, and Contemporary Politics of Education

Much of what is found in contemporary public schooling contains legacies from the Cold War (see Blount, 1996; Lugg, 2003). Public schools still expect that students should exhibit a high degree of gender conformity, and schools can be intensely homophobic (Jordan, Vaughan, and Woodworth, 1997; Malinsky, 1997). These expectations are reflected in all manner of student and faculty policies, as well as curricula materials. As Beverly, who is a parent, discovered:

> I've seen handouts come home, and it's like, you know, like the 1950s. The girl is baking the cake, and I had some questions about that. You know, gender role questions. What are you teaching them about what it means to be a girl and what it is to be a boy? What are you teaching them about what it means to be in a relationship? About what it is to have a family? (Kozik-Rosabal, 2000, p. 5)

Besides maintaining limited notions of gender performance, many public schools give little if any accurate information regarding sexual orientation and the lives of actual queer people (Fontaine, 1997; Tenney, 1995). While the state of Massachusetts has implemented a model program that addresses issues of sexual orientation (Remafedi, 1994a), other states "have laws requiring sex education or AIDS education programs in public schools to emphasize that 'homosexual conduct is not an acceptable lifestyle' and is illegal" (Eskridge, 2000, p. 1369). Some states and localities also give parents the option to pull their children out of sexuality education classes, particularly if the information conflicts with their religious beliefs (Eskridge, 2000). Other states and local school boards go even further, banning any mention of "homosexuality" within the public school walls (Tenney, 1995).

One recent development that draws the ire of some parents and parents' rights groups is that of "Gay/Straight Alliances" (GSAs). GSAs are non-curricular school groups that are composed of both "gay and straight" students who meet to discuss issues pertinent to them. Because these groups openly claim students who are queer, they have been highly controversial in some locales, and there have been attempts to ban such organizations. However, GSAs are protected under federal law—under the Equal Access Act—that was originally designed to permit after-school Bible and Christian clubs (Lugg, 2002; Rehder, 2001).

Perhaps the best-known battle over a GSA took place at East High School in Salt Lake City, Utah. Students had been trying to establish a GSA since the mid-1990s. Parents objected to East hosting a GSA, claiming the club would promote immoral and illegal behavior because Utah maintained (and still does) a law banning consensual sodomy (Lugg, 2003; Robson, 2001). When the Salt Lake City school board considered the request for a GSA, legal counsel informed the board that it could not deny the request because East High maintained other non-curricular groups. In legal terms, East High School had established a "limited public forum." The only legal way for the board to ban the group was to ban all non-curricular groups, which the board promptly did. This action provoked a large outcry and anger, much of it aimed directly at the students who had requested the GSA (Robson, 2001). The East High GSA consequently sued in federal court, and a five-year series of court battles began. By the fall of 2000, the East High GSA, which had transformed itself into a curricular-related club called People Respecting Important Social Movements (PRISM),[21] was finally permitted to meet at East High (Rehder, 2001). But this request was granted only after spending several years in court.

Part of GSAs' political appeal is their attempt to provide students with a "safe space" (Bryant, 1999). Safety issues have been a growing concern for some educators and policymakers since the late 1980s. Harassment of queer, suspected queer, and non-queer youth is a long-standing and common problem in U.S. public schools. One study reported that students hear queer-related taunting and name calling six times a day (Storm, 2000). Similarly, a Massachusetts study found that 97 percent of all students heard homophobic comments from their classmates, and 57 percent heard such comments from school staff (in McFarland, 2001). Because it is so prevalent, many adults consider this taunting a rite of childhood and adolescence—and ignore it (Herr, 1997; Jones, 2000; Jordan, Vaughan, and Woodworth, 1997; McFarland, 2001).

This harassment cuts across lines of gender and sexual orientation. As counseling expert William McFarland (2001) noted:

> Homophobia is detrimental to other people in the schools besides gay and lesbian youth. For example, heterosexual boys who do not fit the traditional male gender role (aggressive, controlling, restricted emotions) defined by heterosexism may be punished, ostracized, and abused. These boys may be called "faggots," "fairies," "sissies," "queers," or other derogatory names. ... . Girls also experience pressure to conform to

heterosexist gender stereotypes, and failing to do so is likely to result in abuse. Girls who fail to demonstrate stereotypical feminine traits (complacent, emotional, deferential) may be called "dykes," "lezzies," or other derogatory names. (p. 174)

Given the historic social pressure and expectations for men in general (Chauncey, 1994), a young man is under great pressure to "act like a man." Some public schools reinforce and intensify gender conformity by banning boys and young men from wearing earrings, regulating the length of their hair and mode of dress (Rehder, 2001; Wojohn, 2001). Since male homosexuality is mistakenly equated with femininity (Blount, 1996; Case, 1995; Pharr, 1988; Terry, 1999; Valdes, 1995) and of being "less than a man," young men are on guard for any seemingly "unmanly" behavior. This pressure surrounding gender conformity is so high that one survey found that young men would rather be *punched in the face* than be called gay (Jones, 2000). Clearly young men are the targets of viscous teasing and physical abuse if they do not strictly conform to expectations of gender (MacGillivray, 2000).

Perhaps the most outrageous case of abuse involved Jamie Nabozny who knew he was gay by age 13. So did his homophobic classmates who attacked him with impunity—for years. Between grades 7 and 10, Nabozny experienced repeated verbal and physical violence. He was spat on, urinated on, bitten, punched and subjected to a mock rape in which 20 other students looked on and laughed (Broz, 1998; Bryant, 1999; Robson, 2001). All of these attacks happened on school property, and all were perpetrated by other male students. Nabozny was called "faggot" or "fag" throughout this time. In the grade 10, Nabozny was so savagely kicked and beaten that he needed surgery to stop the internal bleeding and repair extensive abdominal damage (Broz, 1998).

Nabozny repeatedly appealed for help from both teachers and school administrators. His middle school principal, Mary Podlesny, told him that "boys will be boys," and that if Nabozny was "going to be so openly gay, that he had to expect this kind of stuff to happen" (in Broz, 1998, p. 753). After the mock rape, Nabozny's parents attempted to intervene. They were subsequently told by Podlesny, that if their son "was going to be openly gay that he had to expect that kind of stuff" (in Broz, 1998, p. 754). Later in grade 10, one teacher called Nabozny a "fag." When Nabozny was repeatedly abused in high school, his assistant principal, Thomas Blauert, told him that he deserved his mistreatment *because* "he was gay" (Broz, 1998, p. 756). Like his middle school principal and the assistant high school principal, the high school principal William Davis did nothing to protect Nabozny after the student reported incident after incident of

abuse. Between grades 7 and 10, Nabozny attempted suicide twice. He eventually dropped out of school during his junior year (Broz, 1998; Bryant, 1999)
after being informed by administrators that he should go to school somewhere
else (Robson, 2001).

In 1995, Nabozny sued the Ashland, WI, school district in U.S. federal
court for gender (sex)[22] and sexual orientation discrimination, as well as for
violation of his due process rights. The court rejected the claim of due process
violation but agreed that he had experienced discrimination based both on
gender (sex) and sexual orientation. A jury later awarded Nabozny $900,000 in
damages (Broz, 1998; Jones, 2000; Reese, 1997).

The *Nabozny* case clearly illustrates the public school's historic power as the
enforcer of expected norms regarding gender, heteronormativity, and homophobia. Nabozny's schools maintained a dangerously homophobic climate, even in
light of constant physical harm and state laws barring both sex and sexual
orientation discrimination. Nabozny's teachers and administrators, and of
course, the student body knew he was being abused. A few teachers unsuccess-
fully tried to intervene on his behalf (Broz, 1998). Yet, multiple administrators,
regardless of their individual sex, not only failed to help Nabozny, they insulted and
blamed him for the violence. They insisted that he should pass as straight—or
at least "cover" (Yoshino, 2002) his orientation. The public school administrators in the *Nabozny* case followed the historic and legal lines of accepted
administrative and masculinist practice.

The *Nabozny* case also illustrates how devastating a homophobic public
school culture can be for queer children. Nabozny's two suicide attempts are
consistent with research that finds that queer children have much higher rates
of suicidal ideation and suicide (Elia, 1994; Gibson, 1994; Jordan, Vaughan, and
Woodworth, 1997; Remafedi, 1994b). Besides enduring violence and harassment, queer children also frequently respond to the hostile environment by
skipping school, dropping out, running away from home, and engaging in
substance abuse. Those who remain in school usually experience a drop in
academic performance (Jordan, Vaughan, and Woodworth, 1997). In describing
the problems queer children face in attending school, one legal scholar noted,
"schools are notoriously ignorant of, and/or hostile toward, their gay students,
and in some cases school officials permit harassment and/or violence toward
them" (Goishi, 1997, p. 1149).

Some states have tried to stop violence against and harassment and discrimination of queer children and those non-queer children who do not adhere

to rigid expectations of gender. Yet, many of these intended policies are constrained by an inherent policy paradox. While states and locales might be striving to make public schools safer places, the adults working in these schools are not safe from discrimination along lines of gender and sexual orientation (Lugg, 2003). Public school teachers may have tenure (in most instances) and be covered by state antidiscrimination laws (in only thirteen states), but they have fared poorly in the federal court system. The vast majority of teachers lose both their cases, and subsequently, their jobs (Lugg, 2003). And so, the vast majority of public school teachers remain closeted (Harbeck, 1997; Kissen, 1996). Public school administrators, who are largely at-will hires, have even fewer protections. They also have the burden of policing and enforcing historic norms regarding gender and sexual orientation, regardless of their own status (Lugg, 2003). Therefore, some states and locales are expecting the adults to protect students from the violence and harassment that the adults may very well experience.

Educational policy in Utah illustrates this paradoxical point. In the midst of the conflict over East High School's GSA, the State Department of Education enacted a regulation protecting queer students from discrimination (Rehder, 2001). Yet, Utah also maintains laws barring consensual sodomy (see Lugg, 2003). Historically, states with laws banning consensual sodomy have used these laws to demonize and jail queer people (Chauncey, 1994; D'Emilio, 1983; Dayoff, 2001; Eskridge, 1997; Leslie, 2000; Terry, 1999). While in many states these laws cover both queer and non-queer people, only those who are queer are targeted for criminal prosecution (Dayoff, 2001; Leslie, 2000). Additionally, because these states make consensual sodomy a felony (currently in eight states out of fourteen states), queer teachers and administrators are at particular risk in those states (Lugg, 2003). These educators are technically "statutory felons" (Leslie, 2000). This legal distinction makes "coming out," or being open about one's personal life and identity, very difficult for queer educators. A public declaration of identity would threaten licensure, because felons cannot hold a teaching or administrative license (Lugg, 2003). In Utah, queer teachers and administrators are at high risk of job termination because of the criminalization of their status (see Leslie, 2000), but queer public school students are protected under state department of education guidelines (Rehder, 2001). Such a paradox places all Utah administrators, queer and non-queer, in an inconsistent position. They are expected to protect queer students on one hand, while being expected to pursue and fire adult personnel who are suspected of being queer on the other (Lugg, 2003).

This paradox in educational policy also reflects the ambivalence that the American general public has regarding issues of gender and sexual orientation. Currently in the United States, there are limits to what types of gender performances and sexual orientations are politically and/or legally acceptable (Herman, 1997; Lugg, 1999; Stein, 2001). These limits can restrict both queer and non-queer people. For example, many of the venomous and hysterical attacks on Hillary Clinton focused on her very "un-First Lady-like" gendered behavior, especially when she ventured into the realms of policymaking and politics prior to her election as U.S. Senator. Likewise, both then-President Clinton and then Speaker of the House Newt Gingrich heartily endorsed the Defense of Marriage Act, which banned federal recognition of queer marriages at a time when neither was doing a good job of taking care of their own. Nevertheless both men's contempt of queer people and obvious hypocrisy escaped much public comment, given the general public's own discomfort over the possibilities of "gay marriage."

This political ambivalence over gender, sexual orientation, and the stringent boundaries of tolerance is reflected in the politics of education. The ambivalence has also been reflected in the politics of education and educational leadership research. Gender (as performance) and sexual orientation have largely escaped much mention in this literature, and those researchers who do engage in this research are often viewed as working outside of the mainstream. Nevertheless, as we have seen, issues of gender and sexual orientation are a part of the deep structures of public schooling. From issues of certification, to staff hiring and firing, to curricular content, student conduct policies, and extra-curricular activities, gender and sexual orientation are part of the lived daily realities of those who work and learn in U.S. public schools. This study now turns toward an analysis of this situation and offers a possible remedy, before drawing this discussion of gender, sexual orientation, and the politics of education to a close.

Gender, Sexual Orientation, and a New [Queer?] Politics of Education

> It is my contention that, unfortunately, the world will not be safe for women in frilly pink dresses—they will not, for example, generally be as respected as either men or women in gray flannel suits—unless and until it is made safe for men in dresses as well.
>
> —Case, 1995, p. 7

Currently, fourteen states bar consensual sodomy, while only 13 states, under their individual state constitutions, provide equal protection measures under the rubric of either sexual orientation or sexual preference (Lugg, 2003). At the federal level, there are no specific Constitutional or statutory protections for queers who are discriminated against because of their queer status (see Eskridge, 2000; King, 2002). Furthermore, existing civil rights protections—including those covering sex—have been under sustained attack by an activist federal judiciary for well over twenty years (Resnik, 2000; Siegel, 2002).

At the federal level, however, there has been some movement to protect public school students who are harassed for their gender (as performance) under an admittedly expansive reading of Title IX (Eisemann, 2000).[23] This statute bars discrimination based on *sex* in all U.S. schools that receive federal funds (Buckle, 2000; Jones, 2000). Additionally, there may be legal precedent for citing discrimination based on sexual orientation in protecting queer students, thanks to the litigation success of Jamie Nabozny. Yet, to date, his case remains the sole successful case in the federal court system.

At the state and local level, some states—most notably Massachusetts[24]—and local school districts have drawn upon the overwhelming and dismal data[25] concerning queer students and their public school experiences (D'Augelli and Hershberger, 1995; Fineran, 2002; Gibson, 1994; Remafedi, 1994a) and have implemented programs to better ensure queer children's basic safety and well-being (Harbeck, 1997). These programs are an important start and are *exceptional* when compared to other public schools across the nation. Yet, from a QLT perspective, they are highly problematic. By making queer students the subjects of "special protective services," a state or local school board has still reinforced the notion of queer as deviant. Being deemed by the government as "at-risk" or as "essentially troubled" hardly grants liberation. Framed in a different light, non-oppression is not quite the same thing as social justice. Legal scholar Nancy Levit labels this "tolerance lite," or more pointedly, a "hold your nose" form of tolerance (Levit, 2001, p. 875). The "problems" confronting queer children are not that they are queer—on the contrary—the American legal foundations for homophobia, heteronormativity and gender bias generate their problems. Additionally, these protective services may tend to focus on white notions of "queerness" (Kumashiro, 2001; McCready, 2001), which further reinforces societal, racial, and ethnic biases.

Furthermore, by focusing on all queer kids as "deviant," non-queer students are ignored as both the perpetrators and sometime victims of oppression. For example, Brian Seamons, a non-queer high school football player was grabbed by his teammates one day after coming out of the shower. They forcibly tied him to a towel rack using adhesive tape. They also taped his genitals. His teammates then brought a girl that Brian had once dated to view the spectacle. According to Vanessa Eisemann (2000):

> After Brian reported the incident to school authorities, his coach "brought Brian before the football team, accused Brian of betraying the team . . . and told Brian to apologize to the team." The school district, however, responded to the incident by canceling the final football game of the season. Angry about the game's cancellation, Brian's classmates threatened and harassed him. When Brian sought help, school officials told him that he had brought the harassment upon himself by making the initial complaint, and they told him he "should have taken it like a man." The school officials' callous response to Brian Seamons' complaint was most likely rooted in the sexist and stereotypical notion that boys should be "tough." (p. 145)

The Tenth Circuit Court, in *Seamons v. Snow*, 1996, also agreed with the school district, that this specific form of harassment was not a form of sex discrimination under Title IX. The court based its ruling in large part on the fact that the school district has also failed to act when girls were hazed. Consequently, since the school maintained an "equal opportunity approach towards hazing"—ignoring it—there was no constitutional violation (see Eisemann, 2000).

Another weakness in "the protective" strategy is that by targeting queer students, both the queer and non-queer adults working within the school walls are ignored, as is the case in the state of Utah. Again, in a "tolerance lite" political and legal system, tolerance of queers is only permitted to go so far (Levit, 2001). In the vast majority of American states, queer educators can be fired for their status, and they have no legal recourse.[26] Similarly *non*-queer educators can be fired if they are perceived to be queers. This perception also shapes the gender politics of hiring, particularly for leadership positions. As we have seen, educational administration has, historically, been defined as a fiercely masculinist and homophobic field (Lugg, 2003). Consequently a prospective candidate can be viewed either as not "man enough," in the case of men who take a nontraditional approach to leadership or, in the case of women, they can be seen as being "too mannish" or "too tough." In both cases, the aspirant has touched the "third rail" of public school administration—the suspected queer line—and probably won't be hired. Unless males, regardless of their queer or non-queer status, can "pass" as masculinist leaders—the gendered expectation—they may have difficulty in being hired. Female aspirants, regardless of their status, are put into a Catch-22. If they adopt a masculinist approach to a historically masculinist profession, they might not be hired because they are suspected to be queer. But if they follow a "womanist" or feminine path (see Brunner, 1999a), they may be viewed as not being strong enough for the position (Blount, 1998).

Besides limitations in the hiring processes, public school personnel can also be fired for running afoul of a host of homophobic state mandates. In Alabama, one may not "promote lifestyles or activities prohibited by sodomy and sexual misconduct laws." In Arizona, material is barred that "promotes a homosexual life-style" or "portrays homosexuality as a positive alternative life-style." In South Carolina, health education programs "may not include a discussion of alternate sexual lifestyles from heterosexual relationships including, but not limited to, homosexual relationships except in the context of instruction concerning sexually transmitted diseases." In Minnesota, "nothing in the Minnesota Human Rights statutes shall 'be construed to mean that the state condones homosexuality or bisexuality or any equivalent lifestyle or authorizes or permits the promotion of homosexuality or bisexuality in education institutions or requires the teaching in education institutions of homosexuality or bisexuality as an acceptable lifestyle" (all in Eisemann, 2000, p. 132).

Obviously, very few U.S. public schools, whose own historical and legal foundations are also in homophobia, heteronormativity, and gender bias, are well equipped or have the larger political support to focus on these very same issues within their walls (Eskridge, 2000). In most parts of the United States queer citizens live under a system of gender and sexual apartheid—where if their status becomes known, they risk harassment, loss of job, and possible violence (Garland, 2001). This system affects all citizens, queer and non-queer, because *perceived* status is usually the trigger, particularly when it comes to hate crimes (Garland, 2001; Hutchinson, 1999).

Yet, if educators, researchers and policymakers stay too focused on the problematic present, we might miss opportunities for what could be. As stated previously, QLT is expressly future oriented in its approach (Valdes, 1995) and values intersectionality and multidimensionality (Hutchinson, 1997, 1999, 2000, 2001; Valdes, 1995, 1998). Human beings have multiple identities, and we live in highly complex and overlapping social systems. These two understandings must be at the forefront of any QLT guided approach to policy.

One approach to public school policy and politics would call for policies barring the harassment of *anyone*, boys and girls, queers and non-queers, students and adults, for *any* perceived or actual status, including, but not limited, to queer-ness. Furthermore, demands by public school officials that queers assimilate (Yoshino, 1998, 2002), be it covering, passing, or converting would be viewed as bias incidents and consequently prohibited. For example, the prom would be integrated, and if non-queer faculty members discussed their spouses and brought them to school events and functions, so could queer faculty members. Queer staff members would not be threatened with job termination, nor would queer professional staff be threatened with job loss *and* licensure revocation—in those states with laws barring consensual sodomy. Obviously, this is a somewhat conservative approach in that it protects everyone, queer and non-queer, from abuse and harassment regarding gender (as performance) and perceived orientation.

But basic safety, as noted before, is not the same as empowerment. One step toward actual empowerment would be to revise student and professional dress codes under a QLT analysis. One of the most common prohibitions in public schools is that of boys and men wearing earrings and other jewelry (Rehder, 2001), regardless of whether the individual in question is queer or non-queer. Unless such a prohibition is extended to self-identified females, there is little reason to maintain the distinction. Boys (and men) who are "hassled" for wearing earrings are rebuked for wearing historically "women's" jewelry. They are signifying—at least to sexists and homophobes—that they might be "less than men." A proper, if possibly controversial, application of a QLT guided dress code would be to permit students and adults to wear cross gendered attire regardless of the individual's legally defined "sex" (Case, 1995; Franke, 1995; Rehder, 2001). Yet this may be less controversial than it seems. Women and girls have been permitted to do so on a daily basis since the late 1960s and 1970s, without disrupting the order or "good discipline" of public schools.[27] Public schools, as the historic enforcers of gender (as performance) and homophobia and heteronormativity, would do well to reexamine what actually underpins their dress codes (Rehder, 2001). Mary Ann Case's contention at the beginning of this section, while somewhat tongue-in-cheek, gets to the heart of gender as performance. In many respects (and with apologies to Case [1995]), *public schools* "will not be safe for women [or girls] in frilly pink dresses—they [women and girls] will not, for example, generally be as respected as either men or women in gray flannel suits—unless and until … [public schools are] made safe for men [and boys] in [frilly pink] dresses as well" (p. 7).

A more radical and wide-reaching step is to promote a queer-infused curriculum as an expanded understanding of "multicultural education" and across the K-12 spectrum of offerings (see Blinick, 1994; Lipkin, 1994; Williams, 1997). Children already learn about queer people at a very early age (Bickmore, 1999; Kumashiro, 1999), although much of it may be miseducative, to use a Deweyian term. As Kathy Bickmore observed:

> Debates about sexuality-related education in elementary schools tend to hinge on the problem children's vulnerability, their need for protection. Sexuality, and homosexuality in particular, is generally seen to be unsafe content for young children's classrooms. This assumption misjudges what many children already know about themselves and their world. (1999, p. 21)

By reforming the school curricula following a QLT rubric, public school students learn that there are multiple ways to be, including the various ways to be queer and non-queer.

The following is merely a smattering of possible curriculum changes: When the histories of Native Americans are studied, the Berdache, who were men and women who assumed cross-gendered identities, are also mentioned (Miller, 1995; Valdes, 1995).[28] In science classes, when genetics and reproduction are studied, the range of possible combinations between XX and XY are discussed (Greenberg, 1999). When students read "A Raisin in the Sun" they learn that not only was the author, Lorraine Hansberry, an African American writer—she was a lesbian African American writer who was also an early gay rights theorist (D'Emilio, 1983; Katz, 1992; Miller, 1995).[29] When the Holocaust is studied, queers are included in the list of whom the Nazis persecuted (Miller, 1995). When the McCarthy era is studied, students would learn that queers were also subjected to Red-Baiting. They would also examine the duplicity of Roy Cohn, Senator McCarthy's top aide (Miller, 1995).[30] Quite simply, public school students would see a variety of people and their families, who live and lived in various racial, ethnic, class, and religious contexts, who are and were queer and non-queer (Letts and Sears, 1999; Kumashiro, 2001; Sears and Williams, 1997).

Under a QLT guided rubric, sexuality education would become universal, as well as inclusive and accurate (Tenney, 1995), with a focus on adult roles and responsibilities, as well as promoting an understanding of healthy adult relationships. It would also be comprehensive, explicit, and offered at age appropriate intervals, going beyond the mere abstinence-based programs found in many U.S. public schools (Jones, 2002; Levesque, 2000; Ross, 1999; Sears, 1998). Students would learn about sexual maturation, conception and contraception, maintaining sexual health, and how to prevent sexually transmitted diseases.

This approach is congruent with research that shows most Americans (80–95 percent) support fairly extensive sexuality education in public schools (in Lindley and Reininger, 2001; see also Jones, 2002).

Students would also learn about the complex interactions between biology, psychology, and identity, and sexuality education would cover a range of identities including: heterosexual, homosexual, bisexual, intersexual, transgendered, and transsexual. More controversially, under the "compelling state interest rubric," sexuality education would be *compulsory*, and parents would not be permitted to have their children "opt out" of the curriculum (Levesque, 2000; Tenney, 1995). As courts have consistently ruled, parents do not have the right to bar their children's access to vital scientific, sociological, and psychological information—information that may very well save their children's lives, their health, and their sanity, and at minimum, if internalized, keep them from harm (Levesque; 2000; Remafedi, 1994a, 1994b; Robson, 2001; Tenney, 1995). Students have a right to make informed decisions regarding their lives (Ross, 1999; Tenney, 1995). As Roger J. R. Levesque (2000) observes:

> Parental rights still clearly lose their power when they place children's lives at risk for injury and violence. Just as states may intrude in youths' lives to protect them from parental decision making, states have an obligation to infringe on parental rights in the name of protecting their children, especially when parents fail to do so. (pp. 974–975)

Across curricular areas and grade levels, public schools would not be permitted to transmit false information regarding queer people, or non-queer people for that matter. Neither would public schools be permitted to pursue the falsity of silence—that queers simply don't exist—or if they do, that they should be ignored (Jones, 2002; Tenney, 1995). In short, under a QLT educational approach, queer-ness and queer people would become part of the normal daily routine of public schools.

Such an approach to curricula and behavioral codes demands extensive professional development as well as parental and community education (see Sears and Williams, 1997). A QLT approach to educational policy and politics is also sure to trigger a political—or what Valdes calls—"majoritarian" backlash (1998), particularly in more conservative communities. For individuals who believe that sex/gender is divinely dichotomous (see Chiusano, 1996; Kintz, 1997), a QLT approach might be viewed as particularly menacing—threatening and insulting to their religious beliefs, and perhaps, to their children's very souls

(Diamond, 1998; Kintz, 1997; Stein, 2001). As homeschool activist and lawyer Keith Fournier wrote:

> Homosexual living arrangements under the guise of marriage are not only sterile, incapable, and insufficient, they are destructive to the very fabric of our society. The strategy to inculturate active homosexual practice in our society as a favored institution is synonymous with injecting a cancer into a healthy body. Homosexual marriage directly attacks the family which is the most vital cell in society. The family is the first government, the first church, the first school. We must not allow this vital cell, the rock upon which society is built, to be inculturated with a perversion that will destroy it, and with it the future of our children and grandchildren. (in Diamond, 1998, p. 171)

This is a hyperventilated response, to be sure. Yet, the use of the cancer metaphor is striking, exhorting like-minded people to act before it's "too late." It plays a familiar chord—the contagion thesis—or that queer people are the carriers of social pathology (Knauer, 2000; Terry, 1999). Injecting the contagion thesis into the politics of education infers that mere exposure to someone—or some information or fact—might challenge a strongly held theological belief. Consequently, their children might become "contaminated."

> My children ... my children. They're the most important thing to me in my life. And it's that simple. I could not sit back with the knowledge of what they wanted to teach my children. The assault has got to stop. We cannot send our children off on the school bus any more and trust that schools are doing the right thing. Our children and our nation depend on us. And I hope and pray that we are not too late in turning things around.—Shelly Uscinski, parent and Christian Coalition activist. (in Kintz, 1997, p. 74)

But such a rationale, no matter how devoutly believed, has not fared well in court. As the Sixth Circuit Court of Appeals wrote in 1987, in the curriculum case *Mozert v. Hawkins,* "governmental actions that merely offend or cast doubt on religious beliefs do not on that account violate free exercise."(*Mozert v. Hawkins,* 1987; see also *Brown v. Hot, Sexy and Safe Prod. Inc,* 1995). Similarly, those states that maintain bars on mentioning "homosexuality" (queer issues) in public classrooms, except for linking it to disease and criminality, would probably fail the standard established by the Supreme Court in *Epperson v. Arkansas* (1968). Since these laws enforce "traditional" (read theological) notions of morality, they constitute a state endorsement of religion and should fail the endorsement test (see Ross, 1999; Tenney, 1995).

A QLT approach to educational policy and politics has much to offer queer and non-queer students and educators alike. By focusing on intersectionality and multidimensionality, it stresses the various identities each individual can hold. Some of these identities can be shared across identity groupings, enabling seemingly diverse individuals to find common ground. This commitment to intersectionality and multidimensionality also enables QLT to maintain a strong antiessentialist stance. Yet, QLT may engender a fair amount of political hostility, particularly for those individuals wedded to essentialist assumptions involving gender (Valdes, 1995; 1998). Nevertheless, QLT is particularly attractive in moving the focus from "tolerance lite" notions of queer students as being at risk, to students being empowered. It also offers educators working in public schools a way out of the long-standing masculinist box, which shapes much of what goes on.

Conclusion

> My attendance at school has fallen steadily and school has become a place I no longer want to be, mostly, because of the lack of education and acceptance of diversity, but more so, the homophobia among faculty and students. —Adelide Goetz, junior at Cambridge Rindge and Latin High School.
>
> —In Remafedi, 1994a, p. 169

I began this chapter with a deliberately provocative (okay—incendiary) title, followed by a depressing vignette of what one queer student had confronted during her time in public school. Yet, "Sissies," "Faggots," "Lezzies," and "Dykes" is a lived daily reality of queer and more than a few non-queer students. Such language might be a bit harsh to the tender eyes and ears of scholars, but it is a far too common and brutal fare for many U.S. public school students. The least we can do is not look away.

This book is dedicated to exploring various avenues towards building a "new" politics of educational leadership. Yet, as we have seen, when it comes to gender and sexual orientation, public schools, as they engage with these issues, remain stubbornly set in Cold War concrete. Similarly, many mainstream politics of education and educational leadership researchers seem "stuck" when it comes to conducting research involving gender and orientation. While the politics of gender and sexual orientation have shaped and continue to shape public schools in historic and substantial ways, these areas have been under-examined by mainstream politics of education scholars.

Public schools need to move beyond just protecting students and educators from harassment and bullying along the lines of gender and sexual orientation. This is an important first step, and faces some significant legal hurdles in fourteen states, thanks to the interplay of licensure and sodomy laws. Nevertheless, protection or non-oppression is not the same as social justice or for that matter, education. Furthermore, the roles of teachers and administrators need to be reconceptualized, away from the masculinist traditions, which have for too long dominated the culture of public school in general, and administrative practice in particular.

Queer Legal Theory offers us a way to break free from the current oppressive reality when it comes to gender, sexual orientation, and the politics of education. Given its anti-essentialist stance, hostility toward demands that certain people "pass," and its embrace of multidimensionality and intersectionality, it has the potential to offer incredibly rich and nuanced accounts of how these issues "play out" in educational policy and politics. For researchers and theorists who are seeking ways to break free from heteronormative, sexist, racist and class assumptions that undergird much of contemporary educational politics and policy, a QLT approach to educational politics and policy analysis offers exciting (and seemingly limitless) possibilities for a better, more equitable future for all

Notes

This chapter first appeared in: *Educational Administration Quarterly* (Sage), 39, no. 1 (2003), 95-134.

1.　Supreme Court Justice Robert Jackson once remarked that he had "mental reservations ... in teaching of Santa Claus or Uncle Sam or Easter bunnies or dispassionate judges" (in Tushnet 2001, p. 113).

2.　Traditional legal scholars would strenuously object to the notion that courts are inherently political, although this is the basic premise of Critical Legal Scholars, Critical Race Theorists, and Queer Legal Theorists. Such objections have become difficult to maintain in light of the U.S. Supreme Court's actions in *Bush v. Gore* (see Tushnet, 2001).

3.　Some individuals who are intersexed will also sexually develop as both male and female upon puberty. As one intersexed individual recalls "My breasts grew, and so did my facial hair. I began to get intermittent menstrual periods, and intermittent morning erections." (In Potter and Summers, 2001, pp. 155-156).

4.　Surgery to "correct" intersexed individuals is highly controversial in the intersexed community, and is becoming increasingly so in the medical community (Beh and Diamond, 2000). Likewise, sex reassignment surgery in the transgendered community is controversial (See Nye, 1998).

5.   "Strict constructionists" favor originalist interpretations of the U.S. constitution, that is the meaning of the text when it was written in the late eighteenth century. This type of analysis is very problematic for twenty-first century jurisprudence, particularly when one considers at the time that the Constitution was signed, most African Americans were slaves, Native Americans were not citizens and subjected to ethnic cleansing, non-propertied white males could not vote, and all women were either the property of their families or their husbands.

6.   Given that educational administration has long policed gender and sexual orientation (see Blount, 1998, 1999; Lugg, 2003) this recommendation can be hardly seen to be liberatory or for that matter, particularly feminist. Some authors have used the term "feminine" to describe women's style of leadership, which is a bit odd, again, because of the implied essentialism. I would argue that feminine is to masculine as *womanist* is to masculinist. A prime example of an organization with an incredibly high degree of womanist ethos would be the Mary Kay Corporation.

7.   At present (2003), only the Ninth Circuit Court of Appeals considers gender a suspect category. Furthermore, both Judge Posner and Justice Scalia are critical to scathing in their assessments of "gender discrimination."

8.   This understanding of sexual orientation includes those individuals who are intersexed, transgendered, transsexual, or not. Consequently, a transgendered individual may or may not have a heterosexual orientation. Again, sex and gender are not predictive of sexual orientation.

9.   Historically, the term "queer" is the most vicious of insults. Yet in the early 1990s, there was a move by primarily gay and lesbian activists to reclaim the word. As the movement became more diverse, including trans people and intersexuals, queer has become shorthand for lesbian, gay, bisexual, transgendered, transsexual, and intersexual. Its use remains controversial within "queer" circles. To some extent this controversy represents a generational divide. My partner, who came out in the mid-1970s, identifies as lesbian. I came out in the late 1980s–early 1990s, and happily embraced "queer," which horrifies her. Non-queers use the term at their own peril.

10 . There are numerous examples of Gaylegal theorists not "getting it." In the 1980s, Richard Mohr dismissed demands by lesbian feminists and people of color that gay political organizations challenge issues of racial subordination and patriarchal oppression and form coalitions with anti-racist and feminist groups. He deemed such efforts as an "unnecessary and ... wasteful drain on the movement" (in Hutchinson, 1999, p. 15).

11.   The majority of white Americans do not see themselves as "raced"—although this notion flies in the face of history and U.S. jurisprudence. There is burgeoning research in this area called, "Critical White Studies" (See Delgado and Stefancic, 1999).

12.   Hence, to Queer Legal Theorists, the book *Virtually Normal* (1996), by gay conservative Andrew Sullivan, is wildly regressive and oppressive in its politics (see Hutchinson, 2000).

13.   One time when traveling with my partner Mary, I landed in the hospital in Petersburg, Virginia. Not knowing what the climate would be for queers, Mary decided that we should tell the hospital staff we were cousins—a bald-faced and visually unconvincing lie. She is of Lebanese descent, and I am of northern European descent. Still, we did pass, to our utter shock.

14. Elsbree is a very problematic source because his text reflects the racism of the time by white authors of history of education texts. For example, "Sex immorality among schoolteachers has never been countenanced by the public except in a few sections of the South where white school boards ignore it in Negro teachers" (Elsbree, 1939, pp. 536–537). This lacks any citation.

15. For example, female teachers could not be seen riding in cars with men other than their fathers or brothers, they must regularly attend church, cannot be seen or were forbidden from smoking and drinking, and in some areas there were curfews (Elsbree, 1939).

16. The vast majority of the early educational administration programs either barred women or set stringent quotas that limited their numbers. This would be the norm until Title IX was seriously enforced (see Blount, 1998).

17. Faderman (1991), Chauncey (1994), Terry (1999) and Somerville (2000) stress the influence of class, race, and ethnicity as shaping notions of sexuality in general, and homosexuality and heterosexuality in particular. The sexologists' concepts were mired in racial notions of "who was more civilized than thou." Consequently, heterosexual marriage by white males represented the height of civilization (Terry, 1999).

18. One of the historic slurs against queer people is that we are pedophiles. The research overwhelmingly contradicts this notion, yet it remains a popular rhetorical charge employed by opponents to queer civil rights (Diamond, 1998; Herman, 1997).

19. Newspapers would remain silent on the sentences of those who were convicted of a "queer" charge. As lawyer Dale Jennings recalls "At that time several judges were giving homosexuals a choice between a sentence as long as fifty years or castration for sodomy convictions, and the papers printed nothing about it. Or if they did, they wouldn't mention this dreadful choice" (in Alwood, 1996, p. 29).

20. *The Well of Loneliness* (1928), by Radclyffe Hall, was a lesbian novel that was banned in Great Britain in the 1920s, although it escaped the U.S. censors after a successful trial in 1929. The legal cases in both the United Kingdom and the United States of America were sensational, helped along by Hall's own unabashed and courageous lesbianism. While the book is mired in the "wrong-body thesis" and is unbearably dreary, it is the *classic* novel in lesbian history. It was the book to read for generations of lesbians who were in the process of "coming out."

21. Transforming GSAs into curricular-related clubs is a highly effective means of side stepping possible political and legal objections vis-à-vis "limited open forums." By focusing on queer literature, biographies and history, direct links to curricula-related content can be made. In the Utah case, PRISM made links to American government, history, and sociology (see Robson, 2001).

22. Nabozny's lawyer conflated sex and gender and the court did nothing to correct it. Wisconsin has a law banning sex discrimination, not gender discrimination. At the time Nabozny was a student, boys who harassed girls were subjected to the district's discipline policy. Nabozny was harassed by boys, yet the district did nothing. It is because the district failed to act in Nabozny's case, when it did act repeatedly when the victim was a girl, that Nabozny's claim prevailed. It is doubtful that the orientation claim would have prevailed if the gender (meaning biological sex) had been dismissed.

23. In 1997, The U.S. Department of Justice's Civil Rights division issued guidelines extending Title IX coverage to queer students, at least when it comes to same-sex harassment. It re-

mains mute on harassment on sexual orientation, a fine point (see Mayes, 2001). While the current Bush administration has yet to rescind these guidelines, it also has yet to comment as to whether or not these will be maintained.

24. This program did not survive the recession of 2002. Massachusetts eliminated funding for the program due to great fiscal pressure.

25. Generally, queer students are 2–3 times more likely to attempt suicide, and are at greater risk of substance abuse, absence from school, violence, harassment, early parenthood, and of course, dropping out. They are also much more likely to be thrown out of their homes by their parents (see D'Augelli and Hershberger, 1995; Eisemann, 2000; Fineran, 2002; Gibson, 1994; Remafedi, 1994b; and Savin-Williams, 1994).

26. They might have some protections if they have tenure. But of course, like sodomy laws and licensure requirements, this varies from state to state.

27. As a first grader, I signed a petition to over-turn the dress code at my rural PA elementary school—which forbade girls from wearing slacks except for physical education. I found the rule to be completely impractical for a rural, and in the winter, frigid environment. By the time I was in the local public high school, the informal dress code for students included jeans, t-shirts or polo shirts, and sneakers, regardless of gender.

28. The berdache were biological men and women who assumed opposite gender roles. Such individuals, who would later be viewed as either homosexual and/or transgendered by whites, were venerated in most Native American societies. (See Miller, 1995; Valdes, 1995).

29. In a 1957 letter to *The Ladder,* a lesbian magazine, Hansberry observed, "I think it is about time that equipped women began to take on some of the ethical questions which a male-dominated culture has produced and dissect and analyze them quite to pieces in a serious fashion … . In this kind of work there may be women to emerge who will be able to formulate a new and possible concept that homosexual persecution and condemnation has at its roots not only social ignorance, but a philosophically active anti-feminist dogma" (in Miller, 1995, p. 331).

30. Every social movement needs its "Quisling" and Roy Cohn easily qualifies as one for queers during the McCarthy era. He served as Senator McCarthy's right hand man in hunting down suspected subversives, which included Communists, labor activists, civil rights activists, and of course, queers. Cohn insisted he was non-queer, even though he had been repeatedly "outed" since the 1950s. He continued to insist that he was non-queer even when he was dying of AIDS in the mid-1980s (see Gross, 1993).

References

Alwood, E. (1996). *Straight news: Gays, lesbians, and the news media.* New York: Columbia University Press.

Anyon, J. (1997). *Ghetto schools.* New York: Teachers College Press.

Beh, H.G., and Diamond, M. (2000). An emerging ethical and medical dilemma: Should physicians perform sex assignment surgery on infants with ambiguous genitalia? *Michigan Journal of Gender & Law,* 7: 1–63.

Bell, C., and Chase, S. (1995). Gender in the theory and practice of educational leadership. *Journal of Just and Caring Education,*1 (2): 210–222.

Bickmore, K. (1999). Why discuss sexuality in elementary schools? In W. J. Letts, IV, and J. T. Sears, (Eds.), *Queering elementary education: Advancing the dialogue about sexualities and schooling.* (pp. 15–25). Lanham, MD: Rowman & Littlefield.

Blinick, B. (1994). Out in the curriculum, out in the classroom: Teaching history and organizing for change. In L. Gerber (Ed.), *Tilting the tower: Lesbians teaching queer subjects.* New York: Routledge, pp. 142–149.

Blount, J. M. (1996). Manly men and womanly women: Deviance, gender role polarization, and the shift in women's school employment, 1900–1976. *Harvard Educational Review,* 68 (2): 318–339.

———. (1998). *Destined to rule the schools.* Albany, NY: SUNY Press.

———. (1999). Manliness and the gendered construction of school administration in the USA. *International Journal of Leadership in Education: Theory and Practice,* 2(2): 55–68.

Bowles S., and Gintis, H. (1976). *Schooling in capitalist America.* New York: Basic Books.

Britzman, D. (1995). Is there a queer pedagogy? Or, stop reading straight. *Educational Theory,* 45(2): 151–165.

Brown v. Hot, Sexy & Safer Prods., Inc., 68 F.3d 525, 533 (1st Cir. 1995).

Broz, A.N. (1998). *Nabozny v. Podlesny*: A teenager's struggle to end anti-gay violence in public schools. *Northwestern University Law Review,* 92: 750–778.

Brunner, C.C. (1999a). "Back talk" from a woman superintendent: Just how useful is research? In C. Cryss Brunner (Ed.), *Sacred dreams: Women and the superintendency.* Albany, NY: SUNY Press, pp. 179–197.

———. (1999b). Power, gender, and superintendent selection. In C. Cryss Brunner (Ed.), *Sacred dreams: Women and the superintendency.* Albany, NY: SUNY Press, pp. 63–78.

———. (2000). Unsettled moments in settled discourse: Women superintendents' experiences of inequality. *Educational Administration Quarterly,* 36 (1): 76–117.

Bruton, D. (1994). Insisting on ignorance: The paradox of withholding knowledge in our schools. In K. Jennings, (Ed.), *One teacher in 10: Gay and lesbian educators tell their stories,*. Boston, MA: Alyson Publications, pp.177–190.

Bryant, T. J. (1999). May we teach tolerance? Establishing the parameters of academic freedom in pubic schools. *University of Pittsburgh Law Review,* 60: 579–639.

Buckle, David S. (2000). Legal perspective on ensuring a safe and nondiscriminatory school environment for lesbian, gay, bisexual, and transgendered students. *Education and Urban Society,* 32 (3): 390–398.

Burke, P. (2001). Overture. The new history: Its past and its future, in *New perspectives on historical writing,* edited by P. Burke. University Park, PA: Penn State Press, pp. 1–24.

Butler, J. (1990). *Gender trouble: Feminism and the subversion of identity.* New York: Routledge

Cahn, S. K. (1993). From the "muscle moll" to the "butch" ballplayer. Mannishness, lesbianism, and homophobia in U.S. women's sport. *Feminist Studies,* 19, (2): 343–371.

Callahan, R. E. (1962). *Education and the cult of efficiency.* Chicago: University of Chicago Press.

Capper, C. A. (1998). Critically oriented and postmodern perspectives: Sorting out the differences and applications for practice. *Educational Administration Quarterly*, 34 (3): 354– 380.

———. (1999). (Homo)sexualities, organizations, and administration: Possibilities for in(queer)y. *Educational Researcher*, 28(5): 4–11.

Case, M. A. C. (1995). Disaggregating gender from sex and sexual orientation: The effeminate man in the law and feminist jurisprudence. *Yale Law Journal*, 105: 1–105.

Chauncey, G. (1994). *Gay New York: Gender, urban culture, and the making of the gay male world, 1890–1940*. New York: Basic Books.

Chiusano, M. (1996, September 30). Parents' rights. *National Review*, 48 (18): 55–57.

Clifford, G. (1989). Man/woman/teacher: Gender, family and a career in American educational history. In D. Warren, (Ed.), *American teachers: Histories of a profession at work,*. New York: Macmillan, pp. 293–343.

Conklin, A. M. (1927). The school as a new tool. *Journal of Educational Sociology*, 1(2): 93–99.

Crenshaw, K.W. (1991). Mapping the margins: Intersectionality, identity politics, and violence against women of color. *Stanford Law Review*, 43: 1241–1299.

Cruz, D. B. (1999). Controlling desires: Sexual orientation conversion and the limits of knowledge and law. *Southern California Law Review*,72: 1297–1400.

D'Augelli, A., and Hershberger, S. (1995). The impact of victimization on the mental health and suicidality of lesbian, gay, and bisexual youths. *Developmental Psychology*, 31: 65–74.

Dayoff, A.D. (2001). Sodomy laws: The government's vehicle to impose the majority's social values. *William Mitchell Law Review*, 27: 1863–1894.

Delgado, R., and Stefancic, J. (Eds.) (1999). *Critical race theory: The cutting edge* . Philadelphia, PA: Temple University Press.

D'Emilio, J. (1983). *Sexual politics, sexual communities: The making of a homosexual minority in the United States, 1940–1970*. Chicago: University of Chicago Press.

———`. (1992). *Making trouble: Essays on gay history, politics and the university*. New York: Routledge.

Diamond, S. (1998). *Not by politics alone: The enduring influence of the Christian Right*. New York: Guilford Press.

Eisemann, V. H. (2000). Protecting the kids in the hall: Using Title IX to stop student-on-student anti-gay harassment. *Berkeley Women's Law Journal*, 15: 125–161.

Elia, J. P. (1994). Homophobia in the high school: A problem in need of a resolution. *Journal of Homosexuality*, 77 (1): 177–185.

Elsbree, W. S.(1939). *The American teacher: Evolution of a profession in a democracy*. New York: American Book Company.

Epperson v. Arkansas, 393 U.S. 97 (1968).

Epstein, D., and Johnson, R. (1998). *Schooling sexualities*. Bristol, PA: Open University Press.

Eskridge, Jr., W.N. (1994). Gaylegal narratives. *Stanford Law Review*, 46: 607–646.

———. (1997). Law and the construction of the closet: American regulation of same-sex intimacy, 1880–1946, *Iowa Law Review*,82: 1007–1136.

———. (1999). David C. Baum Memorial Lectures on civil liberties and civil rights–*Hardwick* and historiography. *University of Illinois Law Review*, 631–702.

———. (2000). No Promo Homo: The sedimentation of antigay discourse and the channeling effect of judicial review. *New York University Law Review*, 75: 1327–1411.

Faderman, L. (1991). *Odd girls and twilight lovers: A history of lesbian life in twentieth-century America.* New York: Penguin Books.

Fajer, M. (1992). Can two real men eat quiche together? Storytelling, gender-role stereotypes, and legal protection for lesbians and gay men. *University of Miami Law Review,* 46: 511–651.

Fineran, S. (2002). Sexual harassment between same-sex peers: Intersection of mental health, homophobia, and sexual violence in schools. *Social Work,* 47(1): 65–75.

Fontaine, J. H. (1997). The sound of silence: Public school response to the needs of gay and lesbian youth. *Journal of Gay & Lesbian Social Services,* 7(4): 101–109.

Foster, M. (1999). Race, class and gender in education research: Surveying the political terrain. *Educational Policy,*13(1): 77–85.

Franke, K. M. (1995). The central mistake of sex discrimination law: The disaggregation of sex from gender. *University of Pennsylvania Law Review,* 144: 1–99.

Garland, J. A. (2001). The low road to violence: Governmental discrimination as a catalyst for pandemic hate crime. *Law & Sexuality,*10: 1– 91.

Gibson, P. (1994). Gay male and lesbian youth suicide, in G. Remafedi (Ed.), *Death by denial: Studies of suicide in gay and lesbian teenagers.* Boston, MA: Alyson Publications, pp. 7–68.

Goishi, M. (1997). Legal and social responses to the problems of queer youth: Unlocking the closet door: Protecting children from involuntary civil commitment because of their sexual orientation. *Hastings Law Journal,*48: 1137–1182.

Goldberg, M. (2002, July 19). The battle over Bush's judges. Salon.com. From the World Wide Web. http://www.salon.com/politics/feature/2002/07/19/judges/index.html. Last accessed on July 19, 2002.

Gotanda, N. (1991). A critique of "Our Constitution is color-blind." *Stanford Law Review,* 44(1): 1–68.

Greenberg, J. A. (1999). Defining male and female: Intersexuality and the collision between law and biology. *Arizona Law Review,* 41: 265–327.

———. (2000). When is a man a man, and when is a woman s woman? *Florida Law Review,* 52: 745–768.

Gross, L. (1993). *Contested closets: The politics and ethics of outing.* Minneapolis, MN: University of Minnesota Press.

Hall, R. (1928). *The well of loneliness.* Garden City, NY: Sun Dial Press.

Halley, J. E. (1989). The politics of the closet: Towards equal protection for gay, lesbian, and bisexual identity. *UCLA Law Review,*36: 915–976.

Harbeck, K. M. (1997). *Gay and lesbian educators: Personal freedoms, public constraints.* Malden, MA: Amethyst.

Harris, A. P. (1990). Race and essentialism in Feminist Legal Theory: *Stanford Law Review,* 42: 581–615

Herman, D. (1997). *The antigay agenda: Orthodox vision and the Christian Right.* Chicago: University of Chicago Press.

Herr, K. (1997). Learning lessons from school: Homophobia, heterosexism and the construction of failure. *Journal of Gay and Lesbian Social Services,* 7(4): 51–64.

———. (1999). Institutional violence in the everyday practices of school: The narrative of a young lesbian. *Journal for a Just and Caring Education,* 5(3): 242–255.

Hicks, K. A. (1999). "Reparative" therapy: Whether parental attempts to change a child's sexual orientation can legally constitute child abuse. *The American University Law Review*, 49: 505–547.

Hogan, D. (1992). "...the silent compulsions of economic relations": Markets and the demand for education. *Educational Policy*, 6(2): 180–206.

Hutchinson, D. L. (1997). Out yet unseen: A racial critique of Gay and Lesbian Legal Theory and political discourse. *Connecticut Law Review*, 29: 561–645.

_____. (1999). Ignoring the sexualization of race: Heteronormativity, Critical Race Theory, and anti-racist politics. *Buffalo Law Review*, 47: 1–116.

_____. (2000). "Gay rights" for "gay whites"? Race, sexual identity, and equal protection discourse. *Cornell Law Review*, 85: 1358–1391.

_____. (2001). "Intersectionality," "multidimensionality," and the development of an adequate theory of subordination. *Michigan Journal of Race & Law*, 6: 285–317.

Jones, R. (2000). The new minority to protect under Title IX. *The Education Digest*, 65(8): 20–26.

Jones, J. (2002). Money, sex and the religious right: A Constitutional analysis of federally funded abstinence-only-until-marriage sexuality education. *Creighton Law Review*, 35: 1075–1105.

Jordan, K. M., Vaughan, J. S., and Woodworth, K. J. (1997). I will survive: Lesbian, gay, and bisexual youths' experience of high school. *Journal of Gay & Lesbian Social Services*, 7(4): 17–33.

Katz, J. N. (1992). *Gay American history: Lesbians and gay men in the U.S.A.—A documentary history, Revised edition.* New York: Meridian.

Kepner, J. (1998). *Rough news-daring news: 1950s' pioneer gay press journalism.* New York: Harrington Park Press.

King, T. L. (2002). Working out: Conflicting Title VII approaches to sex discrimination and sexual orientation. *U.C. Davis Law Review*, 35: 1005–1044.

Kintz, L. (1997). *Between Jesus and the market: The emotions that matter to right-wing America.* Durham, NC: Duke University Press.

Kissen, R. (1996). *The last closet: The real lives of lesbian and gay teachers.* Portsmouth, NH: Heinemann.

Knauer, N. J. (2000). Homosexuality as contagion: From "The Well of Loneliness to the Boy Scouts." *Hofstra Law Review*, 29: 403–501

Kozik-Rosabal, G. (2000). "Well, we haven't noticed anything bad going on," said the principal. *Education and Urban Society*,32(3): 368–389.

Kumashiro, K. K. (1999). Reading queer Asian American masculinities: and sexualities in elementary school. In W. J. Letts, IV and J. T. Sears (Eds.), *Queering elementary education: Advancing the dialogue about sexualities and schooling.* Lanham, MD: Rowman & Littlefield, pp. 61–70.

Kumashiro, K. K. (2001). Queer students of color, In K. K. Kumashiro, *Troubling intersections of race and sexuality: Queer students of color and anti-oppressive education.* Lanham, MD: Rowman & Littlefield, pp. 1–25.

Lasswell, H. (1958). *Politics: Who gets what, when, how.* Cleveland, OH: Meridian Books.

Law, S. A. (1988). Homosexuality and the social meaning of gender. *Wisconsin Law Review*, 187–235.

Leslie, C. R. (2000, Winter). Creating criminals: The injuries inflicted by "unenforced" sodomy laws. *Harvard Civil Rights-Civil Liberties Law Review*, 35: 102–181.

Letts, IV, W. J., and Sears, J.T. (Eds.) (1999). *Queering elementary education: Advancing the dialogue about sexualities and schooling.* Lanham, MD: Rowman & Littlefield.

Levesque, R. J. R.(2000). Sexuality education: What adolescents' educational rights require. *Psychology, Public Policy and Law*, 6: 953–977.

Levit, N. (2001). A different kind of sameness: Beyond formal equality and antisubordination strategies in gay legal theory. *Ohio State Law Journal*, 61: 867–943.

Lindley, L., and Reininger, B.M. (2001). Support for instruction about homosexuality in South Carolina public schools. *Journal of School Health*, 71(1): 17–22.

Lipkin, A. (1994). The case for a gay and lesbian curriculum. *The High School Journal*, 77: 95–107.

Lugg, C.A. (1998). The religious right and public education: The paranoid politics of homophobia. *Educational Policy*,12(3): 267 – 283.

_____. (1999). *Kitsch: From education to public policy*. New York: Falmer.

_____. (2002). Be careful what you pray for: Religious conservatives, queer activists, and the politics of policy subversion. Unpublished manuscript. New Brunswick, NJ: Rutgers University.

_____. (2003). Our straight-laced administrators: The Law, LGBT administrators, and the assimilationist imperative. *Journal of School Leadership*,13(1): 51–85

MacGillivray, I. K. (2000). Educational equity for gay, lesbian, bisexual, transgendered, and queer/questioning students. *Education and Urban Society*, 32(3): 303–323

Malen, B. (1994). The micropolitics of education: Mapping the multiple dimensions of power relations in school polities. In J.D. Scribner and D. H. Layton (Eds.), *The study of educational politics*. Bristol, PA: The Falmer Press, pp. 147–167.

Malinsky, K. P. (1997). Learning to be invisible: Female sexual minority students in America's public high schools. *Journal of Gay & Lesbian Social Services*, 7(4): 35–50.

Marcus, E. (1992). *Making history: The struggle for gay and lesbian equal rights, 1945–1990*. New York: Harper Collins.

Marshall, C. (1993). Gender and race issues in administration. In C. Marshall (Ed.), *The new politics of race and gender*. Bristol, PA: The Falmer Press, pp. 168–174.

———. (1999). Researching the margins: Feminist critical policy analysis. *Educational Policy*,13(1): 59–76.

———, and Anderson, G. L. (1995). Rethinking the public and private spheres: Feminist and cultural studies perspectives on the politics of education. In J.D. Scribner and D. H. Layton (Eds.), *The study of educational politics*. Bristol, PA: The Falmer Press, pp. 169–182.

Mayes, T.A. (2001). Confronting same-sex, student-to-student sexual harassment: Recommendations for educators and policy makers. *Fordham Urban Law Journal*, 29: 641–682.

McCready, L. (2001). When fitting in isn't an option, or, why black queer males at a California high school stay away from Project 10. In K. K. Kumashiro, *Troubling intersections of race and sexuality: Queer students of color and anti-oppressive education*. Lanham, MD: Rowman & Littlefield, pp. 37–53..

McFarland, W. P. (2001). The legal duty to protect gay and lesbian students from violence in school. *Professional School Counseling*,4(3): 171–180.

Miller, N. (1995). *Out of the past: Gay and lesbian history from 1869 to the present*. New York Vintage Press.

———. *Sex-crime panic: A journey to the paranoid heart of the 1950s*. Los Angeles, CA: Alyson..

Moore, C. R. (1947, December 19). Sexual behavior in the human male, book review. *Science*, 106: (2764): 622–623.

Mozert v. Hawkins County Bd. of Educ., 827 F.2d 1058 (6th Cir. 1987).

Nabozny v. Podlesny, 92 F.3d 446 (7th Cir. 1996).

Nagel, J. (2000). Sexualizing the sociological: Queering and querying the intimate substructure of social life. *Sociological Quarterly*, 41(1): 1–17.

Necsu, E. D. (2000). CLS stands for Critical Legal Studies, if anyone remembers. *Journal of Law and Policy*, 8: 415–453.

Novick, P. (1988). *That noble dream: The "objectivity" question in the American Historical Association*. New York: Cambridge University Press.

Nye, J. L. (1998). The gender box. *Berkeley Women's Law Journal*, 13: 226–256.

Oncale v. Sundowner Offshore Services, Inc. 523 U.S. 75 (1998).

Orfield, G., and Yun, (1999). *Resegregation in American schools.* Cambridge, MA: The Civil Rights Project, Harvard University.

Pharr, S. (1988). *Homophobia: A weapon of sexism.* Little Rock, AK: Chardon Press.

Pinar, W. F. (1998). *Queer theory in education.* Mahwah, NJ: Lawrence Erlbaum Associates.

Potter, Z., and Summers, C. J. (2001). Reconsidering epistemology and ontology in status identity discourse: Make-believe and reality in race, sex, and sexual orientation. *Harvard Blackletter Journal*, 17: 113–196.

Randall, E. V., Cooper, B. S., and Hite, S. J. (1999). Understanding the politics of research in education. *Educational Policy*, 31(1): 7–22.

Reese, S. (1997). The law and gay-bashing in schools. *Education Digest*, 62(9): 46–49

Rehder, T. (2001). Discussion and expression of gender and sexuality in schools. *Georgetown Journal of Gender & the Law*, 2(2), 489–509.

Remafedi, G. (Ed.) (1994a). *Death by denial: Studies of suicide in gay and lesbian teenagers.* Boston, MA: Alyson Publications.

———. (1994b). The state of knowledge on gay, lesbian and bisexual youth suicide. In G. Remafedi (Ed.), *Death by denial: Studies of suicide in gay and lesbian teenagers.* Boston: Alyson Publications, pp. 7–14.

Resnik, J. (2000). The programmatic judiciary: Lobbying, judging, and invalidating the Violence Against Women Act. *Southern California Law Review*, 74: 269–293.

Rhode, D. L. (1993/94). Adolescent pregnancy and public policy. *Political Science Quarterly*, 108(4): 635–670.

Rivera, R. (1999). Our straight-laced judges: Twenty years later. *Hastings Law Journal*, 50: 1179–1198.

Robson, R. (2001). Our children: Kids of queer parents and parents and kids who are queer: Looking at sexual minority rights from a different perspective. *Albany Law Review*, 64: 915–948.

Ross, C. J. (1999). An emerging right for mature minors to receive information. *University of Pennsylvania Journal of Constitutional Law*, 2: 223–275.

Rousmaniere, K. (1997). *City teachers: Teaching and school reform in historical perspective.* New York: Teachers College Press.

Rudy, K. (2000). Queer studies and feminism. *Women's studies, 29* (2): 195–217.

Rush, S. E. (1997). Equal protection analogies—identity and "passing": Race and sexual orientation. *Harvard Blackletter Journal*, 13: 65–106.

Savin-Williams, R. C. (1994). Verbal and physical abuse as stressors in the lives of lesbian, gay male, and bisexual youths: Association with school problems, running away, substance abuse, prostitution, and suicide. *Journal of Consulting and Clinical Psychology*, 62: 261–269.

Scagliotti, J., (Executive Producer), and Schiller, G. (Director) (1986). *Before Stonewall: The making of a gay and lesbian community*. [Motion picture] Before Stonewall, Inc. Jezebel Productions: New York.

Scientists' Committee on Loyalty Problems (1949, June 24). Loyalty and security problems of scientists: A summary of current clearance procedures. *Science*, 109(2843): 621–624.

Seamons v. Snow, 84 F.3d 1226 (10th Cir. 1996).

Sears, J. T. (1997). *Lonely hunters: An oral history of lesbian and gay southern life, 1948–1968*. Boulder, CO: Westview Press.

_____. (1998). Teaching and researching sexualities in a socially responsible manner. In J. T. Sears and J. C. Carper (Eds.), *Curriculum, religion and public education: Conversations for an enlarging public square*. New York: Teachers College Press, pp. 161–176.

Sears, J. T., and Williams, W. L. (Eds.) (1997). *Overcoming heterosexism and homophobia: Strategies that work*. New York: Columbia University Press.

Sherman, D., and Repa, T. (1994). Women at the top: The experiences of two superintendents. *Equity and Choice*, 10(2): 59–64.

Siegel, R. B. (2002). She the people: The Nineteenth Amendment, sex equality, federal, and the family. *Harvard Law Review*, 115: 947–1046.

Smith-Rosenberg, C. (1989). Discourses of sexuality and subjectivity: The new woman, 1870–1936, in M. Duberman, M. Vicinus, and G. Chauncey, Jr., *Hidden from history: Reclaiming the gay and lesbian past*. New York: Penguin, pp. 264–280.

Somerville, S. B. (2000). *Queering the color line: Race and the invention of homosexuality in American culture*. Durham, NC: Duke University Press.

Stein, A. (2001). *The stranger next door: The story of a small community's battle of sex, faith, and civil rights*. Boston, MA: Beacon Press.

Storm, A. L. (2000). Developing tolerance for gay, lesbian students. *School Administrator*,57(2): 42–44.

Sullivan, A. (1996). *Virtually normal: An argument about homosexuality*. New York: Vintage Books.

Tenney, N. (1995). The Constitutional imperative of reality in public school curricula: Untruths about homosexuality as a violation of the First Amendment. *Brooklyn Law Review*,60: 1599–1651.

Terry, J. (1999). *An American obsession: Science, medicine, and homosexuality in modern society*. Chicago: University of Chicago Press.

Trebilcock, J. (2000). School board control over teacher conduct. *Tulsa Law Review*,35: 445–472.

Tushnet, M. (2001). Renormalizing *Bush v. Gore*: An anticipatory intellectual history. *Georgetown Law Journal*, 90: 113–125.

Tyack, D., and Hansot, E. (1982). *Managers of virtue: Public school leadership in America, 1820–1980*. New York: Basic Books.

Valdes, F. (1995). Queers, sissies, dykes, and tomboys: Deconstructing the conflation of "sex," "gender," and "sexual orientation" in Euro-American law and society. *California Law Review*: 3–377.

_____. (1997). Queer margins, queer ethics: A call to account for race and ethnicity in the law, theory, and politics of "sexual orientation." *Hastings Law Journal*, 48: 1293–1341.

_____. (1998). Beyond sexual orientation in Queer Legal Theory: Majoritarianism, multidimensionality, and responsibility in social justice scholarship or legal scholars as cultural warriors. *Denver University Law Review*, 75: 1409–1464.

Williams, W. L. (1997). Multicultural perspectives on reducing heterosexism. In J.T. Sears and W. L. Williams, *Overcoming heterosexism and homophobia: Strategies that work*. New York: Columbia University Press, pp. 76–87.

Wojohn, P. L. (2001). Out-speech: The First Amendment and sexual orientation. *Georgetown Journal of Gender & the Law*,1(2): 305–320.

Yoshino, K. (1998). Assimilationist bias in Equal Protection: The visibility presumption and the case of "Don't Ask, Don't Tell." *Yale Law Journal*, 108: 485–571.

_____. (2002). Covering. *Yale Law Journal*, 111: 769–939.

7

Re-Radicalizing the Consciousness in Educational Leadership: The Critically Spiritual Imperative toward Keeping the Promise

Michael E. Dantley

Introduction

Much has been written about the role of spirituality and the leadership of schools (Dantley, 2003a, 2003b, 2003c, 2005a, 2005b; Shields, Edwards, and Sayani, 2005; Starratt, 2003) as well as the need to create schools that exemplify the principles of democracy and equity (Darling-Hammond, 1997; Foster, 1986; Giroux, 1997; Meier, 2002). Several scholars in educational leadership have argued that one of the ways for schools to become spaces where democracy is clearly evident is for those who lead in those places to operate from a spiritual epicenter (Oldenski and Carlson, 2002; Shields, Edwards, and Sayani, 2005; Dantley, 2005c). Work in critical spirituality (Dantley, 2003b, 2005c) and leadership argues that school leaders who function under the auspices of their spirits are able to bring about the radical reconstruction of schools if they do so from a critically spiritual perspective. The radical reconstruction of schools portends the existence of learning communities where democracy and the equitable treatment of all students, the adults who teach them, and the families the students represent, are normative.

The term radical is used extensively in this chapter because in many ways the revolutionary attitude and actions that once were a part of the genesis of the notions of social justice and education have seemed to have lost their incisive edge. Notions of social justice, when originally introduced to the educational leadership discourse, troubled the field through the acrid interrogation of the issues of race, class, gender, sexual orientation, and other signifiers of identity. The critical question of who benefits from the sedimented practices of educational leadership was proposed to motivate scholars and practitioners alike to grapple with the myriad instances of inequality that plagued the education of African American, Latino/a and children of poverty. The interrogation of hegemonic administrative practices, under the banner of social justice, highlighted the undemocratic ways in which schools had traditionally been administered and the heinous results of the miseducation of children of color and poverty that had been allowed to prosper in American schools. Given the ubiquitous nature of racial, social class, gender, ability, and sexual orientation discrimination, the field of educational leadership cannot trivialize notions of social justice and democracy. Interestingly enough, it appears that the phrase "social justice" has become a fixture in the educational leadership vernacular. While this may appear to be the quintessential placement of the social justice discourse, one could rightly propose that the general acceptance of the notion of social justice in the educational leadership conversation has caused it to lose some of its counter-hegemonic edge. What seems to be the case is that whenever rebellious counter-narratives and once seditious concepts and ideas become a part of the common language of any field, they pay a very high price for acceptance; they have, in some way, been co-opted in order to enjoy a space in the privileged discourse.

Critical spirituality offers to this process of radicalization and reformation an underpinning for transgressing the hegemonic ways in which education is usually carried out in our society. The reason this is so is because critical spirituality is an amalgam of the tenets of critical theory and African American spirituality and both demand that reflection, resistance, and reconstruction of the hegemony take place where American institutions such as public schools are concerned. The purpose of this chapter is to briefly outline the tenets of critical spirituality, to juxtapose critical spirituality against the notions and the agenda of right wing conservative Christianity and to then argue how the aligning of critical spirituality with democracy and social justice can help to radically reform schools.

The Tenets of Critical Spirituality

Critical spirituality includes critical self-reflection, deconstructive interpretation, performative creativity, and transformative action. Each of these four components of critical spirituality work together to cause school leaders to become reflectively conscious as well as to become grassroots activists or organic intellectuals for the progressive reconstruction of schools. The element of critical self-reflection requires the school leader to consider ways in which the rituals and performances in schools marginalize those who on account of their race, social class, gender, sexual orientation, ability, or religion find themselves outside of the dominant cultural group that is given legitimacy in the public schools. "It asks that leaders, through a moral imperative, interrogate their behaviors and those of the school systems they serve to disclose those sedimented and often systemic rituals that perpetuate undemocratic practice in the system" (Dantley, 2005c, p. 509). Deconstructive interpretation involves the application of a critical theoretical lens to oneself and the system of the educational process. It is during this phase of critical spirituality that the school leader asks how she was so socialized as to embrace her personal positions on issues of race, class, gender, sexual orientation, religion, and other markers of distinction and identity. This question reveals the historical and social constructions in the school leader's experiences that have influenced her to believe what she does and to respond and build her professional practice the way that she does. "Applying a critical ideological frame after critical self reflection asks educators to seriously consider the interests embodied in the process of education and how these interests may be challenged, changed, or sustained in order to provide an emancipatory reality in public schools" (Dantley, 2005c, p. 510). Performative creativity involves the use of a radical or progressive imagination, grounded in hope, to envision a radical reconstruction of the educational process. What this component of critical spirituality does is to take the results of the reflection and the interpretation to a point of creating strategies and transformative practices to bring about reform in schools. A reimagining of places called schools demands that the school leader release herself from the vestiges of a traditional understanding as well as interpretation of schools in order to facilitate the recreation of educational sites that are grounded in a democratic motif. Creativity and authorship are both exceptionally spiritual activities, and the school leader who is serious about imagining a new way to educate our children must have the courage as well as the hope to visualize the process and the results of the process leading to schools that are equitable and democratic for the entire learning community. Finally, transformative action takes all of this process from the context of "naval gazing" and moves it into manifestation. Here the school leader politicizes the whole critically spiritual endeavor and strategizes with others as to how to pull off this newly imagined place called school. The goal of operating from a critically spiritual center is not only so that school leaders will facilitate learning communities where students will acquire academic skills and intellectual acuity through the teaching/learning process, but that students would also, through what Paulo Freire (1972) calls reading the word and the world, become activists whose goal is the radical transformation of society and its institutions. In fact, the very act of becoming literate, according to Freire, becomes a political one.

Literacy, according to Freire, is critically linked to an activist agenda of seeing a purer form of democracy existing in our society. Through literacy, students would have the skills to critically interrogate or read written transmissions, decipher spoken language, and deconstruct visual and nonvisual texts to ascertain the degree to which they either enhance or retard the exercise of democratic practices in society. What is vitally important, however, when considering enacting a Freirean agenda for social reconstruction is the necessity to grapple with the way to define democracy and democratic practices. Schools are sites of contested topography where the various voices and constituencies of the learning community are all vying for legitimation. School leaders that operate from a critically spiritual center understand the necessity to legitimate the multiple voices of the learning community, even though many or most may be in a state of constant contestation with one another, within a democratic context. The next section of this chapter will offer three scholars' definitions of democracy. Each could be useful in a critically spiritual leader's work to bring about a radical reconstruction of what happens in schools.

Three Scholars' Definitions of Democracy

Marable (1996) defines democracy as a process. He says that democracy is a dynamic concept and particularly argues that people of color have a distinct way to think about and define democracy. Marable argues that people of color have radically defined the nature of democracy. He says:

> We assert that democratic government is empty and meaningless without active social justice and cultural diversity. Multicultural political democracy means that this country was not built by and for only one group—Western Europeans; that our country does not have only one language—English; or only one religion—Christianity; or only one economic philosophy—corporate capitalism. Multicultural democracy means that the leadership within our society should reflect the richness, colors, and diversity expressed in the lives of all our people. (p. 96)

Further, Marable argues that multicultural democracy offers all citizens the ability to achieve full self-determination which might involve what he calls territorial and geographical restructuring.

Multicultural democracy embraces a feminist or womanist vision of society. Such a perspective takes into consideration,

> the patterns of subordination and exploitation of women of color—including job discrimination rooted in gender, race and class, rape and sexual abuse, forced sterilizations, harassment and abuse within the criminal justice system, housing discrimination against single mothers with children, the absence of pay equity for comparable work, political under-representation, and legal disfranchisement—combine to perpetuate a subordinate status for women within society. (p. 96–97)

For Marable an agenda for political liberation is impossible to achieve unless it embraces the empowerment and the emancipation of women in society. He contends, "Men must learn from the experiences and insights of women if we are to liberate restraints which deny us our rights as Americans and free human beings" (p. 97).

According to Marable, three of the four components of multicultural democracy are a commitment to an active position on social justice and diversity, the ability to achieve self-determination, and the embracing of a feminist or womanist perspective. It seems that all of these, to be achieved, demand an interfacing with one's spiritual dimension. There is no sense of self determination or how that process is to begin as well as course or flow without a genuine understanding of the self and especially the self in the context of others. Critical spirituality engages the process of understanding and deconstructing the self through reflection, critique, and interrogation.

West (2004), in discussing notions of democratic practice concluded that, "Democratic individuality requires mature and free persons who confront reality, history, and mortality—and who shun innocence, illusion, and purity" (p. 82). Critical spirituality serves as the underpinning for a leadership in schools that facilitates an environment that promotes students becoming both mature and free. What is most interesting about this process of building spaces called schools that promote the maturity and freedom of students is that such notions seem to be diametrically opposed to the traditional ideals of education. If anything, for traditional education, notions of maturity only include physical growth and the linear progression of acquiring requisite academic skills certain celebrated gatekeepers have established as the measuring rod of academic success. Traditional notions of student growth may hint at maturity, especially as many curricula and scope and sequence documents laud the acquisition of critical thinking skills for students. However, critical thinking is usually located in the deciphering of an established set of facts, ideas, and predispositions as opposed to the serious interrogation of values, ideals, and sedimented practices that are often reified in the minutia students are asked to embrace. The notion of freedom is an alien one to those who generally serve as leaders of our schools. Freedom is linked often to permissive, rambunctious, and out of control settings as opposed to places where students are invited and in fact, challenged to think outside the box, to question and inquire about those things that are accepted as fact and to suggest alternate ways of thinking and perceiving rituals and practices that have been granted a heretofore monolithic demeanor. This allows for the mature and free individual to confront the history, reality, as well as the mortality that West argues is vital to the demonstration of democracy. Schools have traditionally eschewed this kind of confrontation as they believe that such activity might lessen the proper perpetuation of the society's goals and the cultural reproduction schools have traditionally performed. But if democracy involves the deconstruction of illusions and untenable notions of purity in order for citizens to grapple with the realities of communal living, then schools must become those spaces where students are encouraged to ask the very penetrating questions about the customs and prevailing predispositions that underpin much of the dominant culture schools are called to reproduce. Part of this process demands that schools and their leadership wage a war against the kind of nihilistic thinking where the possibilities of actually living in a democratic society are concerned. Schools have to muster the necessary courage to allow the learning community to deal with the often muted malaise many feel because the realities of democracy are seldom witnessed and more often than not are abridged because of a capitalistic, imperialistic, and colonizing motivation that grounds behavior and performance in our society. West is very helpful in capturing the realities of this malaise. He offers:

> This disaffection stems both from the all-too-true reality of the corruptions of our system and from a deeper psychic disillusionment and disappointment. The political discourse is too formulaic, so tailored into poll-driven, focus-group-approved slogans that don't really say anything substantive or strike at the core of our lived experience, the lack of authenticity of discourse—and the underlying lack of gravitas, of penetrating insight and wisdom on the part of politicians—is numbing. But we must keep in mind that the disgust so many feel comes from a deep desire to hear more authentic expres-

sions of insights about our lives and more genuine commitments to improving them. (p. 64)

It is in forging a democratic space and the facilitation of a democratic citizenry that the intersection of critical spirituality and educational leadership is best displayed. Because this nihilistic spirit to which West so articulately speaks is so entrenched in the citizenship discourse, it is imperative that a spiritual remedy be suggested that will have the impetus to shatter the wall of disillusionment and offer counter-narratives to the ones presently voiced by those who sincerely desire to see democracy and genuine citizenship enacted throughout the culture of the United States but who feel hopeless to bring it to pass.

Gutmann (1987) helps us to understand notions of democracy and citizenship when she puts into perspective the dichotomy between what she calls a state of individuals and a democratic state. Examining this dichotomy is important when defining citizenship in a democratic society. Gutmann argues that the difference between a state of individuals and a democratic state is that the democratic state recognizes the worth of political education in "predisposing children to accept those ways of life that are consistent with sharing the rights and responsibilities of citizenship in a democratic society" (p. 42). She further suggests that within the realm of educational authority is the responsibility of providing members of the learning community with an education that will allow them to participate in democratic politics, "to choosing among (a limited range of) good lives, and to sharing in the several sub-communities, such as families, that impart identity to the lives of its citizens" (p. 42). Whether we choose to perceive it this way or not, the idea of being able to make decisions among a number of choices that are purported to lead to the acquisition of good lives demands embracing the spiritual nature of our existence. Of foremost interest is the whole notion of the good life and what that actually means. Our spirits help to define for us the nature of good and assist us in differentiating good for us as individuals and good for us as members of a community.

Ross (2002) in discussing the right and the good causes us to more deeply consider the issue of what may be implied in the whole notion of the good life. He says that often rightness is based upon some kind of productivity. He argues, "The first form this attempt takes is the attempt to base rightness on conduciveness to the advantage or pleasure of the agent" (p. 478). When one does this, such thinking flies in the face of the fact that often notions of duty are grounded in the "observance of the rights and furtherance of the interests of others whatever the costs to ourselves may be" (p. 478). Ethicists have alleged that observing the rights of others never results in a loss of happiness for the agent. But Ross argues, "As soon as a man does an action *because* (italics author's) he thinks he will promote his own interests thereby, he is not acting from a sense of its rightness but from self-interest" (p. 478). So while it is self - efficacious to consider the choices essential to one living even a modicum of the good life, it is also vitally important that those decisions take into account the lives of others. To do that demands an engagement with one's spiritual dimension.

Distinguishing between Critical Spirituality and Conservative Religion

The spiritual dimension of our lives does a number of things. First, it provides for us ontology as well as teleology to ground us. What this means is that our spirits help to inform our sense of being and the reason or purpose for our being. Second, our spirits motivate us to embrace connectivity with others. It compels us to move beyond the confines of individualistic reasoning and hedonistic impulses but pushes us to consider the "Other" and the efficacy of being in relationship with the "Other." Third, our spirits help to inform our sense of what is moral and ethical.

Spirituality, unlike religion, is not concerned with codifying ethereal practices into a monolithic institutional structure. In fact, critical spirituality motivates leaders to interrogate the ways in which institutional spaces, like schools and codified religion, perpetuate notions of racism, classism, sexism, ableism, and homophobia among a number of other undemocratic practices. Herein lies a major difference between institutionalized religion and critical spirituality; religious organizations, especially conservative, fundamentalist religious organizations, are in the forefront of a campaign to maintain the hegemony that celebrates the perpetuation of what is often called, "the American way". This ideology praises the traditional roles and positions on notions of race, class, and gender generally believed and espoused by European American men. Religious conservatives are assisted in this work through the labor of neoliberals who find that conflict around any one of these issues must be eschewed in favor of establishing a color-blind, all inclusive melting pot, totally ignoring the need to celebrate difference and the multicultural nature of our society. Apple (2001) comments, "For a rapidly growing segment of the conservative population, God's message to all of us is to turn to both capitalism and tradition" (p. 22). Leaders in conservative religious circles have openly supported a "right wing" agenda in an effort to assert that such an agenda would bring the country back to its foundation and its cultural roots. The proponents of this return to our historical foundations forget that at the time when these roots were established only men were able to participate in the cultural rituals and white, land-owning men at that. Women, both Black and White were subservient to the demands and impositions of men, they were also deligitimated and African American men were only three-fifths of a human being. This is the cultural context that many of the religious right wish to see replicated in our current times.

It is important to note that not all religious institutions necessarily embrace a conservative position or are committed to the stabilization of the cultural status quo. However, the most vociferous voices regarding the ways in which the dominant culture should remain are coming from those of the religious right. Apple is very helpful in explicating this notion of the conservative right's blatantly clear position. He notes:

> My own interest is grounded in a similar politics; but I want to explore how organic connections are now made between people's daily lives and *conservative* (italics, author's) religious movements, since these are the ones increasingly dominant today and these are the ones that seem to be exceptionally powerful in polarizing our beliefs about schooling currently (p. 28).

What Apple argues is that many conservative religious spokespersons articulate a growing belief that only through a commitment to a market economy as well as a return to an "Edenic" past will our schools, children, the community, and indeed the nation be "saved."

Along with this is a rising need for those from conservative religious circles to serve as gatekeepers and the monitors of how society is either promoting or lessening the power of hegemonic rituals and practices. Religion is taking on a surveillance function much like what Foucault (1984 as cited by Rabinow) offers in his treatise on the panopticon or hierarchical surveillance. The conservative religious devotees are attempting to serve as the police of the prevailing cultural mores that often marginalize and disenfranchise those who are outside of their realm of acceptance and approval. Foucault offers:

> Discipline fixes; it arrests or regulates movements; it clears up confusion; it dissipates compact groupings of individuals wandering about the country in unpredictable ways; it establishes calculated distributions ... it must neutralize the effects of counterpower that spring from them and which form a resistance to the power that wishes to domi-

nate it; agitations, revolts, spontaneous organizations, coalitions-anything that may establish horizontal conjunctions. (pp. 208–209)

If we correctly locate the conservative religious right as a discipline, in the way Foucault defines a discipline, that is, as a vehicle for establishing parameters and boundaries on acceptable thinking and behavior along with sanctions for disobedience and resistance to the established religious hegemony, then we can see how the agenda established by this group of fundamentalists is purposed to fix, regulate, and order human multiplicities. Dantley (2005b) offers a decidedly different perspective where religion and especially Christianity is concerned. Being a pastor of a Christian church as well as a scholar in educational leadership, he couches his deconstruction of the traditional Christian dogma and behavior from deeply personal experiences. He says:

> Spirituality grounded in a progressive interpretation of the Christian faith is one that motivates the believer to bring about radical change in society and culture. For many, spirituality linked with a traditional religious expression, emphasizes docility and acquiescence to the structures and rituals of the dominant society. It is claimed by some that Christian spirituality is best demonstrated by compliance with the status quo and blind acceptance of the authority stemming from established cultural institutions. (p. 130)

Dantley's position regarding a progressive interpretation of the Christian discourse is in sync with West's (1999) notions of prophetic Christianity. West writes about the synoptic vision of the prophetic Christian tradition. He offers that this synoptic vision, "speaks with insight and power to the multiform character of human existence and to the specificity of the historical modes of human existence. Its moral vision and ethical norms propel human intellectual activity to account for and transform existing forms of dogmatism, oppression and despair" (p. 371). This position is diametrically opposed to that which is assumed by the religious conservative right.

What conservative religious right proponents often miss is the radical and indeed revolutionary position Jesus espoused in his life and in his written message. He makes it very clear that his mission was to deconstruct the prevailing hegemony and to establish a new order, one that was egalitarian and dealt forthrightly with the inequities and injustices that were often perpetuated and celebrated by the religious establishment. What is obvious through the religious right discourse is a watering down of the radical, revolutionary nature of the message of Jesus. In fact, Dantley argues, "Political and social systems have watered down Christ's revolutionary message in order to create Christian religious institutions displaying strict obedience, an absence of critical reflection, and an acceptance of the status quo. In many ways, this perverted hermeneutic of Christ's teachings has informed the preservation of the hegemony" (p. 131).

Before leaving this obvious dichotomy between the position of the religious right and that of a more progressive interpretation of the biblical canon, it is important to assert that spirituality is neither progressive nor conservative. Spirituality can be used to establish evil rituals as well as democratic and egalitarian ones. What is essential to any political positioning of one's spirituality is the vehicle through which the spirit is informed and nurtured. There is an epistemological grounding that informs how the spirit motivates or activates our ways of perceiving and thinking, our behavior, and even professional practices (Hafner and Capper, 2005). When an educational leader's spirituality is grounded in a critical spirituality then the epistemological grounding for her way of behaving is founded on a critical, prophetically pragmatic way of perceiving and functioning. What this means for schools is exceptionally interesting. This means that the educational leader's motivation for connectivity with others, sense of purpose and mission, and perspectives on what is morally and ethically right are all based on notions of the undemocratic nature of asymmetrical relations of power and the interests that are being served through a commitment to a capitalist, market-driven ideology. Given that predisposition, leaders who subscribe to critical spirituality have a heightened sense of the various ways schools perpetuate in a denigrating way class differences as well as cultural distinctions (Dantley, 2005b, p. 137). What is also a part of these educators' thinking is the fact that schools not only perpetuate the exigencies of the prevailing class struggle but also engage the oppression suffered by others based on race, gender, sexual orientation, religion, and ability, as well as other markers of social and/or cultural distinction. In fact, educational leaders, who operate from a critically spiritual center, would facilitate schools where teachers are encouraged to create lessons that "address the immediate naming of oppressive situations, create through a critical imagination ways to rectify these marginalizing circumstances, while concomitantly addressing the more teleological and ontological issues surrounding why these debilitating conditions came to exist in the first place" (Dantley, 2005b, p. 137). School leaders who ground their professional practice in critical spirituality can embrace the creation of democratic schools through the use of Marable, West, and Guttman's notions of democracy and forge an alliance between these notions and their own predispositions to the use of critical spirituality.

Four Outcomes of Aligning Critical Spirituality
and Democratic Citizenship

Schools that see the marriage of critical spirituality and the notions of democracy will produce four specific outcomes. First, these schools will have students who are encouraged to achieve self-determination with the only caveat being that the self-determination is embraced within the context of community. Second, these schools will be sites where students are engaged in active commitments to social justice and diversity. Third, students will have the freedom to confront and critique realities and to then imagine and construct new ones. Fourth, these schools will be safe places for students to understand the rights and responsibilities of their personal citizenship. Let us see how each of these is produced from the intersection of critical spirituality and notions of democracy.

Self-determination is a highly spiritual endeavor. It demands that serious critical self-reflection takes place. What must happen in schools where self-determination is emphasized is that the entire school becomes a place where students are challenged to examine themselves, their motivations, their predispositions, prejudices, ways of thinking, and other core issues that define them. Critical self-reflection applauds the unraveling or the revelation of the genuine self with its multiple facets and nuances. Deep, critical reflection asks students and those who are working with them to analyze their positions on issues of race, class, gender, and other markers of distinction and to seriously consider from where these notions have emanated. Self-determination in the context of democracy is impossible without seriously considering the host of others who are in the community. Essentially, self-determination is not a celebration of hedonism or Epicureanism but rather the self is constructed within the context of others. What becomes right for the self is always determined by its effects on the lives of others. Rawls (1999) offers some assistance in understanding this communitarian context and the exploration of what is individually right or the crux of one's self-determination. He says:

> The many associations of varying sizes and aims, being adjusted to one another by the public conception of justice, simplify decision by offering definite ideals and forms of life that have been developed and tested by innumerable individuals, sometimes for generations. Thus in drawing up our plan of life we do not start de novo; we are not required to choose from countless possibilities without given structure or fixed contours. So while there is no algorithm for settling upon our good, no first-person procedure of choice, the priority of right and justice securely constrains these deliberations so that they become more manageable. Since the basic rights and liberties are already

firmly established, our choices cannot distort our claims upon one another (pp. 493–494).

Critical self-reflection is one of the components of critical spirituality and clearly positions one's pursuit of personal determination through a democratic or communitarian context. Dantley (2005c) argues:

> A psychology of critical self-reflection involves the educational leader coming to grips with his or her own identity and juxtaposing that against the identity of the learning community. That is, the school leader comes to understand who he or she is first personally and then in a social context. This entails leaders' grappling with issues such as their personal predisposition and belief systems on matters of race, class, and gender and their individual sources of motivation and purpose as well as their coming to grips with the social construction of their individual identities (p. 503).

Given this definition of critical self-reflection, when a school leader facilitates an environment that emphasizes the ability of students to engage in a process of self-determination, then the atmosphere of the school must be established where the students fully understand that their individual ability to enhance themselves is never at the expense of someone else. One of the markers of critical self-reflection is the understanding that no one is an isolate. We are all connected to one another in some fashion and therefore we become responsible and accountable to one another even if we are pursuing what we have determined to be the good for us as an individual. Concomitantly, critical self-reflection demands that the individual, while pursuing self-determination, clearly engages in a process that neither demeans nor dehumanizes others in her/his pursuit. In fact, part of the process of self-determination includes unmasking those rituals and procedures that deliberately marginalize and disenfranchise others in order to personally gain or profit. So when a school leader embraces critical spirituality and marries it with establishing a democratic school, then the whole notion of individuals having the freedom and the right to pursue their own destiny and establish their own path in society is only confined to taking into account their accountability to others. This accountability is characterized as individuals pursuing their own self-determination in a democratic context that liberates others along with themselves from inequitable and discriminatory practices but also frees these same individuals to seek what is the good and perfect will for themselves.

There is one other facet of critical spirituality that intersects with the democratic notion of self-determination, that is, performative creativity. Dantley (2005c) defines this component of critical spirituality in this way:

> Performative creativity takes reflection and interpretation beyond introspection into action. It is in the process of performative creativity that educational leaders develop strategies designed to use the information gleaned through critical self reflection and deconstructive interpretation, laced in hope, to craft the transformative practices to bring about reform in the schoolhouse. (p. 513)

The conjoining of performative creativity with democracy takes these notions out of the realm of merely being musings and ideas into strategic action. What this implies is that the school that embraces self-determination as a clear demonstration of democracy will encourage students to pursue these notions of self-identity and self-discovery in a communitarian context but will also encourage these same students to actualize or to operationalize their thinking and reflecting. So the school then becomes a site of activism. The intellectual work of the students in schools that are guided by leaders who subscribe to the combination of critical spirituality and democracy is tied to their personal sense of identity and purpose, their teleology as well as their ontology along with their clear understanding of their accountability to others and then to a strategic plan of implementing what they have envisioned. This is an exciting prospect, for the school actually becomes the breeding ground where creativity and imagination flourish. But these two are nurtured and find a safe space to exist within a context of community and democracy. So, students are encouraged to dream. They are encouraged to envision themselves as change agents or as contributors to society but must also envision themselves as the preservers of democracy while in the process of attaining their self-determined paths and ideals.

Another result of schools aligning critical spirituality with democracy is that these schools can become active sites where diversity and social justice are predominant. Because critical spirituality demands the deep, introspective grappling with all forms of marginalization, schools that operate from this focus cannot help but deconstruct the various ways that the school and those who operate in it perpetuate, either knowingly or unwittingly, the hegemonic rituals and practices that regularly disenfranchise those who are outside of the cultural mainstream. One of the intriguing aspects of schools becoming democratic spaces through the use of critical spirituality is that the academic labor of the teachers and students is contextualized in an activist persuasion. Issues of race, class, gender, sexual orientation, ability, age, and religion are not hidden but become the fodder for study, discussion, and intense investigation. Essentially, the school becomes the place where students find themselves working to ensure their own liberty while concomitantly pursuing intellectual and academic endeavors. In effect, the two become so intertwined that it is difficult to see the difference. These schools will have faculties that clearly mimic the racial and ethnic make up of the student body. But those kinds of physical characteristics are not enough. Teachers and administrators who operate in these schools will have demonstrated a commitment to activism where social justice is concerned as well as a dedication to aligning intellectual work with social justice praxis. Scheurich and Skrla (2003) argue, "but the type of classroom change that has to happen in order for children who have not been well served in the past to have culturally respectful classroom experiences depends for its success on changing teachers' awareness of their own, most often hidden and unexamined beliefs about the children they teach" (p. 49). From this self-examination and really coming to grips with the ways in which they have been socialized, teachers in these democratic schools will couch their pedagogical practices in a critical theoretical perspective that not only deconstructs the performances and rituals of schools and society that perpetuate asymmetrical relations of power but also investigates and strategizes ways to bring those debilitating practices to an end. So essentially, the school becomes another vehicle to mount civil rights activism designed to bring about the radical reconstruction of not only schools but the society that surrounds them. The school becomes an active site of social justice promotion as well as a living example of the celebration of cultural, ethnic, and racial difference. School leaders in these kinds of schools make decisions predicated on the extenuation of a diverse and socially just environment. For them the matter of what is morally right has everything to do with how a decision or some institutional ritual perpetuates the egalitarian treatment of all people regardless of background, physical characteristics, or cultural identity. Certainly, school leaders cannot make decisions on such premises if they have not come to deal with their own positions on the issues of race, class, gender, and other markers of distinction.

Finally, a school leadership couched in the notions of critical spirituality and democracy will facilitate a place where students and all those in the learning community will become critical citizens or active participants in the flourishing of democracy. These school leaders will have come to grips with what it means for them as well as others to be citizens in a democracy. They will be able to

clearly articulate the difference between consumerism and citizenship that
Wallis (1995) has so ably defined. Wallis says that citizenship has been replaced
by consumerism. It has become the collective activity and in fact, "consumerism
has invaded and even usurped our civic life" (p. 155). Wallis continues, "Political participation has waned dramatically, just as the rituals of consumption have
come to dominate more and more of our social life. Politics has become a
spectator sport, as sports have become totally subjected to the power of money
and advertising" (p. 155). Genuine citizenship involves the public discourse
over ideas and the creation of public policy. Citizenship in a democracy is much
more than casting a ballot. It is all about helping to determine who should
actually be on the ballot and whether their positions and platforms adequately
respond to the needs of the citizenry. Citizenship also involves interrogating
and critiquing policy, literally being cognizant of the issues and engaging in
public debate about these matters. Lakoff (1996) defines a liberal model of
citizens that fits admirably well with the marriage of critical spirituality and
democracy. To liberals, according to Lakoff, the model citizen is one that is
empathetic, helps the disadvantaged, protects those who need protection,
promotes and exemplifies fulfillment in life and takes care of himself so he can
do all of this. Lakoff continues:

> Model liberal citizens are those who live a socially responsible life: they include socially
> responsible professionals; environmental, consumer, and minority rights advocates;
> union organizers among impoverished and badly treated workers; doctors and social
> workers who devote their lives to helping the poor and the elderly; peace advocates,
> educators, artists, and those in the healing professions. (p. 173)

If democratic citizenship involves being able to confront both reality and
history, then schools must become those places where the concerns and issues
of contemporary times are not ignored and assumed to exist only outside the
walls of the schoolhouse. Neither can these contemporary issues be assumed to
have emanated outside of some historical context and grounding. Students must
be given the opportunity to confront and challenge the historical discourse that
marginalizes and excludes those who don't perpetuate the traditional American
historical grand narrative. Not only must citizens be allowed to confront such
historical untruths, but they must also have the opportunity to interject into the
historical discourse those parts of the narrative that have been selectively
excluded. Citizens in a democracy have voice and their voices must be legitimated and included in the cultural discourse. School leaders who combine

critical spirituality with the creation of democratic schools understand the more responsible and critical definition of citizenship and work to create an institutional atmosphere that welcomes a critical pedagogical, and dialogic methodology in the classroom.

References

Apple, M. W. (2001). *Educating the "right way": Markets, standards, God, and inequality.* New York: Routledge Falmer.

Dantley, M. E. (2003a). Purpose driven leadership: The spiritual imperative to guiding schools beyond high-stakes testing and minimum proficiency. *Education and Urban Society,* 35(3): 273–291.

————. (2003b). Critical spirituality: Enhancing transformative leadership through critical theory and African American prophetic spirituality. *International Journal of Leadership in Education: Theory and Practice,* 6(1): 3–18.

————. (2003c). Principled, pragmatic, and purposive leadership: Reimagining educational leadership through prophetic spirituality. *Journal of School Leadership,* 13: 181–198.

————. (2005a). African American spirituality and Cornel West's notions of prophetic pragmatism: Restructuring educational leadership in American urban schools. *Education Administration Quarterly,* XLI: 651–674.

————. (2005b). A Christian view of spirituality and educational leadership. In Shields, C. M., Edwards, M. M., and Sayani, A. (Eds.). (2005). *Inspiring practice: Spirituality and educational leadership.* Lancaster, PA: Proactive Publications; pp. 129–144.

————. (2005c). The power of critical spirituality to act and to reform. *Journal of School Leadership,* 15: 500–518.

Darling-Hammond, L. (1997). *The right to learn: A blueprint for creating schools that work.* San Francisco, CA: Jossey Bass Publishers.

Foster, W. (1986). *Paradigms and promises: New approaches to educational administration.* Buffalo, NY: Prometheus Books.

Freire, P. (1972). *Pedagogy of the oppressed.* New York: Herder and Herder.

Giroux, H. A. (1997). *Pedagogy and the politics of hope: Theory, culture, and schooling.* Boulder, CO: Westview Press.

Guttman, A. (1987). *Democratic education.* Princeton, NJ: Princeton University Press.

Hafner, M., and Capper, C. (2005). Defining spirituality: Critical implications for the practice and research of educational leadership. *Journal of School Leadership,*15: . 624–638.

Lakoff, G. (1996). *Moral politics: How liberals and conservatives think.* Chicago: University of Chicago Press.

Marable, M. (1996). *Speaking truth to power: Essays on race, resistance, and radicalism.* Boulder, CO: Westview Press.

Meier, D. (2002). *In schools we trust: Creating communities of learning in an era of testing and standardization.* Boston, MA: Beacon Press.

Oldenski, T., and Carlson, D. (Eds.) (2002). *Educational yearning: The journey of the spirit and democratic education*. New York: Peter Lang.

Rabinow, P. (Ed.) (1984). *The Foucault reader*. New York: Pantheon Books.

Rawls, J. (1999). *A theory of justice*. Cambridge: The Belknap Press of Harvard University Press.

Ross, W. D. (2002). The right and the good. In Cahn, S. M. and Markie, P. (Eds.), *Ethics: History, theory, and contemporary issues*. New York: Oxford University Press, pp. 477–486.

Scheurich, J. J., and Skrla, L. (2003). *Leadership for equity and excellence: Creating high-achievement classrooms, schools, and districts*. Thousand Oaks, CA: Corwin Press, Inc.

Shields, C. M. , Edwards, M. M., and Sayani, A. (Eds.) (2005). *Inspiring practice: Spirituality and educational leadership*. Lancaster, CA: Pro Active Publications.

Starratt, R. J. (2003). *Centering educational administration: Cultivating meaning, community, responsibility*. Mahwaw, NJ: Lawrence Erlbaum Associates.

Wallis, J. (1995). *The soul of politics: Beyond "religious right" and "secular left."* San Diego, CA: Harcourt Brace and Company.

West, C. (1999). *The Cornel West reader*. New York: Civitas Books.

———. (2004). *Democracy matters: Winning the fight against imperialism*. New York: Penguin Group.

8

Student Engagement and Academic Achievement: A Promising Connection

Joanne Chesley

Introduction

I hear and think. I see and I remember. I do and I know.
—Confucius

I have very fond memories of my days as a Home Economics teacher when teaching was joyful and stimulating, less restrictive, and child centered. Actually, I had never planned to teach Home Economics; for this was the era of expanding women's rights, and choosing this field in some way seemed like a seback, somehow settling for what my mother or grandmother might have been relegated to. So though I went on preparing myself for a career in textile science, my direction began to change during student teaching. I "adopted" a wonderful mentor (not my supervising teacher), who from day one, taught me the importance of helping young people find their own strengths, teaching them to have confidence in themselves, regardless of their life situations, and acknowledging the sky as the limit. I admired the way she "propped kids up," sort of boosting their personal esteem. Sometimes this was seen in a simple compliment, sometimes a request of a student (students have always felt special when selected to take something to the office for the teacher) and sometimes it was handing a student (who would least expect it) her car keys to get the food supplies for the day's nutrition lesson. I learned early in my career to create growth opportunities for children who often are not afforded these same experiences at home; children whose parents struggle to discover their own personal identity, social capacity, and realized potential, much less trying to help their children with these tasks.. We took students to restaurants, teaching them appropriate etiquette. We escorted them on field trips to see how garments are produced, food products packaged, and fibers are extruded into yarn. We wanted them to understand their world—the clothes they wear, the foods they eat, and the many "tourist" attractions in their own city. We produced fabulous fashion shows with lights, local news cameras and action set to "Axel F" and other music selected by the students. The young men and women made the garments they modeled. They directed the make-up and dressing rooms, sold the tickets, built the stage set, helped to write the script for the moderator, and hosted the after-party for their teachers, parents, and friends. I saw these kids blossom; kids who had never taken charge of anything at school (many have leadership experiences at church, where their teachers and peers do not get a chance to witness this talent). I saw huge smiles as they styled down the runway showing off the garments they had made (some they even designed) for an auditorium full of people from the school community. Some children never see their names on printed programs and never hear their names called out to receive applause. I saw young Black males (you could say, "discards" from other teachers' classrooms) develop pride in their work, and pride in themselves. We worked steadfastly to insure that these children could tell their children one day, stories of memorable, positive, life-altering school experiences. We believed this would make the difference for so many. We knew that any of these children, though from low income homes (most of them) could achieve whatever goals they would set for themselves, as long as someone cared enough to help them develop something of their own and a strong sense of purpose.

My students made and sold knock-off Cabbage Patch dolls, experimented with diverse cultures' foods, and hosted an international food tasting for their favorite teachers. They participated in outdoor education. They learned the importance of working on a team. The outdoor experience stressed the importance of regular attendance, punctuality, preparedness, and character development. They learned the importance of being there not just for their own development but that others now depended on them. Teachers began to notice the difference. Students who were once shy and retreating were becoming more socially competent and more confident. The students' so-called risk factors became less a point of discussion for them and for school administrators, who began to look at the students' participation, their engagement, and their newly developed sense of purpose for coming to school, rather than seeing them through the deficit lenses they had always used.

New Populations Mean New Connections

Interpersonal connections are very important for people of all ages. Students need to feel and be connected to their schools through activities, friendships, and stories of success. As a matter of fact, they need to know that their very presence there has something to do with the success of the whole place. When this is not felt, student alienation can and will occur.

As schools have become more diverse, student alienation has increased dramatically, which may also imply that students are a lot less resilient than they once were in their schools. This appears to be so, because of the models that most schools buy into, those being the Cultural Difference and the Teacher Expectation models (Au, 1980; Villegas, 1991). These models assert that culture serves as a predictor of a child's success in school. They further claim that a child's success depends on his or her ability to balance or compromise familiar cultural patterns with new and uncomfortable cultural patterns. These models assume that a parent's lot in life will give a good indication of the child's potential for success. They posit that the more the student is like his or her teacher, the greater the chance for high achievement, since there is less discontinuity in experiences and resources, and fewer problems with culture transfer. For many students of color, most of whom are poor, success therefore, according to such a construct, will be contingent on their ability and willingness to accept values of the majority population which controls the curriculum and the operant rules for success. For far too many children of color, having to make choices such as this, leads to inner conflict, anger, withdrawal, and alienation—and any one of these can lead to school dropout.

Our promise to children, when we appealed to Thurgood Marshall in the 50s marched for freedom in the 60s, and escorted them to "white schools" in the 70s was to provide the best opportunity for an excellent education. Fifty years after the momentous Supreme Court decision however, students of color still report feelings of alienation in desegregated schools that were formerly white (Lyons and Chesley, 2004). Very little attention has ever been paid to this topic, and in turn, we have seen record numbers of students dropping out of school over the last fifty years—the period in which we aspired to a more equitable and free education for all.

Alienation: Condition and Causes

Alienation is a term used in research to describe the condition of being separated from society, fragmented, or discontinuous. Some studies suggest that the alienated person is to blame for his own condition, contending that he is not very assertive or outgoing, gets left out of a lot of activities in which his contemporaries participate, and displays little initiative. Eventually he goes into a shell and grows to be more and more a recluse and becomes angry, aggressive, and uneasy to be around. Whatever the case, an alienated person is often considered socially incompetent (Cairns et al., 1988, 1994; Carter, 1998; Luther, 1991; Ryan and Grolnick, 1986). This view however seems to place all of the blame on the affected person, rather than on the environment within which that person attempts to function.

Other studies have tried to explain alienation through cultural difference theory (Claerbaut, 1978; Davis et al., 1970; Eisenhart, 1989; Fisher, 1981; Fordham and Ogbu, 1986) suggesting that it is not so much about personality traits as described above, as it is the kind of social and cultural exposure to which a person has had access, and that there are differences in these pieces of social capital, along ethnic and gender lines.

Fromm (1941, 1995) hailed as one of the pioneers in this research, would tell us, however, that both views are shortsighted and in many ways inaccurate. His work analyzes organizational structures that force people to conform, silence them, and thereby achieve a superficial sort of harmony and efficiency. Fromm says that we are surrounded by an "atmosphere of subtle suggestion which actually pervades our whole social life...one never suspects that there is any order which one is expected to follow" (Fromm, 1941, p. 190). While this automaton conformity is occurring, the individual suffers; he is not free to express thoughts, act on his own creative agenda, or just be who he really is. The person who is timid, less resilient, or lacks self confidence, begins to conform to the organization, with every opportunity he gives up, where he could have used his own critical thinking and innovation. Fromm's work finds that when this condition reaches a certain point, the individual finds it best to alienate himself from the mainstream. In doing so, he begins to believe that he has no role there, no power, and that little about the organization has meaning for him. For the most part, he would rather be away from those who seem to be thriving there. He actually entertains thoughts at times of destruction, not caring any longer about the place or the way he is perceived by others there. Fromm says, "the individual ceases to be himself; he adopts entirely the kind of personality offered to him by cultural patterns and he...becomes exactly as all others are and as they expect him to be" (pp. 208–209). Here we see the five aspects of alienation that Seeman (1959), studied some twenty years later: Powerlessness, meaninglessness, normlessness, isolation, and self-estrangement. Alienation can be characterized by any one or any combination of these aspects. A brief explanation of each follows.

1. Powerlessness is the self-expectancy that one's own behavior cannot determine outcomes.
2. Meaninglessness is the individual's inability to understand the events happening around him, even those in which he is engaged.
3. Normlessness refers to a person's belief that ignoring the rules and codes of social conduct will get him some reward. Generally such thinking occurs when the struggle to meet goals has been constantly thwarted by those in authority, leaving the person to feel defeated. The term also applies to the state of the larger environment, where the collective standard is weakened when people find they are not able to attain the prescribed goals.
4. Isolation is a personal decision to become detached from the organization or group.
5. Self-estrangement refers to a feeling that the circumstances of society are negatively impacting one's own worth. He is not sure where to place the blame and feels unable to plan and make decisions because of his present state of confusion.

Ring the bells that still can ring
Forget your perfect offering
There is a crack in everything
That's how the light gets in
　　　　—Leonard Cohen

Student Alienation: Its Vicious, Spiraling Effects

Students are alienated in schools for the same reasons people are alienated in society. Cities, organizations, and schools spend enormous number of hours and dollars transforming people and places, creating things shiny and new, often with no consideration for the disenfranchised. How do these reforms address the needs of the least connected and least advantaged? How will the decisions being made improve the lives of the poor, the forgotten, the lonely, the ignored, the addicts, and the abandoned? Where is the justice?

While alienation certainly has its roots in dysfunctional comformity-driven organizational structures (Fromm, 1941) that strangle the life from its members, alienation is also a residual effect of harsh social complexities—drugs and guns, welfare mentality, health issues, low income, poor self esteem, low expectancy by others, premature parenting, despair, high unemployment, lack of support for dreams, negative ethnic identity, unidentified or unclear lifegoals, lack of involvement in wholesome activities, victimization, and discrimination—to name the more common factors (Cairns, 1988; Cairns and Cairns, 1994; Carter, 1998). We know the data. We know that while students of color make up only 34 percent of the adolescent population, they comprise 67 percent of the juvenile detention population. We know that Black youth are 9 times more likely to be incarcerated than White youth for violent offenses, and 48 times more likely to be incarcerated than White youth for drug related offenses. We know that 20 percent of Black males between 18 and 26 are currently in prison (Children's Defense Fund, 2004). We just don't always translate these compelling statistics and extend the discussion beyond what's on the surface in order to better understand what it all means.

Let's take a look at how this insidious phenomenon that exists in our schools plays itself out for one segment of the population—Black males. Many teachers don't understand that the Black males sitting before them are an endangered (not dangerous) population, and that on any given day, at any hour outside of the school day, by virtue of racial profiling (which is rampant), this Black male student can be approached by a law officer and accused of a crime—"just because!" For those Black males who are less school-engaged and less culturally connected, this means that they must fight to survive. And so they develop that tough exterior to protect themselves, a kind of resilience (though not a constructive form), and in so doing, are labeled belligerent, which seems to give permission to some people in authority to ostracize, criticize, and even demonize these students. A correct response then, on the part of the Black males enduring this discrimination, is to increase their resistance which is demonstrated in their code language, head and hand gestures, clothing, haircuts, music choices, disrespect toward others, drug use and other evidences of self-destructive behavior. All of this now serves only to heighten the level of fear experienced by their teachers, especially many middle-class white teachers. It also engenders alienation by the teacher. The widespread "infection" caused by this single sociocultural dilemma is phenomenal. The effects are realized across the entire school population and climate, causing almost total alienation of these students and others who happen to look like them. In fact the effects are extended to the communities and the world at large, via popular media outlets and political spokespersons. But right here at school, there are rippling effects of a negative sort. A young, "intelligent" Black woman, thinking about her future, looks at these guys and gives up the dream of a nuclear family—a family like the one in "My Wife and Kids," or "The Cosbys." She is actually embarrassed by their behavior and often "disses" her "brothas" to express her disappointment and her own "do it for myself" sense of confidence. Often in the integrated school, she considers that there are few Black guys "her equal." The "intelligent" Black male suffers too. He now is alienated by his own brothers who have labeled him a "nerd" or "oreo" or some other insulting term to suggest "selling-out," the term that suggests that being smart is "actin' white." Black males from middle class, formally educated homes have a mission—to emulate the success they see in their own parents. Their goal is not to show up brothers who have not had the benefit of parental modeling. But, that's not all. Even white girls have a role in this play, often using their "white female privilege" to make a play for the very guys that Black girls don't want to date, but still don't want White girls to date either. In the mind of the Black female, it is like they (white girls) are "tasting the forbidden fruit" and then spitting it out, just to say they've had a taste. The divisive force of alienation continues as we see Black girls develop animosity toward their white female peers, suggesting that they are *using* Black men and *being* used by them. This Black male, often a self-proclaimed "thug" may relish this attention from white females in this integrated setting where he is not accepted on other levels. He is not viewed as intelligent because the crotch of his pants is at his knees; he is feared because his "brothas" on TV who look like him are dangerous, and he is not likely to be invited to represent the school at any functions because ... well... just because.

By no means are Black students the only victims of school alienation. Alienation is not always talked about by the people who are most affected or by anyone for that matter. It is not always met head on, as in the case of the so-called belligerent Black male. For many, it is one of those silent killers—killing enthusiasm and the will to press on, in an environment of hostility and invisibility. Alienation is the condition of the invisible—and there are a lot of invisible kids in our schools.

It is very interesting to note the difference in the ways students perceive their social circles and settings, by virtue of their own selves—their own identities. As I recall, from my days as an assistant principal in a high school, students use terms such as dweebs, dorks, wannabes, gothics, smart people, soccer girls, country, thugs, Mexicans, Black kids, and White kids to describe each other. Interestingly though, the kids who are not seen as popular or smart, will be sure to include those groups—the popular and the smart, in their list or discussion. On the other hand, the popular and smart don't even bother to list people much outside of their own realm of friendship and status. It is as if the "others" do not exist. The smart and popular don't see a need to figure them into their world—what can they possibly learn from them or gain socially from them?

One of the ways I observed these chasms forming in the high school was through the segregation of students who needed "special" classes. These special classes included language for non-native English speakers, competency math for those who did not score high enough on the state exam, various cross categorical EC classes for students who just didn't quite perform at the "norm," academically or socially. There were Honors and Advanced Placement classes for the smart kids—classes that were generally 95 percent White, in a school where Black students made up 28 percent of the population and Latino and Asian students made up another 6 percent. "Other" classes included chorus, theatre, and orchestra, where the curriculum in these courses was often not reflective of anyone's culture but that of children from European descent. I recall Black students choosing the Gospel choir if such was available (and often it was available just so the "other" choir did not have to venture into Black music), where they would relate to pieces like, "O Happy Day." This was preferred to choosing Chorus, where they sang songs such as "All Through the Night" and "On a Clear Day." While the latter songs are perfectly good selections for anyone to learn, we might take heed to Tatum (1997) who says young people need to share experiences with their own, to explore the issues of ethnicity, and exclusion, and oppression with each other. They need to know if they are alone in this, or if this is the way of the world. So sometimes the "traditional" choices made by students of color reflect their need to find identity and share identity with those most like them by virtue of ancestry. And with regard to alienation in schools, yes, it does present a bit of contradiction for some.

I have discussed only a few examples of alienation that begin in our schools and transfer to the larger society, creating societal dilemmas that seem to only spiral back to the lives of our children, and the stability of family life. Perhaps equally as alienating in schools today are the issues of sexual preference and orientation. I am less able to discuss this from a first hand view, for when I served as a school administrator, teachers and students were still not free to be who they were, or say what they believed about sexuality if it was outside of the heterosexual norm. I and others could only speculate that certain teachers and students (thought to be gay or lesbian), whose friendships were few, and demeanors retreating, must have felt a bit alienated.

Other children affected include children from Mexico, Haiti, Ethiopia, Vietnam, Iran, and hundreds of other countries where political relationships with the United States result in their inferior status here in this country, and in our schools. Others affected by alienation are those in special education classes, competency level classes, children who are overweight, children who are not viewed as physically attractive, newcomers who are considered "country" or those who are just not popular because they are odd or awkward. Children in these categories make up a large number of the dropout statistics each year.

Our promise to reduce dropout must then see us engaged in the transformation of hearts and minds. School leaders must work to create environments where kids feel accepted and liked by others. We must also work to inspire a deeper sense of care, respect, and love in our teachers and staffs. These are the people that students encounter on a regular basis. They make the difference by the words they say to students, the forgiveness they extend, and the social and cultural understanding around which their work is framed.

It matters not how strait the gate,
How charged with punishment the scroll,
I am the master of my fate;
I am the captain of my soul.
> —William Ernest Henley

Social Engagement and Feelings of Acceptance

I have been interested in this topic of school engagement for a while now. My work as a school principal helped me to choose this as the focus of my dissertation (Carter, 1998). In short, what I learned from that research was this: The students who dropped out were the least connected in their schools. For them school activities would have provided a necessary support system, a vehicle for affiliation. There were two groups, each mirroring the other on usual demographic parameters (age, SES, GPA). Among the group that eventually dropped out, participation in extracurricular activities was at 29 percent, and that 29 percent participated in only one activity during the time in high school. Among those who remained in school and graduated, despite the same low academic averages, the same aggression assessment scores, the same economic status, the extracurricular participation rate for them was 84 percent, and this group (average) participated in two or more school clubs, activities, or sports during the four years in high school (or five years for repeaters).

Too many educators fail to consider the connection between the social and the academic. All too often the impact of the school's climate, the demeanor of the teachers, and the attitude of the community toward the students are ignored, resulting in achievement lags, disenfranchisement, and worst yet—school dropout. Some of this understanding that once was there for Black children (who make up the largest percentage of students experiencing school failure in the United States) was lost with the integration of schools. Black teachers in Black schools encouraged students to join a club, sign up for a sport, or compete in a math competition. They expected them to be well rounded. The principal expected them to attend student functions. The teachers knew the community; they knew the parents. They found it easy to comfort and provide assurance to a student who was new to the school or one who was just shy. That teacher took it upon herself or himself to help that student to blossom, and this was done through the social and the academic. The landmark *Brown v. Board of Education* decision, though not intentionally, resulted in several negative impacts for Black children—all having to do with their sense of affiliation and pride in the schools in which they would end up. Very few white students were asked to move to a Black school—to make a huge cultural adjustment. Those that did, were generally "experiments"—a small number of volunteers, whose parents agreed to let them model "the right thing to do" for other white citizens. Black students however, lost the benefit of 38,000 Black teachers who were not only teachers to these students, but surrogate parents, counselors, disciplinarians, and advocates for these children (Lyons and Chesley, 2004). White teachers, all too often were unprepared to serve in any of these roles for children of color. In addition to being ill-prepared, many were also resistant to teaching Black children, who were in the class by court order, but were never addressed, assisted, or taught. Integration has surely proven itself for most of the reasons it was initially designed to do. Some scholars (Davidson, 1996; Pollard, 2002; Tatum, 1997) however, have questioned whether the socialization factor, or lack thereof, has taken its toll on the success of many Black students. They argue that school is the main arena where students learn the meaning of a society's social categories such as race, multiracial families, ethnicity, and social economic status in order to understand and construct their own personal identities. They assert that students cannot be adequately educated without being taught these concepts and given opportunities to discuss these in the formal setting of a classroom. We know that this is not done in America's classrooms, especially since the onset of one of the most conservative administrations and narrow-minded judicial climates in our history.

The climate of a school, particularly as it impacts the success of students of color is also affected by a number of other factors, including disproportionately higher numbers of disciplinary actions, harsher disciplinary actions, low teacher expectations, tracking into low level classes which leads to inadequate college preparation, stereotyped views by teachers, inappropriate placement of Black students in special education classes, unfamiliarity with learning styles, and teachers' lack of education and disinterest in the multifaceted history, values, and traditions of Black people.

School Engagement and Black Students

In our investigation (Lyons and Chesley, 2004), Jim Lyons (my mentor and friend) and I talked with thirty-six current and recently retired African American high school principals in North Carolina and Alabama to find out if they perceived the climate of integrated schools to be conducive to Black student success. One of the specific interests we had was that of Black student engagement as an indicator of true integration and student attitudes of acceptance. They were asked the following questions:

1. Do you believe that African American students generally have full and equal opportunities to serve in high school leadership roles today?
2. Do you believe that African American students normally will seek student leadership positions in integrated high schools?
3. In which student organizations or clubs do African American students tend to seek leadership roles?
4. In which student organizations or clubs are African American students most likely to participate?
5. In which student organizations or clubs are African American students least likely to participate?
6. Do African American students have an equal opportunity to be selected for cheerleading squads where the criteria for selection is likely to be subjective (size, beauty, charm, agility) versus objective (knowledge of school, smart, great voice, ability to learn and teach routines, punctual, regular attendance, previous athletic experience).

The principals' responses reflect their actual student membership in clubs and organizations—approximately 325 students per each of 36 schools (Lyons and Chesley, 2004). The study found that African American students are underrepresented in terms of participation in school organization and activities. The opportunities for participation included Honor Society, Beta Club, student government, subject-related clubs, vocational organizations, Junior ROTC, service clubs, debate teams, yearbook, school paper, band, choral group, baseball, football, basketball, golf, tennis, soccer, track and field team, and cheerleading squad. African American students participated to a high degree (meaning 60 percent or more) or very high degree (80 percent or more) in only three of these "traditional" venues for school participation. These include band, basketball, and football. However, these students also participated at high levels in organizations that are of specific interest to them, including the student NAACP, Black History Month Club, Gospel Choir, and others along these lines (Lyons and Chesley, 2004). These findings on African American school participation are consistent with previous findings by Clotfelter (2002).

Reasons for African American Student Choices Regarding School Engagement: A Recent Study

Why do African American students tend to select the same small number of clubs and activities in most integrated high schools? You may recall that earlier I attributed some of this to the premise posited by Dr. Tatum (1997)—that of ethnic identity. In this research that we did with the principals and students, looking at the effects of *Brown* fifty years later, the students told their principals some of the reasons for their choices, and all of the reasons are related to the issue of student alienation. They say they are "reluctant to even join organizations that do not have other African Americans, for fear of being ostracized by friends." Clotfelter (2002) says this is also true for White students considering majority African American organizations. The students also say that they have a disadvantage in gaining admission to honor societies where the criteria are a combination of academic achievement, character, and attitude. They believe that teachers often make it difficult for them and even refuse to sponsor them, weighing in subjective considerations such as "bad attitude" or "too outspoken." Thus, due to differences in culture, values, manners, behavior, and communication patterns, a student who meets the academic requirement can be kept out because of the presumable "character flaws."

The most troubling of all extra-curricular organizations or clubs in integrated schools since school integration began in the south is cheerleading (Lyons and Chesley, 2004). We found that only one-third of the schools represented by the principals had integrated cheerleading squads. The other twenty-four had either an all-Black squad or an all-White squad. This is also disturbing since our schools are no longer just Black and White. Why are the other students of color not represented? Principals reported that this activity is not always about skill and that the decisions are always "political, emotional, subjective, and cumbersome" (Lyons and Chesley, p. 309). I learned too, that other reasons for non-participation by African American girls include economics. Many report not being able to afford the attire, the trips, the training camps, and even see requiring some of these as a way of keeping them out. Principals added that sometimes the expectation on the part of the parent cheerleading booster clubs is that the girls live in the same community to establish camaraderie to make it convenient to share rides to practice. The principals have also observed that parent leaders, when serving as judges for "try-outs" often use very narrow cultural references as guidelines for expectations—references that reflect their own physical orientation and preferences—references that omit and even denigrate the beauty associated with African American or Haitian or Latino or females, and as a result, these girls never get their opportunity. This obviously suggests that principals must be more involved in the dismantling of socially unjust traditions. While the promise of *Brown* has not come to full fruition in any of the arenas of education, it may be *better* realized in the academic arena than in the social arena. We could argue that this is acceptable, that if one had to be neglected, it should be the latter. We should never, though, negate the importance of the social setting where learning takes place. At the same time, we might keep in mind what Tatum tells us—that every now and then, what seems to be separation or alienation (on face value) is really a purposeful, liberatory experience that affirms self-identity and ethnic identity. "All of the Black children sitting together in the cafeteria" should not necessarily imply that the student body is separatist, but that the Black children, or any other self-selected group of students, have chosen to pull away from the whole group in an effort to think, share, process, empathize, and criticize in a safe space.

What We Can Do to Increase Student Engagement in Schools

Administrators have the power to turn the school on its head, to totally upset the applecart when necessary. Sure we teach our prospective principals to involve others in decisions and to seek consensus when possible. But you know, there are times when you just have to do the right thing, and sometimes you don't have forever. Forever would mean ignoring the lives of children who need an opportunity now. Forever would mean denying students their right to learn and experience success now. Sometimes the principal has to be the principal, and say "We will no longer do business that way." She has to be able to look at her coaches and club advisors and say, "The tryout policies here are unjust and we will not abide by them any longer." She has to say to the yearbook advisor, "Awarding grades on the basis of ad sales is discriminatory, when many of our students do not have those connections in the community yet." The principal must attend cheerleading tryouts. She must read and analyze the policies and procedures and call for changes as she sees fit, to ensure a more socially just process. She should be sure that the cheerleading selection committee and the parent booster club are representative of the school with respect to ethnicity. She must ensure that gender and sexual orientation are not barriers to a student's involvement in school activities. Principals absolutely must stick their noses in other people's business. Schools, for too long, have allowed departments, clubs, and sports to establish their own expectations, with no regard for a total school ethos about justice and equal opportunity. Principals must, with faculty and community, establish that ethos, and must model and uphold it in every curricular and co-curricular activity. The principal must teach teachers to model and uphold this ethos of justice and equal opportunity. She must look for examples of it when observing the teacher's class. She must look for examples of it when attending school football games, deciding on student recognitions, and reviewing the disciplinary referrals for the week.

The principal must have this on her mind and in her heart, with every school walk through, consistently assessing the quality of access in the school—the degree to which the school and all of its programs and activities are inviting to each and every child.

The principal must talk with the students to determine how they feel about the school, its social climate and perception of receptivity. Principals should encourage students to be honest in their comments about the school's social life. This information should be shared with faculty and decisions should be made to address areas of weakness. Principals should also encourage, rather, they should personally invite those students who are not involved in the activities of the school, to get involved. Perhaps no one has ever invited that child. Principals, at times, need to ask central office for assistance. This assistance could be financial, where funds are needed to support expanded student involvement. The assistance might also be in the human relations realm, where teachers or students are taught skills for improving relationships with people whom they see as different. Yes, this is a mammoth task, added to the formal curriculum responsibilities held by school administrators. The reality is, though, that paying due diligence to these school climate issues actually makes the job of boosting student achievement easier.

Students who love their schools, who are full of school spirit, who hold positions and feel a sense of power and significance there, just do better! They have a reason for being. There is meaning to the work. They feel accepted and supported, and that's contagious! School environments that promote student involvement foster resilient students—students who learn to get past the bad times, students who learn to deal with tough, narrow-minded people, and students who set goals for themselves because they have come to understand their own abilities and possibilities.

Summary: Our Promise

Students want their school experiences to be rich and rewarding, to be productive and engaging, the way many of us remember or wished for. Our promise to children should be just that—to give them schools where they are fully accepted, where they are invited to participate, and supported in their contributions. Our promise to children should be that school is the place children learn to reach outside of their perceived limitations to realize the greatness God had in store for them upon birth, and that we—the adults, the professionals, will not stand in the way of that realization, but do all we can to help each child fulfill their innermost dreams.

References

Au, K. H. (1980). Participation structures in a reading lesson with Hawaiian children: An analysis of a culturally appropriate instructional event. *Anthropology and Education Quarterly*, 11(2): 93–115.

Cairns, R. B., Cairns, B. D., Neckerman, H. J., Gest, S., and Gariepy, J. L. (1988). Social networks and aggressive behavior: Peer support or peer rejection? *Developmental Psychology*, 24: 815–823.

———(1994). *Lifelines and risks: Pathways of youth in our time*. London: Harvester Wheatshaft.

Carter, J. C. (1998). The relationship between at-risk students' resilience and dropout behavior. A dissertation presented to the University of North Carolina at Chapel Hill.

Children's Defense Fund. (2004). Retrieved December 11, 2005 from www.childrensdefense.org/education/juvemile/factsheet/boys/aspx.

Claerbaut, D. P. (1978). *Black student alienation: A study*. San Francisco, CA: R&E Research Associates, Inc.

Clotfelter, C. T. (2002). Interracial contact in high school extracurricular activities. *The Urban Review*, 34: 25–46.

Davidson, A. L. (1996). *Making and molding identities in schools: Student narratives on race, gender, and academic engagement*. Albany, NY: SUNY Press.

Davis, S. C., Loeb, J. W., and Robinson, L. F. (1970). A comparison of characteristics of Negro and White freshmen classmates. *Journal of Negro Education*, 39: 359–66.

Dean, D. G. (1961). Alienation: Its meaning and measurement. *American Sociological Review*, 26: 754–75.

Eisenhart, M., (1989). Reconsidering cultural differences in American schools. *Educational Foundations*, 3(2): 51–67.

Fisher, S. (1981). Race, class, anomie, and academic achievement: A study at the high school level. *Urban Education*, 16: 149–73.

Fordham, S., and Ogbu, J., (1986). Black students and school success: Coping with the burden of acting white. *Urban Review*, 18: 176–206.

Fromm, E. (1941). *Escape from freedom*. New York: Rinehart and Co.

———. (1995). *The fear of freedom*. New York: Routledge.

Heussenstamm, F. K., and Hoepfner, R. (1971). Black, white and brown adolescent alienation. Paper presented at annual meeting of National Council on Measurement in Education, New York.

Luther, S. (1991). Vulnerability and resilience: A study of high risk adolescents. *Child Development*, 62: 600–616.

Lyons, J., and Chesley, J. (2004). Fifty years after Brown: The benefits and tradeoffs for African American educators and students. *The Journal of Negro Education*, 73: 298–313.

Middleton, R. (1963). Alienation, race, and education. *American Sociological Review*, 8: 973–977.

Newmann, F. M. (1980). Organizational factors and student alienation in high school: Implications for theory for school improvement (Report No. NIE-G-79-0150). Washington, DC: National Institute of Education.

Orfield, G. (2001). *Diversity challenged*. Cambridge, MA: Harvard Educational Review.

Page, R. M., (1992). Feelings of physical unattractiveness and hopelessness among high school students. *The High School Journal*, 75(3): 150–55.

Pollard, D. S. (2002). Who will socialize African American students in contemporary public schools? In W.R. Allen, M.B. Spencer and C. O'Connor (Eds), *African American education: Race community inequality and achievement*. Kidlington, Oxford: Elsevier Science, pp. 3–21.

Ryan, R.M., and Grolnick, W. S. (1986). Origins and pawns in the classroom: Self-report and projective assessments of individual differences in children's perceptions. *Journal of Personality and Social Psychology*, 50: 550–558.

Seeman, M. (1959). On the meaning of alienation. *American Sociological Review*, 24: 783.

Tatum, B. (1997). *Why are all the Black kids sitting together in the cafeteria?* New York: Basic Books.

Villegas, A. (1991). *Culturally responsive teaching (The Praxis Series: Foundation for Tomorrow's Teachers, No.1).* Iowa City: Educational Testing Service.

Part Two

Narratives of Education Leadership

9

"Who's Afraid of the Big Bad Wolf?" Facing Identity Politics and Resistance When Teaching for Social Justice

Camille Wilson Cooper and Charles P. Gause

Faculty members who are committed to social justice in education must often confront student resistance in their classrooms. As social justice educators, we strive to co-create, along with students, democratic classrooms where each participant feels empowered to share their perspective, engage in constructive debate, and contribute to each other's learning. Social justice educators also work to encourage students to critique self, schools, and society. We scrutinize the prevalence of racist, sexist, classist, and homophobic practices in schools, and we also examine inequities related to ability and language. As part of our instructional practice, we push our students outside of their comfort zones with our instructional methods, materials, and assignments. We strive to inspire our students to think, speak and act critically while drawing upon courage, moral fortitude and political savvy (Bartolome, 1994; Cochran-Smith, 1997; Cooper, 2003; Darder, 1991; Ladson-Billings, 1994; Nieto, 1999; Oakes and Lipton, 1999).

Social justice educators also acknowledge the need for every class participant to feel valued and validated given their personal and professional backgrounds. Indeed, if students are asked to lead their school communities in a democratic way that engages and empowers all teachers, staff, students, and families, educational faculty members have the responsibility to do the same. Despite these democratic goals, fostering democratic classrooms is challenging when social justice educators are confronted with students who do not understand, resist, or blatantly counter social justice aims in education.

Our confrontations with sharp student resistance in our educational leadership program has led us to acknowledge that for better or worse, most classrooms are not pure and true democracies—faculty members have and use professorial authority (Knight and Pearl, 2000; Obidah, 2000). Thus, we must consider the influence of our authority as we promote open and inclusive learning.

In this chapter, the literature addressing democratic education, critical pedagogy, and race in higher education informs our analysis of the challenges we face as two young faculty members of color who mediate students' resistance to social justice teaching. We draw from our experience working in a graduate educational leadership program in a historically White Southern university. We explore the sources of conflict we have with our students, which pertain to three areas of divergence: our positionality, epistemology, and praxis. Brief vignettes are included to illustrate this discord and reveal opportunities for good teaching.

Self-examination of our teaching, our relationships with students, and our social location within the academy culminates in our discussing ways to advance democratic teaching in higher education. Specifically, we stress the need for social justice educators to use critical and liberatory pedagogies and engage in what we call *collaborative activism*. Doing so will help re(create) democratic learning communities for students preparing to be educational leaders. Finally, we consider the courage and commitment faculty members need in order to honor democratic education objectives, despite facing identity politics, student resistance, and the non-democratic norms of academia.

Social Justice and Democratic Education

Education has historically been a source of liberation for oppressed groups—the "great equalizer"; yet schools too often function as sites of social and economic inequality (Anderson, 1988; Giroux, 1988; Quantz, Rogers, and Dantley, 1991). Teaching for social justice attempts to confront this disturbing paradox and break entrenched and destructive cycles of social reproduction. We as social justice educators, therefore, regard teaching as a political, liberatory and transformative act—an act that is linked to educators' civic responsibility to foster democracy. Thus, social justice and democratic education go hand in hand.

Democratic education involves educators empowering students to engage in free and open discourse and offering consistent opportunities for students to engage in inquiry, reflection, critique, and ultimately, social transformation (Knight and Pearl, 2000; hooks, 2003; Nagda, Gurin, and Lopez, 2003). These practices align with critical and liberatory pedagogies that teach students to understand how matters pertaining to race, class, gender, language, ability, and/or sexual orientation influence social systems and one's power, authority, privilege, or oppression. Moreover, these pedagogies challenge students to question taken-for-granted cultural scripts and norms, and recognize that knowledge; values and traditions are socially constructed and culturally relevant (Banks, 1996; Lawrence, 1996; Nieto, 1999; Obidah, 2000).

Overall, critical and liberatory pedagogies blatantly counter notions of value-neutral education or standardized education (Lawrence, 1992). Moreover, since these approaches view education, and teaching, as political praxis, implementing them requires social justice educators to possess a "political and ideological clarity" (Bartolome and Trueba, 2000, p. 279; Cooper, 2003) that helps them maintain the commitment and courage needed to do this work.

Preparing Transformative Educational Leaders

Emphasizing social justice and democratic education is particularly salient to the preparation of educational leaders (Brown, 2004, 2005; Cambron-McCabe and McCarthy, 2005) since schools are institutions of social reproduction that reify anti-democratic structures and practices. Educational leaders are charged with guiding instruction; advancing student learning; supporting and enhancing the work of teachers; engaging families from increasingly diverse cultural, economic, and linguistic backgrounds; and managing building sites and budgets. This work, if done effectively, requires educational leaders to possess a range of organizational and interpersonal skills. It further requires them to develop productive relationships based on trust, understanding, and collaboration. Yet, for educational leaders to promote social transformation and build school communities that are anchored in democratic norms and structures, they must also view education through a critical lens that compels them to question the status quo, implement equitable school reform, and "transform present social relations" (Cambron-McCabe and McCarthy, 2005; Brown, 2004, 2005; Lawrence, 1995; Larson and Ovando, 2001; Quantz, Rogers, and Dantley, 1991, p. 103). As Brown (2005) states:

> If leadership is the enactment of values, the preparation programs must include approaches that enable preservice leaders to challenge their own assumptions, clarify and strengthen their own values, and work on aligning their own behaviors and practice with these beliefs, attitudes and philosophies. By exposing aspiring school leaders to information and ideas they may resist, leadership programs can assist students in stretching beyond their comfort zones to a deeper consciousness of equity. (p. 156)

This approach to leadership preparation aligns with the idea of encouraging students to embrace and embody "critical transformative leadership" (Quantz, Rogers, and Dantley, 1991, p. 98), which, like teaching, is a political practice. Critical transformative leadership constitutes viewing of schools, not only as sites of social reproduction, but also as sites of cultural and political resistance where leaders use their positional power to promote democracy and empower various stakeholders, including marginalized students and families. Through collaborative methods, leaders then develop inclusive governing structures and communities (Larson and Ovando, 2001; Lopez, 2003; Quantz, Rogers, Dantley, 1991).

Educators' Call to Action

Preparing critical transformative leaders in higher education starts with faculty members who are willing and able to draw upon critical, culturally relevant, and counter-normative pedagogies. Indeed hooks (2003) states:

> We need mass-based political movements calling citizens of this nation to uphold democracy and the rights of everyone to be educated, and to work on behalf of ending domination in all its forms—to work for justice, changing our educational system so that schooling is not the site where students are indoctrinated to support imperialist white-supremacist capitalist patriarchy or any ideology, but rather where they learn to open their minds, to engage in rigorous study and to think critically. (p. xiii)

This call to action is one that leaders, teachers, and students at all academic levels should heed. Education faculty members, however, are specifically well positioned to catalyze intellectual and political change given the autonomy and academic freedom the academy affords us.

An important first step to promoting social justice and change is to co-create democratic learning communities with our students. Faculty members should use classrooms (offices, research sites, and other potential places of learning) to join students in mediated discourse that thwarts dominant racist, classist, and sexist ideology. We should also challenge students to identify, confront, and critique their cultural politics, while also examining their beliefs about the nature and function of public schools. Students must feel free and be willing to exit their comfort zones for learning's sake by participating in hard conversations. The success of this exchange only works if faculty members ensure that all students feel respected and safe from retribution.

Students' willingness to be vulnerable and take risks in a democratic learning community must be matched with faculty members' efforts to do the same. As Palmer (1998) posits, "the courage to teach is the courage to keep one's heart open in those very moments when the heart is asked to hold more than it is able so that teacher and students and subject can be woven into the fabric of community that learning, and living, require" (p.11).

In addition, we as faculty members must be mindful of our positions of authority, and the tendency for traditional student-teacher power dynamics to infiltrate our learning spaces despite our desire to empower students and to be co-learners (Nagda, Gurin, and Lopez, 2003; Obidah, 2000). Indeed, the patriarchal and inequitable forces of the society we critique are the same forces that can propel social justice educators to lose sight of our power, heed or silence students' voices, affirm or denigrate their identities, and value or dismiss their life experiences (Knight and Pearl, 2000; Nagda, Gurin, and Lopez, 2003; Obidah, 2000).

Validating the voices, perspectives, identities, and experiences of all students—both the privileged and the marginalized—is vital to honoring the tenets of democratic education. By implementing critical, liberatory pedagogies, our classrooms and other instructional arenas become democratic sites where we lead by example, and show images of,

> teachers as transformative intellectuals who usurp traditional notions of power and authority in the classroom and allow intellectual and critical spaces to exist wherein students may make meaning and find power for themselves. (Obidah, 2000, p. 1040)

Race, Teaching, and the Politics of the Academy

The paradox of teaching for social justice in higher education—which comprises revered institutions grounded in patriarchal, Anglocentric norms—challenges any faculty member striving to use critical, liberatory pedagogies. Faculty members of color doing this work, however, must confront a second paradox: that of being disproportionately oppressed, devalued, and scrutinized by the same structures, institutions, and social norms that we work within, critique, resist, and encourage others to defy.

Faculty members of color, regardless of ideological orientation and instructional style, usually work in settings where some colleagues and students implicitly question or explicitly challenge our professional qualifications, intellect, professorial authority, scholarship, and political agenda (Antonio, 2003; Baez, 2003; Bonner, 2004; Hamilton, 2002; Lawrence, 1995; Tate, 1994;

Thomas, 2001). From the time we enter our university hallways, others are suspicious of us and look to us to prove our worthiness among them. Their suspicions, stemming from ignorance and racist stereotypes and assumptions, force us to carry an undue burden as we navigate through a layer of academic politics that our white colleagues are spared, regardless of whether we have equal or superior credentials, experience, and levels of productivity.

Scholars exploring issues of race and the professoriate further pinpoint the tendency of faculty of color to: receive less mentoring by senior colleagues; be expected to engage in all service activities regarding diversity and culture; conduct less rigorous and relevant research, and teach courses that are less substantive, but more entertaining than white faculty members (Antonio, 2003; Bonner, 2004). Overall, the treatment many faculty members of color receive in the academy from university colleagues can vary from indifference to blatant hostility: from patriarchal shepherding to well-intentioned but demeaning tokenism. At the same time, students' racial and cultural biases also shape their interaction with faculty members of color in and out of classrooms.

White students, especially those who have never had teachers or professors of color, often expect professors of color to inflate grades and maintain low standards of student performance and be deferential or passive toward them. If such behavior is not demonstrated, students tend to show subtle or explicit defiance that is expressed via negative classroom discourse, course evaluations, and/or hostile out-of-class interactions (Bonner, 2004; Hamilton, 2002; Tate, 1994). As an African American professor explained to a White colleague:

> With all due respect, sir, when you try to take control of your class, the students accept it. Maybe they're grateful for it. When I try to take control of my classes, I get student evaluations that say "I'm mean," "I'm intimidating," "I make them uncomfortable," "I force my opinions on them." (Hamilton, 2002, p. 32)

Such sentiments represent the experiences that many faculty members of color have with students who voice differential, and often biased, perceptions of them.

Indeed, faculty members of color are often constructed as the proverbial "big, bad wolf" who should be feared, monitored, and corralled. The skepticism, disdain and/or intimidation some White faculty members and students feel toward faculty members of color often intensifies when faculty members of color infuse critical, liberatory pedagogies in their teaching and scholarship. Whereas White faculty members tend to be highly regarded for examining issues of race, faculty members of color who do so are perceived as overly subjective, promoting a self-interested scholarly agenda, or having a chip on our shoulder (Bonner, 2004; Hamilton, 2002; Tate, 1994; Thomas, 2001). Thus, being a social justice educator of color becomes what Hamilton (2002, p. 36) calls an "intractable dilemma."

Furthermore, since critical and liberatory pedagogies by their nature challenge the status quo, they naturally threaten the interests of faculty members and students who wish to preserve the current power structure, thereby protecting their privilege. Faculty members of color who explicitly approach teaching and scholarship as liberatory political praxis can seem even more menacing. Our marginalized identities lend to our illuminating marginalized voices and perspectives. We then struggle to help others see this as a significant epistemological and pedagogical contribution.

This struggle for validation is ironic given academia's aim to generate new ideas and knowledge and grant all faculty members academic freedom. Yet, Tate (1994) reminds us that within the academy, ideas, texts, and scholarship that "construct reality in ways that legitimize privilege" are most honored (p. 248). Social justice educators of color offer counterstories and counterscripts that, for Whites and other privileged groups, "strips them of authority" (Tate, 1994, p. 262) and compel them to face uncomfortable truths about society, culture, and themselves. This type of social disruption is uncomfortable, but it is done to promote social progress and political change. It is also democratic because it empowers marginalized groups, and it brings forth additional voices, perspectives, and realities thereby benefiting the public good.

The combined virtue and intractability of promoting critical and liberatory pedagogies present faculty members (of all racial and cultural backgrounds) important challenges and questions for consideration. Four questions of particular significance include:

1. How can social justice educators co-create democratic learning communities?
2. How can we make critical and liberatory pedagogies more relevant and meaningful to students preparing to be educational leaders?
3. How can we more effectively engage students, regardless of their ideological background or levels of resistance, in educative, caring, and respectful ways?

4. How can faculty members of color retain the courage and commitment to
    teach for social justice despite the patriarchal and Anglocentric norms of
    the academy?

In the following sections, we address the questions above by drawing upon
our experiences as tenure-earning faculty members of color who promote social
justice education. To contextualize our perspectives, we first overview our
positionality and professional background. We then offer two examples of our
encounters with resistant students, which have inspired us to examine and
strengthen our use of critical, liberatory pedagogies.

Teaching from the Margins

To generate the questions stated above, we examined ourselves as social justice
educators of color. We reviewed a variety of data, including: course evaluations,
student email correspondence, student work, written correspondence to each
other, and personal journals. As a result, we determined that three areas of
divergence contribute to our conflicts with students: our positionality, epistemology, and praxis.

We are young, tenure-track faculty members of color. We both hold doctoral and other advanced degrees from tier-one research institutions, and we
were both mentored by highly distinguished education scholars. Together, we
have ample experience in leading, teaching, researching and evaluating K-12
schools situated in a range of geographical, political, and cultural contexts.

Additional elements of diversity contribute to our positionalities. We are
both African American--one female, one male; one heterosexual, one same
affection loving; one from the West Coast; one from the South, one non-
Christian, one Christian; both outspoken faculty members; both users of
theories rooted in social transformation, critical race, and feminist lenses. We
value forms of knowledge that are experiential, transformative academic,
culturally relevant, and thus, often contested (Banks, 1996; Delpit, 1995;
Ladson-Billings, 1994; Nieto, 1999). Furthermore, our praxis is rooted in
traditions of social justice, community, advocacy, and political struggle and
resistance.

We teach in a graduate educational leadership program. As faculty members
in a public and historically White university in the South, we have met consistent resistance from our White, conservative, Christian students. We have also
faced resistance from a handful of students of color and those who consider

themselves more liberal. Most of our students are middle class, married educators who live in predominantly white communities and work with mostly White colleagues, though many serve culturally diverse school communities. Our students (both White and of color) tend to value forms of traditional Anglocentric and Westernized knowledge. Their praxis, by their own explanation, is typically rooted in traditions of caring (Noddings, 2003), efficiency, polite civility, and a sense of moral righteousness steeped in their Judeo-Christian beliefs.

In addition, many of our students are wary of regional outsiders, those with alternative gendered identities, and non-Christians. Many have never dealt with people of color in positions of authority and/or have never had a teacher of color in their entire schooling experience. We, therefore, assault some students' senses and sensibilities. At best, students are taken aback by our instructional practice, at worst, they are offended.

The student resistance we have faced has come in the forms of both verbal and non-verbal communication, including: students boldly glaring at us with hostility during class, rolling their eyes and huffing and puffing, and blatantly disengaging from dialogue and activities. It has further manifested itself via impolite and disrespectful emails, snide comments whispered to other students within our earshot, and looks of utter shock on the first day of class when students realize we are the professor and not a student or a clerical or janitorial staff member. Overall, our areas of divergence are apparent in classroom discourse, course evaluations, and out of class interactions. Our relationships with students (and colleagues) are further influenced by the fact that we are part of a small cadre of faculty members who are helping to racially integrate our institution.

Facing resistance has been frustrating, tiring, and at times painful. Still, we are committed to doing our personal and professional best. Our key challenge involves engaging resistant students in a way that respects them, yet honors the tenets of critical, liberatory pedagogies. We address this challenge in the remainder of the chapter.

Counterstories: Snapshots of Student Resistance

While research *on* women and people of color in educational leadership is growing, the narratives and critical analyses *of* women and faculty members of color in educational leadership programs are stagnant, particularly works that chronicle the experiences of those who serve in predominately White institutions or in the American South. We, therefore, offer brief vignettes as counter-stories that help illustrate the terrain that many social justice educators must confront and negotiate to be effective.

Assault with a "Black Eye"—Reflections from C.P. Gause

Getting students to understand they too must undergo a transformation in order to transform schools is a great struggle (Gause, 2003). Based upon my experiences, many students have difficulty negotiating their own cultural politics, especially when they are faced with receiving instruction from me, a black male Ph.D., which many have never encountered. In addition, I am 5' 10" and 255 pounds. More often than not, many of my students (white, African American, and Latino) have articulated that I am the first African American male they have experienced as an instructor in their entire academic career. This profound realization as a new professor was my first black eye experience.

Most of my students come to the academy seeking answers for how to work with culturally and linguistically diverse populations; yet, when faced with individuals in the professoriate who have the ability to articulate and decon-struct modernist thinking that hinders those populations, it becomes difficult for students to negotiate their own social locations and critique relevant information.

As a black male academician, it appears to me that critical perspectives regarding the intersection of race, class, and gender affront many of my students' Judeo-Christian and southern values. Instead of "behaving as if the issues aren't there" (Rusch and Marshall, 1996, p. 25), I infuse cultural studies in the leadership discourse of our educational leadership preparation program, and I address issues surrounding democratic schooling (Gause, 2005). I do this work not because it is a line item within the mission statement of my department: I engage in this work because it is at the core of my being, it is who I am and what I believe. I am leading and living for social justice. Still, this approach is problematic for most of my conservative students even though they, as educators, are trying to respond to the large influx of Latino and Asian immigrant students in local schools, and respond to other shifting urban populations.

The contradiction between why students say they enter an educational leadership program and what they are open to learning and engaging hit me very hard during my first year in my current academic position. In the midst of a seminar, titled Leadership for Teaching and Learning, I was blind-sided by students' blatant remarks regarding inequities in education. Comments from a group of students enrolled in this Master of School Administration course included: "If parents can't afford to live in neighborhoods with good schools that's their problem," "we pay enough taxes to fund all schools," and "I work two jobs to pay private school tuition."

Upon hearing these remarks, I challenged the students to recognize the biased assumptions and unexamined privilege embedded in their comments. While doing so, I shared frameworks situated within critical race theory and social justice, yet some students engaged in side-bar conversations and made comments that could be perceived to be disrespectful, challenging, and confrontational. I previously informed this group, on more than one occasion, I believed education was a liberatory practice and that teaching for me was a form of activism. That night I continued by presenting my vision of leadership: to bring a level of criticality to the dialogue and discourse surrounding leadership preparation that would challenge the present notions regarding schooling and the politics of local education agencies, and that this could only be done through the "language of possibility and critique" (Giroux, 1988; Quantz, Rogers, and Dantley, 1991, p. 105).

I further informed this group that I believed in developing learning communities that understood that democracy was messy, provocative, and required the participation of all voices in the dialog. After assisting the students in understanding the power of language, I reminded them that the language that I utilized was purposive to challenge the hegemonic paradigms of schooling (such as those echoed in their earlier remarks) that continue to disenfranchise and marginalize students of color, those in poverty, and those who articulate alternative gendered identities.

This type of discussion was not anything unusual for me. I presented this rhetoric in all my previous courses in order to help students understand that "what they see" may not really be "what they see." I knew my positionality would contribute to some level of resistance among the students; however, I thought the South had begun its "great transformation," particularly after the death of Southern conservative ideologues like Strom Thurman. Thus, I hoped my students would be more receptive than they were.

The class was comprised of white and black females and males. The age representation was late 20's to early 50's, and the group represented a spectrum of classroom teachers, district level personnel, and acting assistant principals. Many in the group had spent the majority of their academic career and personal lives in and around the state of North Carolina; however, I thought given the bombardment of popular thought and various educational paradigms that had been presented to these educators through print and digital media, they would somehow be more open-minded, global thinkers. Instead, I began to see in these students several problematic themes that I saw in previous classes that I taught. The students' responses were rooted in language often associated with Christian fundamentalism and exclusionary politics. I realized these students did not want to engage in the language of critique or possibility because they assumed it would challenge their beliefs.

After class that evening, as I got in my car, I overheard a group of black and white male and female students, dismissively state in reference to me: "He's just an angry black man." Wow! What a statement. This was my second black eye experience. I was appalled, disturbed and hurt by such a comment. My passion for education coupled with how I situate my purpose—as a teacher/activist—was perceived to be one of anger—bestial anger.

I spoke to some of my colleagues about my group of students, and many of them (including an African American female, a Jewish female and two white males) spoke of the issues regarding this particular student cohort. My colleagues and I discussed how previous courses the cohort had taken with White professors also talked about diversity, change, and difference, without causing such uproar. Then, we all began to realize that many of our students never had an African American male professor. In fact, many of these students, particularly the doctoral students, had called for our department to be more inclusive and representative of the populations they served.

After several conversations, my colleagues and I also realized that students who are asked to confront issues surrounding racism, sexism, ageism, and gender identity by a white male or female respond differently than when asked to do so by an African American male or female who presents critical content. Within my seminar, I happened to not only be an African American instructor, but the first black male tenure-track faculty member in the history of my department. Now we are really talking about an eye-opening experience for all of our students. This realization was my third black eye experience.

"Making" White People Feel Uncomfortable: Reflections from C.W. Cooper

Teaching according to principles of critical and liberatory pedagogies involves constantly pushing students out of their comfort zones. Though the literature on critical pedagogy is filled with calls for educators to create "safe spaces" in their classroom, I feel any space where people with different amounts of power and authority interact and dialogue can never be entirely safe— comfortable, respectful, and secure most of the time, but not safe if safe means protected from insult, injury, or risk taking (Knight and Pearl, 2000; Obidah, 2000).

Indeed, democracy that comprises representation of multiple perspectives is not safe: nor is fostering democratic discourse in classrooms where students engage in frank dialogue about racism and other forms of oppression. My teaching experiences (and former experiences as a student) have shown me that a classroom's social climate can become palpably uncomfortable and potentially unsafe without adequate professorial leadership and mediation. Moreover, facing identity politics and student resistance in my classes have reminded me that despite my position of professorial authority, *I* do not always feel safe—especially since teaching for social justice means serving as the target of White people's anger. My positionality—socially, as a young, African American woman, and politically, as an untenured faculty member who educates many students who are also in professional positions of power—contributes to this feeling.

Teaching a class on the theories of educational leadership during my second year as an assistant professor forced me to think about my and my students' discomfort and risk taking. This class was a small, doctoral level course that included teachers, counselors, assistant principals, and principals: five students were White, four were African American. We were wrapping up a unit on critical race theory in this course designed to introduce students to various theoretical paradigms. The students had read Lopez' (2003) article on critical race theory and the politics of education several weeks earlier. The article, which critiques the colorblind approach to educational leadership and stresses the permanence of racism in U.S. schooling, served as a hard-hitting but palatable examination of racism for most White students. Still, a 30-something, White, female teacher in the class spent three weeks challenging, resisting, and attacking the article via online discussions and in two class sessions.

One evening, this student raised her hand while simultaneously interrupting me mid-sentence as I was speaking to another student to demand that the whole class revisit the article. Prepared with the article, she turned the pages and emphatically read an excerpt with a tone of disbelief and disgust. She quoted:

> The only difference between racism today and of the past is that modern-day racism is more subtle, invisible, and insidious. Popular beliefs such as color blindness and equal opportunity have only served to drive racism underground, making it increasingly diffi-

Canada's multicultural rhetoric

cult for people of color to name their reality. Racism now requires tangible proof of its existence: hate crimes, lynching, hate speech, burning crosses, or other physical assault…Without this external proof, racism is difficult to affirm (Lopez, 2003, pp. 82–83)

The student went on to discredit Lopez' assertion. She insisted that children of all races in her school were treated equally, and she could not believe that our society had not progressed. She referred to the success of Colin Powell, Oprah Winfrey, and Condoleezza Rice as symbols of social change. I explained how these rare examples of high profile, wealthy African American figures did not negate the existence of racism in everyday America, nor the racist ideology that shapes this nation's culture and institutions.

While I was looking directly at the student and addressing her, she whipped her head to the side completely disregarding me and proclaimed, "I want to hear from everybody else!" She asked the whole class what they thought of Lopez' thesis, and before anyone could respond, she looked specifically at three African American students (two females, one male) seated side-by-side and asked, "Do *you* all think it's true?" The students emphatically replied, "Yes!" The other white students sat quietly with looks of trepidation. I thought the African American students' response would serve as the "tangible proof" the White student was seeking and thus diffuse her frustration, but it didn't.

The student began yelling at me as she explained that she was tired of the course material that "just focuses" on the "problems" of racism, sexism, and educational inequity. She asked, "When are we going to start talking about solutions? I want to know what I can do to help." In addition, she demanded that "if" racism is still so prevalent, I give her solutions for solving racism instead of "dwelling" on its negative implications.

I, like my student, was frustrated and angry at this point in the class—not because she was challenging critical race theory, or even because she was invalidating the standpoint of her African American peers (thereby substantiating Lopez' claim). I was upset because I perceived a White woman capitalizing on her privilege and disrespecting me because she felt inconvenienced by the existence of racism.

Despite my personal feelings, I tried my hardest to appear calm and unaffected, but tension was building in the class and within me. At last, the student, with tears swelling up in her eyes, conceded: "I guess what I'm trying to say is that, if what this article says is true, it makes me very uncomfortable." Ahh…at last, she spoke her truth! I was relieved that she acknowledged her distaste for the article was not about the lack of racism in schools, but about the fact that the article challenged her reality.

After the student's statement, silence filled the room for several seconds, and I searched my mind for an appropriate response. I said to the student, "Well, all I can say—and I'm not trying to be mean—but the purpose of this article and the rest of this literature that discusses racism and inequality is not to make white people feel good!" Seconds later I followed with, "And, it's not meant to make white people feel bad."

I went on to explain how critical theory does not aim to attack individuals, but rather critique groups and social structure, and to situate discussions of inequality in broad historical and political contexts. I admitted that discussing this literature would continue to push us all out of our "comfort zones," but it was needed. Finally, I explained: "Before we can solve racism, we have to understand it. I'm asking you to be uncomfortable for a while, keep an open mind, and try to reach a greater understanding." I also asked the students to trust me.

We concluded the class by watching the first segment of the documentary, *Matters of Race* (PBS, 2003), which highlights the social conflict and refueled racism that is emerging in North Carolina as the state experiences rapid demographic change. The documentary contains a relatively recent recording of a former North Carolina school principal calling African Americans "niggers," and a Latino state school board member crying as she admits that some racial groups "hate each other." The video poignantly complemented the course reading, and it was an effective antidote to the student's resistance. The documentary *showed* the realities behind critical race theory, and I could tell that it was thought provoking and touching for everyone. Furthermore, it helped diffuse the student's frustration, and it inspired her to become more receptive to critical viewpoints.

Despite the negative feelings and vulnerability that I felt during that class meeting, I left feeling proud that my student had the courage to speak out and wrestle with important material. Her words and interactions, though unpleasant, created a "teachable moment" that I used to bring us together as a learning community.

Analysis

This current age of educational consumerism has led many educators to pursue higher education in order to gain certification, employment, and promotion rather than enlightenment (Levine, 2005). Thus, wrestling with deconstructive philosophies, sociocultural contexts, and structural inequality—ideas that challenge the thinking and lifestyles that many educators enjoy—is not a priority or preference. Several of our students strike us as approaching their graduate education as educational consumers rather than practitioner-scholars. Our tendency as social justice educators to forge ahead with critical instructional approaches when they clearly are not welcomed by all has caused us to question the role of democratic practice in instruction. As we later elaborate, the power of our vignettes inspires us to view our teaching and scholarship as collaborative activism. We are particularly driven to do so because of the students who construct our identities as the "big bad wolf" versus agents of change and democracy.

While our practice and pedagogy have proven effective and insightful for many of our students, there is much more work to be done. This era of educational accountability, globalization, and market competition has created aspiring educational leaders who are concerned more with "the bottom line," than with developing free thinking members of society. Democratic education and freedom have been reduced to the ability to achieve academic standards and acquire material goods, wealth, and power without critiquing the consequences of inequity, greed, and inequality. Given the effects of free market fundamentalism on American culture, schools are looking less like sites of democracy and more like capitalistic prizes of transnational corporations.

Students (many of whom are current educational practitioners) who enter graduate programs often say they wish to find ways to reform schools, and many of them find it difficult to engage in a discourse that moves beyond school reformation. The technical aspects of schooling are many students' greatest concern given their pressure to implement so many political mandates. Moreover, because schools are hegemonic reproductions of the larger society, engaging graduate students in the discourse of power, knowledge, and pedagogy creates tension. Moving them from the language of reformation to that of transformation is often viewed as counterproductive, but, if schools are to be sites of democracy, this is the path of liberation.

Social justice is not a new hot topic, as many of our K-12 aspiring educational leaders would like to assume. Rather,

> It has always been at the vital center of democracy. Indeed, the struggle to broaden the application of equitable democracy from a few wealthy White men to everyone regard-

less of her or his gender, race, ethnicity, class, sexual orientation, disability, culture, or home language is the heartbeat of democracy. (Scheurich and McKenzie, 2006, p. 9)

Part of our obligation in using critical, liberatory pedagogies is to help students heed the call to action that involves seeking social justice so public schools can live up to their democratic purpose.

Four central questions have guided our self-inquiry and reflection. The questions pertain to how social justice educators can use strategies to co-create learning communities; make critical and liberatory pedagogies more relevant; effectively engage students regardless of ideological background or level of resistance; and finally, maintain the courage and commitment needed to do this work.

We have concluded that teaching for social justice and democracy first requires that educators possess clarity about themselves and their commitments. It entails infusing dialogue, reflection, and critique in our teaching methods, while also incorporating an array of materials, including multimedia and popular culture sources. Offering students experiential educational activities that promote understanding and empathy for marginalized populations is also essential, as is fostering humor and a sense of hope, despite the serious nature of education and transformative leadership.

Our vignettes illustrate some of the pedagogical features we recommend, but, most of all they serve as reminders that we must be open to approaching our students as partners in the struggle for educational and social transformation. This requires standing our ground while also striving to create a learning community founded on mutual respect, trust, and validation of all learners' experiences and identities.

Indeed West (2004) argues that "three crucial traditions fuel deep democratic energies," including those that involve "questioning of ourselves," having a "prophetic commitment to justice—for all peoples," and possessing an "inner strength provided by the tragicomic commitment to hope" (p. 16). He further explains that, "The tragicomic is the ability to laugh and retain a sense of life's joy—to preserve hope even while staring in the face of hate and hypocrisy—as against falling into the nihilism of paralyzing despair" (p. 16).

Conclusion: Engaging in Collaborative Activism

All of the strategies mentioned above form the basis of what we call *collaborative activism*—a democratic education approach that unites educators and learners in

raising consciousness and rupturing the status quo in order to socially deconstruct, politically transform, and share a sense of hope.

　　Collaborative activism is the essence of transformative leadership. As two
transformative, African American, social justice educators who view ourselves
from social locations that include alternative gendered identities, we realize that
first and foremost we must: engage in a discourse of leadership for social justice;
deconstruct the "grand" narratives reified by media and texts by telling our
counterstories; and, create a space that situates educational leadership within the
context of the prophetic spirituality that is an important part of the African
American experience (Dantley, 2003; Lawrence, 1996; West, 1993).

　　As faculty members of color, we are underrepresented in American higher
education. We make up just over 10 percent of full-time undergraduate faculty
(Antonio, 2003), and the statistic is far less at the graduate level, particularly in
educational leadership preparation programs. Our small numbers speak to the
very inequities and forms of oppression we strive to counter, which is daunting.
As we work to decolonize and co-create democratic classrooms we must not
tire in our efforts and thereby continue to engage the process of democratic
education as liberatory practice. Partnering with others to engage in collaborative activism will help renew our energy, courage, commitment, and spirit.
Finally, engaging in collaborative activism through our teaching, mentoring,
political advocacy, and scholarship will also position us to not be the feared, big
bad wolves, but rather, the educators who help blow down walls and houses of
inequity.

References

Anderson, J.D. (1988). *The education of blacks in the south 1860-1935*. Chapel Hill: University of
　　North Carolina Press.
Antonio, A. L. (2003). Diverse student bodies, diverse faculties. *Academe*. American Association of
　　University Professors. http://www.aaup.org/publications/Academe/2003/03nd/
　　03ndanto.htm. Accessed: November 16, 2005.
Baez. B. (2003). Outsiders within? *Academe*. American Association of University Professors.
　　http://www.aaup.org/publications/Academe/2003/03ja/03jadbaez.htm. Accessed: No-
　　vember 16, 2005.
Banks, J.A. (1996). The canon debate, knowledge construction, and multicultural education. In
　　J.A. Banks (Ed.), *Multicultural education, transformative knowledge, and action: Historical and contem-
　　porary perspectives*. New York: Teachers College Press.

Bartolome, L. I. (1994, Summer). Beyond the methods fetish: Toward a humanizing pedagogy. *Harvard Educational Review*, 64 (2), 173–194.

Bartolome, L.I. and Trueba, E.T. (2000). Beyond the politics of schools and the rhetoric of fashionable pedagogies: The significance of teacher ideology. In E.T. Trueba and L.I. Bartolome (Eds.) *Immigrant Voices: In search of educational equity*. New York/ UK: Rowman & Littlefield.

Bonner II, Fred A. (2004). "Black professors: On the track but out of the loop." *The Chronicle of Higher Education* 50, no. 40. http://chronicle.com/temp/email.php?id=dql1or2 m38lt8ei5v0datc57vkd6ej4l. Accessed: June 24, 2004.

Brown, K.M. (2005). Social justice education for preservice leaders: Evaluating transformative learning strategies. *Equity & Excellence in Education*, 38, 155-167.

Brown, K.M. (2004). Leadership for social justice and equity: Weaving a transformative framework and pedagogy. *Education Administration Quarterly*, 40(1), 77-108.

Cambron-McCabe, N. & McCarthy, M. (2005). Educating school leaders for social justice. *Educational Policy*, 19(1), 201-222.

Cochran-Smith, M. (1997). Knowledge, skills, and experiences for teaching culturally diverse learners: A perspective for practicing teachers. In J. Irvine (Ed.), *Critical knowledge for diverse teachers and learners*. Washington, DC: AACTE, pp. 27–88.

Cooper, C. W. (2003). The detrimental impact of teacher bias: Lessons learned from African American mothers. *Teacher Education Quarterly*, 30 (2): 101–116.

Dantley, M. (2003). Principled, pragmatic, and purposive leadership: Reimagining educational leadership through prophetic spirituality. *Journal of School Leadership*. *13* (2): 181–198.

Darder, A. (1991). *Culture and power in the classroom: A critical foundation for bilingual education*. Westport, CT: Bergin & Garvey.

Delpit, L. (1995). *Other people's children. Cultural conflict in the classroom*. New York: New Press.

Gause, C. P. (2005). Navigating the stormy seas: critical perspectives on the intersection of popular culture and educational leader-"ship." *Journal of School Leadership*, 15(3): 333–342.

———. (2003). Transforming leaders, creating communities: changing schools through transformative leadership, Commentary-Miami University, *Department of Educational Leadership-Electronic Journal*: http://www.units.muohio.edu/eap/departments/edl/eduleadership/anthology/RCI/COM03002.html.

Giroux, H. (1988). *Teachers as intellectuals: Toward a critical pedagogy of learning*. Grambin, MA: Bergin & Garvey.

Hamilton, K. (2002). Race in the college classroom. *Black Issues in Higher Education*, 19(2): 32–36.

hooks, b. (2003). *Teaching community. A pedagogy of hope*. New York. Routledge.

Knight, T., and Pearl, A. (2000). Democratic education and critical pedagogy. *The Urban Review*, 32(3): 197-226

Ladson-Billings, G. (1994). *Dreamkeepers: Successful teachers of African American children*. San Francisco. CA: Jossey-Bass.

Larson, C., and Ovando, C. (2001). *The color of bureaucracy: The politics of equity in multicultural school communities*. Belmont, CA: Wadsworth/Thomas Learning.

Lawrence, C.R.III (1996), *The word and the river: Pedagogy as scholarship and struggle*. In Crenshaw, K. et. al(Eds.). *Critical Race Theory: The key writings that formed the movement*. (pp. 336-351). New York. New World Press.

Levine, A. (2005). *Educating school leaders.* Washington, DC: The Education Schools Project.

Lopez, G. R. (February, 2003). The (racially neutral) politics of education: A critical race theory perspective. *Educational Administration Quarterly*, 39(1): 68–94.

Nagda, B.A., Gurin, P. and Lopez, G.E. (2003). Transformative pedagogy for democracy and social justice. *Race, Ethnicity and Education*, 6(2), 165-191.

Nieto, S. (1999). *The light in their eyes: Creating multicultural learning communities.* New York: Teachers College Press.

Noddings, N. (2003). *Caring: A feminine approach to ethics and moral education*, second edition. Berkeley: University of Californa Press.

Oakes, J., and Lipton, M. (1999). *Teaching to change the world.* Boston, MA: McGraw-Hill College.

Obidah, J.E. (2000). Mediating the boundaries of race, class, and professorial authority. *Teachers College Record*, 102(6): 1035–1060.

Palmer, P. (1998). *The Courage to teach: Exploring the inner landscape of a teacher's life.* San Francisco, CA: Jossey Bass.

Public Broadcasting Station (2003). *Matters of race.* Documentary.

Quantz, R., Rogers, J., and Dantley, M. (1991). Rethinking transformative leadership: Toward democratic reform of schools. *Journal of Education*, 173(3): 96–118.

Rusch, E. A., & Marshall, C. (1996). *Troubled educational administration.* Paper presented at the annual meeting of the American Educational Research Association, New York.

Scheurich, J., and McKenzie, K. B. (2006). The continuing struggle for social justice: 2006 Politics of Education Association Yearbook. *Educational Policy.* 20(1): 8–12.

Tate, W. F. (1994). From inner city to ivory tower: Does my voice matter in the academy? *Urban Education*, 29(3): 245–269.

Thomas, G. (2001). The dual role of scholar and social change agent: Reflections from tenured African American and Latina faculty. In R.O. Maboleka and A. L. Green (Eds.), *Sisters of the academy: Emergent Black women scholars in higher education.* Sterling, VA: Stylus.

West, C. (2004). *Democracy matters. Winning the fight against imperialism.* New York: Penguin Press.

———. (1993). *Race matters.* New York: Vintage Press.

10

Beyond Generic Democracy: Holding Our Students Accountable for Democratic Leadership and Practice

Charles P. Gause, Ulrich C. Reitzug, and Leila E. Villaverde

Introduction

This chapter is the beginning of many lengthy conversations addressing the ethical, moral, and philosophical (re)articulation of the language of democracy, leadership, and democratic education. Our purpose is to share where we started, where and how we decided to evaluate/critique how democracy is currently defined given the current sociocultural and political climate within the United States and how to better "make sense" of these constructs to effect change in educational leadership preparation programs locally and globally (although we are not there yet). We engage in the first difficult steps of questioning and articulating here. In subsequent works we engage in discourse analysis to inform our pedagogical practices as a means of holding our students accountable to the department's statements of commitments. [1]

The chapter's structure/process centralizes conversation as a scholarly endeavor; it focuses on dialogue as a primary medium for theorizing and praxis. Why? We believe important discussions are dismissed in the search for legitimacy, in the narrow compliance with bureaucratic standards, and in including the canon at the expense of new or emergent literature and because this inquiry has implications for pedagogy. The three of us will engage in a series of discussions, both online and in person, addressing language/terminology, mainly ideas initially (and its effects on how we envision our roles in schools and in other educational contexts). We critically assess our visions of leadership, foundations, and democracy with interdisciplinary catalysts that force us to rethink the nature of our practice, the call to action, and the ethical referent that defines our concern for humanity.

The text in the chapter recreates our discussions with continuous interjections from each of us, accentuating through mostly the use of typography and image what each stressed, questioned, whispered, screamed, pondered, or engaged. The use of typography and the play of space within the page are crucial in the translation and documentation of actual conversation among us, as scholars and educators in the field. We wanted to communicate the intensity of engagement with the issues and the degree of critical inquiry experienced through the repositioning of dialogue as a main vehicle for transformative learning, yet we found it incredibly difficult to even get past defining democracy or figuring out how students would know and live it. Scholarly and experiential work is cited throughout the text as it pertains to the issues we raise, in other words, we are theorizing in our speech, not to validate, but to push the use of theory in the everyday, in who we are, and who we hope our students will be as educational leaders. In rearticulating the language of democracy, leadership, and democratic education we are also taking great liberty to challenge the reader's assumptions/expectations of how it is best to receive or produce knowledge. We intend to chart new territory in the construction of leadership scholarship with what follows as the initial steps. We ask these questions: What is democracy? What type of democracy do we envision?, and How do we hold our students accountable for such democracy?

What Do We Mean by Democracy?

UR: Democracy is not so much a condition that we achieve, as an ideal toward which we strive. It is more than a form of governance; indeed, it is a way of life. Dewey (1916) noted that democracy includes a whole range of "associated living" and occurs in the various realms of social and cultural life (p. 87). For me, democracy has to do with inquiry, discourse, equity in participation and outcomes, and determining the common good. My own personal definition of democracy is, "a way of living that requires the open and widespread flow and critique of ideas, with an overriding commitment to determining and pursuing the common good."

LV: Democracy is a social experiment, a practice instituted through a hierarchal system of oppression and denial, at least so far in the United States. It was quite clear from the writings of James Madison and George Washington that democracy was neither meant to be publicly participatory or representative. It was only intended for those that were considered "educated," who had access to formal systems of schooling and wealth. These individuals would be capable of reasoning present and future decisions. Democracy analyzed in this way is heavily invested in controlling the unknown future over leading/living in the present. Fear and arrogance limit the possibility of an engaged citizenry.

UR: Before we dismiss or embrace democracy, I think we need to distinguish conceptually "which democracy" we're talking about. For example, my description of democracy (see previous) refers to an idealized notion of democracy, that is, what democracy is like when it's what it should be. A second conception, as reflected in your response, Leila, is democracy as it currently and historically has been practiced in the United States., that is, as a "social experiment" rife with oppression, exclusion, hierarchy, and the tyranny of the majority. A third conception of democracy, also evident in your response, Leila, is democracy as the "great white fathers" of our country saw it. I don't think we should dismiss the idea of democracy because of historical and current flaws in how its been implemented and practiced. Although I don't want to be ahistorical, the issue may not be as much whether democracy has been good or bad in the past, but rather, whether there is hope for a better practice of democracy in the future.

LV: Rick, you have a point, it's important not to be immobilized by what democracy has been, yet at times it's like quicksand … one keeps trying to get out of it and gets dragged back in.

CPG: Rick and Leila, I believe democracy moves beyond the purist notion of the people's ability to self-govern. The concept of democracy, for me lies within the intersections of faith and passion.

LV: So you're looking at democracy as an embodied notion, something we enact and carry with us daily…true, if not it falls by the wayside.

CPG: Yes, I do believe it is an embodied notion, Leila. Why? Well, in my efforts to situate my social location within the context of educator and interlocutor, I must also deal with the psychological ramifications of over three hundred and fifty years of enslavement of Africans, Amerindians, and indigenous people. My black male identity is formed out of those who were enslaved by individuals who framed this democratic experiment (Gause, 2005a). Interesting enough they believed in freedom from the "almighty" (king) but not for the "all mighty" (people). The people's understanding of self-rule rests upon our commitment to the ideas of freedom, justice, and expression. The faith in overcoming adversity to be seen, heard, and recognized. According to Barber (2002),"It is the new democratic realist who sees that if the only choice we have is between the mullahs and the mall, between the hegemony of the religious absolutism and the hegemony of market determinism, neither liberty nor the human spirit is likely to flourish" (p. 6).

UR: I think that raises an interesting issue: should the democratic process of inquiry, discourse, and equitable voice determine the common good, or should we accept the "ideas of freedom, justice, and expression" as intrinsic ends of democracy?

Still Waters Run Deep

The current sociocultural political climate in the United States, the renewing of the Patriot Act, disaster relief or lack there of, terrorism and homeland security, the demonization of those in poverty, and the privatization of free public education led us to ask ourselves the following question: What type of democracy do we envision?

LV: The type of democracy I wish to see and be a part of is closely aligned to what Lummis, Mouffe, Laclau, Chomsky, and others refer to as radical democracy. Not that a new adjective solves the pragmatic dilemmas of democracy, nonetheless its literature engages democracy through its most essential elements: "*demos*-the people with *kratia*-power" (Lummis 1996, p. 22). It stresses the importance of people having the power to govern themselves. Radical democracy encompasses numerous social spheres/collectives needing/producing continuous interchanges of various knowledges/ways of knowing, critiquing and problem solving, engaged and participating in and through venues that collectively sustain the whole. Leadership resides in each of these dynamic collectives and steps up as needed. These collectives are not static groups; instead these are as complex as the individuals that are part of them. There is no central power, a temporal one, maybe. Instead, power resides in multiple nodes throughout a group, community, and/or society. The school, classroom, community organization, or any other learning environment can be a rich node through which to exercise and enact the elements of democracy.

CPG: As a creative educational leader who espouses and believes in education as the praxis of freedom (hooks, 1994) my perspective of democracy lies within my practice. I take this unique approach because just as slavery began as an economic experiment, so too American democracy. As a member of the Black

Diaspora, my lineage is not disembodied from the fabric of American democracy. West (2004) posits:

> The American democratic experiment is unique in human history not because we are God's chosen people to lead the world, nor because we are always a force for good in the world, but because of our refusal to acknowledge the deeply racist and imperial roots of our democratic project (41).

Because the personal is political and because I view my role as a teacher/activist within a framework that my perspective of democracy cannot be de-linked from what I do as a teacher/activist in the academic space; I envision democracy as the interconnections that lie within the quest of knowledge, the faith that our humanity exercises as we navigate the manifestations of our destinies.

Dead or Alive: Where Does Democracy Exist?

LV: Picking up from an earlier comment CPG made…democracy exists within as an enacted daily practice as people interact, communicate, relate through daily professional, personal, or social routines and issues. It does not operate top down or bottom up, but through multiple networks or rhizomes. In my present cynical state of mind, this sounds idealistic. I'm perhaps having a failure of imagination as to how this would operate nationally or even statewide. It seems unfathomable on a large scale since a base necessity for this type of interchange is respect for self and other regardless of identity politics. As a society we have been trained/socialized through abstract individualism to be suspicious of the other and of the collective. Even through a mutually supportive network of struggles, discussions, dissentions, and innovations, power exists. The question would then be how does a radical democracy not fall prey to the abuse of power?

UR: If it truly were a "mutually supportive network of struggles, discussions, dissentions, and innovations," then I think an intrinsic system of checks and balances might keep the abuse of power at bay. However, when the linkages in the network break down, or it becomes no longer mutually supportive, it leaves open the door for the abuse of power. I think a current problem is that, in schools and society, we do not even have a common ground/purpose around which to develop a mutually supportive network. Both our society and our schools lack a noble vision that can unite people. That makes us all guilty.

LV: Yes, there is also a breakdown between the rhetoric of what schools and society say are prioritized values and their practices. Because we navigate these daily we have to both own our complicity and our responsibility to turn the tides, so to speak.

CPG: We have to believe change is possible...I believe in education as a practice of freedom (hooks, 1994), democracy must exist in institutions that encourage human beings to transform our environment, communities, neighborhoods, and schools into arenas where dialogue, discourse, and dissent are not silenced but celebrated.

UR: So, what are "these institutions"? Aren't the institutions we are trying to transform the same ones in which democracy must exist (i.e., neighborhood communities and schools)? And, how do we "celebrate" dialogue, discourse, and dissent when, increasingly, even in families and neighborhoods, all topics dealing with sociocultural or political issues must be avoided in order to keep the peace? Which, of course, makes for boring family reunions and cocktail parties.

LV: Undoubtedly, unless we accept discomfort as part of the process of reaching a deeper understanding and exploration of what is doable, possible, or necessary, then we perpetuate the status quo.

Terms of Endearment: Dialogue and Discourse

UR: So what do inquiry, discourse, equity, and the common good have to do with democracy and, what do we mean by these terms? Let's start with discourse. In his volume, *Democracy and Education*, Dewey (1916) called attention to the "great diversity of populations, of varying languages, religions, moral codes, and traditions" (p. 82) that exist in society. He argued that in order for the interests of all to be served in a democracy, there must be a widespread sharing of experiences and perspectives. This, of course, occurs through written and oral forms of discourse. Discourse in a democracy, must be inclusionary of all people (i.e., all need to have access to the conversation), and all perspectives must be equitably considered. At the heart of discourse are diverse and competing perspectives. As a result, democratic discourse will be filled with dissensus, disagreement, "social discord" (Goodman, 1992, p.10), and "bringing democracy to life...[will always be] a struggle" (Beane and Apple, 1995, p. 8).

Strike (1993) argues that in resolving disagreements in democratic discourse, the "strongest argument" [as opposed to the strongest/most powerful person] should prevail. Determining the strongest argument requires a more systematic process than is likely to frequently be found in public discourse. Specifically, determining the strongest argument requires inquiry—the gathering of data, perspectives, and formal knowledge to inform the deliberation on an issue. Inquiry and discourse, although democratic processes; however, can be used to serve ends that are not democratic, but rather exclusionary. Beane and Apple (1995) note, "One of the contradictions of democracy is that local populist politics do not always serve democratic ends" (p. 9). For example, supposedly democratic means of governance and a concern for "the common good" have resulted in the historical and continued exclusion of people of color, gays, lesbians, and others from full access to American society. Thus, the conception of "the common good" that is pursued in a democracy must have at its core a concern for the equitable treatment of all individuals and groups.

CPG: Rick, in order to get at "the common good" dialogue has to be a central component. Dialogue is two-way interactive sharing and visiting, which changes our context or us. As this communication takes place and remains ongoing, discourse develops. Discourse is not just rhetoric; it is socially and culturally grounded. I strive to teach students that discourse is a politically centered, loaded conversation. Taking such risks within the classroom learning environment has at times produced difficult pedagogical moments. In several of my experiences, students resist engaging in dialogue oftentimes because they do not want to consider others' points of view. I often remind them that democracy in its concepts considers the voice of dissent. So I encourage them to consider plurality and to border cross.

LV: Exactly, a radical democracy requires plurality, valuing others as a basic practice, respecting others' opinions, and willingly engaging in dialogue about ideas, past and present steps/strategies, and possibilities. It also requires patience and understanding especially through differing viewpoints emphasizing the space for dissent, contradiction, and resistance. This is not, however, a plea for rationalism or an assumption that dialogue is only possible through a sophisticated ability to reason. This would reinforce both Marxism and Rational Humanism's appeal to logic and rationality. I'm not supporting anti-intellectualism either, by no means; I'm simply trying to challenge the assumptions of how an informed, so-called educated people are to represent themselves. Radical democracy privileges a "free" exchange of ideas and the need/desire for mobilization from and through varying and diverse groups of people. In this dialogue, neither consensus nor agreement is the end goal, yet the process of the not yet is. It intends to put into action the exercise of an imperfect emancipatory project of access and change.

UR: I agree with both of you, but I think we must also look at our own practice as faculty to make sure that we are not silencing or excluding the perspectives of students who come from conservative/right wing/fundamentalist perspectives. How do we implicitly and explicitly silence them in our classes? Isn't simply knowing what our perspectives are an implicit act of silencing, given our privileged status as professors? In other words, does our practice of democracy in our university classes feel democratic to students who embrace ideologies that are different than ours?

LV: Great questions! We also have to consider student perception which some times differs greatly from what we are trying to do. Are we compromising our own enactment of democracy, our own professional/ intellectual authority by sometimes privileging students overwhelmingly? I think it's an interesting balance to sit, be, in the space between reclaiming the authority that is always challenged for those of us that are faculty of color or women and the sharing of that borrowed authority.

Whatever Happened to One Size Fits All?

UR: While I believe strongly in the goodness of democracy in its idealized state, I recognize the world as an imperfect place and democracy as a flawed concept in its implementation at all levels. As noted at the outset, democracy is not so much a condition that we achieve, as an ideal toward which we strive. Thus, a key issue is whether a partial or flawed practice of democracy is superior to other forms of governing and ways of life, or whether the side effects of imperfect democracy outweigh its benefits. Relatedly, at which stage of partial/flawed implementation is a democracy no longer democracy? At which point does it become some other entity that leads us down paths that are counterproductive to us as a human people?

The flawed implementation of democracy emanates from many factors, among them:

- cognitive factors: our inability to properly gather, process, and weigh all the information required to make appropriate decisions;

- personal factors: arguing for our own personal vested interests during democratic discourse while placing the common good on the back burner;
- power factors: the majority, those with the most forceful voices, or those with the most power get their way;
- apathy or inattention factors: people do not care enough to participate in the discourse, or they do not understand the significance of issues that are in the public discourse, or they simply are not paying attention and thus do not use their opportunity to participate in the discourse around an issue;
- ideological factors: the intentional as well as inadvertent distortion of information by politicians, the media, and others to promote ideological agendas;
- political factors: using a self-serving and shifting conception of democracy as a political tool to promote our personal and/or ideological interests (e.g., "bringing democracy to the Iraqi people" while simultaneously repressing voice and restricting personal rights and freedoms in our own country);
- efficiency factors: it is impossible to adequately consider all publicly relevant issues.

Flawed democracy leads to:

- the tyranny of the majority;
- false positives (i.e., incorrect outcomes of inquiry and discourse);
- a version of democracy that's named "democracy" by its perpetrator, but may well resemble dictatorship or some other form of authoritarianism more than democracy *North Korea*

LV: These bullet points, in and of themselves, provide great filters to analyze current events in these last few years in the United States.

CPG: When it comes to my pedagogical practices, students, at the beginning of my classes, often believe my approaches are flawed until they begin to deconstruct their own assumptions.

According to Knight and Pearl (2000):

> We present six attributes of democracy that have been generally recognized and apply them to education: (1) the determination of important knowledge; (2) the nature of educational authority; (3) the ordering and inclusiveness of membership; (4) the definition and availability of rights; (5) the nature of participation in decisions that affect one's life; and (6) equality. We add a seventh—an optimal learning environment made available to all students—that derives logically from the other six. (p. 198)

I would like to focus on the seventh attribute—an optimal learning environment. I have placed in all of my course syllabi the following: "this syllabus may be amended at the discretion of the professor to provide optimal learning experiences." I single out this line at the beginning of the semester with all students so they will understand that there is no finality regarding the construction of the syllabus because I must consider their voice, positions, and perspectives. Upon our initial meeting I then take all of the information and begin to construct a "living and breathing" document from which to operate. Students at first are taken aback and then realize that the syllabus can be changed at any time to suit the needs of the individual as well as the collective. This unto itself is democratic and quite liberating for most students only after they become willing participants in the development of a democratic classroom.

Holding Our Students Accountable

LV: The second question, "how should we hold our students accountable for such democracy?" is where the rubber meets the road, so to speak. I see the classroom as a much clearer space for the actualization of radical democracy, a possible site for the practice and exercise of ideas, values, actions, and visions/commitments. These ideas are products of radically different interactions between all those involved, ones based on equal human value and respect. One of the things I reiterate in class is the purpose of the pedagogical space. As I see it, anything can be studied, researched, and analyzed in the classroom, in the confines/boundaries of the classroom space. If these liberties are not given to the pedagogical space, we run the risk of making the classroom, and education in general, a process of mimicking the status quo and rubber-stamping the best replicas. Too often we present education as a packaged process where students just fulfill the requirements and expect to successfully graduate, without regard to quality or innovation. If we truly want to hold students accountable to independent thinking, taking ownership of their learning process, exercising a lively interchange of ideas, and not always knowing the answers, yet fulfilling rigorous intellectual study and committed activism, then this means we have to change the way we teach, the way we interact with students, and what we expect from students. The ability to stay the course or have the courage to create a new path may be one of the biggest hurdles we have yet to face; it's difficult to negotiate the silences, uncomfortable conversations, numerous revisions, personal attacks, and political repercussions.

The first step is to be well versed in whatever version of democracy one commits to, then to envision possible applications in the classroom, from assignments to class structure, to student responsibility, to extending the boundaries of the classroom, to questioning/reflecting/modifying the course as a group while you work on needed consensus, action, and transformative learning.

CPG: According to Hopkins (1997) education is considered to be the most accessible means for achieving social, political, economic, and cultural liberation in the United States. This traditionalist view accepts the idea that public schools are vehicles of democracy and social and individual mobility. Educators and laypersons alike believe that the nature of public schools is the major mechanism for development of a democratic and egalitarian society (Hopkins, 1997).

Gutmann and Thompson (1996) posit:

> In any effort to make democracy more deliberative, the single most important institution outside government is the educational system. To prepare their students for citizenship, schools must go beyond teaching literacy and numeracy, though both are of course prerequisites for deliberating about public problems. Schools should aim to develop their students' capacities to understand different perspectives, communicate their understandings to other people, and engage in the give-and-take of moral argument with a view to making mutually acceptable decisions. These goals, which entail cultivating moral character and intellectual skills at the same time, are likely to require some significant changes in traditional civic education, which has neglected teaching this kind of moral reasoning about politics. (359)

We must hold our students accountable by shifting them from this traditionalist view of education and democracy. To teach, learn, and lead democratically requires constant participation with and in change. Critical change occurs with significant self-sacrifice, potential alienation/rejection, and costly consequences. As educators, we must do justice to the larger social/public responsibility of our positions/roles. Because schooling is such a substantial process in identity formation, educational leaders must confront the need and exercise courage in making educational changes for social justice. In (re) crafting the education of leaders we must demystify change/courage/risk as we (re)imagine the language and fluency of multiple discourses in the rediscovery of democracy and social justice to prepare teachers and principals for the echo boomers and their children.

Pedagogical Implications

CPG: Teaching is political as well as a liberatory practice. I believe our nation's freedom depends upon the development of exciting and enticing democratic learning communities where the pursuit of knowledge is the primary objective. According to hooks (2003)

> We need mass-based political movements calling citizens of this nation to uphold democracy and the rights of everyone to be educated, and to work on behalf of the ending of domination in all its forms—to work for justice, changing our educational system so that schooling is not the site where students are indoctrinated to support imperialist white-supremacist capitalist patriarchy or any ideology, but rather where they learn to open their minds, to engage in rigorous study and to think critically. (p. xiii)

I believe that this can only occur through democratic education and at the heart of democratic education is teaching. Teaching is who I am and through my scholarship and service I strive to create opportunities for aspiring educational leaders and members of the public community to journey with me in the pursuit of *logos* and *mythos* that will transform our society and well-being.

Teaching that is dynamic, engaging, and transformative cannot be reduced to technique. The teacher's personality, desire, understanding of self and others, and ability to bring a lesson to life entails more than the ability to deliver texts, concepts and "how to" lessons. According to hooks (1994) "teaching is a performative act. And it is that aspect of our work that offers the space for change, invention, spontaneous shifts, that can serve as a catalyst drawing out the unique elements in each classroom" (p. 11). Because I believe learning takes place within a classroom that is spontaneous and ever-changing, I strive to create a "safe" space within our learning/classroom community so that students will begin to engage who they are as educators and future transformative leaders.

This often places students outside of their comfort zone. I challenge students to critique assumed cultural scripts and positions of power and authority. I invite them to engage in inquiry that questions, investigates, analyzes, and evaluates assumed paradigms. It is in this liberatory practice that our learning community learns to be holistic as it deconstructs "notions" of entitlement, whiteness, and privilege. In the development of a democratic classroom, I encourage students to reflect upon one of hooks' (1994) most powerful statements regarding vulnerability and empowerment: "any classroom that employs a holistic model of learning will also be a place where teachers grow, and are empowered by the process. That empowerment cannot happen if we refuse to be vulnerable while encouraging students to take risks" (p. 21).

Empowering self and others takes great courage. I encourage risk-taking by modeling the process. Palmer (1998) posits, "the courage to teach is the courage to keep one's heart open in those very moments when the heart is asked to hold more than it is able so that teacher and students and subject can be woven into the fabric of community that learning, and living, require" (p.11). I often deconstruct my own identity and praxis during our classroom seminars. I share my challenges and triumphs as an educator with students openly. I want students to know that the journey of the self towards self-knowledge is a never ending process and that I, too, must navigate and negotiate the intersections of race, class, and gender to better teach and serve the academic and public community. I also strive to communicate to our students that teaching is a political act and often times confronting your own beliefs as well as the beliefs of others is a struggle. As hooks (1994) asserts, "teaching was about service, giving back to one's community. For Black folks teaching—educating—was fundamentally political because it was rooted in antiracist struggle" (p. 2).

Final Thoughts

CP: This non-traditional/post-formal chapter explores through conversations the meaning of democracy and how we hold our students accountable in our educational leadership preparation program. We began this journey knowing that American democracy is under re-construction. This re-construction is situated within globalization, sociocultural politics, free market enterprise, and evangelical fundamentalism. Gause (2005b) writes and offers the following questions:

> We are educating in a time of expanding globalization whose impact we witness via 24-hour digitally mediated discourse. How are schools and educational leaders keeping up with this global transformation? What type of impact does this transformation of schools from sites of democracy to "bedfellows" of consumerism have upon the school and much larger global community? How are the "souls" of schools affected? In the journey of school reform are educational leaders acknowledging that the "process of schooling" is filled with "cultural politics"? How are educational leadership programs

preparing future school leaders? Are educational leadership preparation programs equipping schools' leaders for the "journey of the self" or for the "journey of the soul"? (p. 242)

As we further our investigation into this project we ask that you the reader engage in dialogue with us utilizing the aforementioned questions as a platform of discussion. There is a need for a citizenry who will respond to knowledge in ways that will benefit not only formal/informal organizations/institutions and communities, but the social order as well, this is the essence of participatory democracy. We believe the role of the educational leader in the twenty-first century is to facilitate the development of inviting, engaging and dynamic learning communities that (1) break up fallow ground, (2) transform the human condition, and (3) create spaces for open dialogue. Transformation is re-creating who we are to better serve humanity.

LV: One would hope enough collective courage exists to make this tangible and accessible. We need to look at what we can do with our students, in classes and in our department, not only assignments, but experiences as well.

UR: If this is really a democracy and we are bringing in other voices…particularly the voices of our students; however there are only three voices speaking at the moment…we understand the limitations of this text.

LV: I'm not sure I follow this, Rick. Is democracy an inclusion of all voices, or access to and balance of the voices that exist, at least as it pertains to us three?

CPG: It is up to the various readers to bring in themselves, who they are and their various ideological and pedagogical orientations to this conversation. This is the democratic experiment at its best.

LV: So we invite any reader to join us at:

(http://beyondgenericdemocracy.blogspot.com).

Our conversations are just getting off the ground.

Notes

1. The Department of Educational Leadership and Cultural Foundations is governed by Statement of Commitments that articulate the development of a just and caring democratic society in which schools serve as centers of inquiry and forces for social transformation.

These belief statements and learner outcomes are the basis for our pedagogical practices as advocates of social justice, as well as situate our research and scholarship as forms of activism. You may view this document at http://www.uncg.edu/elc.

References

Barber, B. (2002). Beyond *Jihad* vs. McWorld. *The Nation.* http://www.thenation.com/doc/20020121/barber. Accessed 3/2/2006.

Beane, J. A., & Apple, M. W. (1995). *Democratic schools.* Alexandria, VA: ASCD

Dewey, J. (1916). *Democracy and education.* New York: Macmillan.

Gause, C. P. (2005a) The ghetto sophisticates: Performing black masculinity, saving lost souls and serving as leaders of the New School. *Taboo: The Journal of Culture and Education,* 9(1): 17-31.

————. (2005b). Guest editor's introduction: Edu-tainment: Popular Culture in the making of schools for the 21st century. *Journal of School Leadership,*15(3): 240-242

Goodman, J. (1992). *Elementary schooling for critical democracy.* Albany, NY: SUNY Press.

Gutmann, A., and Thompson, D. (1996). *Democracy and disagreement.* Cambridge, MA: Harvard University Press.

hooks, bell. (2003). *Teaching community: A pedagogy of hope.* New York: Routledge

hooks, bell. (1994). *Teaching to transgress: Education as the practice of freedom.* New York: Routledge.

Hopkins, R. (1997). *Educating black males: Critical lessons in schooling, community, and power.* Albany, NY: State University of New York Press.

Knight, T., and Pearl, A. (2000). Democratic education and critical pedagogy. *The Urban Review,* 32(3): 197-226.

Lummis, C. (1996). *Radical democracy.* Ithaca, NY: Cornell University Press.

Palmer, P. (1998). *The courage to teach: Exploring the inner landscape of a teacher's life.* San Francisco, CA :Jossey Bass.

Strike, K. A. (1993). Professionalism, democracy, and discursive communities: Normative reflections on restructuring. *American Educational Research Journal* 30(2): 255-275.

West, C. (2004). *Democracy matters. Winning the fight against imperialism.* New York: Penguin Press.

11

Margaret Haley as Diva: A Case Study of a Feminist Citizen-Leader

Kathleen Knight Abowitz and Kate Rousmaniere

Introduction

This chapter is about educational leadership, gender, power, and citizenship. In it, we propose a feminist model of leadership in education that allows for ambition, incorporates power, and discusses leadership as performance. We introduce the notion of diva citizenship (Berlant, 1997) as a leadership model for women who work for and with others by actively disrupting current systems of educational practice.

We use the term citizen-leader in this chapter to signal both the importance of active political citizenship and the ways in which this type of civic action paves the way for others to act in the politics and governance of the school. T.S. Marshall (1998) defines political citizenship as "the right to participate in the exercise of political power as a member of a body vested with political authority" (p. 94). Political citizenship in the United States is often seen in a most limited and limiting way, associated with the act of voting. Parker notes that we have an "impoverished notion of citizenship that involves little more than civic voyeurism—watching other people (elected representatives) act like citizens" (Parker, 1996, p. 121). Similarly, participation in educational institutions can take on the same spectator role: watching the federal government, legislators, school administrators, and locally elected school representatives shape schooling processes and outcomes. In this chapter we want to emphasize a notion of citizen not as mere witness but as active participant. This chapter has particular concern with the active participation of women and racial and class-based minorities in schools, for it is the interests of these individuals and groups that many public schools still largely ignore.

Schools are a domain of public life that is heavily populated by women as workers, but less often as formal leaders. Conceptions of active political citizenship are crucial in the educational realm, where women have long been standing in the front of classrooms but only recently have stepped outside of those classrooms into informal or formal leadership roles. In using the term citizen-leader for this context, we signal an expansive meaning of leadership beyond formalized titles or hierarchical forms. For example, teachers exhibit citizen-leadership when they step out front and "speak truth to power" about inadequacies in schools by publicly framing an educational problem for others to hear and examine in a new way. In this age of top-down educational reform that emphasizes testing over learning, and punishment over relation, teachers are sorely in need of more creative models of citizen-leadership.

The notion of diva citizenship comes from postmodern feminist Lauren Berlant (1997) and provides a provocative way to think about positioning women and other historically marginalized peoples as citizen-leaders in educational sites. Through a case study of the life of early twentieth-century teacher union leader Margaret Haley (1861–1939) (see Rousmaniere, 2005), we mine the construct of diva citizenship to show how feminist and postmodern ideas of public voice and leadership might be conceptualized for schooling, particularly to be used by women, people of color, and the poor—all groups historically underserved by schools.

Margaret Haley stands as a model of diva citizenship in education. The founder of the first American teachers' union, a passionate advocate for structural school reform and for the authorization of teachers' voice in educational policy, Haley had a distinctive and dynamic leadership style and vision that incorporated the attributes of what we call diva citizen-leadership. Certainly many of these characteristics were Haley's response to her own historical context; thus we do not hold Haley as a rigid model for educational leaders in other contexts who face different barriers and challenges. Still, as a woman excluded from avenues of political power, who responded to that exclusion in particular ways, Haley offers a model of political activism that is a useful way of rethinking power, leadership, and citizenship in educational reform.

The chapter is organized in the following manner. First, we introduce the idea of citizenship by exploring feminist theory's different approaches to the topic of political participation in democratic life, and educational leadership as a particular form of that participation. Feminist citizenship theories have explored in depth the transgressive leap from private to public that has defined feminist citizenship. Schools represent a particular site in which private, domestic interests and bodies of children meet public interests and agendas, and teachers—and other educators—occupy a bridge between the public and private worlds because educating and caring for children is still "women's work." Feminist theories of educational leadership, which we briefly survey in this section, bring into focus the ways in which women's leadership has been theoretically configured as it has negotiated this private/public domain.

We then turn to the notion of diva. The figure of the diva is grounded in the feminine, in women's positions and performances in public life, typically as singers or starlets on-stage. In performing as divas, women act: they use their voices, bodies, and minds to put themselves in the public eye. Similarly, when Berlant (1997) uses Anita Hill as a diva citizen par excellence, she is highlighting Hill's simple and powerful move of speaking the truth, of standing up and using voice, body, and mind to name a problem—notably, a "public" problem that many in our patriarchal society wish to dismiss into the "private" realm: sexual harassment. We draw on the work of postmodern and other critical feminists and trace out five characteristics of the diva citizen-leader.

Next, we turn to our case study, and mine the life and work of teacher and union activist Margaret Haley to show how a diva citizen-leader makes educational change. Finally, we summarize the ways in which an educator as diva can transcribe a marginalized identity into a more powerful one through a postmodern feminist model of citizen-leadership, exploring both the problems such a model might solve, and also anticipating the sort of problems such a model will create.

Feminist Notions of Citizenship and Educational Leadership

> Citizenship has existed for nearly three millennia; with very minor exceptions, women have had some share in civic rights in the most liberal states for about a century. This juxtaposed contrast has sometimes been explained by the argument that citizen-ship, particularly in its civic republican mode, is a status invented by men for men. (Heater, 2000, p. 203)

Only until very recently have women been citizens in any full sense of the term, and the feminist scholarship on citizenship—its historical patterns, theoretical foundations, and social constructions—reveals the ways in which gender still marks patterns of civic participation. Since citizenship has been historically a practice enjoyed by one certain group in our society, the very meanings of the term are "delimited conceptually by falsely universalizing one particular group's practice of it" (Jones, 1998, pp. 222–223). In other words, the ways in which we envision the activities, practices, and dispositions of *the citizen* and the political realm are layered with gendered and patriarchal meanings.

The feminist scholarship on citizenship is rich and diverse. Feminist notions of citizenship can be understood as occupying three basic theoretical positions or camps: liberal feminism, difference feminism, and postmodern feminism (Dillabough and Arnot, 2000). These positions do not represent "pure" categories but general, often overlapping theoretical locations. Liberal feminists, also called humanist or equality feminists, are occupied with the simple yet fundamental challenges of integrating women as full citizens, using the current social meanings of citizen without troubling the potentially negative, gendered implications of the term itself. Liberal feminists, as scholars and activists, address the barriers to women's full participation as citizens. Redistributing family responsibilities, for example, would free up women to engage in democratic work outside the home. Assuring that all women, no matter where they worked (in an office, in the home, in a factory), have adequate health and Social Security insurance would provide women with the full benefits that civic membership should provide. Liberal feminists in education have fought for the inclusion and success of girls in areas of study typically seen as the domain of boys, such as upper-level math and science courses, or traditionally male vocational programs like computer technology, building trades, or aviation technology (see Kaplan, 2003).

Liberal feminism, at first glance, looks like a promising path for women educational leaders. For many years, the idea that women were essentially (biologically, morally, and in all other senses) different from men had justified the laws and norms that kept women out of educational leadership and policy decision making. The history of the teaching profession bears out how a feminized identity was used to diminish teaching as real work. The occupation of teaching became feminized in the late nineteenth century in order to draw upon a pool of workers who could be paid less than men and who could be told what to do by men administrators. Central to this new occupational identity was the expectation that women teachers worked out of care for children—that their work was public mothering, a labor of love, a natural feminine gift—and not a "real" occupation. Teaching was not work but a self-sacrificing mission that was not deserving of money or power (Rousmaniere, 1997). Liberal feminists argue that if these differences between men and women could be minimized in rhetoric and leadership performance, women could achieve educational equality. Liberal feminists originally argued that to be effective leaders, women had to learn how to be like men—to take on male traits of assertiveness and independence in their leadership. Early liberal feminist theorists on women in leadership argued that simply removing the structural and procedural impediments to leadership positions, and teaching women how to gain power like men would achieve equality. Discrimination itself was irrational and could be averted procedurally if egregious barriers were eliminated and women were urged to adopt the traits of male leaders, since these were the traits that were determined to be "natural" to successful leaders. (Shakeshaft, 1989)

Some critics of liberal feminism argue that fighting for equality is inadequate, "because, within the existing patriarchal conception of citizenship, the choice always has to be made between equality and difference, or between equality and womanhood" (Pateman, 1992, p. 20). Difference feminists are concerned with reconstructing our conceptions of citizenship to include traditionally female values (caring, nurturance), making space in the public sphere for the important values and activities of women as care-givers, home-makers, and sustainers of community life. Elshtain (1998) points us to the heroine of Sophocles' drama *Antigone* (447 B.C.E), who rather than allowing her brother to be dishonored by the state, defies the political ruler for her family's honor and duty to the sacred human rite of burial. Elshtain asserts that although women in Antigone's time were denied the rights and duties of citizenship, she is an example of an "active historic agent, a participant in social life who located the heart of her identity in a world bounded by the demands of necessity, sustaining the values of life-giving and preserving" (p. 371). Jones states, "Citizenship has to be redefined to accommodate women's bodies in their concrete, historically changing forms....[constructing citizenship] that encourages the articulation of interests and the pronouncement of authority in voices of many registers" (Jones, 1998, p. 229).

Rather than perceiving gender difference as a deficiency on the part of women, feminist theorists advance women's difference as a sign of superiority. For difference feminists, the problem lies not with making women accepted and acceptable as citizens; the problem is with the meanings of citizen and public life. Educational theorists such as Noddings (1992) and Roland Martin (1992) advance similarly positioned versions of difference feminism in education, advancing modes of relationality and community, formerly associated with the women's domain of home and civic life, to be incorporated into school structures, curriculum, and moral education. Drawing on social psychology research that claims that women and men see life differently--women through a lens of care and interdependence and men through a lens of rights and independence (Gilligan, 1982)--difference feminist educators argue that women educational leaders prioritize relationships over authority, work through collaboration and not competition, and make explicit their responsibilities to children and to human relationships. Difference feminists argue that women's leadership is guided by an ethic of care, and women leaders create "relational leadership" and a "circle of empowerment" that is based in attending to the day-to-day realities of schools (Irwin, 1995; Regan and Brooks, 1995). These characteristics are then advanced as more appropriate for leaders in a democratic school system (Shakeshaft, 1989).

While difference feminism in educational leadership has made a positive impact by showing the ways in which both "feminine" and "masculine" traits are needed in real school leaders, the construct of male/female leadership can still lead to gender stereotypes and can serve to perpetuate power imbalances that are typically not diagnosed as problematic by difference theorists. By applauding gendered leadership traits, difference feminists run the risk of reaffirming a long organizational history of women educators' confinement to caring work in classrooms, and men to higher paying, higher prestige leadership work in administration. Difference feminists' calls to make administration more "caring" still leave the burden of change on women, as they struggle to change a powerful cultural ideology that effective administration is about power and authority, and not about care.

Postmodern theories of feminist leadership have disrupted the trait-based binary of a "men's" and "women's" style of leadership. Jill Blackmore claims that such a discourse sets up new universalizing norms that idealize women as being self-sacrificing, averse to public ambition, and universally bonded to the private world of children. The notion of a "women's style of leadership" also creates a false category of women that ignores class and racial divides and political differences between women. And most importantly, the emphasis on women's traits as leaders "diverts attention away from the politics of workplaces and labour process research." (Blackmore, 1999, p. 60) Such theories perceived "the glass ceiling" "as a barrier to be penetrated rather than deconstructed in order to seek out what it constitutes, why and how has it been maintained" (Blackmore, 129). In short, theories of women's ways of leading simply reverse the sexism of traditional theory. As Jackie Blount has argued, "To say women should be school administrators because of their sex is just as dangerous as the time-honored practice of insisting that only men be leaders" (Blount, 1998, p. 162).

Postmodern critiques that examine how power works in educational politics open up new conceptions of educational leadership. Crys Brunner draws on the metaphor of warriors to make sense of the lives and work experience of women school superintendents, as they learn to explore the "battleground" of educational leadership. She notes how battle metaphors pervade educational talk—from teachers being "in the trenches" to "fighting the good fight" for educational reform. She argues that women educational leaders are warriors because they fight for children; they are also warriors because they have entered a domain from which they and their beliefs have been historically excluded (Brunner, 2000). Brunner's use of the metaphor of warrior moves away from identifying gender traits of caring or not-caring and begins to examine how woman leaders negotiate power in a hostile territory that is not of their own making.

Postmodern feminist theory in citizenship and education seeks to trouble the dualisms between equality and difference feminisms, and "recognize more plurality in politics and society and focus on key questions around voice, identity, and discourse" (Dillabough and Arnot, 2000, p. 24). Skeptical of positions on either side of the debate, they find liberal feminism too locked into discourses of rights, reason, and universal citizenship, and difference feminism too vulnerable to essentialized notions of difference that are regressive to efforts for equality and recognition. Through deconstructing the *feminine* as well as the *citizen*, postmodern feminist Lauren Berlant (1997) offers a way to re-think women's roles in educational leadership.

Diva citizenship

As a postmodern feminist, Berlant aims to deconstruct contemporary dominant notions of citizenship and public life and to reconstruct models of political agency appropriate for women and other groups who are still marginalized. Her concept of "diva citizenship" provides a model of narrating the truth of oppressed people and groups through performances that utilize the necessary drama of such a narration.

> Diva citizenship occurs when a person stages a dramatic coup in a public sphere in which she does not have privilege. Flashing up and startling the public, she puts the dominant story into suspended animation; as though recording an estranging voice-over to a film we have all already seen, she re-narrates the dominant history as one that

the abjected people have once lived sotto voce, but no more; and she challenges her audience to identify with the enormity of the suffering she has narrated and the courage she has had to produce, calling on people to change the social and institutional practices of citizenship to which they currently consent. (Berlant, 1997, p. 223)

Enacting this model of political agency that hopes to shape the power of the diva toward the goals of social justice, Anita Hill countered dominant constraints of family-values citizenship when she testified against Clarence Thomas in an effort to show that the workplace is a public space in which women's so-called private, sexual, and economic vulnerabilities are exposed (Berlant, p. 227). For Berlant, diva citizenship exists in acts of pedagogy, risk, controversy, and struggle in response to emergencies—threats to human dignity, like slavery, or sexual harassment—that are embodied, and first experienced as personal, intimate, and private. Diva citizenship exists in acts of public pedagogy about conditions of oppression or exclusion, acts which transgress the public/private divide and are historically embedded in systemic relations of power. Diva citizenship is political action in the sphere of counterpublics "in which it is hoped that the poesis of scene making will be transformative, not replicative merely" (Warner, 2002, p. 122).

Mamie Till Bradley, mother of Emmett Till, provides another example of diva citizenship. After her son was brutally murdered by White racists in Mississippi in the summer of 1955, Ms. Bradley turned her private suffering into public outrage. "This 33-year-old Chicago resident 'wanted the whole world to see' what had happened to her son" (Feldstein, 1994). "She insisted that his battered body appear in an open casket at the funeral" (in Hill Collins 2000, p. 194). Ms. Bradley did not retreat into a secluded grief but took to the streets in the months and years after her son's death, working to make her son's death meaningful in light of the larger sufferings of the Black nation. Now, in retrospect, Emmett Till's death marks the beginning of the Civil Rights Movement in America, and Till Bradley as one of its noted citizen-leaders. Hill Collins documents the power of Black mothers who fight on behalf of their own, and their neighbor's, children. "Raising their Black children in racist environments fosters new views of motherhood for many of these women. This is an entirely different understanding of political activism and empowerment than fighting on one's own behalf" (Ibid).

The Black feminist concept of "womanist" furthers the notion that black women's political activism evolves from a cultural standpoint of oppression and marginalization. "Womanist" characteristics are based in the realities of how

Black women have historically had to resist and advocate for themselves and their communities. Alice Walker, who coined the term womanist, described its origins in black folk expressions of mothers to their self-confident and aspiring female children, "You acting womanish," or, like a grown-up woman. To be called womanish was, according to Walker,

> usually referring to outrageous, audacious, courageous, or willful behavior. Wanting to know more and in greater depth than is considered "good" for one. Interested in grown-up doings. Acting grown-up. Being grown-up. Interchangeable with another black folk expression: "You trying to be grown." Responsible. In charge. Serious.(Walker quoted in Ropers-Huilman and Taliaferro, 2003, p. 157)

A diva is deliberately womanish in that she is acting powerfully or courageously in a way that is not befitting a person of her station. A girl-child struggling to assume adult roles and responsibilities may be accused of acting womanish. A woman citizen-leader, assuming the diva stance, is also performing a courageous act that will seem, to some, out of the bounds of normalcy or appropriate behavior.

Like a girl acting womanish, a diva is assuming power by her own initiative and performance. A contemporary diva is powerful not in spite of her marginalized location as woman or woman of color, but through the cultivation of the power that such marginality can provide.

Diva typically implies a lead performer of celebrity status, one whose power and influence within her profession allow her to dictate the terms of her performances, "asserting control over her peers and putative directors. … She cultivates a personality that befits such attention: a magisterial and confident pose, elegant diction, graceful movements, and a studied indifference to the mundane and tedious elements of daily life." (Jung 1999, p. 4–5)

The diva constructs herself through an aesthetic performance of self—a self that may be, in the contemporary diva's world, an utterly feminized icon of conventional beauty and grace. Yet divas twist the feminine into a commanding source of authority through their performance *as* powerful people. Jung writes, "this aesthetic power provides [the diva] with autonomy, security, capacity for growth, and the ability to effect profound improvements in the lives of others." (Ibid. 8). The aesthetic, performative power of the diva ironically derives from her exclusion from normal channels of power. "From marginality comes the potential for alternative resources." (Ibid.) The diva is inherently a performer, and one in whom the performance allows a liberating and autonomous force.

In sum, we wish to make use of the construction of diva citizenship as a model for educational leadership. Five characteristics describe our model of diva citizen-leadership.

1. Diva citizens are people who are structurally disenfranchised. They are marginalized from both power and information about power. They lack the status and authority of traditional leaders, and they gain power by disrupting the structure in part through the force of their own personal will.

In describing Black feminist activist work, Hill Collins speaks to the "power of self-definition and the necessity of a free mind"—the role that a conscious-ness of freedom plays in resistance and agency (2000, p. 285). The diva citizen performs and gains power in her marginalized status through a strength fed by an evolving consciousness of freedom and human dignity.

2. Diva citizens gain authority and voice through performing gender in a way that may both underscore gender "differences" and also twist gender norms, making them obvious and ironic as the limitations and falsities of these "differences" are seen in the performance.

Diva starlets like Diana Ross and Madonna perform gender in ironic ways—they may project an image of supreme beauty, grace, and femininity, but they are known for their steely personal power and control over their perform-ances, their money, their image, and their lives. Divas are akin to difference feminists in that they are not engaged in a project of apeing men or masculine ways of engaging in public life. They are unafraid to use their unique experi-ences *as* women to articulate their public voice.

3. Diva citizens disrupt the norm. Their transgression into the public sphere, their manipulation of gender roles, and their use of humor, irony, and bombast lead them to disrupt public notions of normality, undermining laws, common assumptions and rituals.

The diva is a construct that has traditionally transgressed gender norms in powerful ways—women who inhabit femininity but use it as a tool to disrupt the normal. Anita Hill, in her polished lawyer suits, channeled her cool profes-sionalism into a testimony so jarring in its intimacy and truth that it shook "the ground of collective existence" (Berlant, 1997, p. 223). While sexual harassment was, in the intimate spheres of gendered life, a "normal" occurrence that women have learned to subtly resist or silently tolerate, Hill disrupted this oppressive normalcy by undermining the sacred halls of the U.S. Senate with her descriptions of sexual misconduct of her former boss and now Supreme Court justice.

4.   Diva citizens may have strong, dynamic and often difficult personalities. They have an attitude, a combination of ego, audacity, talent, strength, and chutzpah that combine to set them apart from many women and from people with power. They have ambition—they want to be successful, to lead, to have power, to influence others. Their ambition can be accompanied by a single-focus, domineering, autocratic leadership style, a domineering and assertive way of being that can be exclusive and difficult.

5.   The history of women's political participation and activism is typically narrated as cooperative, relational work that is characterized by solidarity and the communal networks which embed the single activist in a larger associational web (see Eisler, 1987; Welch, 1990). As progressive educators, we go against the grain to hold up a model of political activism and leadership that is characterized in part by its acknowledgment of the benefits of individual strength and the singular ambition to influence others. While we understand the limits of the diva citizen—progressive politics cannot survive without cooperative, communal models of political work—there are many moments in schools and in public life at large that call for the diva's assertive, near domineering power. Diva citizens work for the good of others. Originating outside of power, their motivation is to make power available to others from the margins. They have a strong understanding and respect for the every day struggle of every day people, and their leadership is informed by resistance strategies and a "logic of survival" intended to obtain dignity for ordinary people amongst the institutions and policies they did not build. (Bettina Aptheker quoted in K. Jones, 1993, pp. 114-116).

Ours is a reconstructed model of the diva, in which a disenfranchised person uses the performance of a diva in order to bring attention to a suffering or an injustice that is being silently, duplicitously tolerated by the majority, rather than to herself alone. Theologian Katie Cannon (1985) describes the importance of a biblical faith in the prophetic tradition that helped Black women to "devise strategies and tactics to make Black people less susceptible to the indignities and proscriptions of an oppressive white order" (in Hill Collins, 2000, p. 213). While prophets have traditionally been men, their courage, audacity, and truth-telling power make them a likely parallel to the model of diva citizenship that we construct here. Diva citizens, like prophets, lead resistance efforts and loudly testify to the injustices of our society. Like the examples of martyred prophets such as Martin Luther King or the historical Jesus, divas also take many public risks in inhabiting this role.

There are many cultural moments that demand the performance and work of diva citizens. In what follows, we describe an historical moment in which a diva citizen emerged from the ranks of an immigrant family and school-teacher vocation to become a powerful activist for public schools. In examining this case of diva citizen-leadership, we show how one woman used this model to make progressive change for schools.

Margaret Haley: Diva Citizen-leader

Born in 1861 into an Irish immigrant family in rural Illinois, Margaret Haley became a country school teacher at age sixteen. She later moved to Chicago where she taught in one of the city's poorest school districts for over a dozen years before she joined the newly formed Chicago Teachers' Federation in 1897, an organization founded and led by women elementary teachers for the purposes of protecting their pension and improving working conditions in city schools. Haley immediately led the Federation into the heart of urban school politics by directing a successful legal challenge of corporate tax deductions that had emptied the city school board coffers. In 1900 Haley left the classroom to become the paid business representative, lobbyist, and administrative leader of the Federation, a position which she held until her death in 1939.

During Haley's tenure, the Federation fought for increased salaries, a stable pension plan and tenure laws, and it led investigations into teachers' working conditions and school funding. Haley negotiated an unprecedented affiliation between teachers and the Chicago Federation of Labor and led her organization to become Local 1 of the newly formed American Federation of Teachers. Haley worked at the national level too, traversing the country to promote political activism among the nation's predominately female teaching force, and pressuring the powerful, administrator-dominated National Education Association to include the representation of women teachers.

An early critic of what she called the "factoryization" of education, Haley fought not only for teachers' rights as workers but also for teachers' authority to shape the classroom into a caring and supportive environment for children. Echoing John Dewey's faith in the school as a potential agent of social change, Haley believed that the classroom teacher could be the center of humanitarian reform. If the school could not "bring joy to the work of the world," she argued, then "joy must go out of its own life, and work in the school as in the factory will become drudgery." (Haley in Reid, 1982, p. 286) Haley's progressive vision to make schools more humane was embedded in a larger vision to make the American political system more democratic, and she also campaigned for electoral reform, the revision of city government structures, women's suffrage, and school finance reform.

Margaret Haley covered a wide range of political playing fields, linking teachers with labor, the feminist reform movement, municipal reform, and progressive education. At the height of her political activism (1900–1920) she was constantly in the news of Chicago and educational politics, butting heads with captains of industry, challenging autocracy in urban bureaucracy and school buildings alike, arguing legal doctrine in state courts, and urging her constituents into action. Contemporaries described Haley as a dynamo of integrity who "flung her clenched fist" into the faces of men in power (Sandburg, 1915).

Margaret Haley fought for power and voice in the name of citizenship, and she did so by hurling herself from the sidelines of the political playing field into the fray, using her identity as a disenfranchised woman teacher to assert her rights on behalf of children, women, and working people. Throughout her political career, she disrupted, disobeyed, annoyed, and enflamed the early-twentieth-century narrative of how women teachers should behave, who should direct school policy, and what roles educators should play in a democracy. In so doing, she pulled the world of the school, and the lives of children and women teachers into the public political discourse.

Margaret Haley lived out the five characteristics of diva citizenship that we delineated above: she was disenfranchised from avenues of power by both her identity and her occupation; she performed her gender identity as a woman teacher in order to achieve power; she was audacious, outrageous, and fearless; she was ambitious and domineering; and she committed her life's work to improving the day-to-day experiences of teachers and students in schools. Her work as a leader was one of disruption and twisting of norms as she wormed her way from the outside of political legitimacy into the halls of power. We examine her life and work through the five characteristics of a diva citizen-leader outlined above.

One: Diva citizens are people who are structurally disenfranchised, and who gain power by disrupting the structure in part through the force of their own personal will.

In 1900, women's capabilities as citizens were constrained by their inability to vote and by their relegation to low paying and marginalized occupations, absence of information and access to the public sphere, and inaccessibility of political and economic information. While all women suffered this marginality, some were more excluded from public discourse than others: white middle-class women maintained some informational access and power as a result of their class and racial status, while African American women and immigrant and working class women had much less access. Irish American Catholic women in early-twentieth-century America stood in a particularly marginalized location, barely one foot up from their African American and darker-skinned immigrant peers. Even those who had fought their way into the security of such civil service positions as teaching were still marginalized by their ethnic identity (Ignatiev, 1995; Roediger, 1991). In turn-of-the-century Chicago, a large proportion of elementary teachers were Irish Catholic women, and this group identity worked against their attaining political or social legitimacy.

Most elementary teachers in 1900 Chicago worked in under-funded, over-crowded schools, and they had little or no voice in their school management or curriculum design. As women, they could not vote in state elections until 1913, or in federal elections until 1920. Although by the turn of the century, women urban teachers across the country had reaped some benefits such as the pension, higher salaries, and the right to work after marriage, they faced the encroaching authority of centralized city school administrations that emphasized economic efficiency and accountability for educational expenditures. The gendered dynamics of new school administration was not lost on teachers, most of whom were women who worked under an increasing bureaucracy of higher paid men. Haley joined other progressives in her critique of the new school system as being built around "the ideal of the industrial factory system, which made the man at the top the only person with power, and the thousands below him the mere tools to carry out his directions" (Haley in Reid, 1982, p. 86).

Margaret Haley saw such power inequity as the source of all educational problems: the persistent cost cutting of school administrators was driven by wealthy city business interests that maneuvered tax cuts, corrupt deals, and deflated civil service budgets in order to enhance private interests at the expense of the public. Citizen activism was the answer to this problem. In both schools and society, Haley championed political reform in which citizens would be the democratic vanguard against "the political machines and the entrenched vested interests of the city and state" (Haley, 1911, p. 118). Citizens needed to be prepared to take on this new guardianship, and it was the double role of the school to both train future citizens for this task and prepare current citizens to protect the school. Teachers played the central role in this calculus of civic defense, but teachers were disenfranchised from political work, economically marginalized, and woefully ignorant of their own rights. Women teachers were systematically socialized to think of their work as a natural female occupation that deserved little pay or recognition, and they were dangerously ignorant about basic economic practices. Haley argued that teachers needed to develop their own "science of political economy" which would educate them about their own economic rights and make them more alert citizens (Haley, 1901a). Her vision was to educate women teachers into power: the Chicago Teachers' Federation was founded in part for women teachers to study law and to learn how to participate in the political structures that marginalized them. As a leader, Haley acted as educator by providing teachers with access to information about state laws, economic and legal principles, educational theory, and political processes. She taught teachers about the rights that had been denied them in order to change the public world from which they had been excluded. Only by organizing together in educative groups to study economics and political processes could women teachers gain power—both power over their own consciousness and in the halls of the government.

Two: Diva citizens gain authority and voice through performing gender in a way that may both underscore gender "differences" and twist gender norms.

Excluded from political power as a woman and as a teacher, Haley used both of these identities to claim authority. She played on the image of moral authority of the schoolmarm, but instead of the punishing paddle, she drew on a more nationalist metaphor of the warrior. Haley's public image itself was a double imagery of female selflessness and masculine military valor. Like Joan of Arc, with whom she was often compared, reporters inevitably described her by both her femininity as a school teacher and simultaneously by her inherent masculinity as a union powerhouse from Chicago. Reporters described her as both a petite feminine schoolteacher and as a searing politician; she was one of Chicago's "Five Maiden Aunts," and she was a "lady labor slugger" who "stirred

Chicago upside down until she had her way." (Hard, 1906) She was one of the women in politics who were "Soldiers in Second American Revolution," wrote one reporter, who simultaneously described her as "a trim little woman" with "soft brown hair . . . whose blue eyes are soft except for the occasions when she is excoriating some especially repellant abuse, some dishonest politician or some time-serving interest." But she was "absolutely, entirely feminine," assured the reporter, who described her as "A Joan of Arc setting her helmet on straight before the battle—but none the less a Joan!" (Synon, 1914). Describing her own political tactics, Haley twisted President Theodore Roosevelt's imperialist and masculine dictum, "Speak softly and carry a big stick" into her own version of public leadership: "I didn't have a big stick," she recalled, "But I had a little one with nails in it" (Haley in Reid, 1982, p. 230)

Haley began her autobiography with the simple phrase of a humble schoolteacher: "I never wanted to fight" (Haley, 1935). But whether she ever wanted to or not, fighting turned out to be what Margaret Haley did best, and she seemed to enjoy doing it. Battle imagery pervades her autobiography which she called "Battleground." In this memoir, she recalled, "that, like all crusaders, I have stormed in where kings and courtiers feared to tread. I have beaten my fists, and sometimes my head, against stone walls of power and privilege. I have railed at mayors, at governors, at legislators, at presidents of great universities. I have banged machine-guns in defense of certain basic principles" (Haley in Reid, 1982, p. 3). Nor was she reluctant to draw on even more visceral imagery. When describing the teachers' first victory over a despised education bill, she wrote that the women teachers in the Federation "had tasted blood, and we liked the taste" (Haley in Reid, 1982, p. 40).

Haley carefully monitored her image, creating a complex identity that balanced traditional female gender roles with more dynamic and masculine roles of the citizen, patriot, and military hero. Throughout her forty years of public life, she relied on a strategy to publicly justify her very unfeminine public life by continually claiming that she was not looking for trouble, thereby placing the weight of the trouble on the offending party. If it was not her intention to create a problem, then the problem must have existed there in the first place, whether it was undemocratic processes or unqualified leaders. Like a classroom teacher forced to punish a badly behaved boy, she justified the severity of her actions by the seriousness of the problem. This tactic allowed her to spin the teachers' fight into a dramatic battle between the sexes where prim and proper schoolmarms took on cigar-smoking bureaucrats. In these popular images, teachers' labor claims—for salary increases, rights to decision making, and so on—were downplayed and the moral highroad of the lady schoolteacher was promoted. Illustrating a battle in the National Education Association (NEA) where Haley had won the right of classroom teacher to have a voice in that organization, one newspaper portrayed the teachers' victory in a cartoon where Margaret Haley was the stern and upright schoolmistress behind her desk overlooking the schoolboy versions of two male university presidents and NEA leaders, Charles Eliot and Nicholas Murray Butler. The image of the prim and moral schoolmarm who was also a domineering force over masculinity re-fashioned traditional gender roles into a powerful political force.

Three: Diva citizens disrupt the norm.

Distinctive about Haley's work was that she did not *break* the law, but rather *used* the law even as she as a woman was denied her rights to the law, and as a teacher was conceived as passive, almost domestic figure with no interest in politics or law. By pulling women teachers into discussions about law, she disrupted normative assumptions about citizenship, moving women into men's spaces and reaching for men's power. In so doing, Haley "shattered the simple world view of clear dichotomies, sharp boundaries, and established expecta-tions" and accomplished what Marjorie Garber calls a "category crisis"—a "failure of definitional distinction, a borderline that becomes permeable." (Garber, 1992, p. 17). Furthermore, as her opponents organized to discredit Haley, she further disoriented them by fighting back, drawing on humor, mockery, and irony.

The Chicago teachers were constantly reminded that they had no role in public decision making. One elected official told Haley that "when you teachers stayed in your school rooms, we men took care of you," but when they left that sanctity for the political world, they should expect to be punished (Haley in Reid, 1982, p. 72). Public officials echoed the popular press by sharply disap-proving of the teachers' political work to revise tax laws to raise more money for schools, arguing that the problem of taxes was "outside the teachers' province" and that it was "impertinent for public employees to lobby to get more pay for themselves" (Herrick, 1971, p. 103.) Men educational and political leaders expressed their horror at the notion of women teachers claiming any sense of authority, and they organized quickly to delegitimate Haley. When she first spoke up at the NEA meeting in 1901, the first time a woman or classroom teacher spoke up at such a meeting, Commissioner of Education William T. Harris denounced her and advised the crowd to ignore everything said by that "grade teacher, just out of her classroom at the end of the school year, worn out, tired out, hysterical." Haley responded by mocking him. She pled guilty to being a common classroom teacher and admitted that if what she had just done was hysterical, then she hoped it would be contagious so that teachers all over the country would rise up and claim their rights (Haley in Reid, 1982, p. 133).

As her work continued, she faced lawyers and legislature who yelled at her, tried to bribe and threaten her, and made sexual innuendos about her. Haley took advantage of these behaviors by unveiling them to public view. In her speeches and writings, she belittled the enemy, reinforcing her larger portrait of corporate corruption by rhetorically creating an image of hordes of greedy politicians and "oily" lawyers who "bared fangs" at her (Haley, 1911, p. 81). She described the bizarre length to which the captains of industry would avoid facing the small citizen calling for justice, regaling teachers with stories of corporate lawyers hiding in closets to avoid her, legal forms that vanished in thin air, and grown men who turned pale at the sight of the diminutive Haley. She carefully documented official's harassments and bribes and she hired a stenographer to coolly record everything that was said in public meetings, including the curses, to use later in public testimonies (Haley, 1911, p. 120; Winship, 1902).

Haley also developed a popular practice of allowing the opposition to speak at a Federation meeting, thereby presenting the enemy in full view of the antagonistic membership. Male officials who naively volunteered to explain politics to the women teachers found themselves on a stage in front of hundreds of well-educated women, only to be teased and humiliated by them. Sometimes, Haley reflected, "the enemies of a cause do it far more good than do its friends" (Haley in Reid, 1982, p. 36–37). Indeed, Haley increasingly promoted the image of women teachers as tough minded, independent women who would not put up with men, thus crafting a new image of the woman teacher. In one of the Federation monthly bulletins, for example, an article explained why so many Federation teachers were single. It wasn't because they could not get husbands, but because

> they do not care to be bothered with taking care of big, stupid men. They enjoy their freedom and independence and the knowledge that they are members of the most useful and important of callings...why should she descend from this high estate to become the keeper of a blundering, self-sufficient male animal who will have to be watched all the time to keep him out of mischief? ("Why Our Schoolmarms Don't Get Married," 1907.)

Four: Diva citizens may have strong, dynamic and often difficult personalities.

Dynamic, wildly popular on stage, and highly articulate, Haley was also widely criticized as being a demagogue and an obnoxious colleague. Men were not her only critics; many women claimed that Haley was a devious leader who had an abrasive personality and who was self-centered and conceited. Haley's contentious leadership style aggravated other teachers who on a day-to-day level who found her to be opinionated and bull-headed, incapable of compromise, and unwilling to work in any organization that she could not control. One opponent in the Federation charged that Haley was "a dangerous leader" who "hypnotized" members into acquiescence and who believed that people who did not take her point of view had simply not thought enough about the issue. Other teacher leaders charged Haley with undermining other groups if they did not do what she wanted and freely promoting social gossip, innuendo, and manipulation to denounce opponents. She was suspicious about other teacher organizations, including the American Federation of Teachers, which she helped to create, seeing them as encroaching on her own authority, and she criticized their leaders as being politically naïve, inconsistent, and unprepared for the difficulty of political combat (Rousmaniere, 2005, pp. 114-118).

One of her methods of maintaining power was her skill at parliamentary procedure, which she used to disarm her opponents in formal meetings and to force her own issues. Another skill was her ability to obsessively record and recount years of legislative detail, a tendency described by one observer as "forensic combat." She spent years forging connections with reporters, judges, and politicians and documenting the evidence retrieved from them. Such tactics enhanced Haley's power but also furthered the public image that the Federation was not a struggling little organization of lady schoolteachers but an entrenched insider power broker (Wattenberg, 1936. pp. 112-113).

Haley was unapologetic about her character, describing herself as someone whose only flaw was her unbridled passion for justice. Ultimately, she crafted her image as a solitary figure, even as her life's work was the development of democratic processes for teachers. She worked closely and respectfully with only two other women—Catherine Goggin, who shared the leadership of the Federation with Haley until her death in 1916—and Ella Flagg Young, the famous Chicago school administrator. But in her autobiography and public writings, Haley primarily described herself as working alone and accomplishing victories alone, ignoring the collective work of the hundreds of women teachers who made up her organizations.

Five: Diva citizens work for the good of others.

Haley's life goal was to make public the plight of public education. She did this through complex legislative battles through which she revealed corporate and political graft and by publicly describing the desperate physical and social conditions faced by thousands of children and teachers in city schools. She spoke constantly about underserved children, exhausted teachers, soulless curriculum, and nonsensical school management policies that crippled efforts to improve schools. She revealed to the public the role of economic interests in schools and argued that these interests worked at the expense of the humane education of children.

Haley made education a public issue, and in so doing, she changed the shape of American educational politics forever. She drew teachers out of the isolated nineteenth-century schoolhouse and into a cohesive labor unit committed to school reform and teachers' professional development. She encouraged women teachers to take on their own political education, and urged them to step into the public sphere, even as law and social custom excluded them from it.

All of this she did out of her inherent belief that schools were the heart of the civic organization, and the teacher was its steward. "The cause of the teacher is the cause of the people and vice versa, and their common cause is that of the children," she wrote in 1901 (Haley, 1901). The driving force behind all of Haley's activities was her vision of citizenship—that women, teachers, parents, and children had the right and responsibility to be involved in the democratic process and that only education would lead them into that process. In the years before women could vote, and before most Americans even earned a high school diploma, Haley asserted that women public school teachers were citizens who were obligated not only to teach citizenship but to engage in public policy decisions. Teachers' responsibility was to preserve the academic freedom and public nature of schools, guarding against those private interests that tried to exert influence in public schools. She saw the ongoing battles over school funding and administrative control over public schools as nothing less than a battle for the soul of American democracy.

Caveats, Conclusions

The diva creates her image through performance, spectacle, and a public moral critique; she thus creates a new icon of power. There are, of course, appropriate limits on how this power might be usefully taken up in progressive work to reform schools. Diva citizen-leadership should not replace models of cooperation and solidarity-building; it should punctuate, ignite, and inspire such coalition-building. To do so, the diva will need to contain her raw ambition at times and will need to consider the needs of others with whom she leads. This will be a considerable challenge for true divas like Margaret Haley.

But many of us who may not be "true" divas can *perform* diva citizenship in the same way that Anita Hill did—in decisive moments, we are sometimes called upon to publicly speak the truth, in the face of risk to our selves, our job stability, our professional status, and our futures. In these times, the truths of marginalized students, parents, and teachers in schools are whispered, but shouldn't we be shouting? Diva citizen-leaders can provide models and inspiration for those who wish to proclaim their struggles to receive a quality education as public problems. In these times of Title IX rollbacks, standardized high-stakes testing, increasing privatization, and continued struggles to adequately fund public schools, the performance of divas is needed now more than ever. The diva citizen-leader can help bring attention to persistent problems that are right in front of us but which we cannot see. The diva citizen-leader brings her rage, courage, and strength to help us see, with new eyes, the problems of equity and funding that Haley sought to solve and that we continue to battle.

References

Berlant, L. (1997). *The queen of America goes to Washington city: Essays on sex and citizenship.* Durham, NC: Duke University Press.

Blackmore, J. (1999). *Troubling women: Feminism, leadership, and educational change.* Philadelphia: Open University Press).

Blount, J. (1998). *Destined to rule the schools: Women and the superintendency.* Albany: State University of New York Press.

Brunner, C.C. (2000). *Principles of power: Women superintendents and the riddle of the heart.* Albany: State University of New York Press.

Cannon, K. G. (1985). *The emergence of a Black feminist consciousness.* In L. M. Russell (Ed.), *Feminist interpretations of the Bible.* Philadelphia: Westminster Press, pp. 30–40.

Dillabough, J.-A., and Arnot, M. (2000). "Feminist political frameworks: New approaches to the study of gender, citizenship and education." In M. Arnot and J.-A. Dillabough (Eds.), *Challenging democracy: International perspectives on gender, education, and citizenship.* New York: Routledge/Falmer, p. 21–40.

Eisler, R. T. (1987). *The chalice and the blade: Our history, our future.* Cambridge: Harper & Row.

Elshtain, J. B. (1998). "Antigone's daughters." In A. Phillips (Ed.), *Feminism and politics.* New York: Oxford University Press, pp. 21–40.

Feldstein, R. (1994). "'I wanted the whole world to see': Race, gender, and constructions of motherhood in the death of Emmett Till." In J. Meyerowitz (Ed.), *Not June Cleaver.* Philadelphia: Temple University Press, p. 263–303.

Garber, M. (1992). *Vested interests: Cross-Dressing and cultural anxiety.* (New York: Harper, 1992).

Gilligan, C. (1982). *In a different voice.* Cambridge: Harvard University Press.

Haley, M. (1901). Correspondence, August 3, 1901. Chicago Teachers' Federation files, box 36, folder 1. Chicago Historical Society.

———. (1911). Autobiography manuscript. Chicago Teachers' Federation files. Chicago Historical Society.

———. (1935) Autobiography manuscript. Chicago Teachers' Federation files. Chicago Historical Society.

Hard,W. (1906). Chicago's five maiden aunts, *American Magazine,* 62. pp. 481-489.

Heater, D. B. (2000). *History of citizenship.* Allandale Online Publishing. Minneapolis: University of Minnesota Press. Available online at: http://www.netLibrary.com/ebook_info.asp?product_id=43246.

Herrick, M. (1971). *The Chicago schools: A social and political history.* Beverly Hills: Sage Publications.

Hill Collins, P. (2000). *Black feminist thought: Knowledge, consciousness, and the politics of empowerment,* second edition. New York: Routledge.

Ignatiev, N. (1995). *How the Irish became white.* New York: Routledge.

Irwin, R. L. (1995). *A circle of empowerment: Women, education and leadership.* Albany: State University of New York Press.

Jones, K. B. (1993). *Compassionate authority: Democracy and the representation of women.* New York, Routledge.

———. (1998). "Citizenship in a woman-friendly polity." In G. Shafir (Ed.), *The citizenship debates: A reader* Minneapolis, MN: University of Minnesota Press, pp. 221–247 .

Jung, J. A. (1999). *The diva at the fin-de-siècle.* University of California, Los Angeles: Unpublished doctoral dissertation. UMI #9947019.

Kaplan, M. D. G. (2003, 13 January). Fly girl. *New York Times,* 4A, p. 32–34.

Marshall, T.S. (1998). "Citizenship and social class." In G. Shafir (Ed.), *The citizenship debates: A Reader.* Minneapolis: University of Minnesota Press, pp. 93-111.

Martin, J. R. (1992). *The schoolhome: Rethinking schools for changing families.* Cambridge: Harvard University Press

Noddings, N. (1992). *The challenge to care in schools.* New York: Teachers College Press, p. 5, reprint from *Chicago Examiner.*

Parker, W. C. (1996). 'Advanced' ideas about democracy: Toward a pluralist conception of citizen education. *Teachers College Record,* 98(1): 104–125.

Pateman, C. (1992). "Equality, difference, subordination: The politics of motherhood and women's citizenship." In G. Bock and S. James (Eds.), *Beyond equality and difference: Citizenship, feminist politics, and female subjectivity.* New York: Routledge, pp. 17–47.

Regan, H. B., and Brooks, G. H. (1995). *Out of women's experience: Creating relational leadership.* *Thousand Oaks, CA:* Corwin Press.

Reid, R. L. (Ed.) (1982) *Battleground: The autobiography of Margaret A. Haley.* Chicago: University of Illinois Press.

Roediger, D.R. (1991). *The wages of whiteness: Race and the making of the American working class.* New York: Verso.

Ropers-Huilman, B., and Taliaferro, D. (2003). "Advocacy education: Teaching, research, and difference in higher education." In B. Ropers-Huilman (Ed.), *Gendered futures in higher education.* Albany: State University of New York.

Rousmaniere, K. (1997). "Good teachers are born, not made: Self-regulation in the work of nineteenth-century American women teachers." In *Discipline, moral regulation and schooling: A social history,* edited by Kate Rousmaniere, Kari Dehli, and Ning de Coninck-Smith. New York: Garland Publishing.

———. (2005). *Citizen teacher: The life and leadership of Margaret Haley.* New York: SUNY Press.

Sandburg, C. (1915). Margaret Haley, *Reed's Mirror,* December p. 445.

Shakeshaft, C. (1989). *Women in educational administration.* Newbury Park, CA: Sage Publications.

Synon, M. (1914). Women in politics are soldiers in second American Revolution. *Chicago Daily Journal,* February 2, p. 3-4.

Warner, M. (2002). *Publics and counterpublics.* New York: Zone Books.

Wattenberg, W. W. (1936). *On the educational front: The reactions of teachers' associations in New York and Chicago.* New York: Columbia University Press.

Welch, S. D. (1990). *A feminist ethic of risk.* Minneapolis. MN: Fortress Press.

"Why our schoolmarms don't get married. " (1907). *CTF Bulletin,* 6(40).

Winship, A.E. (1902). A woman's victory for schools. *Everybody's Magazine,* 7(4).

12

Unpacking on a Long Journey Home:
A Lesson on Race, Identity, and Culture

Rochelle Garner

Introduction

This chapter was first written upon my return from an educational research and cultural tour in Ghana, West Africa. As I reflect upon this cultural immersion, I continue to find myself unpacking this educational experience by rereading and reexamining the "text" and the many lessons I learned on the ideology of race, identity, and culture. As you read the words in italics throughout this essay, it reflects my stream of consciousness writing this essay, as I am writing a story within a story. As noted by Berger and Quinney (2005) narrative scholars of various stripes seem to concur with the proposition that lived experience can be understood through the stories people tell about it. Stories are ways not merely of telling others about ourselves but of constructing our identities, of finding purpose and meaning in our lives. It is in the telling when "we remember, we rework and reimagine the past, reflect back upon ourselves, and entertain what we have and could become" (Berger and Quinney, 2005). Without discounting the narrative, however, Gubrium and Holstein argue, "researchers should allow 'indigenous voices [to] have their own say' without abandoning their authorial obligation to 'complement and contextualize the explication of informants' accounts, or non accounts as the case might be'" (Berger and Quinney, 2005).

The Awakening of My Journey

I woke up early one morning and asked myself, "Am I crazy, or have I just lost my mind? My husband and my son are in Bermuda and I'm here! I could be cooling out on the beach in Bermuda." Then thinking to myself, "It's only been 2 1/2 weeks and I still have 5 1/2 more weeks to go, whew!" The best thing that I could say to myself was, "No, you're not crazy and yes, Rochelle you can do this." There is no question that some days seemed longer than others being so far away from home; especially, being in an environment and culture which was very different from my home. I survived this pilgrimage home, and returned back across the Atlantic safely to see family and friends as I had prayed. *Home still lingers, where is home?*

In reflecting on my journey, I realize there are so many pieces to the puzzle where I could begin because of the complexity of the culture, while at the same time I can reflect on the richness of the culture, which magnified and unfolded before my eyes. *Home still lingers, I had been waiting all of my life to go home, and finally I was there. Where is home?* As I reflect on the culture, I remember clearly sending postcards to family and friends saying, "We truly have a rich heritage of strong and talented people. You must make the journey!" *Yes, I had finally made it, so others must come.* Today, I will still say the same to family and friends because I have been *home*, to the Motherland, the cradle of civilization, breathed the air, and witnessed the people, *my people,* working hard everyday just to make ends meet. When I think of my grandmother and how strong she was as an African-American woman, I recognized the linkages between my grandmother and the women in Ghana who exemplified the same extraordinary strength. *Home still lingers, I made it home.* Watching the women go about their daily busy lives, going "to and fro" to the market or in the village, many of them carrying their baby on their back with some type of object on their head, and not breaking a stride in their step was unbelievable to me. I realize this was the way of life for many of the Ghanaian women and for them to partake in this "unbelievable experience" was just another "painless" day of getting the job done. Interestingly enough, I said, "painless," however, I never stopped to ask one woman whether or not she experienced any pain carrying a load on her head and her baby on her back (it could have been a bucket of water, a basket of food, fabric or anything that needed to be moved from one place to the other). *Nevertheless, I did not bother to ask her if I could help. Oh my goodness, the thought never crossed my mind.* Now, I wonder what the response would have been if I had asked the women if they felt any pain, or if I could assist them. Would the women have looked at me and laughed, or would they have given me an honest answer. *Since the women are very direct in their communications, I think they would have answered me whether I would have liked the response or not.* Whenever I return, I will pose the question. *Home still lingers.*

When I think of the strength of the people, women's images are first and foremost in my mind. Not only do I think of the women, but I also think of the young girls who are taught at an early age to carry a baby on their back as they are being prepared for motherhood. Although these young girls have yet to experience the physical labor of carrying a baby in their womb, they experience many forms of motherhood by physically carrying their sibling on their back and helping to care for other siblings (some of these girls are as young as six and seven years old). One afternoon, I sat and had a conversation with one of the women professors in her office, and she shared with me a story about a conversation she overheard between her six-year-old daughter and seven-year-old friend. The seven-year-old told the six-year-old that she was not concerned about learning very much in school because her mother had told her that she would find her a rich man to settle down with and marry. The professor of English, who is a single mother shared with me other "cultural beliefs or ways" about women, such as if a woman is highly educated and not married by a certain age, she would be seen as unmarriageable.

Many women in Ghana are still expected to carry out traditional roles of being a wife and mother, along with doing everything else which was made clear by some of the women whom I interviewed. Several women in different interviews repeated the same words, "Women are expected to do everything, even if she has a job or career. She's still expected to cook, clean and take care of the children." Perhaps, educated women would be perceived as "unruly" and one who would possibly ask a lot of questions of her mate. On the one hand, I can see how this could be very true since I perceive patriarchy to be a dominant system in Ghanaian culture. On the other hand, when I think of the Queen Mother's authority in the villages, it makes me wonder what is real and what is perceived?

Did you say Queen Mother?

Many of the Queen Mothers may not have a formal education, and the way the decisions are made in the villages may be very different from an environment where professional women work outside of the village. As I have shared this thought about the possibility of women leading differently, the idea of a complex culture sheds more light on the subject. So, I must continue to raise the question, how do women lead? Who makes what decisions and when? *Home still lingers, and I must keep asking these questions.* Especially, since several different Ghanaians told me that Queen Mothers carry the title but do not have as much clout as people would have one to believe.

On the other hand, as I have learned, Queen Mothers are responsible for development in the village. The roles between what would be considered *traditional* Queen Mothers could vary from Queen Mothers who have been assigned this role outside of the village. These women do not necessarily have to live in the village or be Ghanaian; yet, they have been entrusted by the village to carry out the role of Queen Mother. In *Across the Water*, Dillard (2003) shares her story as a Queen Mother and a particular experience she had in calling a community meeting. Dillard (2003) notes,

> A community meeting can be called at any time by the Chief, Queen Mothers and/or Elders of the village. But this meeting was a bit unusual for me as it was the first community meeting that I'd called on my own that was being held without the presence of the village Chief.

> I called on the community to understand the spiritual nature of life itself: As each of us had been granted by the Creator the gift of life on this day, we also had a responsibility to this community of Mpeasem. And service to this community was our "rent for living" (Edelman, 1992). One of my major responsibilities as nkosua ohemaa is in helping to develop and provide the best possible education for the children of Mpeasem, the ultimate future leaders of the village. But I reminded them, too, that this was not my work alone: It also belonged to them. That the privilege of having a preschool right in the center of the village brought with it the responsibility for not only sending their children to school, but also to paying their school fees as well. In this way, we needed to see development as a cooperative endeavor. Recounting our accomplishments so far, I reminded them of the many projects that had been requested and suggested by them—from planting flowers around the school building to electricity to an income generating farming project. The work of the development is for all of us to do, given our special talents and always on behalf of the children. "This is all I have to say," I said, a traditional way of conclusion. The crowd clapped with enthusiasm. But even in their applause, I knew my words in English were not understood.... I felt sadness and frustration in knowing that ever in a place where I hold an honored leadership role (and where people "know" me), my words were really a symbolic act: Where they were literally heard, they were not literally understood. My message was lost on the very people I wanted to touch with my words .... Yes, it was my desire to have my words "understood" in a literal way. But God reminded me in that moment that words don't belong to me, and are always created for any given occasion and for a divine purpose. ...on this day, it wasn't the literal purpose that was the work, the purpose that we are most often rewarded for as academics. Instead, it was a spiritual purpose. These words, while not understood literally by most people of the Mpeasem community, were used this day to set the tone, to open the spiritual environment of the gathering. My reason for being there was not to "profess" or to even share the details of the various development projects, but to spiritually gather the people

As an African-American woman and college professor, Dillard's role and responsibility may be very different from the traditional Queen Mother who was born in Ghana and lives in the village. The vast nuances of culture in any given society can be quite different, yet, there are certain similarities that distinguish various cultures. Culture, hence, can be described as an "integrated set of norms or standards by which human behaviors, beliefs, and thinking are organized" (Pai and Adler, 2001). Yet, culture can be conceptualized as a "set of dynamic, productive, and generative material (and immaterial) practices in the regulation of social conduct and social behavior that emphasize personal self-management (i.e., the modification of habits, tastes, and style), political affiliation, and trans/national identity" (McCarthy, Giardina, Harewood, and Park, 2005). To say the least, the Queen Mother's leadership in Ghana, and leadership of professional women outside the village can still be considered quite different; yet similar, but culturally complex. *Home still lingers, I'm still lingering for home.*

Whose Research Is It?

When I went to Ghana, I had already determined my topic: "Women in Leadership in Higher Education and Government." As I shared this topic with some of the Ghanaians, several raised the question, "Are you interviewing the Queen Mothers?" *Oh no, here we go again.* My immediate response was "No" and to be quite honest, I had not even thought of them as it related to leadership—the type of leadership I had in mind anyway. The questions I kept getting about interviewing the Queen Mother made me think about the subject deeper. *It was a brief "deeper," because of the complexity of the culture, and how I was thinking of leadership and then integrating the Queen Mother's leadership was too much for this trip. Whew!* I am happy I stayed focused on dealing with a topic more familiar to me, especially due to the length of time I was in Ghana.

My research in Ghana served to be an enriching experience for the two months I was there. Prior to leaving for Ghana, a Ghanaian student gave me the name of his aunt who was an economist. He told me that she would be a good person to interview and she could assist me with names of other women to interview. *Initially, it was a little unsettling to think that I was traveling so far, and did not have a list of people's names to interview. I listened to my spirit and told myself that it would all work out, and it did.* After meeting with my contact person, she gave me names of other women, and the domino effect unfolded as I talked with some of these women.

Because of time, I chose to interview women in leadership positions who were immediately available or willing to make time for me. I interviewed eight women; half of the subjects were in higher education and the other half served in government. By the end of this research project, I had gathered more names of women than time would allow me to interview.

Identifying with the Unidentified: A Humbling Experience

When I went to visit my first informant, Mrs. Benine, I had to wait approximately 20–30 minutes before I could deliver my letter to her that was given to me by my Ghanaian friend Amaj, who was also a doctoral student. I walked into Mrs. Benine's office to find it quite cool with air conditioning (which is a real luxury since the country was experiencing a serious energy crisis), as I looked around the office I noticed many manuals and documents on shelves and stacked in various other places including the floor. Immediately, I thanked Mrs. Benine for allowing me the opportunity to see her without an appointment, then I gave her the letter and she read it while I waited silently staring at her and wondering what type of response I would receive. Amaj wrote her a letter introducing me and asking her to provide me with the assistance I needed with my research project. After she finished reading the letter and looked up at me, I made eye contact and quickly reiterated the purpose of my research and my interest in interviewing her. We set an appointment for the following week. After this initial meeting, I realized how lucky I was because Mrs. Benine was on her way out of the country for the duration of my stay in Ghana. Mrs. Benine, by Ghanaian standards is considered a "Big Woman." By my estimation of American standards, she's a very "Big Woman." In American pop culture, we would probably say she has a lot of "clout" and she makes "bank." The terminology of "Big Woman," as it is used by Ghanaians, acknowledges women who have very high rank or status in society. Mrs. Benine is an economist with the Ministry of Finance.

In the interview, I learned that Mrs. Benine handles economic affairs for Ghana to the extent where she determines which international organizations are allowed to do business or provide economic assistance to the country. Mrs. Benine travels around the world meeting with different organizations and attending various conferences for her job. At the time of our interview, she was on her way to the United States, which would be followed by a trip to Portugal and Spain for other conferences.

Mrs. Benine shared with me various aspects of her life and career, which at one point brought tears to my eyes as she talked about how she had a well installed in her home village in the Central Region. On one occasion, Mrs. Benine went to visit her village, which she does as often as possible, and she asked for a glass of water while visiting. When she received the water, she noticed that it was muddy. Mrs. Benine said that she was surprised to see the muddy water that came from the village stream. This was the same stream the village had gotten water from since her childhood. Now, the water was no longer safe or healthy to drink. When Mrs. Benine returned to her office in Accra, she contacted a company that provided foreign-aid, which could help support the village by installing a well with clean water. After this project was completed, she heard sentiments of dismay by the village people saying, "What do we need a well for? We have been drinking from the stream all of our lives, and how can she come in here and install a well as if our water is not good enough?"

Several months later, Mrs. Benine returned to the village. The village people ran to her car as it entered the village, even the youngest of children singing songs of "praise and thanks." Mrs. Benine told me that there were many different people in the crowd from small babies who did not know her to the village elders shouting, "Thank you." Wondering why suddenly the people were now very happy with the well, someone in the crowd told her, "Thanks for the well, our stream has run dry." By the time Mrs. Benine finished telling me this story, we were both teary-eyed. *A lesson I learned that day is that the human spirit transcends race, ethnicity, identity, and culture and it does not matter how we define ourselves when human dignity and suffering are involved—it's the one element that connects many of us and tells us there is compassion and caring for the very things that make a difference in our lives and we both understood this that day.*

The Researcher Being Researched: Their Eyes Were Watching Me

Mrs. Hawkins, another protégé and mentor of Mrs. Benine's graciously allowed me an interview to discuss her leadership with the Public Service Commission. She is the first woman to serve as a member of the Commission. When I called Mrs. Hawkins to arrange a meeting, she asked, "Where are you, and how soon can you get here?" I replied that I was at the University of Ghana, and it would take approximately one hour to get down town to her office. She agreed that it was okay. Admittedly, I was quite surprised she was willing to see me so soon. *So, I told myself that my previous informant had already brought it to her attention that I would be calling.* Once again, I felt quite lucky since my driver, Micah, was already waiting for me to take me out on appointments for the day. I only expected my interview to last for about an hour, however, it turned into a three-hour interview. *Yes, the Ancestors were working with me that day!*

I arrived at the Public Service Commission and checked in with the security officer for directions on how to find Mrs. Hawkins's office. When I walked into her office, she walked from around her desk, welcomed me and shook my hand. She offered me a seat on the couch and sat down in a chair across from me. Mrs. Hawkins, a tall slim-figured woman was dressed in American style business attire, unlike the traditional African clothing many of the other women wore.

Immediately, I began my script and told Mrs. Hawkins about my research interest and how I got her name as a contact person although she had already been informed of this information. *Today, I wonder how fast the news spread of an "African"-American being in Accra to interview women in leadership.* Mrs. Hawkins began sharing her career path and how she got to her current position. Throughout our three-hour conversation there were many interruptions by people calling on the telephone or stopping by to see her, while observing and meeting me. At one point, Mrs. Hawkins told me that I must meet her daughter whom she called on the telephone and told her to come and meet me. Ten minutes later, Mrs. Hawkins's daughter entered the office and greeted me with a warm embrace. She stayed for a few minutes and then told me she had to go back to her computer class. At another point, Mrs. Hawkins received a phone call from her sister who wanted to borrow money as she explained to me after she hung up. I watched Mrs. Hawkins take some money from her purse, count it and put it in an envelope so it would be ready when her sister arrived. An hour later, her sister arrived to pick up the money and stayed for a while chatting with us. *I'm glad I had my tape recorder.* As the three of us sat and talked, a lady came into the office with food ordered by Mrs. Hawkins. We had yam patties with a sweet onion and tomato stew, and cassava balls. The Ghanaian dishes for lunch were very spicy and quite delectable. Fortunately, I liked everything on the menu since there were some dishes I had tried during my stay in Ghana that did not agree with me or I did not agree with how the meals tasted. Somewhere during my journey, I was informed that Ghanaians are not very happy when you do not like their food and do not eat it. *Whew! I'm glad I made it through that meal.* After lunch, we wrapped up our discussion and Mrs. Hawkins shared with me places where I should travel while in Ghana. She also gave me names of several other women whom she recommended that I interview. *Unfortunately, time was not on my side to conduct those interviews or travel to the other places that were recommended.* By the time we finished talking, I realized that I needed to leave so that I could get back across town for another appointment at the University of Ghana.

This interview made me think a lot about the "other researching the other" who arrived to conduct the research. Our "othering" is relative in the sense of coming from two completely different cultural systems and lifestyles; yet, we bonded as women despite our cultural differences and nuances. We were not really "others," we were "subjects" learning about one another. There were moments when I felt as if I had found home by the warm embrace of these Ghanaian women, and I felt these women felt comforted that I had come from America to learn about their lives. As Collins (2000) notes about Black women's self-definition, she states that rather than defining self in opposition to others, the connectedness among individuals provides Black women deeper, more meaningful self-definitions. Geertz (1995) discusses field research by stating that it is not a matter of working free from the cultural baggage you have brought with you so as to enter, without shape and without attachment, into a foreign mode of life ... it is a matter of living out your existence in two stories at once. Often, I felt myself between the two stories, I had read about Ghana and I had heard many stories from people who were Ghanaian and American, yet, I found myself immersed in a cultural situation learning and listening to the voices of these women who were sharing their stories about everyday life for them. It is clear that no matter how much people try to prepare you for a cultural experience that you will not come to know the "real" lessons until you have lived through the experience. *Home still lingers, I want to go home. I wonder what stories I would have gathered had I stayed longer?*

I have shared only two stories of the eight women I interviewed. Yet, there were common themes among the way most of these women expressed their lives and leadership. The women in this research study realized early in their lives that a college education would offer a better way of living, rather than a menial way of living or solely depending upon their spouse for support. In many ways, I could relate to how these women valued education and wanted to develop their own source of income. In Ghanaian society, these women lived a privileged life. Despite the fact that they were career women, they admitted that they were still expected to do everything at home such as cooking, cleaning, child-rearing, and taking care of their husband's needs. Challenged with this responsibility, many of the women were able to hire "house-help" to assist them in balancing their lives and managing their family and careers. All of the women hold a four-year degree and most of them hold advanced or terminal degrees, while some of the women have studied in the United States or Europe. Another common theme is the way these women talked about their lives and the importance of spirituality in their lives, which influenced the way in they were able to relate to and work with other people.

Reflections upon the Reflection of the Research: Coming to Terms with Contradictions

In many ways, I honestly tried to leave my Western influences and potential biases at home. Prior to my travels, I was told by several different people who had traveled to the African continent that some Africans would welcome and embrace African-Americans, and there were some people who said that may not be the case. Perhaps, it all had to do with each person's individual experience. For me, I was surprised on the one hand, and on the other hand I was totally shocked by some of the experiences and lessons I learned.

When my feet first touched the African soil, I gave a sigh of relief and said to myself, "I'm glad I'm finally here." I had been waiting and dreaming about this moment for more than half of my life. I had read about the atrocities of slavery in grade school (the little that was taught) and I sought out to learn more on my own. As I grew older, the more I learned about Africa, the more I wanted to see it for myself. Finally, I was there. Once, I began interacting with Ghanaians, I noticed a warm embrace by some of the people, but not all. Even some of the individuals who shared the warmth told me things that I was not expected to hear. For example, I learned that many Ghanaians considered African-Americans as being biracial, based on slavery's miscegenation. One day, I was talking with a male professor whom I had become acquainted with from the University of Ghana, and he explained this idea to me. I decided not to take offense, since I only know of my Native-American and African-American heritage and I still would not think of myself as biracial. Since race is socially constructed, it is a term that is used in the United States, but not to the same extent in Ghana. Many African-Americans, who particularly may be of a deeper brown hue, would probably be offended if someone were to call them biracial. As I explained to the professor that my heritage was of Native-American and African-American origin, he responded by saying, "That's biracial." In turn, I responded, "Well, if you consider that biracial, I guess so. I never thought of defining myself that way."

At another point, I had the opportunity to visit an elementary classroom of fifth-graders at the University of Ghana campus. Most of the children who attended this school had parents who worked at the University. One morning, I walked into a classroom of fifth-graders who were dressed in their Cadet uniforms for the day (these uniforms are similar to the American Boy Scouts and Girl Scouts). The male teacher was also dressed in his Cadet leader's uniform; he greeted me and then introduced me to the class as a Black American. Since I was standing directly behind him, I moved forward, whispered in his ear and said, "I'm African-American." He smiled and changed the introduction and said, "African-American"; then, I heard soft snickers from the students. I thought to myself that maybe it was amusing to them to see someone like me describe myself as African-American, especially since Ghanaians saw me as a "Brunnee." Ghanaians describe a "Brunnee" as an individual of mixed heritage. I learned this word while walking across the campus one day, when some kindergartens saw me with other students and they yelled out "Brunnee, Brunnee." When I asked a Ghanaian student, how could they tell that I was not Ghanaian? He replied that they could tell that I was not Ghanaian by the way I looked, the way I dressed (even if I were dressed in traditional Ghanaian clothes they knew the difference), the way I walked and the way I talked. *Now, how was I supposed to unpack this thing called race and identity at this point? I had traveled thousands of miles across the Atlantic to finally meet "my people" to learn they had names for me that I was clueless of, yet, I was determined to define myself as African-American and claimed the whole continent of Africa my home, since I did not know the point of origin where my ancestors were enslaved and brought across the Atlantic to America. Another lesson learned; what you think of yourself may not always be the same as what other people think of you; therefore, how you define yourself versus the way others think of you is far more important.*

Making the journey to Africa and returning home brought me to a catharsis. At one point in my life, I would define myself by saying that I was born in this country (America), but I am of African descent, or I would say that I am African-American; it just depended on the day of the week. In many ways, I was attempting to recognize my American-ness and at the same time deny it or distance myself from it because of the painful experiences my ancestors endured and in many cases the painful experiences African-Americans continue to endure today. At this point in my life, I will say, "Yes, I am African-American and I'm proud of it!" In thinking about all of this, it causes me to pause and reflect on a conversation I had with some African-American students I met at the University of Ghana who were visiting from another university. I mentioned something about being African-American, and this young man responded by interrupting me saying, "African." His response indicated that he was negating my American heritage. Then, I looked at him again, and said, "African-American."

The many encounters and lessons learned throughout this educational experience taught me that I will neither abandon Africa nor America because they both hold meaning for me and a rich heritage to which my people belong. Standing tall and strong, I cannot deny certain truths which include the fact that America has been built on the backs of many of my African-American ancestors who endured the blood, sweat, and tears. While at the same time, African-Americans have continued to make many other great contributions to American culture and society. What has become clear to me is, if one does not recognize from whence s/he came as an African-American, one will never come to know themselves and will always be searching for an identity. Though the web of identity construction fragments my history, I firmly hold to my proud heritage of being an African-American woman. *Home still lingers. I'll make the journey home again.*

References

Berger, R., and R. Quinney (Eds.) (2005). *Storytelling sociology: Narrative as social inquiry.* Boulder, CO: Lynne Rienner Publishers.

Collins, P. (2000). *Black feminist thought: Knowledge, consciousness, and the politics of empowerment.* New York: Routledge.

Dillard, C. (2003). Across the water. Searching (again) in Ghana for the purpose of the word. Paper presented at the annual meeting of the American Educational Research Asociation in Chicago, IL.

Edelman, M. W. (1992). *The measure of our success: A letter to my children and yours.* Boston: Beacon.

Geertz, C. (1995). *After the fact: Two countries, four decades, one anthropologist.* Cambridge, MA: Harvard University Press.

McCarthy, C., Giardina, M., Harewood, S., and Park, J. K. (2005). Contesting culture: Identity and curriculum dilemmas in the age of globalization, postcolonialism, and multiplicity. In C. McCarthy, W. Crinchlow,G. Dimitriadis, and Dolby, N. (Eds.), *Race, identity, and representation in education.* New York: Routledge, pp. 154–155.

Pai, Y., and Adler, S. (2001). *Cultural foundations of education.* Upper Saddle River, NJ.: Merrill.

13

Making Her Community a Better Place to Live: Lessons from History for Culturally Responsive Urban School Leadership*

Lauri Johnson

A teacher's work does not end in the schoolroom. The needs of the pupil and his after school life ... (and encouraging) an unselfish urge to make his community a better place to live should be her immediate concern.

—Gertrude Elise McDougald Ayer

Urban school districts have historically been sites of vast educational inequalities for students and their families from diverse cultural and racial backgrounds. Longstanding issues include overcrowded, under-resourced schools, outdated curriculum materials, underprepared and culturally insensitive teachers, and a lack of quality health care, social services, and employment opportunities in city neighborhoods. Yet urban schools have also been sites of resistance and have spawned some extraordinary historical examples of democratic and progressive school leaders who have worked against the grain of low expectations, racist curriculum, and structural inequalities endemic in urban education.

These efforts to "lead for diversity" have often been absent from the historical record, however, in part because city school districts have left behind few official records that document the development and influence of progressive curriculum innovations and diversity policies on the day-to-day practices of urban teachers and leaders (Donato and Lazerson, 2000). Through examining alternative sources, however, particularly accounts about schools and schooling in the African American press and ethnic newspapers, the archives of race relations and civil rights organizations, and the oral histories of educational activists, historical portraits of urban school leaders who made a difference emerge—principals, superintendents, teacher union leaders, and community advocates who worked to transform the curriculum, promote equality, and make schooling more responsive to diverse students and their families in cities across the country before 1950 (see, e.g., Johnson, 2003).

This chapter describes the culturally responsive practices of one such leader— Gertrude Elise Johnson McDougald Ayer, the first African American woman to become a New York City principal. I examine her leadership practices in Harlem in the 1930s and 1940s in light of the precepts of "culturally responsive" pedagogy (see, e.g., Gay, 2000; Ladson-Billings, 1994; Villegas and Lucas, 2002) to analyze how she incorporated students' cultural knowledge as a vehicle for learning, fostered the development of sociopolitical consciousness and democratic citizenship in her elementary school, and advocated for social and political reform in the wider Harlem community. In the end I propose some principles of culturally responsive school leadership that highlight the leader's stance as a change agent vis-à-vis the larger community and argue that by reclaiming historical narratives of progressive women leaders such as Gertrude Ayer we might provide inspiration and direction for today's aspiring urban school leaders.

Methodology and Data Sources

This historical case study of a school leader surveyed primary sources from several historical archives to develop a biographical profile and reconstruct Gertrude Ayer's educational philosophy and leadership practice. I studied Ayer's scrapbook, investigative reports she authored, and newspaper accounts and photographs depicting her community involvement and curriculum projects she implemented during the 1930s and 1940s. I also surveyed back issues of African American community newspapers including the *New York Amsterdam News*, the *New York Age*, and journals such as *Opportunity* (the official organ of the National Urban League) and *The Crisis* (the National Association for the Advancement of Colored People (NAACP) journal) for a thirty-year period from 1923 to 1954 to locate Ayer's writings on educational and political issues. Finally, I utilized secondary sources on the history of Harlem, civil rights work and labor organizing in New York City, and Black women's philanthropic organizations to contextualize Ayer's leadership in light of key events in Harlem during the 1930s and 1940s.[1]

Profile of a Culturally Responsive School Leader

Gertrude Elise Johnson was born in midtown Manhattan in 1885, the daughter of Dr. Peter Johnson, one of the first African American doctors in New York City and Mary Elizabeth Johnson, a British seamstress.[2] She attended high school at Girls' Technical High School where she became the school's senior class president and its first African American graduate in 1903. After high school, she earned a teaching certificate and taught for six years before resigning in 1911 to marry Cornelius McDougald, a Harlem attorney, and raise a family.[3] In 1916 Ayer began work around labor issues that affected African American girls and women, first as a vocational counselor and then as industrial secretary of the local Urban League.

In February, 1935 Gertrude Ayer received a temporary appointment as principal of Harlem's P.S. 24 after years of battling the New York City Board of Education's examination system.[4] She assumed leadership of the predominately African American school during the depths of the Depression, when the unemployment rate in the neighborhood was over 60 percent and half of the families were on relief. As the standard of living for Harlem families plummeted during the Depression years, neighborhood health and recreational facilities, educational opportunities, and social services failed to keep pace with community needs. The Harlem public schools, in particular, provided stark evidence of underfunding and neglect by the central school bureaucracy in Brooklyn. Harlem parents complained to school officials about unsanitary and dilapidated school buildings, overcrowded classrooms on double and triple shifts, outdated curriculum materials, the lack of psychological and social work services, and the racial insensitivity of many white administrators and teachers who regarded assignment to a Harlem school as a "punishment" ("Education Hearing," 1935). Despite the increasing racial and ethnic diversity in the New York public schools in the 1930s, school officials had made little effort to diversify the teaching force. By 1935 African American teachers constituted only 2–3 percent of New York City teachers and constituted a minority of the teachers in most Harlem schools.[5]

On March 19, 1935 Harlem erupted in an "uprising" which resulted in $2,000,000 of property damage along 125th St. (the main thoroughfare) and three deaths, including an African American teenager who was shot by the police. Looted stores were owned by White businessmen who lived outside the neighborhood and had refused to hire Black employees (Greenberg, 1997). Although there was official condemnation, community leaders agreed that the "Harlem Riot of 1935" represented a spontaneous outpouring of anger and frustration at police brutality, worsening economic conditions, and ongoing racial discrimination in Harlem. In response, Mayor La Guardia appointed an interracial commission of prominent New Yorkers who conducted a series of community forums to study the neighborhood conditions that led to the "riot."

Gertrude Ayer and several of the teachers from her school testified at these hearings. In the verbatim transcripts from the Commission's education hearings Ayer describes working to gain the trust of parents, establish a more relaxed atmosphere in the school, and provide additional relief services for unemployed families within weeks of her arrival as principal ("Education Hearing," 1935).

In the spring of 1935 Ayer also became one of the pioneers in the Activity Program, an experiment to implement child-centered progressive education in New York City's public elementary schools. The intent of the program was to "shift the emphasis of teaching in the elementary school from subject matter to the child" (Morrison, 1941, p. 5). Students in the Activity Program engaged in experiential learning, self-directed projects, interdisciplinary curriculum, and classroom experiments in "democratic living."

At P.S. 24 the Activity Program incorporated intercultural curriculum, human relations work, and neighborhood field trips because of Ayer's background and interest in this area. When Ayer noted friction between students of West Indian background and those born in the United States, a social studies unit was planned on life in the Caribbean (Ayer, 1963). Parents were invited in to share family artifacts, children decorated the hallways with murals depicting Caribbean scenes, and a school fair was held in which each class contributed plays or musical performances. Parents and students also took school-sponsored fieldtrips to neighborhood cultural institutions such as the Schomburg Center that offered regular lectures on African and African American history and readings by Harlem writers such as Langston Hughes and Richard Wright.

A progressive administrator with a strong ethic of care, Gertrude Ayer created a community-centered school at P.S. 24 (and later as the principal of P.S. 119) where parents were welcomed, material resources were provided for families in need, and the cultural life of the surrounding neighborhood was viewed as a resource. Her commitment to the Harlem schools also included mentoring and promoting the next generation of school leaders. She died in her Harlem home on July 10, 1971 at the age of 86.

The Contours of Culturally Responsive Urban School Leadership

How might Gertrude Ayer's leadership practices in the 1930s and 1940s be characterized as culturally responsive? Although there is little discussion of this concept in the school leadership literature, in multicultural education circles the features of culturally relevant or culturally responsive pedagogy have been articulated and refined over the past fifteen years. Ladson-Billings (1995a;

1995b) built her "pedagogy of opposition" on the shoulders of previous anthropological work that noted a cultural mismatch between students from culturally diverse backgrounds and their teachers, particularly in terms of language and verbal participation structures. Incorporating the work of Irvine (1990) and Perry (1993), Ladson-Billings adopted a micro through macro-level approach to the education of African American students that includes a focus on classroom interactions, school policies, and societal and historical contexts. In Ladson-Billings's (1995b) view, culturally relevant pedagogy rests on three propositions: (a) students must experience academic success; (b) students must develop and/or maintain cultural competence, and (c) students must develop a critical consciousness through which they challenge the status quo of the social order. In her now classic study of eight exemplary teachers of African American students, Ladson-Billings offers specific examples of how these teachers incorporated local cultural knowledge and community members' expertise into the classroom to improve student achievement and engaged students in social action projects for collective empowerment (Ladson-Billings, 1994; 1995a; 1995b; see also Tate, 1995).

In their model of culturally responsive teaching, Villegas and Lucas (2002) describe culturally responsive teachers as those who: (a) have a sociopolitical consciousness; (b) affirm views of students from diverse backgrounds; (c) are both responsible for and capable of bringing about educational change; (d) embrace constructivist views of teaching and learning; and (e) build on students' prior knowledge and beliefs while stretching them beyond the familiar (p. xiv). Gay and Kirkland (2003) emphasize the critical consciousness aspect of culturally responsive teaching, arguing that teachers must know who they are as people, understand the contexts in which they teach, and question their knowledge base and assumptions. They posit that these qualities are as impor-tant as developing effective instructional techniques (p. 181). In sum, most approaches to culturally relevant or culturally responsive instruction not only utilize students' culture as a vehicle for learning, but also teach students how to develop a broader sociopolitical consciousness that enables them to critique the cultural norms, values, mores, and institutions that produce and maintain social inequities (Ladson-Billings, 1995b, p. 162).

Surprisingly, there have been few attempts to apply this culturally respon-sive framework to the study of leadership practice in urban schools. Those efforts that come closest have been a series of recent case studies of African American women principals (see, e.g. Dillard, 1995; Reitzug and Patterson,

1998; Bloom and Erlandson, 2003). Collectively, the women leaders profiled in these studies emphasize high expectations for student academic achievement, an ethic of care (or what Reitzug and Patterson, 1998, term "empowerment through care"), and a commitment to the larger community. Lomotey (1989) also found that the three African American principals he studied in the 1980s had a deep compassion for their students and a commitment to the educability of African American children in general. Alston's (2005) characterization of Black women superintendents as "tempered radicals and servant leaders" extends this ethic of care and commitment to the entire school district in her depiction of African American women leaders who serve the community but are not afraid to "rock the boat."

Other recent studies that illustrate aspects of what I am terming "culturally responsive leadership" include Scheurich's (1998) description of the core beliefs and organizational culture of "HiPass" schools led by principals of color in the border region of Texas. These include the leaders' beliefs that all children can succeed, the child-centered and "loving" nature of the schools, and the valuing of the "racial culture and first language of the children."[67]

When placed side-by-side with revisionist historiographies of African American educators before 1960 (see, for e.g., Siddle Walker, 2001), these recent case studies of African American school leaders provide a historical continuum of culturally responsive practice for African American students. In contrast to previous historical studies that largely portrayed African American teachers in segregated schools as victims of oppressive circumstances, Siddle Walker (2001) emphasizes the agency of African American teachers who sought to be involved in community events and served as role models for students by being upstanding members of the community; remaining devoted to "teaching well," putting in the extra hours to ensure that African American students had the support they needed; caring about the whole student and holding them to high expectations; relating the curriculum to the students' needs; and receiving community support for their efforts.

Two aspects of "culturally responsive leadership" that have received little attention in previously published case studies, however, are detailed descriptions of how school leaders have incorporated the history, values, and cultural knowledge of students' home communities in the school curriculum and worked to develop a critical consciousness among both students and faculty to challenge inequities in the larger society. In the remainder of this chapter I will discuss ways in which Gertrude Ayer infused cultural knowledge and progressive teaching methods into her school and remained active at challenging injustice in the schools and the larger society until the end of her life. This focus on the cultural and critical consciousness aspect of Gertrude Ayer's leadership conceptualizes the "culturally responsive urban school leader" as public intellectual, curriculum innovator, and social activist.

School Leader as Public Intellectual

Calls for educators to reconceive their educational role as public intellectuals instead of technicians and bureaucratic agents (see, e.g., Giroux, 1985, 1990) fail to recognize the rich historical legacy of African American educators like Gertrude Ayer (and many others) who *were* public intellectuals during the first half of the twentieth century (see also Murtadha and Watts, 2005). Ayer's leadership practice provides a vivid example of Foster's (1989) notion of the school administrator as a transformative intellectual. She authored journal articles and investigative reports, organized community forums, wrote a regular column on education in the *New York Amsterdam News*, and campaigned tirelessly for school reform in the public arena throughout her 43-year career as an educator and community leader. She gained early attention for her essay "The Double Task: The Struggle of Negro Women for Sex and Race Emancipation" (McDougald, 1925) that appeared in the landmark issue of *Survey Graphic* that launched the "New Negro" literary movement in Harlem in the 1920s. In this essay Ayer analyzed the socioeconomic problems, as well as societal contributions, of four groups of Harlem women, from wealthy to working class. Challenging the monolithic and stereotypical way in which African American women were perceived by White America, Ayer called for a more accurate representation of Black women's strengths, talents, and challenges. Today this article continues to be cited and read in women's studies courses as an early- twentieth-century example of African American feminist or "womanist" thinking (Guy-Sheftall, 1995).

Ayer also wrote about the historical role of Black teachers in the African American community (McDougald, 1923a), the need for more sophisticated vocational guidance for African American students (McDougald, 1923b), and argued against the use of corporal punishment, which was widely practiced in the Harlem schools in the 1930s. In her regular column on women's issues in Harlem's *New York Amsterdam News* she even urged parents not to physically punish their children.[7] Throughout her career Ayer maintained the view that education was as much an art as a science. Although she took further coursework at Hunter College, Columbia University, and City College over the years, she never received her Bachelor's degree. Upon retirement Ayer would remark that she had few regrets about not getting a degree, because in her words: "Too many people with B.A.'s only know their subject matter and don't know how to teach." ("Human Principal," 1954). Although she lacked formal academic degrees, Ayer's stance as a Black woman intellectual situated her as an "outsider within" (Collins, 1991) intellectual circles in New York City. She drew on both her training as an educator as well as her lived experiences as an African American woman to carve out a public space to discuss issues of race and gender in the Harlem community.

School Leader as Curriculum Innovator

Ayer's educational philosophy aimed to develop African American students' intellectual abilities as well as their responsibility as global citizens by centering them in their history and culture. Witness her thoughts on the role and responsibility of African American teachers to develop a "socio-political consciousness" in students:

> It is the high duty of the Negro woman teacher to teach the Negro youth to maintain a critical attitude toward what he learns, rather than to lay emphasis on stuffing and inflating him only with the thoughts of others.... Hers is the task of knowing well her race's history and of finding time to impart it in addition to all other standard facts required, and to impart it in such a way that the adolescent student will realize: 1. That, in fundamentals he is essentially the same as other humans. 2. That, being different in some ways does not mean that he is inferior. 3. That, he has a contribution to make to his group. 4. That, his group has a contribution to make to his nation, and 5. That, he has a part in his nation's work in the world. To stimulate this spirit is the most lasting and far-reaching phase of the Negro teacher's work. (McDougald, 1923b, p. 770)

In the mid 1930s, Ayer embraced a robust approach to progressive education and the "project method" of curriculum emanating from Teachers College, Columbia University probably because it dovetailed with her own child-centered and humanistic philosophy of education.[8] At P.S. 24, which became one of nine Activity Program schools studied and cited for excellence by the New York City Board of Education, Ayer advocated learning experiences that approximated those in real life. The students tended community gardens, engaged in problem-solving activities, learned math while running school businesses and managing individual savings accounts, chaired student-run conferences and discussion groups, and incorporated multiple forms of writing as part of their project-based activities. One class in the school created their own "school city" based on the government of New York City, complete with judges, sanitation squads, election inspectors, and the replication of other city functions ("Woman Principal Runs School Like a 'Big City,'" 1935). At P.S. 24 Ayer also established the first child guidance services in Harlem and a health and dental clinic for students. Her school became a center for community services in the neighborhood, approximating the model of today's "full service" schools.

Ayer also believed in incorporating community "funds of knowledge" (Moll, 1992) into the classroom and encouraged Harlem residents to share their expertise with students. When she left P.S. 24 to become the principal of Harlem's P.S. 119 in 1945 she invited neighborhood carpenters, butchers, and grocers as experts into the school in order to overcome what she termed the "blackboard curtain" between teacher and student and to show children that there were sources of learning outside books. In her words, "The informality helps teachers too. Sometimes they develop a lot of resistance to being a human being."[9]

African American history was an integral element of her child-centered curriculum. In an article that appeared in *Freedomways*, a civil rights journal published in the 1960s, Ayer reminisced about the Activity program and some of her former elementary school students (Ayer, 1963). One of her students had become a lawyer, another a banker, another a dentist, another a taxi driver, and one a famous writer. James Baldwin had attended Harlem's P.S. 24 in the fifth and sixth grades. In Ayer's words:

> I vividly remember his haunted eyes and his slim physique. He was active in school affairs but never intrusive…. He is using his great talent to convey the sufferings of the Negro Americans and to exhort the white American to examine what his thoughts and acts have made of him. We like to think that the study his class made of the lives of great Negro heroes in American history inspired him to take an active personal part in the present struggle. (p. 381)

Gertrude Ayer's instructional leadership remained child centered even after the Activity Program was scuttled in the late 1940s when progressive education came under attack as "intellectually soft" and "subversive" in the wake of the red baiting of prominent progressive educators during the Cold War era (Johnson, 2002). Photographs and newspaper accounts of Ayer throughout the 1940s and early 1950s portrayed her as focused on the children: intently listening to a young girl reading a storybook, talking one-on-one with children

in the school lunchroom (the first school cafeteria in Harlem), and greeting
children as she escorted visitors through the school.

School Leader as Social Activist

Like other African American women educators who were political activists in
Harlem during the 1930s and 1940s, Gertrude Ayer incorporated her work as an
educator as part of a larger project for racial justice and community uplift
(Johnson, 2004). After World War I thousands of young African American
women migrated from the rural South to northern cities like New York City,
Philadelphia, Chicago, Detroit, and Cleveland in search of job opportunities. In
her role as industrial secretary of the New York City Urban League, Ayer
undertook the first study to document the inequalities experienced by African
American women who had assumed employment in New York City's factories
and shops after World War I ("A New Day for the Colored Woman Worker,"
1919). In the 1920s Ayer organized laundry workers with Rose Schneiderman of
the Women's Trade Union League and worked with Socialist Frank Crosswaith
on the Negro Labor Committee to end discriminatory practices in the labor
unions.

As a school leader her social activism included promoting intercultural education and race relations work in Harlem. In the fall of 1934 she brought the
Teachers College course on Race Relations to the 135th Street branch of the
New York Public Library in Harlem. During World War II, Ayer organized
intercultural education workshops for parents and teachers when the Washington Heights neighborhood experienced racial tensions between Jewish and
African American residents.[10]

Throughout her life Ayer also gave generously of her time to philanthropic
work, an avenue utilized by African American professional women throughout
the country in the nineteenth and early twentieth century to provide leadership
in community development and uplift (see, e.g., Hine, 1994). She raised money
for the Harlem Utopia Club's neighborhood house for child welfare, spoke in
cities throughout the Northeast to support the school camp scholarship fund,
and recruited teachers as mentors in an afterschool program she started for
African American girls in Harlem.[11]

After retirement from the New York City Public Schools in 1954, Ayer
continued to make her community a better place to live until the end of her life.
She chaired a committee on consumer problems in Harlem. She spoke at
community forums on "Labor's Responsibility Towards Integration in the New

York City Public Schools." She continued to write her column in the *New York Amsterdam News* on the Harlem schools. At the age of 80 she came out of retirement to provide a workshop for Black and Puerto Rican women teachers who wanted to become New York City administrators ("Negro, Puerto Rican Tutors Flock to Supervisor Classes," 1964). In short, she "walked the talk" as an urban school leader who worked to make her school and the surrounding community more responsive and equitable for her African American students and their families.

Lessons from History for Culturally Responsive Urban School Leadership

Gertrude Ayer came of age as a school leader during a historical time and place of intense political activism. Harlem in the 1930s and early 1940s was populated by a spectrum of political organizations, from mainstream groups like the Urban League and NAACP to radical organizations like the Socialist and Communist parties. Progressive Harlem politicians like Adam Clayton Powell, Jr. led daily pickets on 125th Street to block the entrances of stores that refused to hire Black employees. Tenant organizers staged strikes to protest Harlem's exorbitant rents. In 1941 labor organizers like A. Philip Randolph, Frank Crosswaith, and Layle Lane mobilized thousands of Black New Yorkers in the fight against segregation in the military and national defense industries through the March on Washington Movement (MOWM). School reformers like Lucile Spence and the Harlem Committee of the Teachers Union of New York City fought for new school construction, the incorporation of African American history in the curriculum, and Black representation on the school board (Johnson, 2004). Ayer's democratic leadership was situated within a network of African American intellectuals, labor organizers, religious leaders, politicians, and community activists (and some White political activists as well) who provided intellectual support, organizational and material resources, and constituted a critical mass of progressive reformers bent on structural change in the schools of Harlem.

My point here is that leadership for social justice in general, and culturally responsive school leadership in particular, must be viewed within the historical, social, and political contexts in which it is practiced. How it becomes actualized, then, might vary across particular contexts. In today's milieu where there is increasing interest in staking out the theory and practice of leadership for social justice, stories of school leaders from different geographic regions and historical periods who "made a difference" for culturally diverse students and their families can help to establish a historical continuum of democratic and socially just leadership practice across contexts. For instance, although much of the history of African American teachers and administrators has focused on schools in the South, recent historical case studies have begun to fill in the gaps of leadership practice in predominately Black schools in northern cities during the 1940s through the 1960s (see, e.g., Danns, 2002, 2003; Randolph, 2004). By focusing on particular historical periods of community activism in urban school reform, we might ask: How have school leaders interfaced with larger community efforts for social change? How have these larger social movements in turn influenced school reform efforts? What does it mean to "lead for diversity" in a particular place and time?

In the current high stakes, accountability-driven policy environment in the United States where urban schools are pressured to raise test scores and standardize curriculum, there is little support from city, state, and national educational officials to incorporate multicultural curriculum and institute diversity policies in urban districts. Some would argue that culturally responsive leadership in the current U.S. context requires urban school leaders to respond to the underlying causes and results of the racial achievement gap in their schools. But, I would argue, school leaders also need models of how they might challenge the status quo of inequitable assessment practices, incorporate students' cultural knowledge into the school curriculum, and work with parents and community activists for social change in the larger community. At a time when diversity efforts have dropped off the agenda in many school districts, presenting historical counternarratives of culturally responsive school leaders like Gertrude Ayer can help point the way.

I use this case study, along with other historical narratives of progressive women leaders, in my course on Women in Educational Leadership at the University at Buffalo. I also ask the aspiring school leaders in the course to interview women leaders from diverse backgrounds and develop their biographical narratives. Through analyzing and critiquing the lived experiences and leadership practices of current woman leaders through a cultural lens, my students learn both the theory and practice of culturally responsive urban school leadership—how to form alliances with community organizations to bring local cultural knowledge into the classroom; use their political savvy to garner economic, medical, and social service resources for the families in their schools; and join with parents, community activists, and progressive politicians to agitate for educational equity in the larger society. By reclaiming and revoicing the historical narratives of progressive women leaders like Gertrude Ayer, as university educators we keep the promise of democratic and culturally responsive leadership alive for the aspiring urban school leaders of today and tomorrow.

Notes

*   A slightly different treatment of this work appeared in Johnson (2006).

1.   Archival research for this chapter was conducted at the Schomburg Center for Research in Black Culture, New York Public Library; the New York City Board of Education archives, Special Collections, Teachers College, Columbia University; and the United Federation of Teachers (UFT) archives, Robert Wagner Labor Collection, New York University.

2.   In our current understanding of race, Ayer could be considered of "mixed" racial background because her father was African American with American Indian ancestors and her mother was white and British. However, by all historical accounts (including her own), she affiliated culturally as an African American and lived, worked, and married within the African American community. The differences in the way that the White media and the Black press discussed her accomplishments at the time are instructive about U. S. racial views in the 1930s. African American newspapers across the country were laudatory and proud of her struggle to attain the principalship after years of battling the New York City system. *Time* magazine, on the other hand, used racist terms like "ragged Negro moppets" to describe the children at P.S. 24 and emphasized what they termed Ayer's "light skin" and "kinkless" hair. See, for example, "Mrs. Gertrude Ayers Appointed Principal" (1935) and "Harlem's First" (1935).

3.   Ayer notes that she was required to quit her teaching position because the New York City Board of Education did not provide maternity leave at the time. See Scrapbook, GEA papers.

4.   Although she passed the written examination, Ayer was initially denied her principal's license on the ground of "insufficient meritorious record" because a former white principal under whom she served as Assistant Principal did not rate her highly enough on the examiner's form. On appeal, Ayers pointed out that she had received consistently high ratings from the same supervisor on her semi-annual ratings and raised the issue that an administrator could not be given high ratings for one purpose and a low rating for another based on the identical service record. She won her appeal, and was permanently appointed principal of P.S. 24 in February 1936. In retrospect, Ayer's permanent appointment the year after the Harlem Riot Commission might be an instance of what Critical Race Theorists term "interest convergence"—that Whites will promote advances for Blacks only when they also serve White interests (Bell, 1995). With increased scrutiny on the Harlem schools, there was mounting pressure on the New York City Board of Education to appoint a Black administrator in Harlem. See "Principals' Ratings Must Jibe," and "First Negro Woman Wins Principal Post," Scrapbook, GEA papers.

5. Estimates of the number of Black teachers in the New York City schools in the 1930s range from 500 to 800 because as a result of their "colorblind" policy the New York City Board of Education claimed they did not compile statistics on the race of New York City students or faculty (See Tyack, 1974, p. 226). In her article on the occupational roles of African American women, Ayer notes that there were approximately 300 African American women teaching in Harlem. At P.S. 24 there were only three African American teachers amongst a faculty of 24. See McDougald (1925).

6. Scheurich (1998) terms these schools "hybrid" because of their incorporation of certain aspects of the dominant Anglo culture (e.g., using high stakes tests to drive instruction).

7. See "Child Training," Scrapbook, GEA papers.

8. William Kilpatrick's "project method" involved the development of purposeful activities tied to a child's interests and needs. He argued that students should apply classroom knowledge to meet real community needs. See Kilpatrick (1918).

9. Gertrude Ayer, Schomburg Clipping File, 1925– 1974, Sc 000,388 –1, Schomburg Center.

10. "Why a Teacher Should Also Serve as a Social Worker," Scrapbook, GEA papers.

11. See *The Harlem Project*, box 18, file 1, IHRC 114, Immigration History Research Center, Anderson Library, University of Minnesota.

References

Alston, J. A. (2005). Tempered radicals and servant leaders: Black females persevering in the superintendency. *Educational Administration Quarterly*, 41(4): 675–688.

Ayer, G. (1919). "A new day for the colored woman worker: A study of colored women in industry in New York City." New York: C. P. Young.

———— (1963). Notes on my native sons— Education in Harlem. *Freedomways, III*: 375–383.

———— "Child training—spare the rod and spoil the child–vicious propoganda," Gertrude Ayer Scrapbook, Gertrude Elise Ayer Papers, 1931–1966, Schomburg Center for Research in Black Culture, New York Public Library.

———— "Human Principal," *Newsweek*, July 5, 1954. Gertrude Ayer, Schomburg Clipping File, 1925–1974, Sc 000388-1, Schomburg Center for Research in Black Culture, New York Public Library.

———— "Why a teacher should also serve as a social worker; Elise Macdougald Ayer in 2-fold service." Gertrude Ayer Scrapbook, Gertrude Elise Ayer Papers, 1931–1966, Schomburg Center for Research in Black Culture, New York Public Library.

Bell, D. (1995). *Brown v. Board of Education* and the interest-convergence dilemma. In K. Crenshaw, N. Gotanda, G. Peller, and K. Thomas (Eds.), *Critical race theory: The key writings that formed the movement*. New York: The New Press, pp. 20–45.

Bloom, C., and Erlandson, D. (2003). African American women principals in urban schools: Realities, (re)constructions, and resolutions. *Educational Administration Quarterly*, 39(3): 339–369.

Collins, P. H. (1991). *Black feminist thought: Knowledge, consciousness, and the politics of empowerment*. New

York: Routledge.

Danns, D. (2002). Black student empowerment and Chicago school reform efforts in 1968. *Urban Education*, 37(5): 631–655.

———. (2003, April 21–25). Thriving in the midst of discrimination: Educator Maudelle Bousfield's struggles in Chicago, 1920–1950. Paper presented at annual conference of the American Educational Research Association, Chicago.

Dillard, C. B. (1995). Leading with her life: An African American feminist (re)interpretation of leadership for an urban high school principal. *Educational Administration Quarterly*, 31(4): 539–563.

Donato, R., and Lazerson, M. (2000). New directions in American educational history: Problems and prospects. *Educational Researcher*, 29(8): 4–15.

"Education Hearing, April 4, 1935." E. Franklin Frazier papers, Moorland-Spingarn Research Center, Howard University.

"First negro woman wins principal post," Sc Micro R–4842, Gertrude Ayer Scrapbook, 1931–1966, Schomburg Center for Research in Black Culture, New York Public Library.

Foster, W. (1989). The administrator as transformative intellectual. *Peabody Journal of Education*, 66(3): 5–18.

Gay, G. (2000). *Culturally responsive teaching: Theory, research, and practice*. New York: Teachers College Press.

———, and Kirkland, K. (2003). Developing cultural critical consciousness and self-reflection in preservice teacher education. *Theory into Practice*, 42(3): 181–187.

Giroux, H. A. (1985). Teachers as transformative intellectuals. *Social Education*, 49(5): 76–79.

———. (1990). Curriculum theory, textual authority, and the role of teachers as public intellectuals. *Journal of Curriculum and Supervision*, 5(4): 361–383.

Greenberg, C. L. (1997). *Or does it explode? Black Harlem in the Great Depression*. New York: Oxford University Press.

Guy-Sheftall, B. (1995). *Words of fire: An anthology of African-American feminist thought*. New York: New Press.

"Harlem's first," *Time*, February 18, 1935, p. 56.

Hine, D. C. (1994). "We specialize in the wholly impossible": The philanthropic work of Black women. In D. C. Hine (Ed.), *Hinesight: Black women and the re-construction of American history*. Bloomington: Indiana University Press, pp. 109–128.

Irvine, J. J. (1990). *Black students and school failure*. Westport, CT: Greenwood Press.

Johnson, L. (2002). "Making democracy real": Teacher union and community activism to promote diversity in the New York City public schools—1935–1950. *Urban Education, 37*(5): 566–588.

———. (2003, November 6–9). Making a difference: Leadership for social justice in historical perspective. Paper presented at the annual convention of the University Council of Educational Administration, Portland.

———. (2004). A generation of women activists: African American female educators in Harlem, 1930–1950. *Journal of African American History*, 89(3): 223–240.

———. (2006). "Making her community a better place to live": Culturally responsive urban school leadership in historical perspective. *Leadership and Policy in Schools*, 5(1): 19–36.

Kilpatrick, W. H. (1918). The project method: The use of the purposeful act in the educative process. *Teachers College Record,* 19(4): 319–334.

Ladson-Billings, G. (1994). *The dreamkeepers: Successful teachers of African American children.* San Francisco, CA: Jossey-Bass.

———. (1995a). Toward a theory of culturally relevant pedagogy. *American Educational Research Journal,* 32(3): 465–491.

———. (1995b). But that's just good teaching! The case for culturally relevant pedagogy. *Theory into Practice,* 34(3): 159–165.

Lomotey, K. (1989). *African-American principals: School leadership and success.* New York: Greenwood Press.

McDougald, E. J. (1923a). The Negro and the northern public schools. *The Crisis,* 25(6): 262–265.

———. (1923b). The Negro woman teacher and the Negro student. *The Messenger,* 7: 769–770.

———. (1925). The double task: The struggle of Negro women for sex and race emancipation. *Survey Graphic,* VI(6): 689–691.

Moll, L. C. (1992). Funds of knowledge for teaching: Using a qualitative approach to connect homes and classrooms. *Theory into Practice,* 31(1): 132–141.

Morrison, C. (1941). *An appraisal of the Activity program: A preliminary report of the survey of the curriculum experiment with the Activity program in the New York City elementary schools.* Albany, NY: State Education Department.

"Mrs. Gertrude Ayers Appointed Principal," *The Chicago Defender,* February 1, 1935, p. 1.

Murtadha, K., and Watts, D. M. (2005). Linking the struggle for education and social justice: Historical perspectives of African American leadership in schools. *Educational Administration Quarterly,* 41(4): 591–608.

"Negro, Puerto Rican Tutors Flock to Supervisor Classes," *The Amsterdam News,* March 7, 1964, p. 28.

Perry, T. (1993). *Toward a theory of African-American student achievement.* Report No. 16. Boston, MA: Center on Families, Communities, Schools and Children's Learning, Wheelock College.

"Principals' Ratings Must Jibe," Gertrude Ayer Scrapbook, Gertrude Elise Ayer Papers, 1931–1966, Schomburg Center for Research in Black Culture, New York Public Library.

Randolph, A. (2004). The memories of an all-Black northern urban school: Good memories of leadership, teachers, and the curriculum. *Urban Education,* 39(6): 596–620.

Reitzug, U.C., and Patterson, J. (1998) "I'm not going to lose you!" Empowerment through caring in an urban principal's practice with students. *Urban Education,* 33(2): 150–181.

Scheurich, J. (1998). Highly successful and loving, public elementary schools populated mainly by low SES children of color: Core beliefs and cultural characteristics. *Urban Education,* 33(4): 451–491.

Siddle Walker, V. (2001). African American teaching in the South: 1940–1960. *American Educational Research Journal,* 38(4): 751–759.

Tate, W. (1995). Returning to the root: A culturally relevant approach to mathematics pedagogy. *Theory into Practice,* 34(3): 166–173.

Tyack, D. B. (1974). *The one best system: A history of American urban education.* Cambridge, MA: Harvard University Press.

Villegas, A. M., and Lucas, T. (2002). *Educating culturally responsive teachers: A coherent approach.* Albany: State University of New York Press.

"Woman Principal Runs School Like a 'Big City.'" (1935). Gertrude Ayer Scrapbook, Gertrude Elise Ayer Papers, ScMicro R-4842, Schomburg Center for Research in Black Culture, New York Public Library.

14

The Power and Limits of Small School Reform: Institutional Agency and Democratic Leadership in Public Education

Lori Chajet

The influence of social class characteristics is probably so powerful that schools cannot overcome it, no matter how well trained are their teachers and no matter how well designed are their instructional programs and climates.

—Richard Rothstein, 2004

My faith in the possibility that education can serve as a vehicle for individual transformation, and even social change, is rooted in an understanding that human beings have the ability to rise above even the most difficult obstacles, to become more than just victims of circumstance.

—Pedro Noguera, 2003

How can schools make a difference? Some argue schools worsen existing inequalities, others that they have no power to change them, and others that they are young people's only hope. While educational theorists and researchers engage in this debate, urban school administrators and teachers live it on a daily basis. Faced with students whose experiences are shaped by poverty and racism, working in under-resourced and over-regulated schools, each decision they make is a reflection of where they stand on this question. For some the work of overcoming the odds is left to students themselves; for others overcoming the odds *is* the work of schools. It is the latter group of educational leaders who create schools that enact *institutional agency*; that is, they work from a clear understanding and critique of the reproductive functions of education within the United States (Apple, 1990; Bowles and Gintis, 1976; Giroux, 1997) but do not allow that understanding to represent what it far too often does: determinism without hope. They believe in, and are committed to, the mediating role schools can play (Apple, 1995; Aronowitz and Giroux, 1993; Fine and Weis, 2001; Freire, 1998; Giroux, 2001) and so they use their power to question, redefine, and act.

This chapter brings together the theory of institutional agency with everyday practice to question the role schools can play in the struggle for social justice. First it looks inside of Bridges,[1] a small public high school that takes seriously the promise of democratic schooling and, in doing so, expects not only administrators but also teachers and students to be leaders. Second, it presents the post-secondary experiences of graduates of this school to understand both the power and the limits of such a commitment.[2] Together, the two parts speak to the debate of whether schools can make a difference and, more pointedly, to aspiring educational leaders hoping to develop their own visions—without illusion—of what democratic education *can* look.

Bridges: Institutional Agency in Practice

Graduation, June 25, 2004 (field notes)

Fifty-seven students, predominately Latino and African-American, stand tall in their blue and white graduation gowns before a cheering crowd. Their 12th grade literature teacher, who also taught them humanities in 9th and 11th grades, welcomes everyone in both Spanish and English and delivers a speech that he jokes about having revised three times, just as students' assignments were expected to be throughout high school. He presents students' own words from reflective pieces they wrote: "Bridges School has been like my second home for four years"; "What makes Bridges special is the warmth of the community where everyone is helping each other"; "Bridges School has meant a lot to me because of the way the school is structured…teachers care for students and are there whenever you need extra help." And he then comments, "What these students recognize is that community doesn't just happen because people are in the same place. Community has to be built on purpose. At Bridges we have built community through small classes, advisory, group work, close relationships with parents, after school help… And it is not just one community: each class, each grade, the whole school, the neighborhood, your families, are all interconnected communities. And you are part of a community of small schools—a movement that is spreading." His advice to them as they take their next step: "Wherever you are next year, build community for yourself…Get to know your professors and co-workers. Make friends. Join a political organization. Do community service. Study in groups. Spend time with your families. And keep in touch with your Bridges friends and teachers."

There is no valedictorian; rather all graduates are invited to speak. Fifteen choose to, among them: special education students, students with straight A's bound for com-

petitive colleges, students who struggled to get Cs, males, females, Latinos and Afri-
can Americans. Their words underscore the themes their literature teacher addressed:
community, relationships, academic rigor, and the importance of speaking up.

It is a long graduation—lasting over three hours—despite the small size of the
graduating class. It is a metaphor: the school takes its time educating those students
it has; it thinks about each one deeply, wanting to recognize their individual
strengths. No one is anonymous—no one walks away without saying good-
bye—over 90 percent move on to their next step: college.

Bridges is both typical and atypical of urban high schools. Its population, while smaller in size (516 students, grades 7–12), is no different demographically than neighboring comprehensive high schools[3]: upwards of 80% qualify for free lunch, 26% for special education services[4], 60% are Latino, 28% African American, 6% Asian, and 6% White. There are no admission requirements to enter the school—no test scores looked at, essays written, interviews had[5]. With funding comparable to other similarly populated city high schools, Bridges faces struggles common to urban schools—ill-equipped science labs, small pools of qualified teacher-candidates particularly in math and science, limited social support services for students,[6] among others.

While these realities qualify Bridges as a typical urban school, there are others that make it distinctly atypical. It is a part of a movement of small schools in New York City, established in the mid- to late-1980s,[7] that provides an important example of institutional agency in practice. Educators, recognizing the devastating effects that the policies, practices, and structures of large traditional schools were having on low-income students of color (Anyon, 1997; Fine, 1991; Kozol, 1991; Nieto, 2000; Valenzuela, 1999), and the unequal educational outcomes that resulted (Orfield and Yun, 1999), reconceptualized schooling: the knowledge that got taught, the roles of teachers and students, relationships with families and communities, student groupings, and the meaning of assessment. The small schools they created, Bridges included, functioned despite the system they were in—one which was increasing expenditures for jails while decreasing them for education, neglecting the widening funding gap between urban and suburban schools, and allowing urban drop-out rates to soar (*CFE v. State of NY*, 1999). And they functioned despite prevalent reforms which ran counter to the goals of democratic education (Aronowitz, 1998). In fact, these small schools were a response to such trends, intended as a tool for social justice providing unselective populations of low-income students of color an education most often reserved for the affluent (Anyon, 1980). As Meier (1995), founder of one of the first small schools, argued, "When people think 'those kids' need something special, the reply we offer … is, Just give them what you have always offered those who have the money to buy the best" (p. 49).

Like other small schools, Bridges statistically outperforms its traditional school counterparts (Fine et al., 2005; Foote, 2005; Klonsky, 1995). 85.5% of students who were 9th graders at Bridges in fall 2000 graduated by September 2004,[8] while city-wide only 50.2% of 9th graders from fall 2000 had graduated.[9] Furthermore, while nationwide only 57.4% of Americans (ages 25–29) have some or more college, 82% of Bridges graduates (ages 22–24) do.[10,11] Beyond the numbers—or rather beneath them—lies the real difference between Bridges and typical urban high schools: a commitment to *institutional agency* and a translation of that commitment into practice.

In its aim to provide a democratic education to all students, Bridges redefines "schooling." Structurally, it has made the most of its small size through mixed-ability classrooms, block scheduling, integrated curriculum,[12] advisory, small student loads,[13] teacher collaboration, and a system of performance-based assessment. The culture that ensues can be seen throughout the school. Classrooms are characterized by inquiry-driven collaborative learning, dialogue, and student respect for academic achievement. The hallways feature the fruits of this work—position papers on whether the United States should be at war in Iraq, student-designed math problems on linear inequalities, "additional" chapters to *Their Eyes Were Watching God*. Posters in every classroom display the "Habits of Mind" which teachers use to guide instruction—From whose perspective are we seeing, reading, or hearing? How do we know what we know? Why is this important? Could things be otherwise? The walls are covered with student artwork—paintings with political messages about the under-financing of public schools, racial injustice, and sexism. The principal's office has one wall plastered with photographs of students and staff, another lined with books for teachers, and a third with books for students categorized into genres like "Latino authors" and "social justice." What one does not see is just as powerful as what one does: no metal detectors at the entrance, security guards stationed on each floor, bulletin boards listing test scores, or students hiding in stairwells.

In its commitment to engaging and rigorous education, Bridges prioritizes accountability; but rather than rely on mandated curriculum and assessments, it does so by prioritizing teacher development/collaboration and developing a system of performance-assessment for promotion. Beneath both of these practices lies a commitment to fostering leadership in teachers and students who are expected to speak up, make decisions, and be active forces in the school (Carlson and Gause).

Teachers as Leaders

The founding principal of Bridges was committed to creating a school where all teachers could develop as educators and become leaders. When she herself first became a teacher she was not introduced at her first staff meeting, told if she had a problem to deal with it on her own, and did her lesson planning in partnership with a curriculum guide. It was not until she began teaching in a small school that she came to realize what teaching *could* be. She explained, "I immediately became a part of a group of thoughtful folks who were always talking about their practice, about kids' learning…The principal always gave us interesting stuff to read, teachers welcomed me in their classroom. I felt like I was home. Now I could be a proud teacher…I was learning."

What evolved at Bridges over the years is a reflection of the critique and possibility this principal articulated. Teachers meet in a variety of teams during the school day and weekly for a 2-hour after school meeting[14]: grade teams discuss students and develop strategies to address their needs; curriculum teams plan and examine student work; department teams develop scope and sequences, common approaches to skill instruction, and best practices; and the staff discusses everything from family involvement to school tone. Most meetings are planned and facilitated by teachers themselves.

A glimpse at a few after-school meetings illustrates the translation of the vision into practice. At one meeting the staff set out to explore more closely how the cultural and class differences between themselves and their students affect practice. At another, the humanities team shared literacy strategies, while the science team redesigned 7–12 course content to address more of the sciences. At a third teachers, asked to provide collective feedback on school organization, policy, and teacher support, gave recommendations on everything from managing new testing requirements to retention policies to the budget.
What is clear: teachers are accountable to one another, and moreover, to their students.

Students as Leaders

Bridges's system of performance-assessment is intended to foster both academic achievement and leadership within all students. While New York City has a mandated testing regime of five exams, Bridges, along with a host of other small schools, has taken an active stand against this. Believing such tests are barriers to democratic practices and ultimately a disservice to low-income students of color (McNeil, 2000), many small schools opened with a waiver from them. When the state refused to renew the waiver in 2000, the NY Performance Standards Consortium was formed to regain it. While a variance was eventually awarded,[15] at one point Bridges had to administer all of the tests[16]; it never stopped using its system of performance-based assessment. Twice a year, in all subjects, students are required to create a portfolio, complete a written reflection, and present their work in roundtable formats—3–4 students with 2–3 adults.[17] Additionally, in their senior year students complete performance-assessment tasks and present them to graduation committees[18] in the format most commonly associated with a dissertation defense.[19] The purposes of both roundtables and graduation committees are explained in the principal's letter to participants:

> For most schools throughout New York State the end of the year is a time where student learning is being assessed through state-sponsored standardized tests … At Bridges we believe that learning cannot be sufficiently demonstrated within the confines of tests. This means that our students and teachers are challenged daily not only to prepare for tests, but also to read, write, think, share, explore, solve, create, collaborate, present, question, defend, negotiate, compromise, and, most importantly, reflect upon themselves as learners … Most students would be too scared to expose themselves to the public like this and most teachers too nervous to "put it all out there." … This is not an easy thing to do. Our students' work and our own work is not always as pretty as we want it to be. And no matter how hard they have worked and we have worked, we are never quite satisfied. However, we offer it to the public because it is to the public that we and our students are ultimately accountable.

A glance at the roundtables and graduation committees illustrates the principal's words. In a 9th grade math roundtable Juan, an ESL and special education student, read his reflective piece: he likes projects because he often freezes during tests; he has grown a lot as a student; he is especially thankful to his teacher for pushing him. There were several grammatical errors and it was short. Standing at an overhead projector he then explained a project he did and two sample test problems, demonstrating general understanding but stumbling over math vocabulary. Valencia then presented her work. Her reflective letter was several pages and began: "I am extremely proud of the work in this folder because it shows how I went from getting [Fs] to As in less than five months." New to Bridges, she explained that she began to understand math in this class in ways she never had before. Her presentation of how she used the Pythagorean theorem to construct a stable antenna for a rooftop was evidence of her mastery.

In a 10th grade humanities presentation, portfolios cluttered the tables and there was a lively hum of voices around the room. Handouts summarized the course: a study of the Rwandan genocide, the Arab-Israeli conflict, World War II, and South African Apartheid with a focus on what breeds oppression, how to resist violations of human rights, and the responsibility we have to our communities. As the students reflected on their work, debates that had taken place months before were reopened: What land should Israel concede to the Palestinians? How guilty were by-standers during the Holocaust? One student talked about her struggles with reading while another recounted the long list of books she had read; one student talked about the importance of activism and another about the memorial he constructed to the victims of Hiroshima; some presented a focused critique of the class and others of themselves. At the end their teacher closed the session: "Congratulate yourself on your success but you should also approach each experience with a beginner's mind. Do not wait for a teacher to start your process of inquiry."

In a 12th grade senior graduation committee, Yahaira presented her history research paper. She, along with all of her classmates, had to choose a topic of interest to them, research it with primary and secondary sources, and present it. Yahaira was the only student in the room with a committee of three adults. She focused her presentation on why she chose to study Trujillo's rule in the Dominican Republic—to learn more about her own history—and also focused on the struggles she faced in the research/writing process. She then answered a series of questions: What was the role of the United States? How was U.S. support of Trujillo similar to its support of Bin Laden during the Cold War? What would she advise Bush on foreign policy given what she learned? After over a half an hour of dialogue Yahaira left the room and her committee discussed the paper and the presentation. Opinions varied about specifics, but all agreed that based on the rubric she did an excellent presentation, demonstrated deep understanding, had a well-written paper, and she needed to revise her introduction. Yahaira was invited back into the room and given feedback.

As soon as she left she hugged her friends with relief and then sat down to rework her introduction.

What is clear: all students are active in their learning and are held to high expectations.

The Graduates

> How did we do? What at Bridges prepared you? What worked? What didn't?
>
> — Bridges's Principal

In redefining "school" Bridges's students, who might otherwise have been academically marginalized, are engaged, learning, and persisting through high school. The work of small schools, however, does not end with graduation from high school; in their struggle for social justice they hope to equip their students with what they need to achieve social mobility: a college degree. Thus, what happens to small schools' graduates as they move into post-secondary education is an important, underexplored,[20] window into the power and limits of small schools. While Bridges's graduates may have had democratic experiences in high school, they are not impervious to the host of obstacles college presents to low-income students of color. As one small school's principal posited,

> I know we have given our kids the kind of personalized education that has helped them to be successful human beings over the last four years … *But is what we give them enough?* Will the students be able to overcome the inequities of college? Of the work world? Can they leave their families? Can they make schooling a priority? Will the scholarships be there year after year? Will they be resilient enough? (Littky, 2000, 167)

As noted at the beginning of this chapter, statistically Bridges's graduates persist in and through college at significantly higher rates than national averages (See table 14. 1). They are, for the most part, academically prepared, motivated to learn, and many carry with them the help-seeking orientations (Stanton-Salazar, 2001) needed to navigate the obstacles.[21] The result: significantly higher persistence rates in college.

Table 14.1[22],[23]
College Persistence and Completion Nationwide vs. Bridges

	National (Ages 25–29) (%)	National Black[24] (Ages 25-29) (%)	National Latino (Ages 25-29) (%)	NYC (25 and over) (%)	Bridges (Ages 22-24) (%)	Bridges Black (Ages 22-24) (%)	Bridges Latino (Ages 22-24) (%)
Some College or More[25]	57.4	50.2	31.1	47.8	82	84	83
Associates[26]	12	16	19	5.2	13	16	16
Bachelors	28.4	17.2	10	15.8	35	33	34

At the same time these are not the numbers small schools' educators hoped for; the obstacles more varied and constant than many ever imagined. Looking inside of graduates' journeys reveals a complex story—one which captures graduates' intense desire to learn *and* how trying the journey through college is. Echoed throughout many interviews and surveys were critiques of college teaching, stories of money and family-related stress, and indications of alienation from campus communities. The complexity of these journeys is best narrated by the graduates themselves and so below you will meet three Bridges's graduates, each of whose journeys is representative of many more. Their stories are evidence of the power of institutional agency as well as the enormous obstacles poverty and racism present.

Niki was the first in her family to attend college. Having watched her mother struggle with low-paying jobs and government assistance and her father move between home and prison, she wanted to distinguish herself. She chose to attend a private competitive college just outside of New York City because it was close to home, diverse, and offered her the best financial aid package.

When Niki got to college she immediately became involved in campus life, joining organizations and working two on-campus jobs. Within the first two months, however, she found herself disappointed that she was not learning much academically—"I felt like I was regurgitating everything that they taught ... like [they're] telling me I'm not capable of thinking"—and overwhelmed by financial stresses. She was unable to attend freshmen orientation because it cost extra money; her Tuition Assistance Program (TAP) money was late because of paperwork problems; she could not afford her books; and while she thought she was not going to take out any loans, she had to take out three—"You have problems with everything here and … it always comes back to money."

These trends continued. At the beginning of her second year Niki learned tuition had increased $2,000 but her aid had not. She successfully advocated for more grants and worked three jobs while carrying a full course load. By April of her second year, when she learned tuition was increasing by another $2,000 and that the only additional aid she could secure were loans, she decided to leave. While she liked the community, she felt she was not learning enough to justify taking out another $10,000-plus.

Niki decided the best thing was to transfer to a nearby State school. Though it did not have the best reputation, it was significantly less money and "just a bus stop away." When Niki first arrived at her new college she was disappointed—she missed her friends, she lost eight credits in the transfer, and she had to adapt to a very different environment; but she only had to take out $1,000 in loans a semester and work one job. By the end of the year Niki had adjusted—she had made friends, been offered two TA-ships, and anticipated graduating within four and a half years of beginning college.

Malik was also the first in his family to attend college. He planned to go to a two-year State college several hours outside of the city immediately after high school. However, when financial aid complications arose, and he was faced with an arrest based on false charges, he postponed attendance until the Spring. Come December, with more aid and all charges dropped, Malik was anxious to begin school.

Soon after Malik arrived on campus he realized just how much of an adjustment college life was going to be. He found himself struggling with everything from finances, to academics, to social life. He had to take out two unexpected loans, could not get an on-campus job, and the only off-campus jobs available were too far to travel to without a car. While he had been excited to get back to school-work, he was frustrated with his educational experiences—"You're learning from a book … the teacher talks about what happened in the chapter and that's it for the day … No class discussions … You don't go to your room to talk to someone and say, "You know what I learned today?" And the social life was limited to parties with an abundance of drugs and fighting the dorms were covered in graffiti and had "weed on the floor," and there was a constant police presence. His reaction: "This can't be college … you [go to college to] try to get away from that atmosphere." Despite his disappointments, Malik returned for a second year. However, when he discovered he would have to double his loans to pay the increased tuition, he thought twice. "I [had to] ask myself, "Am I learning anything? … It doesn't feel like [it] … I'm just up here to get the degree," and decided, "It's not worth it."

Anxious to be back in school, Malik immediately turned to the easiest route: a for-profit trade school that promised a fast degree and job security.[27] As soon as he began, and was asked to do elementary school-level work alongside students who had been out of school for upwards of twenty years, he got his money back. But his desire to be back in school did not fade, "If I don't go back to college in January I'll be crushed." So he set out to find work and a new college. He sold everything from donuts to chocolates and put an application into the City University system. When he had not heard back by early January he contacted them and learned his transcripts had never been sent from his previous school; he still owed them $400. As the academic year progressed he saved his money, continued to explore colleges, and did everything he could to resist personal phone calls and abundant advertisements from for-profit trade schools. While tempted by what they promised; he saw them as a trap.

By his third year out of high school Malik secured a spot at one of the city's community colleges. He took four courses in his first semester but having failed the math and reading remedial placement tests only two classes were credit-bearing. While he liked a few of his classes, he wished more were in business and found himself frustrated with the instruction in the remedial courses where one instructor read the newspaper in class and another gave incorrect information. Malik was also disappointed with the campus culture—while he had hoped for a community of learners he found that no one spent time outside of class on campus, "Everyone's pretty much doing their own thing." But he remained focused on his end goal, the degree.

By the end of his first year in community college Malik had placed out of remedial reading[28] but not math and had done well in his other courses. However, several family and financial issues began to surface requiring Malik to take time off. His plan was to re-enroll in the Spring, despite his frustrations, and complete his degree.

Charles,[29] after graduating from Bridges, attended a very competitive private college in New York City. While he knew the coursework at this college would be rigorous, he was excited for the intellectual challenge. Once he began, however, he found that though he was "enthralled" by the scholarly readings and discussions, he was intimidated to the point of being unable to participate in class or complete assignments.[30] While he did not anticipate feeling out of place with a predominately white and middle-class student body, he quickly began to feel the effects of being "different." He was astutely aware of the social and cultural capital his classmates carried with them and more often than not found himself "wallowing in the pits of self-doubt" and "fleeing school" right after class. By the end of his first year, plagued by what he described as "intense writer's-block," Charles had not completed the work for far too many classes. He was dismissed.

Charles decided to accompany his mother, who was recovering from breast cancer, to Florida in hopes of finding a job and his way back to school. With little luck securing work he spent his nights doing what he missed most about school: reading, writing, and soul searching. His first email to me: "After reading 'Letters of a Young Poet' by Rilke, I'm having problems with my supposed craft. I've asked myself MUST I write? Would I die if I didn't write? Would the world even care?" Over the next two months he sent upwards of eight poems on everything from war to love. By January Charles was desperate to be back in school, "The fact that I'm itching to return to school after having it cause so much misery is testament to my desire to learn." The closest school, a community college, was an hour and a half's commute, but he was willing to make it if it meant reclaiming part of his academic identity and intellectual development. His plans were crushed however when he discovered that because he had been living in Florida for only six months he was not a resident and would have to pay out-of-state tuition. "It seems that I will not be going to school this semester," he concluded.

By February Charles set into motion a process to return to New York and to college. He completed an eight-page reflection on why he failed his first year and sent it to admissions and the dean of his original college and completed applications for both State and City schools. In a trip back to New York where he met with anyone he could, he learned that while he could not attend a new four-year college until he completed community college courses he would be afforded another chance at his original college. Further complicating his journey, however, was the fact that having moved to Florida he was no longer a New York resident and thus ineligible for the funding he had initially received. After his mother re-filed her taxes so he could claim "independence," and he moved in with his grandmother, Charles was able to begin again.

Charles returned excited to "right his wrongs." By the end of his third year out of high school he completed a full year of college in much better standing than his first year; he would be able to return the following year. He continued to struggle with many of the same issues he initially faced, but what was different was that Charles reached out for help—to professors, counselors, students. He was clear, "I don't want to fuck this up. Not again—because I would be failing myself—more than anyone else. And I wouldn't know what to do after that."

Conclusions

If education is not the key to social transformation, neither is it simply meant to reproduce the dominant ideology.

—Paulo Freire, 1998

The work of Bridges and the experiences of its graduates lend grounded insights into the debate on whether schools make a difference. The message: though schools can't do it all, they can, and therefore must, do something. Small schools alone can never "do enough" (Littky 2000) to overcome the enormous odds their students are up against; it's not as simple as just "[giving] them what you have always offered those who have the money to buy the best" (Meier 1995) and expecting that the opportunities will follow. At the same time, graduate experiences also reveal that institutional agency does change the odds for many and far surpasses the achievements of their traditional school counterparts.

Determinism without hope is not an option for low-income students of color, nor should it be for schools. Institutional agency needs a more permanent place within the debate on schools as tools of social justice—and more importantly, within the leadership of public schools. Yes, there needs to be more funding for urban schools; yes, there needs to be better social policy for the poor; yes, there needs to be more collaboration among organizations to build toward a movement for social justice. But while we are waiting—and fighting—for those changes, educational leaders need to question what they can do in their own schools to demonstrate a commitment to social justice and equity.

Notes

1. The names of the school, staff members, students, and graduates have been changed.

2. The research for this chapter draws from a larger study conducted between June 2002 and June 2005 on the power and limits of public small school reform as understood through the post-secondary experiences of graduates. Using a multi-method approach to data collection, the study explored the vision and practice of small schools. Made up of an ethnographic school-based component and a graduate follow-up one, the former included participant observation, semi-structured interviews with staff members and students, and document collection. The graduate follow-up study was a three-year "go-along" (Kusenbach, 2003) with six graduates consisting of interviews, campus visits, collection of syllabi and assignments, email, phone conversations, and family interviews. Additionally twenty graduates of the same school were interviewed and ninety graduates surveyed (representing 55 percent of three graduating classes).

3. All data on Bridges is from New York City Department of Education School Report Card, 2003.

4. Bridges has a larger population of special education than most other New York City public schools. Only 13% of the neighborhood comprehensive school is classified as special education.

5. When students enter in 7th grade their test scores, in fact, are below district averages. It is important to note that Bridges has the advantage of working with the majority of their high school students for two years before they begin 9th grade.

6. Bridges does have a corporate sponsor to supplement its programming which it has used, primarily, to hire a college counselor. Additionally it has a Beacon program on site which provides some after-school opportunities for students.

7. These small schools were committed to a common set of ideals and practices. Since then many more small schools have opened; since 2002 upwards of seventy-eight small schools were established. In the process "small schools" have come to mean many things: some test students to enter and some are open to all; some focus on traditional learning and others on project-based learning; some are staff-run and others have traditional governance structure.

8. An additional 11.3% of the original 9th graders were still enrolled.

9. An additional 29.9 % of the original 9th graders were still enrolled.

10. This data comes from my own research rather than Department of Education data.

11. Foote (2005) shows that graduates of similar schools also have higher persistence rates in college. Of the sample she tracked, 78% enrolled for a second year; of those attending 4-year colleges 84% re-enrolled and of those attending 2-year colleges 59% re-enrolled. Nationally

only 73% of students who enter 4-year colleges re-enroll for a second year and only 56% of those who enter 2-year schools do.

12. Bridges began by integrating both history and English as well as math and science. As the school developed, however, it decided to separate the instruction of math and science, believing that it was difficult to maintain the rigor of each discipline throughout high school with an integrated approach.

13. While many schools focus on small class size, Bridges recognizes that it is not only small class size but also the number of overall students that a teacher teaches throughout the week that is important to personalized learning. As such, overall loads range from 40–80 students, with math and science teachers having the higher numbers of students.

14. While this time commitment exceeds the expectation set out in the Union contract, the staff agreed it was necessary and worked it into their School-Based Option plan.

15. In 2005 the Consortium was granted a variance from the State allowing its schools to administer only the English Language Arts Regents and add one other in for students entering high school in 2006. Students entering in 2008 will be required to take two exams and those entering in 2009 to take all five. The Consortium is continuing its fight in hopes to change the conditions of the variance. For more information go to:http://www.performanceassessment.org/.

16. During the time of my research all five exams were being administered at Bridges.

17. Roundtable participants include Bridges's staff, staff from collaborating organizations, student-teachers, and educators from other schools.

18. Committees are made up of educators from both within and outside of the school.

19. When Bridges graduated its first class of students, seniors were required to do a performance task in all subject areas. This policy has changed over the years as different tests were phased in and out. When this research was done there were graduation committees in social studies only; however, when the variance was awarded the school made a commitment to reinstitute committees in other subject areas.

20. There have been two studies to date on small schools' graduates in college. Foote (2005) analyzed college GPAs and persistence rates from year one to year two and Bensman (1995) conducted one-time interviews with graduates of a small school.

21. While this chapter does not provide analysis for why some graduates persisted and others did not, it is worth noting that those who had more access to help at their colleges and those who reached out for it persisted at higher rates than those who did not.

22. National numbers come from 2003 US Census data compiled in "Educational Attainment in the United States: 2003" (US Census Bureau, 2004), and New York City numbers come from 2000 US Census data compiled in Census 2000 Summary File (US Census Bureau, 2000).

23. Statistics on "Some College or More" derived from sample of 90—the graduating classes of 1999, 2000, 2001; statistics on Associates and Bachelors completion derived from sample of 60, as the class of 2001, when surveyed, had not been into high school long enough for degree completion.

24. Defined as African American and Caribbean American.

25. Defined as one or more years.

26. Includes occupational and academic associates degrees.

27. For-profit colleges have grown rapidly in New York State and New York City, serving predominately low-income students of color. Few of them offer degrees—giving certificates instead—and credits from these schools either do not transfer, or transfer to only a select number of colleges. Most overlook prior financial aid debt, offering students loans and Pell and TAP money (Arenson, 2005). Data on loan defaults shows a disproportionate number of borrowers who defaulted were in for-profit schools (Merisotis, 1988). Of Bridges's graduates, 17 percent attended for-profit schools at some point in time.

28. Evidence of the often arbitrary nature of these exams, Malik passed his reading exam at the end of his first semester getting only three questions wrong.

29. Charles's mother got her GED and then Associates degree as an adult.

30. This is a common phenomenon for students of color that Steele (1999) has termed "stereotype threat."

References

Anyon, J. (1980). Social class and the hidden curriculum of work. *Journal of Education*, 162(1): 67–92.

———. (1997). *Ghetto schooling: A political economy of urban educational reform*. New York: Teachers College Press.

Apple, M. (1990). *Ideology and curriculum*. New York: Routledge.

———. (1995). *Education and power*. New York: Routledge.

Arenson, K. (2005). Speedy growth in career schools raises questions. *The New York Times*. July 12, 2005.

Aronowitz, S. (1998). Introduction, in *Pedagogy of Freedom*, New York, Rowman and Littlefield.

———., and Giroux, H.A. (1993). *Education still under siege*. Westport, CT: Bergin & Garvey.

Bensman, D. (1995). *Learning to think well: Central Park East Secondary School (CPESS) graduates reflect on their high school and college experiences*. New York: NCREST, Teachers College.

Bowles, S., and Gintis, H. (1976). Schooling in capitalist America: Educational reform and the contradictions of economic life. New York: Basic Books.

Carlson, D., and Gause, C. (2007). *Keeping the promise: Essays on leadership, democracy, and education*. New York: Peter Lang

CFE v. State of New York. (1999). Available at: http://www.cfequity.org/ns-test1.htm.

Fine, M. (1991). Framing dropouts: Notes on the politics of an urban high school. Albany: State University of New York Press.

———., and Weis, L. (2001). Extraordinary conversations in public schools. *International Journal of Qualitative Studies in Education*, 2(2), 1-27.

———. et al. (2005). *The international network for public schools: A quantitative and qualitative cohort analysis of graduation and drop-out rates*. New York: CUNY Graduate Center. Available at: www.internationalsnps.org.

Foote, M. (2005). *Keeping accountability systems accountable*. New York: New York Performance Standards Consortium.

Freire, P. (1998). *Pedagogy of freedom*, New York: Rowman and Littlefield.

Giroux, H. (1997). *Pedagogy and the politics of hope: Theory, culture, and schooling*. Boulder, CO: Westview Press.

———. (2001). *Theory and resistance in education: A pedagogy for the opposition*. Westport, CT: Bergin & Garvey.

Klonsky, M. (1995). *Small schools: The numbers tell a story*. Chicago, IL: The Small Schools Workshop.

Kozol, J. (1991). *Savage inequalities*. New York: Harper Perennial.

Kusenbach, M. (2003). Street-phenomenology: The go-along as ethnographic research tool. *Ethnography* 4(3): 449–479.

Littky, D., (2000). Life after small schools. In W. Ayers et al. (Eds.), *A simple justice*. New York: Teachers College Press.

McNeil, L. (2000). *Contradictions of school reform: Educational costs of standardized testing*. New York: Routledge.

Meier, D. (1995). *The power of their ideas*. Boston, MA: Beacon Press.

Merisotis, J. P. (1988). Default trends in major postsecondary education sectors. *Journal of Student Financial Aid*. 18(3), 18-28.

Nieto, S. (2000). *Affirming diversity: the sociopolitical context of multicultural education*, third edition. New York: Academic Press.

Noguera, P. (2003). *City schools and the American dream: Reclaiming the promise of urban public education*. New York: Teachers College Press.

Orfield, G., and Yun, J. T. (1999). Resegregation in American schools. The Civil Rights project, Harvard University.

Rothstein, R. (2004). *Class and schools: Using social, economic, and educational reform to close the Black-White achievement gap*. New York: Economic Policy Institute, Teachers College.

Stanton-Salazar, R. (2001). *Manufacturing hope and despair*. New York: Teachers College Press.

Steele, C. (1999). Thin ice: "Stereotype threat" and Black college students. *The Atlantic*. August 1999, 44-54.

U.S. Census Bureau. (2000). Census 2000 Summary File 3, Matrices P18, P19, P21, P22, P24, P36, P37, P39, PCT8, PCT16, PCT 17, and PCT19.

U.S. Census Bureau. (2004). *Educational attainment in the United States: 2003*.

Washington, DC: U.S. Department of Commerce, Economics and Statistics Administration.

Valenzuela, A. (1999). *Subtractive schooling: U.S.-Mexican youth and the politics of caring*. Albany: State University of New York Press.

15

Resisting the Passive Revolution: Democratic, Participatory Research by Youth

Michelle Fine

Over the past quarter century, I have had the good fortune of working with middle, secondary, and university educators, in Philadelphia, Chicago, urban and suburban New York and New Jersey, as well as educators in California, who have dared to lead, for justice, through public education. These administrators and teachers have struggled to create democratic small schools throughout the nation (Calderon, 2005; Fine, 2005; Fine and Powell, 2001; Fine and Somerville, 1998; Meier, 2005; Stovall, 2005; Wei, 2005) for the poorest youth in urban America and have organized for finance equity in school funding (Ladson-Billings, 2006). They have fought against the catastrophic effects of high stakes testing (Cook and Tashlik, 2005; Fine, 2005; Meier, 2005), Eurocentric curricula (Abu El-Haj, 2005; Bigelow, 2006; Nieto, 2006), zero tolerance (Ayers et al., 2001) and tracking systems that disproportionately limit students' access to academic rigor (Anand et al., 2002). I have had the amazing opportunity to work with community and school-based educators who insist that young people deserve to be educated fully about sexuality education (Fine and McClelland, 2006), social history—including indigenous history (Smith, 1999) and to be taught in anti-racist, multilingual and/or transcultural settings (Christensen, 2006; Delpit, 1995; Fine et al., 2005; Hilliard, 1990; Lee, 2005; Peterson, 2006). Some have worked for racially integrated schools that cross zip code lines, and others for neighborhood-based schools to educate immigrant youth and/or youth of color in communities where their parents reside. I have witnessed as educators build study bridges to higher education so that all youth can enjoy the opportunities typically reserved for the elite and educators (collaborating with prisoners) who helped to restore college within prisons, when President Clinton denied prisoners access to Pell grants (Fine et al., 2001; Gangi, Schiraldi, and

Ziedenberg, 1998). I have traveled with educators, parents, and students to newspaper editorial boards, legislative offices, quiet behind-the-scenes meetings and public rallies on the steps of the Capitol to help launch a major successful struggle against high stakes testing in New York State and put in its place instead, an elegant Performance Assessment system.

During a season of neoliberal assault on public education, I have had the joy of witnessing and collaborating with a series of educators throughout the United States who dare to believe that they have a responsibility to exert strong democratic leadership for public education. In the language of Antonio Gramsci, these educators have collectively strategized, with parents, community, and youth, to resist the passive revolution:

> The category of "passive revolution"…qualify[ies] the most usual form of hegemony of the bourgeoisie involving a model of articulation whose aim is to neutralize the other social forces … enlarging the state whereby the interests of the dominant class are articulated with the needs, desires, interests of subordinated groups. (Mouffe, 1979, 192)

Instead, they have undertaken the hard work of critical analysis, collective reflection, strategic networking and "rearticulation"—figuring out what must be, within the very real conditions of what is, understanding that,

> the objective of ideological struggle is not to reject the system and all its elements but to rearticulate it, to break it down to its basic elements and then to sift through past conceptions to see which ones, with some changes of content, can serve to express the new situation. (Gramsci interpreted by Mouffe, 1979, 192)

What I love about working with such educators is that they can't simply theorize, advocate or publish on what "could be." They must tango between powerful Utopian images of educational justice and the stubborn realities of life in real schools—the young faces, educators, systems, communities with whom they labor. In the words of Myles Horton and Paulo Friere, these men and women in schools and communities "make the road by walking." In the words of Deborah Meier, they "build the boat while sailing." Indeed, they are the bricolateurs who pick up the pieces of pain, possibility, passion, and constraint in their schools and the economy, and creatively they remake the world. That is, they exercise the magic of democratic leadership in profoundly unjust times.

In this essay I want to introduce another form of educational leadership—critical participatory action research (PAR) launched by a coalition of educators and youth, with youth researchers as the primary sources of knowedge; youth analyses positioned as fundamental to educational policy, practice, organizing, and leadership. Here you will meet a group of educators and young people from wealth and poverty, suburbs and urban schools, AP classes and special education, who came together to study the race and class injustices that have constituted public education. Supported by superintendents, educators, and community based organizations, once their research projects were complete, they organized to speak back to educators and communities, as well as other youth, about the consequences of these inequities. Ultimately they published and then performed to audiences around the nation their outrage, and their desires. These youth must be included in the net of democratic leaders for public education to whom this book is dedicated.

Participatory Action Research *with*, *by*, and *for* Youth

Enabling youth to interrogate and denaturalize the conditions of their everyday oppression inspires a process of community and knowledge building. Repositioning youth as researchers rather than the "researched," shifts the practice of researching *on* youth to *with* youth—a position that stands in sharp contrast to the current neoliberal constructions of youth as dangerous, disengaged, blind consumers who lack any type of connection. Frustrated, alienated, and angry survivors of discrimination mature into active policy critics and agents engaged in conversation, confrontation, and reform. Legitimating democratic inquiry within institutions as well as outside, PAR excavates knowledge "at the bottom" and "at the margins" (Lykes, 2001; Martin-Baro, 1994; Matsuda, 1995), and signifies youths' fundamental right to ask, investigate, and contest policies that enforce injustice (Torre, 2005).

A methodological stance rooted in the belief that valid knowledge is produced only in collaboration and in action, PAR recognizes that those "studied" harbor critical social knowledge and must be repositioned as subjects and architects of research (Martin-Baro, 1994; Torre, 2005). Based largely on the theory and practice of Latin American activist scholars, PAR scholars draw from neo-Marxist, feminist, queer, and critical race theorists (Anzaldua, 1987; Apple, 1995; 2001; Crenshaw, 1995; Weis and Fine, 2004) to articulate methods and ethics that have local integrity and stretch topographically to sight/cite global patterns of domination and resistance (Katz, 2004).

Our own PAR work spanning the past decade rests on our fundamental recognition that marginalized/oppressed youth carry sharp critique and knowledge about the very mortar of social formations, and that revealing and legitimating this knowledge, significantly challenges existing forms of institutional and structural oppression that have been naturalized as inevitable. Building on prior research, we add a spirit of "radical inclusion," whereby in our most recent project, relatively advantaged youth were invited to study social injustice alongside those who have historically been denied material opportunities. Using resources drawn from the academy, community, and personal experience, radically diverse youth collaboratively investigated the political biographies of privilege and oppression and unearthed the long buried histories of resistance. We have found with this practice, that over time, coalitions of unsuspecting allies erupt within the praxis of inquiry, documentation, speaking back, and reimagining social policies for social justice (Burns, 2004; Guinier and Torres, 2004; Iyer, Leach and Pedersen, 2004; Powell Pruitt, 2004). When PAR collectives are organized as "contact zones," that is, purposely diverse communities that explicitly acknowledge power and privilege within the group, (see Pratt, 1991) and then *use* these differences as resources to further the social justice agenda of the research, there is the potential to produce research that is optically and ethically layered, that addresses issues that otherwise might be left uninterrogated, that pushes boundaries considered comfortable and explodes categories once thought to be "normal" (Torre, 2005). To begin, we take you inside one school-based feedback session:

> *"Now I'd like you to look at the suspension data, and notice that Black males in high schools were twice as likely as White males to be suspended, and there are almost no differences between Black males and Black females. But for whites, males are three times more likely to be suspended than females: 22% of Black males, 19% of Black females, 11% of White males and 4% of white females."* Kareem, an African American student/youth researcher attending a desegregated high school, detailed the racialized patterns of school suspensions to his largely white teaching faculty. Despite many arms crossed in the audience, he continued: *"You know me, I spend a lot of time in the discipline room. It's really almost all Black males."* Hesitant nods were followed by immediate explanations about how in June "it gets Whiter," and "sometimes there are White kids, maybe when you're not there." While some faculty tried to support him, a wave of resistance-to-hear claimed the room. Nonetheless, Kareem turned to the charts projected on the screen, *"You don't have to believe me, but I speak for the hundreds of Black males who filled out this survey. We have to do something about it."*

Contesting the common sense belief that discipline problems are wholly generated by students and the hegemonic belief that disciplinary policies are race neutral, Kareem tried to rearticulate the "problem" of suspensions to his teachers as relational and indeed racial. He invited the faculty to collaborate with him on research to investigate these patterns. Once it was clear that the faculty wasn't likely to take him up on his offer, Kareem took up the persona of the social researcher, reporting the aggregate evidence as a call for action. He explained, calmly, that while the educators might choose to ignore his particular case, they would nevertheless have to contend with hundreds of African American boys who completed the survey and told us the same. He tried to articulate that this is not an individual problem, not race neutral and not separable from the larger school culture. He provided evidence that tore at the ideological representation of the school as integrated and fair. Kareem came to see this school context as ossified, as Franz Fanon has written, "[A] society that ossifies itself in determined form … a closed society where it is not good to be alive, where the air is rotten, where ideas and people are corrupt." (1967, pp. 182, 224-225)

The school was refusing to hear; the air was rotten. Kareem was an engaged member of our Participatory Action Research collective, where we designed critical research to reveal and challenge standard, inequitable educational practices and to rearticulate what could be. In the Spring of 2003, Kareem was asking his faculty for nothing less than educational justice. As a youth researcher on our large scale Participatory Action Research project interrogating youth perspectives on racial and class (in)justice in public schools, Kareem developed, and then taught other youth, the skills of research, collaboration and organizing.

Kendra, a young White student, was a junior attending another public desegregated high school. During the Summer of 2003, Kendra joined a dozen youth, spoken word artists, dancers, educators, lawyers, historians and activists from the New York metropolitan area to study the history of the *Brown v. Board of Education* decision, and the racial inequities that persist to date in public education. Having immersed herself in the history and contemporary struggles for racial justice in education, Kendra created a spoken word piece on the classroom-based racial imbalances that loiter within her desegregated high school. To an audience of almost 800 educators, activists, youth, policy makers, and civil rights organizers, Kendra bridged history and the present:

> *and in the classrooms, the imbalance is subtle,*
> *undercurrents in hallways.*
> *AP classes on the top floor, special ed. in the basement.*
> *and although over half the faces in the yearbook*
> *are darker than mine,*
> *on the third floor, everyone looks like me.*
> *so it seems glass ceilings are often concrete.*

so let's stay quiet, ride this pseudo-underground railroad,
this free ticket to funding from the board of ed.
racism is only our problem if it makes the front page.

although brown faces fill the hallways,
administrators don't know their names,
they are just the free ticket to funding,
and this is not their school. (Kendra Urdang)

Dissecting hegemonic beliefs about desegregation and privilege, Kendra exposed racial inequities in her school, as she challenged the widely held belief that privileged students don't care about injustices from which they benefit.

Kareem and Kendra represent activist scholars of the next generation. Revealing the fault lines of inequity that hold their desegregated schools together, and at the same time, render them vulnerable; these young people have witnessed injustice in schools, researched the policies, practices, and consequences of inequity; disarticulated hegemonic beliefs and worked hard to reimagine schools of justice. Kendra was relatively advantaged and Kareem relatively disadvantaged by equivalent systems. Yet both were stimulated toward critical scholarship to interrupt the "everydayness" of educational injustice. The larger PAR project, with educators from high school and university joining these youth researchers, was designed in the spirit of Michael Apple's (2001) thick democracy as: "a practice that is based in the control of decisions about production, distribution and consumption in the hands of the majority of working people in this country, one that is not limited to the political sphere but to, say, economics and critically gender relations." These young people were engaged in critical research projects that were at once provocative and democratic; rich in theory and activism; analytically wide and locally deep. They were performing democratic leadership ... and their educators—for the most part—cheered them on.

Echoes of Brown: Youth Documenting and Performing the Legacy of *Brown v. Board of Education*

We must contest a particular assumption—that of passivity.

—Apple, 2001, p. 87

In the Fall of 2001, a group of suburban school superintendents of desegregated districts gathered to discuss the disaggregated Achievement Gap data provided by the States of New Jersey and New York. As is true nationally, in these desegregated districts, the test score gaps between Asian American, White American, African American, and Latino students were disturbing. Eager to understand the roots and remedies for the gap, Superintendent Sherry King of Mamaroneck New York invited me and my colleagues from the Graduate Center to join the research team. We agreed, under the condition that we could collaborate with a broad range of students from suburban and urban schools, to create a multi-year participatory action research project.

Over the course of three years of youth inquiry, through a series of "research camps," more than 100 youth from urban and suburban high schools in New York and New Jersey joined researchers from the Graduate Center of the City University to study youth perspectives on racial- and class-based (in)justice in schools and the nation. We worked in the schools long enough to help identify a core of youth drawn from all corners of the school to serve as youth researchers—from special education, ESL, the Gay/Straight Alliances, discipline rooms, Student Councils, and Advanced Placement classes. We designed a multi-generational, multi-district, urban-suburban database of youth and elder experiences, tracing the history of struggle for desegregation from *Brown* to date, and social science evidence of contemporary educational opportunities and inequities analyzed by race, ethnicity, and class (see Fine et al., 2004).

The research was all the richer because it had deep local roots in particular youth research collectives tied and committed to real spaces—the streets of Paterson, the desegregated schools in New York and New Jersey, the community-based activist organization Mothers on the Move (MOM) in the South Bronx, and small schools in New York City—and because we facilitated cross-site theorizing and inquiry to deepen the cartography of inequity we were crafting. We took seriously *deep local work*, and then added in research and organizing that would enable *wide, cross-site analysis*. By blending deep local work with relatively homogeneous collectives, with critical, cross-site analysis, we were able to create what Mary Louise Pratt calls a *contact zone*, in which we could chart critically the uneven distribution of finances, cultural capital, opportunities, hope, despair, and resistance. Documenting inequity through youth research we were also nurturing the tools of critical resistance broadly and deeply in this next generation.

Organized as *doubled resistance*, the Opportunity Gap Project was designed to reveal the presence of deep, historic and sustained injustice in schools, as well as the clever, creative, and exhausting ways that youth of poverty—and privilege—every day resist and negotiate these injustices. Further, this project was designed to provoke action, in discrete and linked sites. (For another example of activist research with youth see, Fine et al., 2005, on *Williams v. California*, a class action lawsuit in which poor and working class youth were, as a class, suing the state of California for inadequate schools, undercertified educators, insufficient books and materials, decaying buildings and less than sufficient intellectual preparation for college; see also Fine, et al., 2003 for a participatory action research project on the impact of college in prison.)

At our first session with close to 50 youth from six suburban high schools and three urban schools, the students immediately challenged/disarticulated the frame of the research:

> When you call it an achievement gap, that means it's our fault. The real problem is an opportunity gap—let's place the responsibility where it belongs—in society and in the schools.

With democratic challenge stirring, we—including the embarrassed adults—quickly changed the name to the Opportunity Gap Project, sheepishly remembering Freire's words:

> The silenced are not just incidental to the curiosity of the researcher but are the masters of inquiry into the underlying causes of the events in their world. In this context research becomes a means of moving them beyond silence into a quest to proclaim the world. (Freire, 1982)

Students met as research collectives within their local spaces, and they also participated in a series of cross-site "research camps," each held for two days at a time in community and/or university settings. Immersed in methods training and social justice theory, spoken word and hip hop music, film and Boondocks cartoons, the camps were designed to explore how to conduct interviews, focus groups and participant observations; to design surveys and organize archival analyses. We worked with historians, lawyers and activists who discussed the history of race and class struggles in public education, the history of the *Brown* decision, civil rights movements, and struggles for educational justice for students with disabilities, second language learners, lesbian/gay/bi/trans and queer youth.[1]

In our early sessions, the agenda and questions were set—in pencil—by the adults. We had determined that we would study the "gap"—quickly reframed by the youth. At the first retreat, we brought in a "wrong draft" of the survey which the young people quickly trashed, revised, and radically transformed, and we set much of the skills building agenda. Over the course of that first weekend, we redesigned the survey to assess high school students' views of Race and Class (In)Justice in Schools and the Nation. Over the next few months, we translated the survey into Spanish, French-Creole, and Braille, and distributed it to 9th and 12th graders in 13 urban and suburban districts. At the second and third camp, another group of youth researchers from the same schools (with some overlap) analyzed the qualitative and quantitative data from 9,174 surveys, 24 focus groups and 32 individual interviews with youth.

After that first session, however, the local research collectives began to take up their local work. Within individual schools, community-based organizations and neighborhoods, the youth research teams determined, with adults, the questions they would study, what they would read, who they would interview, the music they would listen to, and the methods they would deploy to investigate questions of justice and consciousness. The "street life" collective of young men who work the streets in Paterson, New Jersey, facilitated by Yasser Payne, read together a number of excerpts on how scholars represent the "streets" and then culled from contemporary hip hop music how they would chose to represent themselves, as they set up focus group interviews for young men working the streets. The "Mothers on the Move" Youth Researchers group, facilitated by Monique Guishard, read "everything I was reading in my graduate methods course" (Guishard et al. 2003) and brought in articles from youth magazines, contemporary music and spoken word, to develop their theorizing of critical consciousness. In the suburbs, the youth researchers working with April Burns and Maria Torre determined the methods, samples and "spots" for interviews and participant observations in order to capture the full story of desegregated schooling, including the untold stories of internal segregation. April Burns investigated how privileged students think about racial and class injustice, and where their pockets of critical consciousness lie (see Burns in Fine et al., 2004). And in the small urban schools, where Janice Bloom and Lori Chajet taught youth research courses as senior year internships, students collectively determined the questions to be investigated, the methods, readings, the persons to be interviewed, and the products to be generated (see Acosta et al., 2003), the article written by these students about the Finance Equity research project in *Rethinking Schools*. Educators from university and secondary schools joined with students to interrogate questions of justice generated by youth.

All through the three years, across these varied settings, we studied up on the history of *Brown*, Emmett Till, Ella Baker, Bayard Rustin, finance inequity, tracking, battles over buses and bilingualism, the unprecedented academic success of the small schools movement, new schools for lesbian/gay/bisexual/transgender students, the joys, the dangers and "not-yets" of integration. We met with state legislators, organizers, and journalists; read on the growth of the prison industrial complex at the expense of public education, and we reviewed how, systematically, federal policy has left so many poor and working-class children behind.

We collected and analyzed data from the large-scale, broad-based survey moving across suburban and urban schools, and also rich, local material from the site-specific research projects. Designed to dig deep, these local projects included an in-depth study of the causes and consequences of finance inequity; an oral history of a South Bronx activist educational organization (MOM), in which founding members were interviewed by their children and grandchildren; a systematic investigation of the racialized tracking of students in middle school mathematics; cross-school visits, interviews, and senior transcript analysis to document differential access to AP courses and suspension rates by race/ethnicity and track in suburban schools (e.g., the extent to which "test scores" differentially predict enrollment in AP classes by race/ethnicity, see also Revella, Wells and Holme, 2005).

Together we mapped, across urban and suburban lines, the Racial, Ethnic and Class (In)Justices in secondary public schools. We documented structures and policies that produce inequity, the ideologies and youth beliefs that justify the gap, and those spaces within schools and communities in which educators and youth have joined to create extraordinary collaborations to contest the "gap." We wrote scholarly and popular articles, delivered professional and neighborhood talks. We traveled the nation to gather insights, listen to young people and to provoke policy, practice, and change with our research.

Our research, conducted across some of the wealthiest and poorest schools in the nation, confirms what others have found: a series of well-established policies and practices assure and deepen the gap. The more separate America's schools are racially and economically, the more stratified they become in achievement. In our empirical reports on these data we refer to these ongoing sites of policy struggle as Six Degrees of Segregation:

*   urban/suburban finance inequity,

* the systematic dismantling of desegregation,
* the racially coded academic tracking that organizes most desegregated schools,
* students' differential experiences of respect and supports in schools,
* the class, race, and ethnicity based consequences of high stakes testing, or
* the remarkably disparate patterns of suspensions and disciplinary actions (see Fine et al., 2004 for details).

Buoyed by our research findings and participatory process, during 2003 we conducted many feedback sessions in schools (like the opening scene with Kareem) and communities throughout the suburban communities circling New York City, and we presented our material to groups of educators and policy-makers throughout the country.

We found ourselves trapped by obsessive questions pointing to poor youth and youth of color—*What's wrong with them? Even in the same school building, we have a gap? But if we stop tracking how else can we teach students at their "natural" levels?* We grew weary of the volley of critical youth research followed by adult denial. Caught in the undertow of the passive revolution, we needed to strategize a political and educational alternative to radically break the conversation and begin anew.

In the summer of 2003, with the anniversary of *Brown* approaching, we decided to move our critical scholarship to performance. We extended our Social Justice and Social Research camps into a Social Justice and the Arts Institute. We brought together a diverse group of young people aged 13–21, recruited from the same schools and beyond, with community elders, social scientists, spoken word artists, dancers, choreographers, and a video crew to collectively pour through data from the Educational Opportunity Gap Project (Fine et al., 2004), to learn about the legal, social, and political history of segregation and integration of public schools; and to create *Echoes,* a performance of poetry and movement to contribute to the commemoratory conversation of the 50th anniversary of *Brown versus Board of Education of Topeka, Kansas.* [2]

To give you a sense of how we worked—we enter an afternoon session during the summer institute, with feminist lawyer Carol Tracy who was helping the youth researchers/performers historicize the impact of the *Brown* decision on civil rights, feminism, disability rights, and the gay/lesbian movement. Tracy explicated how the *Brown* decision opened doors for girls across racial/ethnic groups, students with disabilities, and gay/lesbian/bi/trans students. Her talk was punctuated by student writing sessions, questions and questions seasoned by the students' original research.

A hot conversation ensued about the new Harvey Milk School—a new small schools in New York City designed to support gay/lesbian/bisexual, and transgender students. The students in the Institute started pressing Carol, "Is this progress … a school for lesbian and gay students? Or is this a step backward into segregation again?" The debate was lively. Most of the young women agreed that all schools should be working on issues of homophobia and that segregating gay and lesbian students would simply be a throwback to the days of segregation.

But then Amir spoke. An African American youth researcher who attends a desegregated suburban school, Amir had shared his deep disappointment with the unmet promises of his desegregated high school. But at this point in the conversation, Amir was inspired to "come out" as a former special education student.

> When we were talking about the dancer [Katherine Dunham] and how she walked off the stage in the South during the 1940s because Blacks were in the balcony, I realized that happens today, with me and my friends—at my high school they put the special education kids in the balcony, away from the "normal kids." They (meaning gay/lesbian students) may need a separate school just to be free of the taunting. Putting people in the same building doesn't automatically take care of the problem.

Amir's poem, "Classification" reveals the connections he made from history, and with the lesbian/gay/trans students at the Milk school:

> *Possessing this label they gave me,*
> *I swallowed the stigma and felt the pain of being seen in a room with six people.*
> *Yeah, it fell upon me and the pain was like stones raining down on me.*
> *From the day where school assemblies seemed segregated*
> *and I had to watch my girl Krystal from balconies …*
> *Away from the "normal" kids*
> *to the days where I found myself fulfilling self-fulfilled prophecies.*
>
> *See I received the label of "special education"*
> *and it sat on my back like a mountain being lifted by an ant—it just can't happen.*
> *It was my mind's master.*
> *It told me I was dumb, I didn't know how to act in a normal class.*

I needed two teachers to fully grasp the concepts touched upon in class,

and my classification will never allow me to exceed track two.

So what is it that I do—

so many occasions when the classification caused me to break into tears?

It was my frustration.

My reaction to teachers speaking down to me saying I was classified

and it was all my fault.

Had me truly believing that inferiority was my classification.

Cause I still didn't know, and the pain WAS DEEP. The pain—OH GOD! THE PAIN!

The ridicule, the constant taunting, laughing when they passed me by.

Amir had been working with us for more than a year, as a youth researcher in his high school and then as a spoken word artist and performer in the Institute. He had never told us about his special education status until that moment. In writing this piece, Amir drew on his experiences as an African American student in a desegregated school, having spent too many years within special education classes. He pulled from three years of our cross-site research findings on rigor/respect/belonging, the history of *Brown* and what he had learned about the dancer Katherine Dunham. With all these strings in hand and mind, Amir argued for a separate school for gay/lesbian/bisexual and transgendered youth in a climate where the price of integration is paid in taunting and physical abuse. In this context of thick critical inquiry, Amir's voice, experience and rage were embroidered into historic patterns of domination and exclusion, contemporary evidence of youth of color yearning for rigor, respect, and belonging.

On May 17, 2004 we performed *Echoes* to an audience of over 800, with video clips of Sonia Sanchez, Arthur Kinoy, and other amazing elders, and the choreography of dancer/choreographer Ronald K. Brown/Evidence. We also published a DVD/book of the work, including all the elder interviews, a video of the Social Justice and the Arts Institute, youth spoken word, detailed commentary by the adult and youth researchers and educators working on educational justice in desegregated schools, speaking on high stakes testing, tracking, and the everyday politics of racism— *Echoes: Youth Documenting and Performing the Legacy of Brown v. Board of Education* (Fine et al., 2004).

Since the performance, these youth researchers have published, lectured, and brought their skills to other social movements for educational justice. With educators, community organizers, advocates, and peers, some have gone on to participate in the Campaign for Fiscal Equity, researching and organizing for finance equity in public schools in New York State. Others have testified in State Legislature for the Performance Assessment Consortium, arguing for multiple forms of assessment in New York State, rather than the single, high stakes testing regime that has spiked the dropout rates for poor and working-class African American and Latino students (Cook and Tashlik, 2005). Those still in high school have brought their concerns about lack of respect, computers, gym, and college-application support back to their schools, communities, peers, and organizations of educational professionals and organizers. White suburban students have launched campaigns for detracking and a serious look at racial inequities in their schools. Educators have developed youth research courses in middle, secondary, and university classes; in schools and in communities; across sites and within neighborhoods (see Anand et al., 2003; Cahill, 2004; Ginwright, 2004; Ginwright and Cammarota, 2002). Together, the collective has presented their research and spoken word pieces at the National Coalition for Educational Activists, the Public Education Network, and the Cross Cultural Roundtable. These youth have learned the skills of thick democracy—to reveal and provoke (see Genoa, 2002). And they understand that their fame and performance means nothing if they stand alone. For in the end, all came to Amir's conclusion, "I had to speak for the others because the silence, oh the silence, is just as bad."

Widening the Web

Democratic Leadership, Critical Youth Research, and Educational Practice

This volume is dedicated to democratic leaders, as keepers of the promise. This essay is an invitation to extend our understanding of leadership and to situate youth as critical players in the radical politics of educational policy and practice. If this volume calls forth public education that challenges social hierarchy, it seems important to position youth questions, knowledge, action, and leadership at the center of the struggle. Critical participatory research by youth is a radical challenge to educational institutions and to the traditions of social research. PAR insists that those who are most fundamentally oppressed/affected by structural inequities construct the questions for the research, produce the knowledge, lead the analyses, determine how the knowledge is distributed, and generate strategic actions.

With PAR, the youth researchers, in coalition with educators and community activists, generated qualitative and quantitative material that reveals the desires and the pain of students in today's public schools. They drew the fracture lines of opportunity and denial. They worked in collaboration with educators, generating questions, critical analyses, power points, performances, and demands for a better tomorrow (Appadurai, 2004).

In the language of Antonio Gramsci, these young women and men exercised their civic responsibilities as organic intellectuals, documented the inequities of current educational practice and committed themselves to creating democracy and justice in and across educational sites. Many educators joined them in these efforts, but as you can imagine ... for the educators it was often a risk. Some were praised; others seen as subversive, perhaps even traitors to the expectation that "professionals" don't critique their institutions, professionals don't ally with students, professionals don't risk. And yet I take inspiration from a well-known democratic leader for justice, who moved the nation with his moral courage. Daniel Ellsberg writes:

> Leakers are often accused of being partisan and undoubtedly many of them are. But the measure of their patriotism should be the accuracy and the importance of the information they reveal. It would be a great public service to reveal a true picture of the administration's plans for Iraq. ... In 1964 it hadn't occurred to me to break my vow of secrecy. Though I knew that the war was a mistake, my loyalties then were to the secretary of defense and the president. It took five years of war before I recognized the higher loyalty all officials owe to the Constitution, the rule of law, the soldiers in harm's way or their fellow citizens....The personal risks of making disclosures embarrassing to your superiors are real. If you are identified as the source, your career will be over; the friendships will be lost; you may even be prosecuted. But some 140,000 Americans are risking their lives every day in Iraq. Our nation is in urgent need of comparable moral courage from its public officials. (Daniel Ellsberg, *New York Times, 2004)*

As Ellsberg suggests, public intellectuals, "leakers," or perhaps we can say critical youth and educator researchers pay a price for speaking, but they also pay a price for silence. The stakes for collusion in war, like (mis)education, can be severe. But in the case of (mis)education (see Woodson, 1977, p. 19), the collateral damage accumulates slowly over time, seeping into communities and across generations. The young women and men of *Echoes*, like their educators, refused to remain silent. And by so doing, they were indeed engaged in democratic, collective leadership—just the kind we need so desperately today.

Notes

1. Many students received high school credits (when a course on participatory research was offered in their schools) and forty-two received college credit for their research work.
2. The 13 youth were drawn from wealthy and economically depressed communities in the suburbs surrounding New York City and within the city, representing the kind of wisdom born in Advanced Placement classes and the kind born in Special Education classrooms. We joined Christians, Jews, Muslims, and youth with no religious affiliation; those of European, African, Caribbean, Palestinian, Latino, and blended ancestries; young people headed for the Ivy League and some who have spent time in juvenile facilities; some who enjoy two homes, and some who have spent nights without a home. We recruited youth interested in writing, performing, and/or social justice from youth groups and public schools in the greater New York metropolitan area including northern New Jersey. We gathered together an intentionally diverse group of young people, together—by gender, race, ethnicity, class, sexuality, (dis)ability, "track;" by experiences with racism, sexism, homophobia, school administrators, social service agencies, "the law"; by (dis)comfort with their bodies, dance, poetry, groups; and so on.

References

Abu El-Haj, T., in Weis, L., and Fine, M. (2005). *Beyond silenced voices*. Albany, NY: SUNY Press, 199–216.

Acosta, N., Castillo, J., DeJesus, C., Geneo, E., Jones, M., Kellman, S., Osorio, A., Rahman, N., Sheard, L., Taylor, J. with help from Bloom, J. and Chajet, L. (2003). Urban students tackle research on inequality: What you thought we didn't know. *Rethinking Schools*. 18(1), Fall: 31–32.

Anand, B., Fine, M., Perkins, T., and Surrey, D. (2002). *Keeping the struggle alive: Studying desegregation in our town*. New York: Teachers College Press.

Anzaldua, Gloria (1987). *Borderlands/La Frontera: The New Mestiza*. Second Edition. San Francisco: Aunt Lute Books.

Appadurai, Arjun (2004). Capacity to aspire: Culture and the terms of recognition. In R. Vijayendra and M. Walton (Eds.), *Culture and public action*. Stanford, CA: Stanford University Press.

Apple, M. (1995). *Education and power*. New York: Routledge.

———. (2001). *Educating the right way*. New York: Taylor and Francis..

Ayers, R., Ayers, W., Dohrn, B., and Jackson, T. (2001). *Zero tolerance*. New York: The New Press.

Bigelow, B. (2006). The line between us. *Rethinking Schools*, 20(3): 56–59.

Burns, A. (2004). The racing of capability and culpability in desegregated schools. In M. Fine, L. Weis, L. Pruitt, and A. Burns, *Off White* (pp. 373 – 394). New York: Routledge.

Cahill, C. (2004) Defying gravity? Raising consciousness through collective research. *Children's Geographies*, 2, 2, 273 – 286.

Calderon, H. (2005). When small is beautiful, *Rethinking Schools*, 19(4): 35–37.

Christensen, L. (2006). Reading Chilpancingo, *Rethinking Schools*, 20(3): 60–63.

Cook, A., and Tashlik, P. (2005). Standardizing small, *Rethinking Schools*,19(4): 15–17.

Crenshaw, K. (1995). Mapping the margins: Intersectionality, identity politics, and violence against women of colour. In K. Crenshaw, N. Gotanda, G. Peller, & K. Thomas (Eds.), *Critical race theory: The key writings that formed the movement* (pp. 357-383). New York: New Press.

Delpit, L. (1995). *Other people's children: Cultural conflict in the classroom*. New York: The New Press.

Ellsberg, Daniel. Truths worth telling. *New York Times*. 9/28/04.

Fanon, F. (1967). *Black skin, white masks*. New York: Grove Press.

Fine, M. (2005). Not in our name, *Rethinking Schools*, 19(4), 11–14.

————., and McClelland, S. I. (Fall 2006). The politics of teen women's sexuality: Mapping the policy environment for sexual and reproductive freedoms, *Harvard Educational Review*. 76, 3, 297-338.

————., and Powell, L. (2001). *Small schools as an anti-racist intervention. Racial profiling and punishment in U. S. public schools*. ARC Research Report, October 2001, 45–50, Oakland, CA.

————., and Somerville, J. (Eds.) (1998). *Small schools, big imaginations*. Chicago, IL: Cross City Campaign for Urban Education Reform.

————., Torre, M., Boudin, K., Bowen, I., Clark, J., Hylton, D., Martinez, M., Missy, Roberts, R., Smart, P., and Upegui, D. (2001). *Changing minds: The impact of college in a maximum security prison*. New York: The Graduate Center. www.changingminds.ws.

————., Torre, M.E., Boudin, K., Bowen, I., Clark, J., Hylton, D., Martinez, M., Missy, Rivera, M., Roberts, R.A., Smart, P., and Upegui, D. (2003). Participatory action research: Within and beyond bars. In Camic, P., Rhodes, J. E., and Yardley, L. (Eds.), *Qualitative research in psychology: Expanding perspectives in methodology and design*. Washington, DC: American Psychological Association, pp. 173–198.

————., Bloom, J., Burns, A., Chajet, L., Guishard, M., Payne, Y., Perkins-Munn, T., and Torre, M.E. (2005). Dear Zora: A letter to Zora Neale Hurston fifty years after Brown. *Teachers College Record,* 107(3): 496–528.

————., Roberts, R.A., Torre, M.E., and Bloom, J., Burns, A., Chajet, L., Guishard, M., and Payne, Y. (2004) *Echoes: Youth documenting and performing the legacy of Brown v. Board of Education*. New York: Teachers College Press.

Freire, P. (1982). Creating alternative research methods. Learning to do it by doing it. In B. Hall, A. Gillette, and R. Tandon, (Eds.), *Creating knowledge: A monopoly*. New Delhi: Society for Participatory Research in Asia, pp. 29–37.

Fullilove, M. (2004). *Root Shock*. New York: Ballantine Books.

Gangi, R., Schiraldi, V., and Ziedenberg, J. (1998). *New York State of mind: Higher education and prison funding in the Empire State, 1988–1998*, Washington, DC: The Justice Policy Institute.

Ginwright, S. (2004). *Black in school*. New York: Teachers College Press.

Genoa, E. (2002). Money for nothing. *The Brooklyn Rail*. http://www.thebrooklynrail.org/poetry/fall02/moneyfornothing.html.

Ginwright, S., and Cammarota, J. (2002). New terrain in youth development: The promise of a social justice approach. *Social Justice*, 29(4): 82–96.

Guinier, L. and Torres, G. (2004) Whiteness of a different color. In Fine, Weis, Pruitt and Burns, *Off White*. New York: Routledge, 411–420.

Guishard, M., Fine, M., Doyle, C., Jackson, J., Staten, S., and Webb, A. (2003). "As long as I got breath, I'll fight:" Participatory action research for educational justice. *Harvard Family Project Newsletter*, May 2003, www.gse.harvard.edu/hfrp/projects.

Hilliard, A. G. (1990). Rx for racism: Imperatives for America's schools. *Phi Delta Kappan*, 71: 593–600.

Iyer, A., Leach, C. and Pedersen, A. (2004) Racial wrongs and restitution. In Fine, M., Weis, L., Pruitt, L. and Burns, A. *Off White*. New York: Routledge, 345–361.

Katz, Cindi. (2004). *Growing up global: Economic restructuring and children's everyday lives*. Minneapolis: University of Minnesota Press.

Ladson-Billings, G. (2006). AERA Presidential Address, San Francisco, CA.

Lee, S. (2005) Learning about race, learning about "America." In Weis, L. and Fine, M. *Beyond silenced voices*. Albany, New York: SUNY Press, 133 –146.

Lykes, M.B. (2001). Activist participatory research and the arts with rural Maya women: Interculturality and situated meaning making. In D.L. Tolman & M. Brydon-Miller (Eds.), *From subjects to subjectivities: A handbook of interpretive and participatory methods* (pp. 183-199). New York: NYU Press.

Martín-Baró, I. (1994). *Writings for a liberation psychology*. Cambridge, MA: Harvard University Press.

Matsuda, M. (1995). Looking to the bottom: Critical legal studies and reparations. In K. Crenshaw, N. Gotanda, G. Peller, & K. Thomas (Eds.), *Critical race theory: The key writings that formed the movement* (pp. 63-79). New York: New Press.

Meier, D. (2005). Creating democratic schools, *Rethinking Schools*, 19(4): 28–29.

Mouffe, C. (1979). (Ed.), *Gramsci and Marxist Theory*. London: Routledge.

Nieto, S. (2006). Thoughts on the 20th anniversary of *Rethinking Schools*. *Rethinking Schools,* 20 (3): 6–8.

Peterson, B. (2006). Crossing borders, building empathy. *Rethinking Schools,* 20(3): 65–67.

Powell Pruitt, L. (2004) The Achievement (K)not. In Fine, Weis, Pruitt and Burns, *Off White*. New York: Routledge, 235–244.

Pratt, M.L. (1991). *Arts of the contact zone*. New York: Modern Language Association.

Revella, A.T., Wells, A. S., and Holme, J. J. (2005). We didn't see color: The salience of color blindness in desegregated schools. In M. Fine, L. Weis, L. Pruit, and A. Burns, (Eds.), *Off-White*. New York: Routledge, 284–301.

Smith, L.T. (1999). *Decolonizing methodologies: Research and indigenous peoples*. London: Zed Books.

Stovall, D. (2005). Communities struggle to make small serve all. *Rethinking Schools*, 19(4): 56–58.

Torre, J. E. (2005) The alchemy of integrated spaces. In Weis, L. and Fine, M. *Beyond silenced voices*. Albany, New York: SUNY Press, 251–266.

Valenzuela, A. (2005) Subtractive schooling, caring relations and social capital in the schooling of U.S.-Mexican youth. In Weis, L. and Fine, M. *Beyond silenced voices*. Albany, New York: SUNY Press, 83–94.

Wei, D. (2005). A little school in a little Chinatown. *Rethinking Schools*, 19(4): 30–31.

Weis, L. and Fine, M. (2004). *Working Method: Research and Social Justice*. New York: Routledge.

Woodson, C. G. (1977). *The mis-education of the Negro*. New York: AMS Press.

Part Three

Popular Culture, the Media, and Educational Leadership

16

Media Literacy:
An Entrée for Preservice Teachers
into Critical Pedagogy?

Stephanie A. Flores-Koulish

Introduction

The longer U.S. public education's "accountability movement" continues, the less our teachers have opportunities to engage students deeply in creative, original thought. Students today are judged as learned by scores received on objective standardized tests. Classroom time is put aside for test preparation and objective content delivery. The result of this pursuit for "high standards" brings us not more well-prepared but passive students, less able to deal effectively with a highly complex, interdisciplinary, intercultural, mediated social world.

Preservice teachers (PSTs) have twice the challenge before them. First, they themselves must become *critical* and at the same time, they need to learn how to deepen their future students' criticality amid the accountability dynasty. It is only in this way that we might one day overturn the objectivity trend. This chapter is based on the premise that PSTs must know how to engage in critical conversation, specifically on media and popular culture for this can help to expand their emerging understandings of critical pedagogy. Media and popular culture are omnipresent, though in the United States we still lag behind in terms of media literacy in our schools, so we are left to conclude that our understandings of our media culture are still immature. While critical media literacy may seem like a futile pursuit given the tenor of the times, it also can be argued that there has never been a more important time to pursue this reconstructive position, for this liberating stance provides a lens through which future teachers might bring students well beyond the cognitively concrete manacles holding them back. Additionally, critical media literacy provides a gateway for students to establish an inquiry stance in the world to potentially bring back aspects of creative, original thought. It is ultimately also a hope that the critical analysis of media culture will one day be typical of U.S. K through 12 curricula.

Before this systemic change can occur however, teachers must be knowledgeable in media literacy curricula and pedagogy. Scant research exists which involves U.S. PSTs and media literacy education (Flores-Koulish, 2004), much less of a critical perspective. Therefore, beyond a theoretical argument, this chapter provides empirical support to show PSTs' emerging connections between critical media analysis and pedagogical comprehension. Herein lies an assistive framework for teacher educators interested and willing to introduce aspects of media literacy within their own instruction. This is accomplished through the qualitative analysis of PSTs' responses to a particular media text: a Madonna music video, "What it feels like for a girl". The analysis highlights how teacher educators can set up a particular analytical context just by choosing the "right" media. Specifically, the participants show how conversation about a Madonna video leads them toward conscientization. Also, this same video allows for the PSTs to acknowledge the subjective viewing experience. And not only do the PSTs reveal what they know, but an analysis reveals where they are lacking in terms of their media literacy abilities (which could be remedied by instruction).

Literature on Media Literacy and Its Connections to Critical Pedagogy

Media literacy education is a critical tool that we can use to experience media differently with democratic and even emancipative implications. Media here include television, technology, film, advertising, and popular culture in general. Media literacy is commonly defined in the United States as "the ability to access, analyze, evaluate and communicate messages in a variety of forms" (Aufderheide, 1993). Alvermann, Hagood, and Moon (2000) explain that media literacy of a critical nature is still defined in various ways depending on whether one uses lenses of postmodernism, feminism, cultural studies, and so on. For the purpose of this chapter, I utilize an eclectic approach in which, beyond the definition above, varying subjectivities are considered within individuals' cultural, political environment, as well as whether individuals choose to resist, ignore, or simply acknowledge hegemonic representations. Media literacy today is powerful as it encourages students to use their cultural landscape to discuss various social issues; namely, how our identities are shaped by a small number of multinational media conglomerates (McChesney and Nichols, 2002).

There are many complementary elements between media literacy education and critical pedagogy. Practicing media literacy naturally encourages a person to identify underlying elements, including power structures and gendered identities (Alvermann, Hagood, and Moon 2000), a pursuit within critical pedagogy. Specifically, in critical media literacy, students learn about media economics and the social power that is held by a very small group of wealthy corporations that controls much of our information and entertainment (McChesney and Nichols, 2002). Operating through the lenses of critical pedagogy endorses the claim that teaching is a political act, which fronts subjective representations of reality. Media literacy enhances a person's ability to "see things differently." Critical pedagogues who employ critical literacy make "decisions that are consciously moral and political" (Kanpol, 1994). They connect curriculum with students' everyday lives, thereby equalizing the typical hierarchy between teacher and student, as well as providing a forum for introspection (Kanpol, 1994).

There are differences among various scholars operating within a critical pedagogical paradigm. According to Stanley (1992), social reproduction theorists claim that education is a force that reproduces hegemony in society working to keep the status quo intact, while resistance theories claim that curriculum has the potential to counter reproductive aspects which these theorists agree are clearly represented in our educational system. Thus, the resistance theorists see a potential for education to act as an egalitarian force. Media literacy education is in line with this stance as it reaches beyond mere critique toward social transformation. The media literacy process requires an analysis of institutional aspects in society: economic, political, social, and even aesthetic. Stuart Hall (2000) claims that mediated fixed meanings are put forth by those in power for ideological promotion, and through media literacy, can be dismantled and thus allow for openings in the attempted set meanings. Beyond analysis, individuals can have a voice by producing media that decode dominant representations and allow for events to carry counter-hegemonic meanings. Media analysis and production together is praxis in critical pedagogy.

Working with PSTs on media literacy thus has the potential to act as an entrée into questioning various institutions and texts, much like is suggested within a critical pedagogical standpoint. Rachel Martin (2001) describes post-structuralism as that which "helps us see our complicity with oppressive ideas and actions differently by seeing power as a web of relations rather than one deterministic force, such as propaganda, that we must overcome" (p. 53). With media literacy too, we see our own complicity with various economic, political, social, and aesthetic purposes of media messages, specifically in media culture. For example, after experiencing introductory media literacy, I have heard people say they are unable to watch television in the same way. However, the aim is not to take away media pleasures. Instead, teachers must learn to delicately balance pleasure with critical analysis, at the same time recognize the struggle that inevitably ensues (Alvermann, Hagood, and Moon, 1999). Luke (2000) claims that the recent evolution of media studies has moved from mere deconstruction toward a valuing of production. She writes that this provides students "with the critical analytical tools to understand reader and viewer diversity of reading positions and sociocultural locations and differences that influence affinities to, or preferences for (and pleasures derived from), particular kinds of media forms and messages" (p. 425). So to increase understandings of power in media institutions and elsewhere, students should practice reading *and* creating various forms of media utilizing a variety of perspectives.

Both Giroux (1994) and Kanpol (1997) discuss the potential of analyzing media cultural texts as a "natural" way for preservice teachers to understand elements of critical pedagogy. By "natural," Kanpol sees that using media cultural texts for critical analysis has the potential to move beyond the nihilistic analysis that commonly occurs in education classes through the complex analysis of schools and towards an investigation of texts that are commonplace and palatable.

Process and Theoretical Framing

The larger qualitative study upon which this chapter is based examined the lives of twenty-five undergraduate elementary education majors to discover their media histories and current knowledge, critical or otherwise, regarding the mass media and media culture (Flores-Koulish, 2004). Through a multiple-choice online survey, participants answered a series of questions geared toward their knowledge, skills, and experiences of media and media literacy. From there, five White women participants volunteered for a more extensive part that included repeated in-depth interviews, which drilled deeper into the areas above. Additionally, the volunteers participated in multiple discussion groups, focusing on topics such as children's media, media literacy pedagogy, media analysis, including screenings, and media literacy curriculum. This chapter focuses exclusively on their conversation following a Madonna music video. The methods and perspectives utilized came from naturalistic inquiry, grounded theory, and critical ethnography.

The video used to promote dialogue included a video of Madonna's banned by MTV, "What it feels like for a girl." I chose this particular video because it attempts to open representations, which Stuart Hall (2000) would say are typically closed off by ideology and power; it tries to uncover *what is* to show *what could be*. I elaborate on the video below.

Madonna as Critical Curriculum

Madonna is a complex character in media culture. The use of irony to produce various representations of Madonna both tweak and sabotage dominant ideological representations of femaleness, gender, and power. Madonna can be read both as modernist and postmodernist (Mandziuk, 1993), placed in typical roles in straightforward ways, yet busting stereotypes and pushing the boundaries of set definitions. Kellner (1995) writes that "Madonna continues to go beyond the borders of the permissible, to subvert and transgress established boundaries in fashion and art. In this sense, the putatively postmodern Madonna is enacting a pop modernist aesthetic" (p. 285/286).

In 1984 she released "Material Girl," which to young women like myself, was interpreted as longing liberation:

Boys may come and boys may go
And that's all right you see
Experience has made me rich
And now they're after me, 'cause everybody's

Living in a material world
And I am a material girl
You know that we are living in a material world
And I am a material girl

The first stanza of this song to me meant that I could live a much different life than my mother's; I was not limited to marrying my high school boyfriend. I could meet many men around the world, and have my own "rich" experiences. Much later alternate readings entered my interpretation. I realized that Madonna was critiquing materialism of the 1980s, all the while mastering marketing and amassing her personal fortune. Additionally, she perpetuated the need for men in women's lives, a heterosexist version of normalcy.

The Madonna video the group viewed, "What it feels like for a girl" (2001) was controversial upon release, nothing new to Madonna, and banned from

MTV. In its only MTV showing, the VJ announces that her video is about "a nihilistic pissed off chick doing things girls are not allowed to do." Its content was similar to the storyline in the film, *Thelma and Louise*: women reclaiming, through the use of force and violence, what they have lost as a result of male hegemony. Beyond nihilistic themes of destruction, there is also a postmodern nod to mundane absurdities. Specifically, Madonna, wearing make-up and high heels sets off, with an elderly woman accompanying her in a sports car, on a male shooting rampage.

Like with many Madonna videos, this one challenges gender stereotypes and subverts dominant representations of women as docile and subservient to men. The contestation over meaning is rendered even more political by MTV's decision not to air the video more than once. The many layers presented here highlight the importance of curricular choices when conducting media literacy. Here Madonna's video presents itself with many critical themes on which to dialogue with a group of young women.

How Madonna Leads Students Toward Conscientization

My purpose in showing this video was to assess the students' ability to engage in the contestation over meaning, to be able to tease out alternative meanings to dominant ideologies presented through everyday media, and thus engage in critical thinking. In other words, does the dialogic practice of media literacy promote what Freire would refer to as "conscientization" or an acknowledgment of empowerment for social equity and change?

Stuart Hall (2000) claims that this process of deconstructing dominant ideologies is difficult to assess in the absence of shared identity. In other words, do female PSTs relate to Madonna and how, and can they begin to see how Madonna subverts gender stereotypes? After viewing the video, Nadia[i] made the following opening comment:

> I think she says a lot. Some of the things are scary and very controversial obviously. You see the 666 numbers on the door flip. You see a lot of things that are referenced to, Satan and stuff like that, so there's that whole controversy. That's been talked about in a lot of classes, I know on this campus. I think a lot of it is about feminism and the constant struggle women have of meeting up and getting accepted and, it's like this whole drastic measure thing. It's one extreme to the next, and how they're constantly fighting for what they think they deserve and equal opportunity, and does anybody know what it feels like to be a woman? And it's (Madonna) expressing her feelings. She goes to an extreme of course, but that's what videos are about, is going to an extreme, and that's her artistic expression. That's how I see it.

Nadia appears to share the meaning the videomakers intended. What is interesting, however, is related to notions of identity. Nadia assumes an "objective" posture, an impossibility according to critical thinkers like Hall, by referring to women in the third person, and thus ostensibly neutering and disempowering herself as a woman in the analytical process. Further investigation is necessary here to determine the root of Nadia's detachment from feminist ideology.

And so while Nadia can name an example of oppressive expression, her identity disengagement with this group—all women, of which she is a member—is somewhat startling and disconcerting. It is as if she has been educated to express the critical without belief of it. Based on this, one could theorize, as Freire (1989) does, that conscientization, or critical awareness is a process, which moves from more basic expressions like Mary Beth's below:

> Just the example with the car ride, like how typically the guys in a car look at the girl and try to pick them up, and that's just typical. Like you don't see, it happens with girls picking up guys, but not as much as guys with girls because physical attraction is so big with guys, looking at the girls, like if they're physically attracted, they'll just go after them, no matter what they think of, or what they want. Typical. But she (Nadia) summed it up pretty good. (laughs)

While Nadia separates herself from feminism, Mary Beth assumes the stereotypical female role. While Nadia is critically detached from the video, Mary Beth is sucked right in, identifying less with Madonna than with the dominant ideological code for gender stereotypes.

The process then might move toward ownership of identity, which is hinted at by Beatrice's comments:

> It made me feel awful inside that I was watching it. I don't know; I think it's both the idea that this happens. I mean, this is what it's like to be a girl, according to Madonna, but also … I don't know, I just felt, I just left, while I was watching it, I had an awful feeling inside that I think it's that I don't want to think that that's what it's like to be a girl. I don't know, it just didn't leave me feeling very good.

Beatrice expresses the alienation and quiescence usually ascribed to someone who would identify with Madonna's message but feels powerless to do anything about it. She expresses a visceral reaction that was not evident in Nadia's above, thereby connecting her more closely with Madonna's identity at least in terms of sentiment, if not by action. It seems that Beatrice therefore inherently believes that the "personal is political," and we are left to question if Nadia (and Mary Beth) feels similarly.

How Madonna Leads Students toward Acknowledging Subjectivity

Further dialogue on the video conveys the PSTs' surprise over complexities present within it. For example, Beatrice asked the group why Madonna brought along an elderly woman, and Nadia replied that it represents women's struggle over time; a solid analysis of this particular signifier. Clearly the students are engaged in critical conversation and dialogue, though with a text that is familiar and safe, not a print-based text that describes convoluted feminist historical contexts, but a different yet common, and more palatable representation of similar sentiments. The range of critical responses in reaction to the video promotes Vygotsky's understanding of the dialogic forum. Knowledge is shared in this social setting (Vygotsky, 1978), which is obvious upon the affirmations given by Mary Beth after Nadia commented above ("But she summed it up pretty good."). This enables them to consider perceptual subjectivities as in Nadia's quote:

> I think a lot of it is up to interpretation too. I've heard a lot of classes analyzing this song when it came out. One person could see the video totally different than another person, and I think that's where it gets into scary grounds, because if a kid's watching it, one kid's going to get something from it that the other might not get, you know? Like when she shot the gun at the cop and water sprayed out, well a kid might miss that water part, you know? So then that brings up violence issues. And it brings up all kinds of stuff, so I think a lot of it is left up to the interpreter, and that's where it gets kind of scary. If it is aired on TV, and a third grader is seeing it, they might not get the feminist struggle women have gone through, and the struggle that women still feel like they're going through for equal opportunity, because I wouldn't get that if I was in 4th and watched that video. I would just get, "Oh there's Madonna riding around in a car being really aggressive, stealing money, shooting at people," you know? Is that what it means to be a woman? You know what I mean? I think like the interpretation leaves so much up to the person and the level of the person. That's kind of scary.

This quote illustrates Nadia's sophistication in terms of media representation. Here, she does not see it as a one-way depiction interpreted by passive viewers as Hall (2000) claims naive media analysts might do. She describes a dynamic postmodern reception process, albeit with paternalistic implications ("That's kind of scary."). One could also argue that Nadia's expressions of fear here further support her practicing of patriarchal analysis.

How Madonna Uncovers What the Students Do Not Know

The depth to which this group of young women analyzed this video was more than I had expected, though their overall media literate deficits also appeared. For example, none of the students was aware that this video had been banned from MTV. This could have furthered their dialogue by considering and comparing many of the violent lyrics and videos by male artists, which aren't banned from MTV. It appeared this group would not agree then with Lugo-Lugo (2001) when she says "if political engagement invariably involves tradeoffs (in this case, the violence), the liberating effect" of Madonna's contradictory constructed representation is well "worth the price of admission" (p. 126). They seem to buy into a more protectionist stance in which no one, man or woman should be representing such behaviors in the media. From this initial analysis they are aware of basic issues of liberation and power but have not yet claimed ownership of and emotional attachment or empathy to these concepts. This highlights their trepidation, whether conscious or not, for political engagement. Perhaps this is a "higher" stage to which one must move for conscientization. Would their consciousness deepen and become active upon exposure to feminist or critical pedagogical literature? Would they suddenly turn their backs on an issue as it continues to push boundaries and offend comfortable middle-class sensibilities? Or would they simply give the professor what he/she wants to hear (Luke, 2000) and then outside in their own future classrooms they would reject the ideas and continue to replicate cultural hegemony that certain artists like Madonna seem to be trying to bust?

Kellner (1995) has found that students are not "naturally media literate, or critical of their culture," though some manifest "a deep involvement in the artifacts of media culture (Mary Beth)," and still others "are often eager to discuss their views, (and) often have interesting insights" (p. 60). Nadia's lack of identification with Madonna's feminist claims, for example, shows that while she can spot and label counter-hegemonic media representations, she has yet to internalize the potential power in Madonna's critique.

Implications and Discussion

This chapter describes the critical conversation that occurred after a small group of PSTs viewed a controversial music video of Madonna's. The process includes elements of media literacy education: access, analysis, and evaluation. Access becomes an important element for teacher educators to note, for appropriate access, or textual choice, promotes thick analysis and evaluation.

Various themes emerged from the PSTs' conversations. First, media literacy dialogue on an appropriately chosen text can lead toward conscientization, though as evidenced here, PSTs are usually at different places in this regard. Also, through the dialogic process itself, viewer subjectivity is acknowledged. And finally, through the research process, teacher educators might spot what students are lacking with regard to media literacy. What these themes illustrate overall is an emerging, if still tentative, ability to ask questions of things that are usually taken for granted, in this case, the media "air" we all breathe. It is just a step toward understanding counter-hegemonic practices that are naturally a part of media literacy. Kanpol (1992) explains that counter hegemony "is a process of meaning making and/or alternative knowledge, the activity, creativity and hope of a possible way out of the determined reproductive aspects of knowledge" (p. 12). Additionally, these participants were in the process of realizing the connections between their knowledge and their future students' knowledge in relation to this particular media culture curriculum. Taken further and under flight of critical media literacy pedagogues, this might lead PSTs to connect with their students with regard to oppression and subordination "with the aim of understanding, undermining, and eventually transforming, these relations" (Kanpol, p. 16). Therefore, media literacy education, a subject matter that serves as curriculum and pedagogy is also an appropriate instrument that can lead toward critical pedagogical awareness and thus, create students who are better prepared to live in our ever-changing complex, interdisciplinary, intercultural, and mediated social world.

Teacher educators can take away from this study a variety of suggestions. First, we should stay aware of popular media culture, looking for texts with multiple interpretations, controversy, and thus, potentially allied critical material. Next, we must integrate these types of texts into our curricula for PSTs and graduate students so they have opportunities to interrogate complex media texts and engage in dialogue on them. The dialogic forum strengthens notions of viewer subjectivity; at the same time it potentially creates critical scaffolds. Therefore, it is crucial for critical media literacy education, but more basic, it becomes a palatable entree for students into general criticality. For this reason, it is also important for teacher educators to meet the students where they are in terms of criticality, and then assist them respectfully forward and deeper. Finally, as an extension, we should offer PSTs strategies for engaging in critical media literacy pedagogy with K through 12 students, and encourage its inclusion in school curricula.

In conclusion, this research contributes to a small body of empirical literature on media literacy education and teacher education. Certain questions naturally remain. How can teacher educators choose media texts that will challenge PSTs' understandings? How will teacher educators negotiate the potential sensitivities that accompany critical media literacy education? How will PSTs translate these interpretive processes for their future teaching, if at all? And finally, perhaps the biggest question that remains: can critical media literacy education thrive amid the current accountability movement in the United States? As stated, there is very little empirical research in this area, and hopefully this study will encourage more visibility to this emerging field.

Notes

This chapter first appeared in: *Teaching Education* (http://www.tandf.co.uk/journals) (Taylor and Francis), 17, no. 3 (2006), 239-249.

1.   Pseudonyms were used for confidentiality.

References

Alvermann, D.E., Hagood, M.C., & Moon (1999). *Popular culture in the classroom: Teaching and researching critical media literacy*. Newark, DE: International Reading Association and Chicago: National Reading Conference.

————. (2000). Critical media literacy: Research, theory, and practice in "New Times." *The Journal of Educational Research, 93*(3): 193–205.

Aufderheide, P. (1993). National leadership conference on media literacy. Paper presented at the Aspen Institute, Washington, D.C.

Flores-Koulish, S. (2004). *Teacher education for critical consumption of mass media and popular culture*. New York: Routledge.

Freire, P. (1989). *Pedagogy of the oppressed*. New York: Continuum.

Giroux, H. (1994). *Disturbing pleasures: Learning popular culture*. New York: Routledge.

Hall, S. (2000). Encoding, decoding. In S. During (Ed.), *The cultural studies reader*. New York: Routledge, pp. 507–517.

Kanpol, B. (1992). *Towards a theory and practice of teacher cultural products: Continuing the postmodern debate*. Norwood, NJ: Ablex.

————. (1994). *Critical pedagogy: An introduction*, First edition. Westport, CT: Bergin & Garvey.

————. (1997). *Issues and trends in critical pedagogy*. Cresskill, NJ: Hampton Press, p.7

Kellner, D. (1995). *Media culture: Cultural studies, identity and politics between the modern and the postmodern*. London: Routledge.

Lugo-Lugo, C. R. (2001). The Madonna experience: A U.S. icon awakens a Puerto Rican adolescent's feminist consciousness. *Frontiers, XXII*(2): 118–130.

Luke, C. (2000). New literacies in teacher education. *Journal of Adolescent and Adult Literacy, 43*(5): 424–435.

Mandziuk, R. (1993). Feminist politics & postmodernism seductions: Madonna and the struggle for political articulation. In C. Schwichtengerg (Ed.), *The Madonna connection: Representational politics, subcultural identities, and cultural theory.* Boulder, CO: Westview Press.

Martin, R. (2001). *Listening up: Reinventing ourselves as teachers and students.* Portsmouth, NH: Boynton/Cook.

McChesney, R. , and Nichols, J. (2002). *Our media not theirs: The democratic struggle against corporate media.* New York: Seven Story Press.

Stanley, W. (1992). *Curriculum for utopia: Social reconstructionism and critical pedagogy in the postmodern era.* Albany, NY: SUNY Press.

Vygotsky, L. S. (1978). *Mind in society: The development of higher psychological processes.* Cambridge: Harvard University Press.

17

Leadership-With:
A Spiritual Perspective on Professional
& Revolutionary Leadership
in a Digital Culture

Glenn M. Hudak

The Context: Leadership-For Goes Online

Increasingly the Internet has become the site of post-America's commerce with its vast pool of information, its capacity for networking and communication, and its ability to provide instantaneous information on global business and political events. Philosopher Hubert Dreyfus (2003) points out that the sheer volume of information on the Web is overwhelming: "at a recent count, it had over a billion pages and it continues to grow at the rate of at least a million pages a day…There is an amazing amount of useful information on the Web but it is getting harder and harder to find" (p. 8). Indeed, when we turn our attention to the context of schooling and the larger educational-political-administrative complex we notice immediately how the Internet, as manifestation of our contemporary digital culture, has become a part of everyday life: more and more we note, for instance, that communications between superintendents, principals, teachers, parents, community leaders, social workers, and health professional occur online. More and more we note that conferencing and networking with colleagues are online. More and more we note that all records and bookkeeping, business transactions, purchasing orders, labor disputes, and labor contracts are conducted online. And while teaching and learning are still primary within the educational community, more and more we note the "library" is primarily online, and we further note higher education setting the pace in pioneering new online efforts in "distance learning" as one way to cut costs and service a larger, more geographically and economically diverse student populations. As such, more and more we notice that the site of the many activities done throughout the larger professional complex of educational workers occurs not in classrooms but rather online.

Without a doubt, the online dimension of schooling in the twenty-first century is altering the daily life for/of the educational workers, and as such altering the terrain of what leadership "means." To address how the Internet is transforming leadership, it would be worthwhile to begin by considering a working definition of "leadership." In the 2002 University Council for Educational Administration (UCEA) presidential address, Gail Furman (2003) presents a succinct and comprehensive account of the current state of affairs with regard to leadership theory and practice. In her address Furman states,

> What I am saying is that the paradigm is shifting; we are experiencing a sort of sea change in the major themes out there, absorbing our attention as scholars. More and more, our scholarship seems to be focusing on the purposes of leadership in schools. (p. 1)

That is, Furman provides convincing evidence from current scholarship on leadership to suggest that there is a paradigm shift in the ways we now conceptualize leadership. The shift is from a traditional leadership paradigm which can be thought of as model *leadership-about* model where: traditional scholarship is about who the leader is; about what the leader does; about how leaders do leadership, and so on. With regard to the traditional paradigm Furman concludes, "in sum, critics say that the traditional scholarship does not serve well as a guide for leadership practice in the 21st century, especially for remedying educational inequities" (p. 2).

In contrast to leadership-about, Furman proposes a *leadership-for* paradigm. Here Furman points out the current research themes cited in leadership journals, themes on: leadership *for* school improvement, learning *for* all children, *for* democratic community; *for* social justice, *for* ethical schools; *for* "valued ends." Furman notes,

> Another way that I think about this shift to what leadership is for is that it suggests a shift from a sort of forward mapping to a sort of backward mapping. Where traditional scholarship focuses on what leadership is, how it is done by whom, often neglecting the why—the purpose of leadership—the new scholarship seems to be engaged in a kind of backward mapping—starting with the purpose of leadership and backward-mapping to figure out how to get there...I suggest that much of the "new" scholarship of educational leadership is an effort to do this backward mapping. (p.2)

Here Furman suggests the way to think of leadership-for is to imagine a sort of backward mapping, where we begin with a moral purpose for leadership, then figure out how to get there. But where is "there"?

> My second claim is that the new scholarship is focusing more and more on the moral purposes of leadership in schools...What do I mean by moral purpose? I mean a sense of purpose in the work of educators that fires the imagination and the heart, that proceeds from a sense of duty and conscious that inspires, that lets us know we are doing something important, something that really matters for children! (p. 3)

It is clear that leadership-for places as primary doing "something that really matters for kids" and where we place the needs of the kids before our own needs. Being moral, for Furman also carries with it a sense of urgency—that this "duty" to help the kids cannot wait. Indeed the word "urgency" comes from the Latin, *urgens,* and Old French, *urgere,* meaning to push, press forward. Moral purpose, then for Furman, implies a forceful pressing forward toward a goal: doing "something that really matters for children."

While a leadership-for paradigm is concerned about the ethics of: justice, critique, care, and profession, Furman (2003) claims that there is a fifth ethic at work here, the "ethic of community."

> It seems to me that none of these ethics, either separately or taken together, say enough about this: The only way to achieve our visions of schooling is to commit to work together on important problems, even with those who are different from us; to commit to communicate and engage in dialogue; to commit to share our stories and respect the views of others; in other words to commit to the processes associated with democratic community in schools...It seems to me that the "ethic of community" is the foundation, the pre-requisite of all other leadership practices that serve the moral purposes of schooling...In sum, I think that to achieve some of the moral purposes we are talking about so much in education—social justice, democratic community, learning for all children—that the practice of community comes first. (p. 4)

Given the discussion thus far it is fair to ask: will the ethic of community be enhanced by online activity? If we bring together two strands of the argument so far—increased online activity in schooling and leadership-for—then we can begin to speculate as to, what happens to our leadership-for efforts, efforts to serve the moral purposes of schooling, when more and more of schooling engagements occur online.

That is, we can see that being online has both a positive and a negative aspect: the up side, I will argue, of this online activity is a greater ability *for* networking, while the down-side, the cost, is a diminished sense of solidarity *with* each other. That is, I will argue in this chapter that increased Internet activities (within reasonable limits) among educational community members seem to enhance a *leadership-for* paradigm, while at the same time increased online activity militates against what I will call a *leadership-with* paradigm; a paradigm that is both moral *and* linked to the "spiritual" (which will be defined in the next sections).

How does online networking enhance a leadership-for model? In his discussion of the Internet, Dreyfus (2003) points out that information online is linked together by "hyperlinks." Hyperlinks "can link any element of information to any other element for any reason that happens to occur to whoever is making the link. No authority or agreed-upon catalogue system constrains the linker's associations" (p. 8). This means that on the Internet information can be brought together in any manner one wishes as there is no traditional hierarchy on the Web where some knowledge and information are more important than any other. Indeed, on the Internet all information is radically equal and available. "There are no hierarchies; everything is linked to everything else on a single level…[As such], the Internet is profoundly disrespectful of tradition, established order and hierarchy, and that is very American" (pp. 10, 12).

This non-hierarchical aspect of being online suggests that when a group of professionals get together to network on a project, all members will have an equal access to information, and an equal voice in the process of deliberation. As such, being online allows for more perspectives to be represented, more voices to be heard, and as Furman (2003) points out, even for dissenting voices to be equally heard. In short, online networking allows for a greater distribution of information and decision making to occur among the members of the online community. That is, one aspect of being online is that it "democratizes" precisely through its ability to "distribute" both information and tasks in a nonhierarchical fashion somewhat similar to the hyperlink. Furman (2003) explains that,

> the distributive leadership perspective suggests that leadership within a school is distributed among many actors. In other words, leadership is not the purview of administrators, but exercised by people in many positions.…There are many different models of distributive leadership, but taken together, they suggest that, not only is leadership distributed throughout the school, but that the total amount of leadership in a school matters, and that leadership multiplies through interactions. (p. 4)

From this passage we can easily imagine how aspects of online networking can enhance distributive leadership activities.

It is obvious then, that online networking is attractive, and indeed, somewhat freeing. In this nonhierarchical, safe, virtual space online members of the community are empowered, freed from tacit relations of power that come from feeling obligated or pressured to say what we think others want us to say. Online, it is possible to breakaway from "group think" and to really be ourselves, to "really" say what's on our mind and respond accordingly to other members. As such, online networking enhances a leadership-for model in that it allows for greater ability for the community to stay on task and to be purposeful in its deliberations with a sense of urgency. All in all, online networking seems to enhance the professional by opening up a public sphere necessary for backward mapping, and more importantly addressing the urgent needs of the moral imperative implicit in the leadership-for model.

Indeed, extending Furman's (2002) argument, the Web would allow for the modernist notion of community as "commonalities" (p. 52) to give way to "a concept of community compatible with the conditions of postmodern life…[where] a promising metaphor of the postmodern community in schools is that of a global community, of an interconnected web of people and cultures who may differ in important ways but who also are interdependent" (p. 60, 61).

But, there is a danger with online freedom. Dreyfus (2003) suggests that the openness to dialogue, to sharing stories, to building community, and to considering all sides of the problem from multiple perspectives,

> opens up the possibility of endless reflection. For, if there is no need for decision and action, one can look at all things from all sides and always find some new perspective. The accumulation of information thus postpones decision infinitely since, as one finds out more, it is always possible that one's picture of the world, and therefore what one should do, will have to be revised. (p. 77)

As such, one danger of online leadership-for is that the very freedom to network and create community comes to produce a proliferation of information where actions can always be deferred for yet another "take" on the problem at hand. Perhaps the element of "urgency" central to leadership-for will be enough to "push forward" the community to act. But, who is to decide when enough is enough information? What will be the criteria? And if leadership is distributed throughout the online community, what will cause the community to leave the comforts of their safe environments online to engage in the risky world of face-to-face politics?

That is, as online activity becomes a part of everyday professional life, we may begin to feel a certain sense of security. In fact, it may come to the point where face-to-face encounters begin to feel somewhat awkward or strained compared to our online "chats." Seeking greater security, at what point does being online become excessive, an obsession, an addiction? Alone, solitary, at our computers, there is no one standing over us, telling us "You're online too much!"

Here Dreyfus's (2003) analysis is alerting us to an even more pressing concern: the very taken-for-grantedness of the Internet in the lives of many in postmodern America. Indeed, the Web has become so much a part of the everyday context of our lives we don't notice how it is transforming us and especially transforming our relations with those closest to us. Dreyfus notes a recent poll that "showed that more than half [of those polled] say computers have led people to spend less time with their families and friends" (p. 102). The Internet is freeing us in many ways but always at a cost; for the price we pay is that

> we are not aware of how we are being transformed, so we need all the more to try to make explicit what the Net is doing for us and what it is doing to us in the process. I've suggested that where meaning is concerned, what the Net is doing to us is, in fact, making our lives worse rather than better. Living one's life on the Web is attractive because it eliminates vulnerability and commitment, this lack of passion necessarily eliminates meaning as well. (p. 102)

At stake, for Dreyfus, is that while the Internet offers greater access to the informational world and less risk in our online interactions/networking (you can say what you want online without have to look at the other person in the eye), the trade-off is that we are losing our "bodies" and with it our "embodied" sense of vulnerability and risk, our sense of strong commitment and passion, and finally meaning in our lives.

Without passion in our lives, without meaning in our work, without a vulnerable body, it is difficult to understand how leadership online can sustain a sense of "urgency" necessary to work toward moral purposes in schooling. The point: the more we are online working *for* school reform the less we are *with* others as embodied participants; the more we are online networking the less we are able to stand-with others, in body, in solidarity in vulnerable, risky situations.

Having said this, it is important to note that I am not claiming that the leadership-for model is wrong or contradictory in some manner. Rather, the point is that online culture of the Web is seductive, in ways discussed. As such, when leadership-for goes online there is a danger that the medium, the Web, transforms our desire for meaningful interconnectedness into something not intended in theory: disembodied leadership. With disembodied leadership what is lost is the necessary ingredient of passion and meaning necessary to standing-with others in struggle. For it's only by standing-with one another, facing the real risks and dangers of politics together, that trust, solidarity, and a sense of "urgency" are formed. With solidarity comes our passionate sense of commitment, commitment that is not only urgent, but also *intense*, commitment in a paradoxically postmodern sense that stretches past the boundary we normally consider as being professional to being revolutionary. As I argue in the last section of this article, "revolutionary" leadership entails a further shift in our thinking from a leadership-for paradigm to a leadership-with; that is, a modality of leadership that is embodied, "spiritual" and "incarnate" in Freire's (1997) thinking rather than virtual.

Reclaiming Spirituality

Increasingly, then, we find a disproportionate amount of our time as educational professionals is spent online not only processing information and networking but also chatting through emails with others within the new post-electronic community. However, while there is nothing wrong with being online or communicating with peers through emails per se, there does come a point of excess where one begins to feel weary and overwhelmed. Ironically, we may have come to a point where all this information and electronic communication online that was supposed to help us in our lives has now become itself a stressful problem. Overwhelmed by the sheer volume of information about our projects to reform schooling, plus all the emails, and all the Spam confronting us as educational workers, daily professional life online is leveled down into a sort of hyper-radical equity where the highs and lows of living meet in the middle and where the question asked doesn't matter as much as the promised sense of *relief* that we can find at the end of a very long day.

Given our consumer-oriented culture, it should come as no surprise that The New Age self-help industry, for instance, has made billions of dollars on offering us relief/the answer/the solution to the stresses in our personal and professional lives, by promising us ways to be more real with ourselves, more spiritual in our workplace, more authentic in our relationships. However, much of the problem with this New Age literature is, as philosopher Charles Guignon (2004) argues, not simply a case of making a buck nor is it simply the case that self-help ideas are wrong, but rather, they are one-sided, truncated, focusing almost exclusively on the personal, on self-improvement, on "me." That is, Guignon explains that oftentimes the very authority of self-help gurus and self-improvement programs are grounded in traditional religious ideas, ideas that originally provided the traditional religious seeker with guidance and direction. However, as Guignon argues, when these traditional religious ideas are removed from their original cultural context, and situated within, say, the context of secular postmodern America, they become truncated, one-sided, losing something of their original meanings and intention. Most often when traditional religious ideas are transported into the New Age cultural industry they are redefined, repackaged, and sold under the heading of spirituality.

What exactly is lost when traditional religious ideas are transported into the New Age inspirational marketplace in the name of being spiritual? Guignon (2004) argues that what is lost in translation from God to "me," is that by turning ourselves, "me," into an authoritative source of direction and insight we paradoxically lose meaning in our lives. Guignon states:

> What is at issue, however, is not whether self-help gurus are connected to a long and rich religious tradition. It is, instead whether the ideals and ways of thinking that originally made sense within that religious tradition are still meaningful when taken out of that tradition and planted in the secularized soil of modernity…What is lost, among other things, is the notion of an authoritative source of direction and insight that I can turn to in order to learn how I should live my life. For when my guide is understood as nothing other than me, it is hard to see what authority this guidance could or should have. (p. xii–xiii)

Traditionally, for example, examining one's life in the Socratic view meant that one's journey of self-examination was about finding one's place within the larger cosmic order of things. It was "cosmocentric in the sense that the cosmos itself determined what things are and how things ought to be" (p. 14).

Later in the Christian tradition, the inner search for self-knowledge meant not stopping with one's quest at finding a "true self," but rather one went inward and upward toward God. As such, Guignon (2004) notes:

> Where Socrates' vision of reality was cosmocentric, Augustine's is theocentric. The center of the universe, the standard and measurement for what is and what should be,

and the very core of our own being as creatures, is the Divine Creator. It follows from this that we only realize our humanity and become what we truly are when we achieve "at-one-ment" with God. (p. 17)

In pre-modern Western traditions the thought that "I" am the center of things was unthinkable. It was only with the Enlightenment and the scientific worldview that separated the outer world from the inner world that authenticity and spirituality come to be associated with self-discovery, with finding the "real" me rather than looking outward toward our connection *with* something outside ourselves. The rub as Guignon argues is that the notion of a "me," as an isolated/individual self is tacitly predicated on the existence of a larger social world. We become who we are in relation to others not in isolation. As such, to be me, authentically "me," implies not just a search for self, for "true" identity, but also, and more importantly an affirmation of the larger social context that props up the very concepts of selfhood. This is why the picture of authenticity and spirituality presented by the self-help industry is one-sided, for the social context and all that it implies are left out of the program.

Going one step further in the argument, although the centerpiece of Guignon's (2004) detailed study is the concept of authenticity, for my purposes it is worthwhile to note that within the modern context there is interweaving between these two concepts, and where we learn that,

The religious origins of these ideas are found in the appearance of the word "spirituality" in practically every area of self-help and inspirational literature. We learn that everyday life is spiritual, that is spirituality in little things, that life is a spiritual quest, and so on and on, usually in a way that is oblivious of the fact that the word "spirituality" as now used is a relatively recent invention, having a clear meaning only in relation to specifically modern conceptions of the aims of life. (p. xii)

In noting the interweaving and reliance of these two terms on each other, we might ask ourselves does this mean that being spiritual means that we are also being authentic? Or is it the other way around? Does being authentic mean that one is spiritual?

Indeed, since I'm not sure whether being spiritual is being authentic or the other way around, I wonder what would happen if we brought together these two modernist terms under the same umbrella, say as, "spirituality-as-authenticity," keeping in mind here that the terms *spirituality* and *authenticity* might be interchanged at any time in the discussion. I apologize for being undecided here, but my concern is less of struggling with which of these two terms has greater priority or of greater value and more with a project of reclamation. For I want to bring these two interwoven terms together in the hope of removing "spirituality" and "authenticity" from the marketplace—from the self-help section—and hopefully to *reclaim* these terms in such a way as to enrich, rather than impoverish our lives.

As I read Guignon (2004) it is obvious to me that he is not about to abandon authenticity, anymore than I want to abandon spirituality. Rather, his (and my) concern is to extend these concepts in ways that speak not only to the authentic (and the spiritual) as personal virtues, but much more importantly as social virtues as well. That is, when we place spirituality alongside authenticity as social virtues we find that both concepts share a similar "intention." Ultimately these two concepts are *not* about "me, me, and a little bit more of me," so to speak, as the self-help industry would have us believe, but rather they are about something "more" than ourselves. They speak to something about our mutual, shared experiences with one another in society. As such, when one reflects as to the meaning of this "shared experience" what comes to mind is that a spirituality-as-authenticity is not the answer to our problems in life, not an answer in the sense it provides *the* solution to difficulties confronting us. Rather I use spiritual-as-authentic in the sense, here, as a conception that refers to an embodied stance, a way of being-in-the-world. Further the particular way we embody the being-in-the-world of spiritual-as-authentic I want to argue is that we *stand-with* the others within a definable social context. That is, spirituality-as-authenticity is a specific mode of positioning ourselves within our social world, and that this particular mode of positioning ourselves within the social context is to stand-with others.

Before I address further the conceptual links between spirituality, authenticity, and leadership in the next section of this chapter, it is important to discuss in some detail the interconnectedness between spirituality and religion. With regard to spirituality, the one thing it is not is religion. While spirituality and religion are related to each other they are not reducible to each other. On this note, let me make three detailed points regarding religion and spirituality.

1.   *To say that religion and spirituality are related means that both religion and spirituality are "embodied stances," ways of our being-in-the–world.* The term embodied is used to refer to "the body" as the primary site of our knowing in the world. For the body, Dreyfus (2003) explains is,

not only our physical body with its front and back, arms and legs, and ability to move around in the world, but also our moods that make things matter to us, our location in a particular context where we have to cope with things and people, and the many ways we are exposed to disappointment and failure as well as injury and death. In short, by embodiment [we] include all aspects of our finitude and vulnerability. (p. 4)

As is apparent from this quote, the body provides us with a more holistic source of our knowing in the world than mere cognitive understanding. To know the world through the body means our being attuned to moods, dispositions, feelings, and things that really matter to us, matter in the sense that through the body we are altered to risks and dangers within a given context. The body then, as finite, vulnerable, and susceptible to risk alters us in a basic way when we are in danger, even before we may be consciously aware of that danger.

As such, to claim that religion and spirituality are "embodied" stances in the world means that both are not solely cognitive, are not solely about calculation, nor about planning out things. Rather, through the body we are able to zero in on risky situations and respond appropriately, and with time we develop greater skill in our interactions with the world. Finally it means we have the capacity, as Dreyfus (2003) claims, to sense the mood of any given social situation. Sensing the mood of a situation allows us to share the situation with others, to create bonds of trust, and even loyalty to one another. This shared mood with other bodies may take the form of compassion, empathy, or social justice.

Indeed there can be neither the religious nor the spiritual without the body. Without the body, religion and spirituality have no life to them. They are absent from a shared mood, and hence without mood they lack any sense of "sharing" the world with other bodies; they lack passion and commitment to those that matter to us.

2.   To state that both religion and spirituality are related to each other also mean that both are grounded in the religious dimension. From our previous discussion, we can say that through our bodies we know the world as having a social dimension and to this I would add, a "religious dimension." Both religion and spirituality share in this religious dimension where our knowledge of the world is ultimately an act of faithful dwelling in the world, for we know "more" about the world we are in than we can explicitly articulate. To step into the religious dimension is to enter the domain of faith, rather than knowledge; to have understanding without knowing the "why" of it all. Dwayne Huebner (1998) poignantly explains this point in his essay, "Education and Spirituality:"

> One knows of that presence, that "moreness," when known resources fail and some-how we go beyond what we were and are and become something different, somehow new…it is this very "moreness," that can be identified with the "spirit" and the "spiri-tual"…Spirit is that which transcends the known, the expected, even the ego and the self. It is the source of hope…One who acknowledges that "moreness" can be said to dwell faithfully in the world…Through the presence of the "other" my participation in the transcendent becomes visible—the future is open if I will give up the self that is the current me and become other than I am. (pp. 322, 323, 329)

Huebner's sense of the spiritual and the religious are very much interwoven. In that, both the spiritual and the religious, with their emphasis on moreness, faith, and an open future, are grounded within the "religious dimension."

The religious dimension, as philosopher John Caputo (2001) maintains, is intimately linked with the future. Caputo, drawing from the work of Jacques Derrida, explains two different notions of the future: the relative future and the absolute future. The relative future is somewhat linear in that we plan ahead our future. But, as Caputo writes, there is another mode of the future that we experience—the absolute future. That is,

> there is another future, another thought of future that is unforeseeable, that will take us by surprise that will come like a thief in the night and shatter the comfortable horizons of expectations that surround the present. Let us call this the "absolute future."…For the relative future we need a good mind, a decent computer, and horse sense, those three; for the absolute future, we need hope, faith, and love, these three…
>
> With the "absolute" future we are pushed to the limits of the possible, fully extended, at our wits' end, and having run up against something that is beyond us, beyond our powers and potentialities, pushed to the point where only the great passions of faith and love and hope will see us through. *With the "absolute future," I maintain, we set foot for the first time on the shore of the "religious," we enter the sphere of religious passion, and we hit upon a distinctly "religious category"* (My emphasis).
>
> The religious sense of life is tied up with having a future, which is something we all have, and the "absolute future" is a basic part of having a future…. By "the religious," I mean a basic structure of human experience and even, the very thing that most consti-tutes human experience as experience, as something that is really happening. (pp. 7–9)

For Caputo we first "step foot on the shores of the religious" with our en-counter with the "absolute future." The religious dimension is not a plan, nor about planning. (Explicitly, I want to note here that the religious dimension is not about backward mapping, which is grounded in a notion of the relative future.) Rather it is in our encounters with that which is radically unexpected—the absolute future—in our lives that we become unhinged, where we sink to our knees praying to be saved. Caputo (2001) argues that as human beings we all have a religious dimension for "the religious sense of life is tied up with having a future, which is something we *all* have, and the 'absolute future' is a basic part of having a future" (p. 9). This sense of a religious dimension-as-absolute future is not only something we all have, but further and most importantly,

> we need to remind ourselves, the religious sense of life would never mean just one thing for everybody, as if it had some sort of common ahistorical, universal, transcendental structure. I try to swear off thinking like that about anything...[For] I have no desire to twist free from such historical situatedness in the name of some purely private religion or of some overarching ahistorical universal religious truth. (p. 9,34)

As such, instead of positing the religious dimension as a universal truth, the same for everybody, Caputo speaks of the religious dimension as a "religion-without-religion." That is, the religious dimension is linked to religious traditions but not reducible to any one of them. Caputo clarifies this point:

> I would rather speak of the religious in people, in all of us. I take "religion" to mean the being-religious of human beings, which I put on par with being political or being artistic. By "the religious," I mean a basic structure of human experience and even, as I hope to show, the very thing that most constitutes human experience as experience, as something that is really happening. I do not confine religion as something confessional or sectarian, like being a Muslim or a Hindu, a Catholic or a Protestant. (p. 9)

That is, the events of the absolute future—as being totally outside our control as these unexpected future events have not yet arrived—cannot be said to be a part of religious institutions per se. Religious traditions provide culturally relevant interpretations of the religious, religion-without-religion. The religious dimension, as a part of what it means to be human, then grounds both traditional religions as well as the spiritual.

3. *To say that religion and spirituality are not reducible to each other means that there are differences.* The distinction I want to make is that spirituality and religion differ in their intentionality. The distinction between religion and spirituality is that the

former intends to "save" us, while the latter's intention is to become "authentic," as I shall explain in the next section.

A defining characteristic of traditional religions is, as Buddhist scholar Frederick Streng (1967) claims, that they all have a "soteriological intention." That is, one primary aim of traditional religious life is "to provide a means to correct an experienced deficiency in human existence, a radically salutary power by which man (sic) is saved from himself" (p. 171). The soteriological intention of traditional religion is to "save" us from ourselves! For, we can ask, what happens if we act, *do* our responsibility, *do* our religious deed for love and social justice—and we *still* screw-up? Sociologist Zygmunt Bauman (1998) reminds us that in premodern religions the hub of all systems was not about sin,

> but that of repentance and redemption. No religion considered sinless life a viable prospect nor proposed a way towards a life without evil…The essence of religious solutions to moral ambivalence, is, so to speak, dealing with it retrospectively— by providing the means of balancing out the burden of a wrong choice. What has been done may be undone—the wrong may be made good again. (p. 3)

The balancing out of a wrong, for making it good again, is accomplished in traditional religious systems by exchanging our freedom for obedience. The obedient sinner could be "saved" by following the path of religious authority.

In sum, we must keep in mind that any conceptualization of spirituality that intents to *reclaim* this term from the self-help industry, and hence enrich our lives, means that we must view spirituality as an embodied stance in the world, as intimately connected to the religious dimension of life, and that its intention is to be authentic. Without these three conditions, any discussion of spirituality is likely to impoverish us.

Authenticity and the Argument for *Leadership-With:* A Freirean Response

By making the distinction between leadership-for and leadership-with, I do not want to claim that one paradigm is "better" than the other. Rather, I want to say that the former model enhances being "professional" while the latter speaks to "revolutionaries" (Freire, 1997). Yes, I want to evoke a word that seems to have gotten lost in the shuffle—the "revolutionary" leader, but not as a heroic figure. Instead when one views leadership from a "spiritual" perspective, as embodied, as linked to the religious dimension, and as authentic, then, one is drawn to the consider the notion of leadership-with. Leadership-with in the sense of *standing-*

with others in solidarity, in communion, and as a witness, as the calling of the "revolutionary."

What distinguishes the professional's calling, then from the revolutionary's calling is that while both act out of urgency, in the case of revolutionary leadership there is an *intensity* of commitment on the part of the leadership that distinguishes it. This is to state that professional and revolutionary leaderships can share the very same commitments: commitments for diversity in community, commitments for social justice, for democratic schools, for quality education for all children, and so on—commitments that many professionals already feel, share, and attempt to live by.

As such, my argument turns not on the commitments held by professional educators nor on ethical purposes aimed at, nor on the urgency of the moral project, but rather on the term *intensity*. For the original meaning of the word *intensity*, which is derived from the Latin, *intensus*, and medieval French word, *intendere*, means "to stretch out, beyond." Indeed, as I read Paulo Freire's (1997) *Pedagogy of the Oppressed* through "spiritual" lenses, I found his articulation of revolutionary leadership suggests a mode of leadership where one's sense of commitment is so intense, where one's actions reflect such intensity of commitment, where one's level of commitment is so strong as to stretch out—push beyond the boundary of what is normally considered being professional. The revolutionary is a professional who is so committed to, is so intense, that the boundary of one's identity as a "professional" is no longer apropos. Indeed, by virtue of its intensity, revolutionary leadership presses beyond the boundary, the limit-situation, of the professional role itself.

To reference the revolutionary moment as a leadership-with model, I will highlight selected passages from Freire (1997). In *Pedagogy of the Oppressed* he observes,

> Revolutionary leaders cannot think *without* the people, nor *for* the people, but only *with* the people. (p. 112)

> In the revolutionary process there is only one way for the emerging leaders to achieve authenticity: they must "die" in order to be reborn through and *with* the people. (p. 113)

> We cannot say that in the process of revolution someone liberates someone else, nor yet that someone liberates himself, but rather that human beings in *communion* liberate each other [my emphasis]. (p. 114)

It is clear that for Freire the revolutionary leader *stands-with* the people.

However, this moment of standing-with is not accomplished online in a postmodern community of interconnectedness; rather it is embodied, embodied to such *intensity* of commitment that the leader must "die" in order to be reborn with the people. This notion of dying is linked to Freire's (1997) emphasis on the "conversion" of the well-intentioned professionals who renounce their own identities to merge with the people. This act of renunciation by the professional is traumatic, and it means, "abandoning all the myths which nourish invasion, and starting to incarnate dialogical action. For this very reason, it would mean to cease being over or inside (as foreigners), and to be in or *with* (as comrades)" (p. 137). Notice Freire's language here, "to incarnate," "as comrades"—these are terms not normally used by professional educators. These terms imply something "more" is in order: a profound sense of releasement, of letting-go of one's ego and stand-with others as comrades. To "incarnate" which comes from the Latin, *incarnare*, to make flesh, means to "embody, to invest with bodily form." To be revolutionary means that we are not just to be urgently committed, but more so, to incarnate means that we embody our commitments with such intensity as to lose one's identity and hence fuse with the people.

This moment *of fusion* with the people is an act of communion, an act that merges both the spiritual and the religious dimension. For,

> at no stage can revolutionary action forgo communion with the people. Communion in turn elicits cooperation, which brings leaders and people to a fusion…This fusion can exist only if revolutionary action is really human, empathetic, loving, communicative, and humble, in order to be liberating. (p. 152)

Is this moment of fusion, a moment of sameness, where difference is erased? One could read it that way, but I prefer to see communion as a moment when the professional's identity is dissolved, into the diverse community that already exists. The emphasis here in not on the community giving up its diversity, but rather the professional being *released* from his or hers; here one is being-for (Bauman, 1998) at the very moment they stand-with the community.

In communion-with the people revolutionary leadership acts in cooperation as a witness standing-with the people in courage to love, with boldness, consistency, and in faith! For Freire (1997) witnessing is an aspect of organization itself where,

> all authentic (that is, critical) witness involves the daring to run risks, including the possibility that the leaders will not always win the immediate adherence of the people…For the revolutionary leaders, organization means organizing *with* the people…[As such], in

cultural synthesis, the actors who come from "another world" to the world of the people do so not as invaders. They do not come to *teach* or *transmit* or *give* anything, but rather to learn, with the people, about the people's world. (pp. 157, 158, 161)

Here, the revolutionary, as Freire suggests, is one who has stretched—gone "*all* the way"—beyond what can be reasonably expected of a professional to such an extent that one is "released" from their professional identity. In this moment of "releasement," one becomes "authentic." That is, authenticity is "this sort of *releasement*," writes Charles Guignon (2004),

[which] means no longer putting ourselves at the center of the picture, no longer letting our egos get in the way in every situation. It points to a way of getting into the swim of what is going on around us without asking where we stand in it all. (p. 165)

There is in the revolutionary a moment where both the "spiritual" (Huebner's moreness) and "authentic" (Guignon's releasement) merge, where we are unable to decide, as Caputo claims, as to which term is primary, the spiritual or the authentic? In either case, the revolutionary moment entails a shedding of one's professional skin, where the professional lets go of trying to have control over the situation. Instead he or she gets into the swim of what is going on around them. This is similar to a moment of "authentic" conversation,

where the participants in the conversation leave behind their self-preoccupations as they give themselves over to the to-and-fro of the discussion…[and where] the locus of the activity as we experience it is not my mind or yours, but rather the "between" made concrete in the issues of the truth of the matter we are discussing. (Guignon, 2004, p. 164–165)

When professional leadership leaves behind its self-preoccupations, especially about success, something strange happens. It lets go of its identity and as such makes a quantum jump from the modern to the postmodern. As Bauman (1998) argues, "identity entered modern mind and practice dressed from the start as an individual task. It was up to the individual to find an escape from uncertainty…'Identity' is a name given to the sought escape from that uncertainty" (p. 82). When the professional is released from being individual, he or she is free to swim in uncertainty with intensity, for better or worse in the face-to-face encounters as revolutionary. Are these professionals profoundly committed, or are they "fanatic"? In the "post" it depends on where one stands within the larger social, historic context of the situation at hand.

From the passages cited by Freire, it is clear that the revolutionary moment is both spiritual as it is authentic, in the sense used throughout this article. If the point of being revolutionary means to act with such intensity so to be released from one's professional identity, then this means that when we view a leadership-for paradigm through the eyes of the spiritual-as-authentic, we are compelled to consider yet another paradigm shift toward a more intense encounter with one another as a leadership-with paradigm would suggest. An intensity of commitment that brings with it a profound sense of belongingness and indebtedness to the wider social context that makes it possible: hopefully, an open and free society. But, there are no guarantees.

Implications for Educational Leadership

In the end, there are still a number of issues to be raised and addressed more fully: who are "the people" referred to by Freire in America today? How does one conceptualize the notion of "the people" within diverse communities? Further, does leadership-with imply that one's revolutionary commitment with the people is so intense, as to actually live with the people, in the same community (see Reed, 2005)? That is, as the professional leadership "converts" to revolutionary leadership and merges with the people, does this mean that one's "home" is not is another location, one different from the people we stand-with? Does this mean, for instance, that leadership now "shops" with the people in the same community? For one aspect of the professional life is that she or he can go "home" at the end of the day and go on the Internet to connect with the global community. But what of the revolutionary with his or her intense sense of commitment to stand-with the people? Where is his or her "home"?

While revolutionaries can and should use the Web, their hearts are not online. Their hearts are with the suffering and the forsaken, indeed,

> for Amos, the name of God is justice, and justice is not a thought but a deed, and its truth is attained only in *doing* the truth, in making justice happen in truth. Justice is not had by talking the talk in solemn assemblies, but by walking the walk in the inner cities. (Caputo, 2001, p. 135)

If this is the case, this suggests that revolutionary leadership involves an almost impossible commitment with others—impossible in the sense that the demands are perhaps beyond reason. If revolutionaries work with economically poor people, then they live with the poor (like Kate Rhee and her work with the Prison Moratorium Project in New York City), *doing* justice in the neighborhood as members who are not only concerned about schooling, but the whole community within which the school is located. For as Mark Warren (2005) asks, "what sense does it make to try to reform urban schools while the communities around them stagnate or collapse?" (p. 133). Revolutionary leadership organizes with the whole community (and its institutions) of which the school is a part. Furthermore, as the boundaries between working and living dissolve for revolutionary leadership we can imagine how the community one works with, then, becomes "home," where one lives. Indeed, as boundaries dissolve, those who are "authentic" revolutionaries would probably not even label their activities as revolutionary. For out of humility, and with a profound, intense sense of love, faith, and social justice they are *released* from our preoccupation over identity.

Further Considerations

Julia Kristeva reminds that we may have come to the point in history where revolution, with a big "R," is no longer possible or perhaps even desirable, given the diffuse relations of power and authority within global economic structures. For first as Kelly Oliver (2004) notes that for Kristeva "within postindustrial and postcommunist democracies we are confronted with a new political and social economy governed by the spectacle within which it is becoming increasingly difficult to think of the possibility of revolt." (p. 219).

And second, in an interview with Kristeva, she makes clear that to view revolution in solely political terms—with a big "R"—is not only dangerous (terrible acts done in the name of revolution) but further, to truncate an important dimension of being human—our capacity to revolt. Kristeva states (2002), "I would like to strip the word "revolt" of its purely political sense. In all Western traditions, revolt is a very deep movement of discontent, anxiety and anguish. In this sense, to say that revolt is only politics is a betrayal of this vast movement" (p. 99). To fully grasp the importance of revolt to our lives and education, we might begin by thinking of revolution as our capacity to turn, to re-turn. Kristeva (2002) continues,

> I try to interpret this word in a philosophical and etymological sense. The word revolt comes from the Sanskrit root that means to discover, open, but also to turn, to return. This meaning also refers to the revolution of the earth around the sun, for example. It has the astronomical meaning, the eternal return. ... It is the idea that being is within us and that the truth can be acquired by a retrospective return, by anamnesis, by memory.

> The return to oneself leads the individual to question his [or her] truth, much like what
> is accomplished with philosophical dialogues, for example Plato's. (p. 100)

Indeed, as I have argued elsewhere (see Hudak, 2005), in *The Republic* education plays a crucial role in the maintenance of the society and ultimately who will lead. Further, and this relates to Kristeva's quote above, Plato writes, "education is the craft concerned with doing this very thing, this turning around, and how the soul can easily and effectively be made to do so" (Grube, 1992, p. 190). As such, education is the craft of turning the soul; of helping the soul find its true orientation in the universe: facing the good.

> Every soul pursues the good and does whatever it does for its sake. It divines that the
> good is something but it is perplexed and cannot adequately grasp what it is or acquire
> the sort of stable beliefs it has about other things, and so it misses the benefits, if any,
> that those things may give. (p. 179)

Every soul pursues the good, however the soul does not know the directionality of the pursuit, and hence the soul needs guidance, guidance to face, be turned toward the good. Robert Cushman (1976) translates this turning of the soul as a *metastrophe,* "conversion." Plato taught that *metastrophe,* "is required as an antidote to counteract the distortion which presently warps and misdirects the soul's vision. The words for 'conversion' or 'to convert' appear at least twenty-one times in Book VII. It is a momentous revolution, which Plato has in mind....Education, as the revolution of the 'entire soul.'" (p. 147). From Plato's perspective we can begin to see that the education of the city's children is more than acquiring information, or even training for one's future occupation, instead it is about revolution: the revolution of the entire soul! That is, while all souls are "called" by the good, so to speak, each soul needs guidance as it makes its "conversion" from looking in the cave to facing the light of the sun. Indeed, for Plato education is an antidote to living a life in ignorance, an unjust life. For ignorance is precisely that soul which has lost its sense of direction, and in "confusion" as it were, loses its sense of where to locate the good—the soul's source of nurturance.

Education is at its root in Western thought, revolutionary; it is about turning, re-turning to memory. Further as Kristeva (2002) continues, "I think that Freud gave a new meaning to this retrospective return by asking psychologically troubled patients to search for memories of their traumas and tell their stories" (p. 100). If education-as-revolutionary is a re-turn, a retrospective return, then where does the revolutionary leader fit in? Revolutionary leadership "returns" to the community, within which the school is located. Here leadership "mirrors" back the community's retrospective memories as a moment of standing-with others. This mirroring is an act of interpretation, of naming, as Freire would have it. And where as Deborah Britzman (2003) writes from a group dynamics perspective, "it is the group that makes the leader, and the leader is a symbolic measure of the knowledge that a group can tolerate" (p. 102). Revolutionary leadership emerges from the group, as embodied, as authentic, and where its stance is one of returning to the community its memory of itself—as a mode of disclosure—as that space where the community can affirm and confront, within tolerable limits, the limit-situations of its existence. Taken as such, revolutionary leadership, leadership-with, is an interpretive stance where, "the leaders cannot provide this interpretation. He or she can model an interpretive stance, a place in space and time and mind where different interpretive voices meet" (Alford, 2004, p. 20). As Alford argues, all leadership provides a "holding environment" for the group, a holding environment whereby the leader mirrors back the community's knowledge of itself for the purpose of introspection, interpretation, and, as Freire would add, praxis.

Notes

* This article is a re-edited, revised, modified, and extended version of "On the Web, on Reclaiming 'Spirituality,' 'Authenticity,' and 'Revolution': An Argument for Leadership-With." *Journal of School Leadership*, November 2005, 15(6): 686–707.

References

Alford, C. F. (2004). Small group and big nations: Politics and leadership from the perspective of the small study group. In *Group dynamics, organizational irrationality, and social complexity: Group relations reader 3*, edited by S. Cytrynbaum and D. Noumair. Jupiter, Fl.: A.K. Rice Institute, p. 5–22.

Bauman, Z. (1998). *Life in fragments*. Oxford: Blackwell Publishers.

Britzman, D. (2003). *After-education*. Albany, NY: SUNY Press.

Caputo, J. (2001). *On religion*. New York: Routledge Press.

Cushman, R. (1976). *Therapeia*. Westport, CT: Greenwood Press.

Dreyfus, H. (2003). *On the internet*. New York: Routledge Press.

Freire, P. (1997). *Pedagogy of the oppressed*. New York: Continuum.

Furman, G. (2002). Postmodernism and community in schools: Unraveling the paradox. In Gail Furman (Ed.), *School as community*. Albany, NY: SUNY Press.

———. (2003, Winter). *The 2002 UCEA Presidential Address. UCEA Review*, Winter, XLV(1): 1–28.

Grube, G. M. A. (1992). *Plato's Republic*. Revised by Reeve, C.D.C. (Trans.). Indianapolis: Hackett Publishers.

Guignon, C. (2004). *On being authentic*. New York: Routledge.

Hudak, G. M. (2005). The inner life of transformation: A philosophic investigation of leadership, media, justice, and freedom. *Journal of School Leadership*, 15(3): 305–332.

Huebner, D. (1998). Education and spirituality. In S. Shapiro and D. Purpel (Eds.), *Critical issues in American education*, second edition. Mahwah, NJ: Lawrence Erlbaum Associates, pp. 321–336.

Kristeva, J. (2002). *Revolt, she said*. New York: Semiotext(e).

Oliver, K. (2004). *The colonization of psychic space*. Minneapolis: The University of Minnesota Press.

Reed, W. (in progress). The bridge is built: The possibilities of community teachers and administrators to reform low-income urban schools. Unpublished manuscript.

Streng, F. (1967). *Emptiness: A study in religious meaning*. Nashville: Abingdon Press.

Warren, M. (2005). Communities and schools: A new view of urban educational reform. *Harvard Educational Review*, Summer, 75(2): 133–173.

18

Halls of Anger: The (Mis)Representation of African American Principals in Film*

Linda C. Tillman

There is a paucity of scholarly literature that documents the experiences of African American[1] school leaders, specifically principals and assistant principals in urban, suburban, and rural school contexts. Additionally, the experiences of African American school leaders particularly in movies and television are also limited. When African American leaders are represented in popular culture, the representations appear in an un-negotiated space. Movies and television series often present White principals as "saviors" and African American principals as ineffective or uncaring leaders who rule by intimidation. Such representations often distort the realities of school leadership and perpetrate a good leader versus bad leader ideology based on race. The perspectives of those considered as "others" continues to be marginalized, leaving readers and viewers with a narrowly scripted version of what educational leadership is and how it is practiced.

The purpose of this chapter is to discuss (mis)representations of African American school leaders in film. Specifically, I address the question: In what ways does popular culture influence the public's perception of the roles of African American school leaders? I begin the discussion with an overview of literature that focuses on representations of school leaders in popular culture. The discussion then shifts to an analysis of two films that focus on African American school leadership, *Halls of Anger* (1970) and *Lean on Me* (1989). I conclude the chapter with a discussion of these two films using Hall's (1980) theory of negotiated and oppositional reading.

Background

Numerous films about schools have focused on the principal or assistant principal as the main character (for example, *The Principal* (1987), *Dangerous Minds* (1995), and *Stand and Deliver* (1988)). However, there are a limited number of films that focus on an African American school leader as the main character. Most recently, the African American principal has been seen as a major character in the television series *Boston Public*. The principal, Mr. Harper, often uses profanity, is constantly frustrated by students, teachers and parents, and is usually seen with a look of despair on his face. Particularly interesting is the manner in which his character is portrayed as ineffective. Rather than serving as an example of a Black principal leader who adopts an ethno-humanist role identity[2] (Lomotey, 1993), or a socially just leader who "interrogates the policies and procedures that shape schools" (Dantley and Tillman, 2005), Harper is seen as a principal who is being led by others in the particular context of Winslow High School. The *Boston Public* world is chaotic, drugs and violence are common, parents are uninformed and powerless, teachers are incompetent, students are out of control, and sorting and tracking is the norm.

One implication of the (mis)representations of principal leadership in the *Boston Public* series is the possibility that the viewing audience will internalize these images and accept them as the reality in every large, urban high school. Educational observers and policymakers have criticized principal preparation programs, and numerous reports have identified problems with the content, scope, focus, and practicality of preparation programs. A recurring theme in the critiques is how these issues can affect the leadership practice of principals (Gates et al., 2003; Levine, 2005). Challenges identified in these reports with respect to principal leadership can be seen in many episodes of *Boston Public* and include maintaining a safe and orderly school climate, recruiting, hiring and retaining highly qualified teachers, the absence of a vision, mission and goals for the school, and student achievement.

There is an absence of a body of scholarly literature that analyzes the representations of principals in film. According to Smith (1999), traditional educational leadership scholarship "fails to tell us how administrators are seen by the general public; or to consider the significance of the images of school administrators that appear in cultural projects designed for a mass audience" (p. 50). Scholars who have written about portrayals of school leaders in films typically place them into categories that are reflective of their television or movie persona (Banks and Esposito, 2002; Burbach and Figgins, 1991; English and Steffy, 1997; Glanz, 1997; Smith, 1999; Thomas, 1998). For example Burbach and Figgins, in their review of a representative sample of films that accurately portray major dimensions of a principal's role, argue that films can be an important medium for viewing the role of the principal. Based on their analysis, the authors note that principals in films are usually cast in minor roles and can be categorized as figures of authority, simple-minded foils, heroes, villains, faceless bureaucrats, and social and emotional isolates. In the films they reviewed, the story line was typically situated in the high school context, the principal was usually a middle-aged, middle-class White male, and the image promoted a stereotypical view of a principal's physical appearance and de-meanor as "somber and businesslike" (p. 53). Burbach and Figgins note that "Missing in their film persona is the range of human emotions that make movie characters complicated and interesting" (p. 53). The authors pose several questions related to the ways that principals are portrayed in films: "Why are principals consigned to the part of movie heavies? Why are well-educated, intelligent professionals characterized as dull-witted and incompetent? Why do those who, according to research, play a key role in creating successful schools show up poorly in film?" (p. 52). While the authors acknowledge the appeal of such images to the viewing audience, they argue that a focus on traditional authority systems and unquestioned compliance to authority is contradictory to school reform theory that suggests more collaborative forms of leadership that include students, teachers, and parents.

Glanz (1997) argues that "Our images and perceptions of principals are influenced largely by popular culture—in particular, movies and television" (p. 295). According to Glanz, "culturally shared cognitive models influence not only how principals are perceived by others, but how principals themselves understand their own professional identity" (p. 295). Glanz viewed twenty television programs and films depicting principals, and used a cultural studies approach to identify three images of principals in films. The *authoritarian* principal employs autocratic administrative practices, rules by intimidation, and is usually male. He cites *Blackboard Jungle* and *Lean on Me* as examples of movies in which the principal is portrayed as an authoritarian, dictatorial leader. The *bureaucrat* principal is primarily concerned with tasks such as reports, scheduling, and conducting meetings, and places managerial aspects of school leadership above the needs of students and teachers. The film *Teachers* is cited as an example in which the principal "places bureaucratic mandates above ethical and moral imperatives related to teaching and learning" (p. 296). The third image, the *numskull* principal, portrays school leaders as "dimwitted dolts who haven't the foggiest notion of what is transpiring in the school" (p. 297). Television sitcoms such as *Welcome Back Kotter*, are examples of the *numskull* characterization where the principals are usually White males who are constantly being outsmarted by students who are more intelligent and more creative. Glanz concludes that even while scholarly literature points to the importance of effective principal leadership, the public's understanding of leadership practice is shaped by popular culture; images are internalized and perceptions are shaped by the "beliefs, viewpoints, and values explicitly or implicitly transmitted by television and cinema" (p. 297).

Smith (1999) notes that contemporary films can shape as well as limit public discourse about effective school leadership and the mission of schools. According to Smith, "Of particular importance is the dissonance between the celluloid images created by Hollywood and the complex and challenging realities in our own communities" (p. 50). Smith examined the representations of school leaders in twenty-eight films "that featured one or more school leaders in major or, more often, minor roles released since the election of Ronald Reagan, who serves as a marker for the re-emergence of an aggressively populist political agenda in the USA" (p. 51). Six images of school leaders emerged from Smith's analysis: (a) the savior; (b) the supportive father; (c) the dupe; (d) the clueless; (e) the opportunist; and (f) the pimp. For example, saviors were considered heroes in films such as *Lean on Me* and *The Principal*. In both films, the viewer is presented with an image of a principal who is assigned to a chaotic school where there is a lack of discipline, disorder, teacher apathy, and student underachievement. In both films, the principal also projects a "take no prisoner" attitude to cleaning up the school, and by the end of each film, the school has experienced a miraculous turnaround.

Smith observes that in the films she viewed, female leaders were portrayed in three categories: politically motivated shrews, benign mothers, or helpmates. She notes, "that there was a blatant sexual (sexist) text in these cinematic messages came as no surprise" (p. 52). According to Smith, films send a specific message about gender, and positive images of female school leaders are absent in many films about schools. She writes,

Partially that absence is a reflection of the approved gendering of behaviors exemplified by administrators or educator-heroes in their various guises (teachers as well as administrators). The good guys are precisely that—guys. They act masculine or, when they are female, they display skills that allow them to assume male privileges. Cast in a positive light, women are not unsexed, but they demonstrate an appropriate degree of toughness. Cast in negative light, they usurp privileges to which they are not entitled and in the process are rendered as shrews. They seem physically constrained by their clothing and emotionally frigid. Denying their [true] nature, they tend to business, rather than children. (p. 63)

While representations of female school leaders in films is problematic, Smith argues that even more problematic in the films is what is not seen. The images of school leaders as principals and assistant principals revealed no collegiality, community building, shared decision-making, or collaboration. Rather, school leadership was defined as effective only when leaders adopted bureaucratic and authoritarian leadership styles and when managerial issues took precedence over the needs of students and teachers. Smith concluded that those who prepare future school leaders must be more attentive to these images, and initiate class discussions about how the images define effective school leadership, as well as the messages they send about race, class, and gender in schooling.

Representations of African American School Leaders

A search for films that focus on Black school leaders yielded five examples in which the principal, assistant principal, or superintendent was an African American: *Halls of Anger* (1970) (African American assistant principal); *Conrack* (1974) (African American female principal); *Lean on Me* (1989) (African American principal, assistant principal, superintendent); *Toy Soldiers* (1991) (African American dean of atudents), and *Dangerous Minds* (1995) (African American principal). In each of these films, African Americans as school leaders are (mis)represented as heroes, authoritarians, and in the case of the African American female assistant principal in *Lean on Me*, "the perfect office wife" (Smith, 1999, p. 56). Interestingly in all of the films, African American principals and assistant principals are viewed as necessary to keeping students (usually African Americans and misfit Whites) in line, ruling the school with a firm hand and establishing that their word is law. These leaders have also been assigned to the schools to "save" the poor, disadvantaged students who would surely be lost were it not for the presence of a strong, no nonsense African American administrator. Like many African American leaders today, the school leaders in these films work in the worst schools that have the worst reputations, in the worst districts, and their primary role as perceived by the White authority (usually superintendents and mayors) is to put out fires and maintain order.

My discussion of the (mis)representations of African American school leaders will focus on two films—*Halls of Anger* and *Lean on Me*. In both films African American school leaders are portrayed as heroes, although from different viewpoints. In my discussion of *Halls of Anger*, I take a negotiated reading of the text (Hall, 1980). A negotiated reading recognizes the contradictory elements in a text but does not accept all of the elements. In my discussion of *Lean on Me*, I take an oppositional reading of the text. An oppositional reading of a text occurs when one's social location is in direct opposition with the dominant ideology being represented in the text. As I posited in a discussion of the television series *Boston Public* (Tillman and Trier, forthcoming), my oppositional reading of *Boston Public* is based on my multiple social positions— university professor (specializing in educational leadership), teaching and administrative experience in an urban school district, and as an African American. Thus, my oppositional reading of *Lean on Me* incorporates issues related to teaching, learning, leadership, and race. My oppositional reading of the text also results from the ways that the film marginalizes the theory and practice of African American school leaders, and trivializes the complexities of education, particularly in large urban school districts with majority African American student populations.

Halls of Anger

> You've got 3000 black kids, 60 white kids, and a war going on.
> —(Tagline for *Halls of Anger, 1970*)

Calvin Lockhart plays the role of Quincy Davis, a former pro-basketball star who is now an English teacher in California. Davis is reassigned, against his wishes, to Lafayette High School as an assistant principal. He is no stranger to Lafayette, having taught at the school during a time when it was orderly, safe, staffed with highly qualified teachers, with students excelling academically and socially. The school has declined significantly in terms of the overall environment, test scores, teacher apathy, and discipline. Lafayette has a majority African American student population with a majority White teaching and administrative staff. As a result of a reapportionment of the district, 200 White students are to be bused to Lafayette and will attend school with 3000 Black students.

Davis is angry about being assigned to Lafayette and tells the superintendent, "I don't want to go back to the ghetto." He questions why a Black man is being ordered to go to Lafayette instead of a White man. The superintendent replies, "You are a Black man and they need you down there, not here." This statement sets the parameters for African American school leadership in this film; it conveys the message that African American school leaders are *only* effective when they work with African American students. The principal, a middle-aged White male. is specific in his instructions to Davis—"In order to teach, we have to stabilize—maintain discipline." When Davis responds that there are other ways to help students and all students must be taught, the principal insists that discipline and control are his main concern. As assistant principal, Mr. Davis is also required to teach an English class. He enters his first class to find disruption, disinterest, and a lack of discipline. J.T., a Black male student, will become Davis's nemesis. While J.T. is smart and has the potential to develop his artistic talents, he refuses to follow rules and is determined to be a formidable foe for Mr. Davis. After a lunchroom disturbance instigated by J.T., the principal warns Davis that he is not doing his job—he is not maintaining control. The principal wants to "get rid of J.T.," but Davis resists saying, "We'd only be passing the problem on to the street." Davis persuades the principal to let him work with J.T. and sets out to save him from the plight he believes so many young Black males face—lack of education, unemployment, drugs, violence, and incarceration. Davis begins to mentor J.T. as well as other Black male students in the school.

Davis also attempts to help the White students who have been bused to Lafayette. While they are more academically advanced than the Black students, essentially they are lost in an unfamiliar and hostile environment. Davis tells one of the White students, "Now you know how Black students feel." Thus, Davis attempts to define himself as a leader who will help all students—Black and White. He constantly questions the school culture, expectations, and perceptions at Lafayette High. He asks, "What does work here? This place is like Disneyland, no standards and teachers don't care." The principal tells Davis that the school is hopeless and "there are no answers." Still hopeful, Davis replies, "If the mold doesn't fit the kids, we need to break the mold." When a representative of the Board of Education comes to "conduct a test to gauge achievement comparative levels in the school," Davis resists this Black-White comparison and tells the representative, "It all depends on what's been available to you." His statement implies that he knows that many Black students will perform poorly on the test, but he also understands they do not possess the social and cultural capital that is viewed as a prerequisite for academic success. When Davis decides to help a group of Black males learn to read, he uses culturally relevant teaching and draws on the students' cultural knowledge (Ladson-Billings, 1995) to teach them the importance of literacy. To balance the story line, a White male student joins the after-school reading group. The viewer is led to believe that although the student is White, he too can benefit from Mr. Davis's culturally relevant instruction and his leadership.

As the film nears an ending, a fight breaks out between Black and White students (again instigated by J.T.), students riot and refuse to go to classes, the principal blames Davis for his failure to control the students, and Davis threatens to leave the school. A Black female teacher tries to talk Davis out of leaving and tells him, "If you leave, these kids have no hope." Davis challenges the principal stating, "You don't care if these students park cars or push brooms for the rest of their lives, but I do." In the end, all is well as J.T. decides to trust rather than resist Mr. Davis the White students also decide to trust Mr. Davis and remain at Lafayette, and all of the students return to classes.

In *Halls of Anger* the Black male assistant principal must resist teacher and student apathy, as well as the authority of the White male principal and central office personnel who maintain deficit perspectives and low expectations of Black students. The involuntarily bused White students pose no problem and are expected to be well disciplined and to excel academically; White authorities are certain these students will set the standards for the school. As assistant principal, Mr. Davis must *save* the Black students and fight to change the negative stereotypes of Black students as uneducable and undeserving of opportunities to learn. The film ends leaving the viewer with the impression that despite the strange ending, Mr. Davis will save the students and the school.

Lean on Me

> A true story about a real hero.
> —(Tagline for *Lean on Me*, 1989)

More than any other film about a Black school leader, *Lean on Me* has been discussed, written about, and taken seriously in both academic and nonacademic contexts. Morgan Freeman plays Joe Clark, the African American male principal of Eastside High School in Paterson, New Jersey. *Lean on Me* is a true story about Clark who is sent to restore order to a school that has been labeled a "cauldron of violence." Clark is not the mayor's first choice to lead the school since he has been branded a troublemaker in the district. However, the state has threatened to take over Eastside High if test scores do not improve, and the mayor is forced to accept the superintendent's recommendation to hire Joe Clark. Clark has no desire to return to Eastside High, having taught at the school twenty years ago. And like Davis in *Halls of Anger*, he asks, "Why send me, why don't you send a White man?"

As the movie begins, viewers see students roaming the halls, stolen goods being sold at the entrance to the school, and an environment that suggests a culture of chaos. The school is ranked last in the state on standardized test scores with only 30 percent of the students passing the minimum basic skills test. Clark's leadership style can best be described as abrasive, bullying, rude, and authoritarian. He begins his tenure as principal by telling teachers, "I want the name of every hoodlum, drug dealer and miscreant who's done nothing but take this place apart on my desk by noon." Shortly after receiving the names, he rounds up 300 students, has security herd them like cattle onto the auditorium stage and tells them to get out of "my school." He warns the remaining students who witness this event that they can expect the same if they do not abide by his rules. His motto is, "If you do not succeed in life, blame yourself; the responsibility is yours." In his first faculty meeting, he tells teachers they cannot teach if they cannot control students. Teachers are not permitted to question Joe Clark or offer suggestions because "In a state of emergency, my word is law," and "there's only one boss in this place and that's me, the HNIC."

Parents are divided over Clark's leadership style and his use of unorthodox tactics to get the results he wants. Some parents welcome his no-nonsense approach and believe he will "save" the students and the school. Other parents disagree with Clark's methods, and when they verbalize their opposition to him, they too become targets of his wrath. In a meeting with parents, he attempts to bully them and tells them it is his way or no way. He tells parents their children are "rotten to the core" and blames them for their children's failures. He admonishes parents to "help your kids with their homework, and *get off welfare*" (author emphasis). Clark then uses religion to further bully parents. He begins to paraphrase scriptures and states,

God told me to come to Eastside and to do whatever I have to do. It doesn't have to
be nice. I gave God my word, and that's why I threw those bastards out, and that's all I
have to say.

He quickly leaves the meeting amid both cheers and boos from parents.
Throughout the movie, Joe Clark clashes with parents, fires qualified teachers,
demeans students, and challenges anyone who has an opinion about the most
effective ways to improve the school culture and student achievement. Clark's
deficit perspective of leading, teaching, and learning affects the entire school
culture. Anyone who does not obey his orders is dealt with swiftly and severely.
The least infraction, such as not knowing the words to the school song could
result in detention for students and reprimand for teachers.

The Black female assistant principal, Ms. Levias does her best to accommodate Clark's every wish. She is efficient, loyal, and rarely questions Clark's
decisions. She is, as Smith (1999) observes, the perfect office wife. Yet midway
through the movie, Ms. Levias becomes so angry with Mr. Clark that she asks
for a transfer. She tells Clark that she can no longer tolerate his insensitivity, his
authoritarian form of leadership and his total disregard for teachers, parents,
and students. Amazingly, Clark appears to recognize his shortcomings and
agrees with Ms. Levias that he has been a little too harsh. However, change is
slow to come and Clark continues his authoritarian form of leadership. In
several consecutive scenes, Clark tells a Black student, "You are a disgrace to
your race," orders security to puts chains and locks on all doors, fights with a
student, tells teachers they are creating a permanent under-class, and continues
to use profanity as though it were an acceptable form of communication in an
educational setting. He begins to carry a bullhorn and a baseball bat which he
uses to enforce rules and get attention. When the assistant principal asks him
what kind of image he is trying to present by carrying a baseball bat, he justifies
his actions stating, "This school is not protected like the White schools."

As the movie nears its end, Clark begins to focus on raising test scores. He
is more tolerant of students, teachers, and parents. He begins to listen to
students. He begins to rely on the expertise and judgment of teachers, and he
loses his temper less frequently. He becomes a school social worker, going to
students' homes, helping parents find jobs, and listening to students' problems.
Miraculously, students now feel comfortable talking to their principal, enjoy
coming to school and are putting more effort into preparing for the state test.
The assistant principal receives the scores from the practice test. They are still

very low, so Clark sets up a peer tutoring program (even while he tells teachers they are incompetent in the presence of students) to get "everyone involved" in test preparation.

In a Wizard of Oz-like ending, Clark is jailed for insubordination, students take to the streets to protest his incarceration because he is "like a father" to them, the new test scores arrive, the students have passed the test, the school board now sees Clark as a hero, a bright light appears in the dark, and everyone begins to sing the song "Lean on Me." In Oz all is well with the world, and a leadership style that disrespects students, parents, and teachers, is non-collaborative and threatening, and sends messages about how to control Black students is perceived to be a model for effective school leadership.

Discussion

African American leaders in both films worked in "halls of anger." The opening scenes in both films showed schools where teachers, students, and parents were angry about the educational and social conditions of their schools. Additionally, both Davis and Clark were angry about the quality of education Black students received in the large, urban school context. While Clark appeared to be angry at everyone and everything, Davis's anger was directed toward an educational system that continued to under-serve and under-educate those students who needed the most support. Additionally, a key focus in each movie appears to be the anger of Black male students. The troublemakers in both films are Black males who are labeled as nonconformists and unreachable and who should be kicked out of school. Black males as "problems" is a familiar theme in schools today as they are disproportionately placed in special education and represent a significant number of the students who drop out of school (Davis, 2006).

As I have noted, a negotiated reading of a text occurs when the reader recognizes contradictory elements in a text but does not accept all of the elements. I critique the film *Halls of Anger* from a negotiated perspective for several reasons. First, the African American assistant principal is not portrayed as a strict authoritarian who is only concerned with the managerial aspects of schooling at the expense of the needs of teachers and students. Rather, Mr. Davis is portrayed as committed to the emotional, social, and academic achievement of students. Like African American principals in the pre-*Brown* era of schooling and like many African American principals today, Davis resisted ideologies and individuals opposed to the education of Black students. Davis fought to give students opportunities to learn by teaching students to read in after school instruction. He used culturally relevant instruction to teach students the importance of literacy, and he constantly attempted to convey the importance of literacy for Black students to the White principal as well as central office personnel. As the assistant principal, Davis also exhibited interpersonal caring by purposefully attending to the psychological, sociological, and academic needs of his students. As I have noted elsewhere (Tillman 2004), the purposeful adoption of a leadership style "intended to address the needs of Black students is contrary to myths of Black educators as uncaring and as unable or unwilling to relate to Black students, particularly those from low socioeconomic backgrounds" (p. 133).

However, there is an underlying theme in the text of *Halls of Anger* that requires an oppositional reading. There is an assumption in the script that only a Black male can work with underachieving, low SES Black students, and particularly Black males. When Davis tells the superintendent to send a White man to Lafayette, the superintendent rationalizes that the students will benefit more from the same-race and same-culture affiliation of a Black male. The subtext is that the leadership skills of Black males and females are only appropriate in certain contexts—all Black or predominantly Black school contexts. There is an additional subtext that suggests that Black students must be controlled rather than educated, and despite whatever unfortunate circumstances may define their lives, school leaders have no obligation to support, encourage, and provide the best possible education for all students. This deficit perspective of the role of school leaders and the purpose of schooling is a persistent theme in education generally and educational leadership specifically today as Black students continue to be concentrated in schools with the fewest resources, the most uncertified teachers, and the lowest test scores (Darling-Hammond, 2005). Additionally, the limited scope of leadership as portrayed in the film is inconsistent with literature on effective school leadership, which suggests that principals play a key role in facilitating the academic success of *all* students, regardless of race, class, or gender (see e.g., Edmonds, 1979; Hallinger and Heck, 1996; Tillman, 2005; Witziers et al., 2003).

An oppositional reading of a text occurs when the viewer/writer's social location puts him/her in direct opposition with the dominant ideology represented in the text. My social location as a university professor (specializing in educational leadership), experience in the urban school context, and as an

African American considers issues related to teaching, learning, leadership, and race. Additionally, I take issue with the ways that the film *Lean on Me* trivializes the education of African American students.

In the film *Lean on Me*, the African American male principal Joe Clark uses a bully pulpit as a leadership style to "deal with" rather than work with, teachers, students, and parents. From a deficit perspective of educational leadership in a predominantly Black school, the tagline for the film is correct. Joe Clark is a hero. He rides into Eastside High School with a baseball bat and a bullhorn and sets out to restore order and improve test scores through an authoritarian, non-collaborative style of leadership. Unlike the African American principals in Tillman's (2004) review of the literature, same race/cultural affiliation did little to positively affect the social, emotional, and academic lives of Black students at Eastside High. An oppositional reading of the text also results from Clark's contentious and unproductive relationships with students, parents, and teachers. As a leader, Clark uses deficit perspectives to demean those individuals for whom he is responsible. Telling students they are a disgrace to their race, telling parents to get off welfare, and telling teachers they are incompetent represents school leadership from a deficit perspective. That is, rather than exhibiting a caring, nurturing, collaborative, and consensus building form of leadership, Clark used deficit theories about Black students and their parents and viewed teachers as subordinates. The one-dimensional aspect of Clark's leadership is contrary to work by Scheurich (1998), Riester, Pursch, and Skrla (2002), and Tillman (2005) which suggests that principals play a critical role in three areas: the social, emotional, and academic success of students; the personal and professional development of teachers; and the inclusion of key stakeholders such as parents in the decision-making process. Particularly troublesome is the image of a Black male leader as the "bad guy" who uses intimidation as the *only* way to bring about an improved school environment and improved student achievement. Proponents of the movie might argue that Clark exhibited caring forms of leadership because his leadership style appeared to shift from strict authoritarian to something bordering authoritarian/collaborative. However, from an oppositional reading of the text, Joe Clark can be seen as gloating about his success and assuming an "I told you so" attitude toward his questionable accomplishments.

Unlike *Halls of Anger*, the film *Lean on Me* with its feel-good song and message of a no-nonsense approach to teaching, learning, and leadership has had a significant impact on the field of education. Several positive reviews of the Joe Clark story have been written (Burbach and Figgins, 1991; Thomas, 19998; Smith, 1999). He is not only seen as a hero but is admired by students, teachers, parents, and leaders. As I was writing this chapter, I informally queried graduate students and colleagues about their impressions of the film. Surprisingly, the majority of the individuals I spoke with had seen the film multiple times and could recite most of the lines in the film verbatim. Each of these individuals had a favorite line. As a form of popular culture, *Lean on Me* has the power to reinforce negative stereotypes about African Americans generally and African American students and leaders more specifically. As a popular culture medium, its influence has been and continues to be profound. While the movie was made almost twenty years ago, *Lean on Me* has invaded the space of the rational and contributed to inaccurate depictions of teaching, learning, and leadership. The image of Joe Clark as a successful leader who knows how to control students and bring order out of chaos returns us to two of the questions posed by Burbach and Figgins (1991): Why are principals consigned to the part of movie heavies? Why do those who, according to research, play a key role in creating successful schools show up poorly in film?

Smith (1999) in her discussion of *Lean on Me* writes that, "villains come in all occupational shapes and sizes; educators aren't the only foils for film fantasies" (p. 64) and asks should those of us who prepare principals be concerned about their images in film. She concludes that as educators we should be very concerned. Elaborating on this point, she writes,

> I found the language of films increasingly intruding into my work space. Colleagues alluded to Joe Clark, wished they could do what he did, and found emotional release in his victories. Parents increasingly talked the language of basics, of tests, of scores, and of toughness as markers in some undeclared war with educational sloth and adolescent rebellion; they used a language that reflected what I had learned at the movies. Politicians referenced films and films referenced the solitary school heroes most likely to capture the attention of a wide audience and *highly unlikely to function effectively in real settings*. (author emphasis) (p. 64)

Smith's comments are instructive and return us to the central question addressed in this chapter: In what ways does popular culture influence the public's perception of the roles of African American school leaders such as principals and assistant principals? It is unlikely that leaders cut from the Joe Clark mold of intimidation will be effective in today's schools. It is also unlikely that Joe

Clark's leadership style will help us to identify specific dimensions of effective leadership practice. Rather, *Lean on Me* represents a form of escape—an escape from addressing the persistent problems that plague large urban schools and the students that attend them. In the real world of teaching, learning, and leadership, Joe Clark would have to do more than carry a baseball bat and bullhorn to fight for increased funding, recruit and retain highly qualified teachers, and facilitate an educational environment that meets the social, emotional, and academic needs of all children. As Shujaa (1993) has cautioned, Joe Clark would have to do more than make sure students are going to school. Joe Clark would have to make sure that students are getting an education.

Notes

*   I would like to thank my colleague, James Trier, who helped me to decide on the title of this chapter.

1.   The terms African American and Black will be used interchangeably in this chapter.

2.   According to Lomotey (1993), a leader who adopts an ethno-humanist role identity manifests the qualities--commitment to students, compassion for students and their families, and confidence in the intellectual ability of students. The primary goal of a principal who assumes an ethno-humanist role identity is "education"--meeting a set of cultural goals.

References

Banks, C., and Esposito, J. (Summer, 2002). Guns, Prozac, and pedagogy: Representations of teachers on *Boston Public*, the first season. *Educational Studies, 33*(2): 236–245.

Burbach, H. J., and Figgins, M.A. (December, 1991). Screen images of principals: A new vision is needed. *National Association of Secondary School Principals Bulletin,* 52–58.

Dantley, M. E., and Tillman, L.C. (2005). Social justice and moral/transformative leadership. In C. Marshall and M. Oliva (Eds.), *Leadership for social justice: Making revolutions in education.* Allyn & Bacon Publishers, pp. 16–30.

Darling-Hammond, L. (2005). New standards and old reform inequalities: School reform and the education of African American students. In J. King (Ed.), *Black education: A transformative research and action agenda for a new century.* Mahwah, NJ: Lawrence Erlbaum Associates, pp. 197–223.

Davis, J.E. (2006). Research at the margin: Mapping masculinity and mobility of African-American high school dropouts. *International Journal of Qualitative Studies in Education (19)*3, 289-304.

Edmonds, R. (1979). Effective schools for the urban poor. *Educational Leadership*, 37, 15–24.

English, F.W., and Steffy, B.E. (1997). Using film to teach leadership in educational administration. *Educational Administration Quarterly*, 33(1): 107–115.

Gates, S. M., Ringel, J. S., Santibañez, Ross, K.E., and Chung, C.H. (2003). *Who is leading our schools?: An overview of school administrators and their careers.* Arlington, VA: RAND Education.

Glanz, J. (1997). Images of principals on television and in the movies. *Clearing House, 70*(6): 295–298.

Hall, S. (1980). Encoding/decoding. In S. Hall, D. Hobson, A. Lowe, and P. Willis (Eds.), *Culture, media, and language: Working papers in Cultural Studies (1972–1979).* pp. 128–138. London: Unwin Hyman.

Hallinger, P., and Heck, R. H. (1996). Reassessing the principal's role in school effectiveness: A review of empirical research, 1980–1995. *Educational Administration Quarterly*, 32(1): 5–44.

Ladson-Billings, G. (1995). Toward a culturally relevant pedagogy. *American Educational Research Journal*, 32(3): 465–492.

Levine, A. (2005). Educating school leaders. Education Schools Project. Retrieved March 30, 2005 from www.edschools.org

Lomotey, K. (1993). African-American principals: Bureaucrat/administrators and ethno-humanists. *Urban Education*, (27)4: 394–412.

Riester, A. F., Pursch, V., and Skrla, L. (2002). Principals for social justice: Leaders for school success for children from low-income homes. *Journal of School Leadership*, 12: 281–302.

Scheurich, J. J. (1998). Highly successful and loving, public elementary schools populated mainly by low-SES children of color: Core beliefs and cultural characteristics. *Urban Education*, 33(4): 451–491.

Shujaa, M. (1993). *Too much schooling, too little education: A paradox of Black life in White societies.* Trenton, NJ: Africa World Press.

Smith, P. (1999). Sex, lies, and Hollywood's administrators: The (de)construction of school leadership in contemporary films. *Journal of Educational Administration*, 37(1): 50–65.

Thomas, R. A. (1998). As they are portrayed: Principals in film. *International Journal of Educational Management*, 12(2): 90–100.

Tillman, L.C.(2004). African American principals and the legacy of *Brown. Review of Research in Education*, 28: 101–146.

———. (2005). Mentoring new teachers: Implications for leadership practice in an urban school. *Educational Administration Quarterly*, 41(4): 609–629.

———, and Trier, J. (forthcoming). *Boston Public* as public pedagogy. *Peabody Journal of Education.*

Witziers, B., Bosker, R. J., and Krüger, M.L. (2003). Educational leadership and student achievement: The elusive search for an association. *Educational Administration Quarterly*, 39(3): 398–345.

19

Critically Examining Popular Culture Representations of Educators

James Trier

In her article "Leadership for Social Justice and Equity: Weaving a Transformative Framework and Pedagogy," Kathleen Brown (2004) argues that the main goal of educational leadership preparation programs should be to develop "critically reflective" administrators who will have the capacities "for both critical inquiry and self-reflection" (p. 91). Brown defines these two main capacities in this way:

> Critical inquiry involves the conscious consideration of the moral and ethical implications and consequences of schooling practices on students. Self-reflection adds the dimension of deep examination of personal assumptions, values, and beliefs. Critical reflection merges the two terms and involves the examination of personal and professional belief systems, as well as the deliberate consideration of the ethical implications and effect[s] of such practices. (p. 91)

In her theorization of how educational leadership preparation programs can engage students in critically reflective experiences as part of their coursework, Brown proposes "a practical, process-oriented model" (p. 79) based on an "alternative pedagogy" (p. 84) that involves students in a variety of critically reflective "strategies." The specific strategies that Brown discusses are (a) writing cultural autobiographies, (b) conducting life histories of older adults' educational experiences, (c) participating in prejudice reduction workshops, (d) keeping reflective analysis journals, (e) doing cross-cultural interviews, (f) taking educational plunges (by visiting an "educational setting" that is unlike any a student has experienced before), (g) participating on diversity panels, and (h) designing activist action plans. Brown explains that these strategies have the collective potential to bring about "transformative learning" in students through "a process of critical self-reflection" that can stimulate students to challenge their "basic assumptions of the world" (p. 89) and, in particular, of the world of educational leadership. Of course, Brown does not argue that these are the only strategies that can accomplish such transformative learning.

Another "critically reflective" course-related strategy that resonates with those that Brown has recommended is articulated by English and Steffy (1997), a strategy captured by their article title, "Using Film to Teach Leadership in Educational Administration." English and Steffy explain that in teaching graduate courses, they have drawn upon film as a "teaching medium" for the purpose of engaging their students in examining core issues concerning educational leadership. They discuss ten films they have taken up with their students, including *Joan of Arc* (1985), *Malcolm X* (1993), *Patton* (1969), *Gandhi* (1982), and *Nixon* (1995). They argue that the films have served as powerful pedagogical texts for a variety of reasons: the films present "a longitudinal view of a leader and decisions in context," "portray a view of artistry in leadership," "illustrate the connection between the leader's belief and values and action," "depict the relationship between cadres and networking," "depict a leader's moral code," and "show discourse on many levels" (pp. 107–108). Essentially, English and Steffy's pedagogical method was to assign students (1) to view the films outside of class; (2) to respond to a series of prescribed questions; and (3) to discuss the films during seminar. The authors conclude that their practice of incorporating films as pedagogical texts was quite productive: students "evaluated their film experience as some of the most difficult but rewarding experiences they have encountered in their course work." They added, "From an instructor's perspective, the excitement students experience in confronting lifelike portraits of leaders in action is both liberating and rewarding. Films can restore a sense of vibrancy and immediacy to discussions of leadership" (p. 114).

Interestingly, English and Steffy did not include any films that offer representations of educational administrators, films such as those that Penny Smith (1999) analyzes in her article "Sex, Lies, and Hollywood's Administrators: The (De)Construction of School Leadership in Contemporary Films." Smith analyzed twenty-eight "school genre films" (as she called them) that appeared between 1982–1995, films such as *Lean on Me*, *The Principal*, *Teachers*, *Ferris Bueller's Day Off*, *Pump Up the Volume*, and *The Breakfast Club*. By doing close readings of these films, Smith divided the representations of administrators into six categories: the savior, the dupe, the clueless, the opportunist, the supportive father, and the pimp. Smith's main conclusion is that very few, if any, positive images of administrators appear in these films: "We had no collegial, community-building activists. There were no proponents of shared decision-making. School climate was dictated from above, not collaboratively constructed" (p. 52).

This close reading of groups of school films for their representations of administrators has been done a number of times by academics (e.g., see Burbach and Figgins, 1991; Dalton, 2004; Glanz, 1997; Pristash, 2002; Thomas, 1998), and without exception, these analyses produce very similar negative categories of representation and arrive at the same basic conclusion that Smith does. Another shared feature of these articles and book chapters is that the authors typically call on other academics to take seriously these popular representations of administrators. For example, Smith states: "We need to disturb, to trouble these images." Presumably, the "we" to whom Smith is referring are her fellow academics. Smith adds, "We need to find ways to bring a discussion on what they are, what they represent, and how they distort discourses about important policy issues to a table that includes more than cultural theorists." Here, Smith suggests a critique of "cultural theorists," which is that discussions about (and deconstructions of) representations of administrators in films only seem to take place in academic articles written by and for "cultural theorists," whereas other "tables" (i.e., pedagogical locations) at which such discussions should take place are in courses that are part of educational leadership preparation programs, courses comprising future educational leaders. Smith concludes by saying, "And we need to find ways to challenge those images with viable, popular culture alternatives" (pp. 64–65). Smith does not, however, offer any examples of the ways that she has engaged her own students in examining cinematic representations of administrators—nor has anyone else, for that matter (e.g., see see Burbach and Figgins, 1991; Dalton, 2004; Glanz, 1997; Pristash, 2002; Thomas, 1998).

In the rest of this chapter, I would like to begin bridging the gap in the literature concerning representations of administrators in films (the "gap" being an absence of discussion about actual pedagogical projects undertaken to engage educational leadership students in examining representations of "screen" administrators). My main discussion will concern a three-hour seminar workshop that I gave when I was a guest speaker for an educational leadership course. The general purpose of the workshop was to introduce students to popular culture representations of educators, students, and schools, and then specifically to engage the students in critically "reading" the representations of educational leaders in selected popular culture "texts." The culminating activity took place after the workshop in the form of a required assignment for the course. It is important to point out here that the activities comprising this workshop were ones that I designed for different critical projects that I enacted with various cohorts of preservice secondary English teachers in a Master of Arts in Teaching (MAT) program. As I have explained in various articles (which I will refer to later on), these projects unfolded over many seminars (sometimes over two academic semesters), which enabled students to engage more deeply in the activities than is possible through a lone workshop. That said, I will never-theless argue that even this one workshop—which I conceptualize as being like the strategies that Brown (2004) has recommended, as well as like the method of film analysis that English and Steffy (1997) have articulated—seems to have had an important effect on the students' perceptions and thinking.

School Films, Readings, and Texts

The workshop that I gave took place on the third seminar meeting of the fall semester of a course titled "Problems of Educational Leadership." The sixteen students in the course were in their first semester of a Master's in School Administration (MSA) program. The professor of the course (who was not present during the workshop seminar) had informed the students that they would be having a guest speaker, and he assigned them to read an article of mine in preparation for the seminar. The professor also explained that there would be a required essay assignment for the following week (I gave them the prompt), and he also assigned them to email him their "reactions" to the workshop within a day or so of the seminar. He informed the students that he would be printing their reaction emails and giving them to me, and as will be seen here, I quote from these emails as I discuss the various activities that I engaged the students in.

I began the workshop by reviewing some of the main elements of the article that the students had read, titled "School Film 'Videocompilations' as Pedagogi-cal Texts in Preservice Education" (Trier, 2003a). I explained that for years I have been collecting what I call "school films," which I define as films that are in some way, even incidentally, about an educator or a student. Some well-known school films are *Mr. Holland's Opus* (1995), *Breakfast Club* (1985), and *Dangerous Minds* (1995); some lesser-known films are *Drive Me Crazy* (1999) and *Foxfire* (1996); some obscure films are *Zero for Conduct* (1933) and *Torment* (1944); and some recent films are *The Emperor's Club* (2002) and *Elephant* (2003). I have about 120 such films in my collection (see Trier, 2000), and new releases of films appear every year, which I eventually acquire (in an obsessive fashion—see Trier, 2005a).

I then discussed that I have designed a variety of critical projects that involved many of these school films. For example, in one project, I introduced preservice teachers to the concept of "techniques of power" through analyses of the film *The Paper Chase* (1973), analyses informed both by Gore's (1998) articulation of eight "techniques of power" and by certain elements from Foucault's (1977) *Discipline and Punish* (Trier, 2003b). Another project involved problematizing preservice teachers' "autonomous," traditional notions of literacy (Street, 1984) by having them read Gee's (1996) articulation of discourses and multiple literacies, and then having them view the film *Teachers* for its construction of literacy. Through close readings of both the academic and cinematic texts, students challenged the film's assumption that literacy is merely the ability to pass standardized tests, and they opened up to a more sophisticated conceptualization based on Gee's definition of literacy as being the mastery of a secondary discourse (Trier, 2001).

Having given examples of some critical projects that I designed around school films, I next explained that one of my main purposes in the workshop was to invite students to reconceptualize their notions of what constitutes "texts" and "readings." We discussed how the term "text" has traditionally been defined as being print document and how "reading" has traditionally been defined as a process that entails discovering an author's intended meaning in *print* texts. I stated that the workshop was premised on a cultural studies conceptualization of "text" as including not only print texts but also such popular culture "texts" as films (Giroux, 2002; Ryan and Kellner, 1988), television programs (Fiske, 1987; Gause, 2005), music (Grossberg, 1992), photographs and drawings (Joseph and Burnaford, 1994), fashion (Fiske, 1989), and so on. To open up the idea of "reading," I introduced Stuart Hall's (1980) theory of preferred, negotiated, and oppositional readings, which I summarized in my article (Trier, 2003a) in this way:

> An arguably simple explanation of these terms would go like this: A preferred reading is one that a text continually works to achieve through its presences and absences (or silences). Viewers who share the dominant ideologies encoded in a text are likely to see the text as the text sees itself. A negotiated reading is one that recognizes the contradictory elements in a text, that does not accept all the elements that fit a preferred reading, that might read some elements in an oppositional way in part, but that does not read in a totally oppositional way. An oppositional reading is an activation of a text that rejects what a preferred reading accepts, resulting in a reading that can indeed

"read the signs" but refuses to follow their direction. Such readings are attuned to the presences and absences (silences) of a text and "read" from an oppositional ideological ground. (pp. 128–129)

After introducing these definitions of "texts" and "readings," I next engaged students in activities that involved them in reading selected popular culture texts. In the following sections, I will discuss each of these activities, and I will quote some passages from students' "reaction" emails (noted earlier) as examples of the effects that the activities had on students. (As the section headings reveal, each activity involves a different popular culture text and focuses attention on a particular kind of reading, in Hall's sense of reading.)

Preferred Readings and Video Box Covers

Earlier, I mentioned that I have been collecting school films for years. When I buy a school film, however, I come to own more than the video: I also acquire the colored box covers that encase the videos. These video box covers are "secondary texts," which John Fiske (1987) has defined as texts that are spawned by and that surround primary texts. (Examples of other secondary texts of films are critical articles, movie reviews, film trailers, and actor interviews.)

For this two-phase activity, I asked students to form four small groups, and I gave each group a packet of photocopies of the same selection of forty video box covers (i.e., each group had the same materials to work with). For the first phase, I asked the students to analyze the video box covers by focusing only on the nonprint elements of the covers (i.e., they should avoid reading the "fine print" that appeared on the covers), and to categorize the covers according to their visual schemes—that is, by the dominant colors and by the human figures depicted on the covers. (Without explaining it, I was engaging the students in semiotic analyses.) The results of the analyses were the same in each group: the video box covers fell into two unmistakably distinct categories that the students easily identified—based on their familiarity of many of the films—as "inner city" school films and "suburban" school films (or what I like to call "inner suburb" school films). The students found that the inner-city school film covers—for example, *Blackboard Jungle, Stand and Deliver, The Principal, Lean on Me, Dangerous Minds, 187, The Substitute*—are dominated by dark colors, mainly pitch-black and blood red, and they feature male teachers or principals as the central figures, usually in aggressive poses, such as holding a baseball bat, grabbing a male student, or standing behind a desk where an automatic weapon rests. In contrast, the suburb school film covers—for example, *The Breakfast Club*, *Pretty in Pink*, *Fast Times at Ridgemont High*, *Welcome to the Dollhouse*, *Heathers*, *Jawbreakers*, *Clueless*, *Can't Hardly Wait*, and so on—glow with bright reds, greens, purples, blues, and pinks, and the central figures are nearly always young, white teens smiling, holding one another, laughing, kissing, and so on. Another important observation at this point was that there were twice as many suburb school films than the inner city school films.

With the covers grouped into inner city and suburb categories based on their nonprint elements, I next sought to have students consider what the covers revealed about the "genres" that the films fall into. To accomplish this, I asked students to analyze the video box covers again, this time by attending to the print text. What the students discovered was that the suburb films fall into many different genres, ranging from light-hearted romances (*Pretty in Pink*), dark-humor comedies (*Heathers*), celebratory youth-rebellion movies (*Pump Up the Volume*), and spoofs (*High School High*). Most of the covers "read" like what most parents probably hope will be the experience of their teenagers as they pass though school and adolescence—at the very worst, maybe a little naughtiness, maybe some teen angst, or maybe the inevitable trials and tribulations of love break-ups and struggles for popularity. For example, the print text for *Ferris Bueller's Day Off* states that the film is about "a rather magical young man" who "gives into an overwhelming urge to cut school," which leads to a lullaby tale of how "life at 17 can be a joy!" The print text for *Sixteen Candles* states that the film is about "your average teen, enduring creepy freshmen, spoiled siblings, confused parents and the Big Blonde on Campus who stands between her and the boy of her dreams." And the print text for *The Breakfast Club* states that the film is about "five teenage students with nothing in common, faced with spending a Saturday detention together in their high school library."

In contrast, the print text of inner city school films typically describes the films as being serious dramas that often involve violence and death. For example, the students observed how all of the inner city covers have negative descriptions of the schools and students, as with the caption for *The Principal*, which includes this statement: "The Principal: He's teaching the students at Brandel High two words . . . NO MORE" (a slogan that echoes the Reaganite "Just Say No" anti-drug slogan, which had become popular when *The Principal* came out in the 1980s). Another example is the film *The Substitute*. Part of the print text reads: "The Most Dangerous Thing About School Used to Be the

Students." For another film titled *Zebrahead*, the caption reads: "If America is a melting pot, its public schools are a white-hot cauldron of conflict."

So, the students analyzed the print elements of these video box covers in relation to their visual elements to arrive at the tentative conclusion that the inner city school is cinematically represented as a dangerous place where the students are the violent enemy that must be subdued by aggressive adults (who are typically white males). In discussing this activity, I pointed out to the students that along with gaining a relatively immediate insight into the school film genre, they had simultaneously been critically analyzing the (semiotic) *process* through which texts work ideologically to bring about "preferred readings."

In their emails to their professor after the workshop, many students revealed a variety of additional insights related to this video box cover activity. One representative example is from a student who wrote:

> Pop culture has helped us become a society that is bombarded with visual images designed to attract as well as distract us. Everywhere you look, messages are being thrown at us in the form of everything from magazine covers, billboards, commercials, tv shows, to book covers and movies. Learning to question those images rather than passively acknowledge their existence is critical to being more aware of the influence others [i.e., what Horkheimer and Adorno (1972) famously termed "the culture industries"] really try to have on our beliefs and the beliefs of others.

In reading this student's response to the video box cover activity, I was struck by how it resonated with the ideas expressed by Douglas Kellner (1995) in his book *Media Culture*. Kellner develops the argument that the significance of media culture texts is that,

> our current local, national, and global situations are articulated through the texts of media culture, which is itself a contested terrain, one which competing social groups attempt to use to promote their agendas and ideologies, and which itself reproduces conflicting political discourses, often in a contradictory manner. Not just news and information, but entertainment and fiction articulate the conflicts, fears, hopes, and dreams of individuals and groups confronting a turbulent and uncertain world. The concrete struggles of each society are played out in the texts of media culture, especially in the commercial media of the culture industries which produce texts that must resonate with people's concerns if they are to be popular and profitable. Culture has never been more important and never before have we had such a need for serious scrutiny of contemporary culture. (p. 20)

My intent here in juxtaposing Kellner's insight with the student's own insight is to suggest that even through a single seminar activity (or "strategy"), students can be engaged to articulate insights that capture, in their own language, the "high theory" insights expressed by academic figures like Kellner. And I think it's a missed pedagogical opportunity not to tap into that pre-existing knowledge and interest.[1]

An Oppositional Reading through a "Videocollage" of *Lean on Me*

In the next activity, I gave an example of an oppositional reading to a text. The text was a school film that most of the students had seen before: *Lean on Me*, arguably among the most famous (or infamous) "principal"-based school films ever made.

I first focused students' attention on the video box cover, which articulates through its imagery and print elements an unmistakable "preferred reading" for the film. On the front side, a quote from a movie critic reads, "It's the 'feel-good' movie of the year." On the back side, there is a photo of the actor Morgan Freeman holding a bullhorn and behind him stands the real-life principal he portrays, Joe Clark, dressed in a white suit and holding a baseball bat. How the film prefers us to read it is signified by the print text that accompanies the photo of Freeman/Clark:

> An extraordinary situation calls for an extraordinary leader. At strife-torn Eastside High School, that leader was Joe Clark. *Lean on Me* is the rousing, fact-based story of high school principal Joe Clark, who armed himself with a bullhorn and a Louisville Slugger and slammed the door on losers at Eastside High School in Paterson, New Jersey. Brought in as a last hope to save the school, he chained the doors shut to keep trouble-makers *out* and strivers *in*. Parents fought him. Teachers fought him. But lots of kids loved him. Clark turned Eastside around, becoming a national symbol of tough-love education and appearing on the cover of *Time*.

One more element of the print text includes a quote from the film: "'If you students don't succeed in life,' says Clark, 'I want you to blame yourselves.' His message is simple: Don't learn excuses. Don't lean on drugs, crime, or anger. *Lean on Me*...and learn."

I next explained to the students that, on my own admittedly oppositional reading of the film, the most ideologically problematic message of the film crystallizes in the very scene from which Clark's "I want you to blame yourselves" quote is lifted. To set up my oppositional reading of this scene (and the film as a whole), I first played the scene on video for the students.

In the scene, Clark, dressed as always in a white suit, is on the stage of the school's assembly hall. Behind him are dozens of students, most of whom are

African American. In the audience are hundreds more students, nearly all African Americans. Clark holds a microphone and faces the students seated in the hall, explaining that the students on stage are drug dealers and users, and that because they "are incorrigible," they are being "expurgated…forever" from the school. At this point, what seems to be two dozen plainclothes security officers (all African American) swiftly remove all the students by physical force from the stage. Moments later, Joe Clark is alone on stage. When the verbal commotion among the seated students dies down, Clark addresses them with a warning and a declaration:

> Next time, it may be you. If you do no better than they did, next time it *will* be you. They said this school was dead, like the cemetery it's built on. But we call our Eastside teams "ghosts," don't we? And what are ghosts? Ghosts are spirits that *rise* from the dead. *I* want you to be *my* ghosts. You are going to *lead* our resurrection by denying expectations that all of us are *doomed* to failure. *My* motto is simple. If you do not *succeed* in life, I don't want you to *blame* your parents! I don't want you to *blame* the *white* man! I *want* you to *blame yourselves*! The responsibility is *yours*!

I explained to the students that though I find Clark's "blame the victim" rhetoric and tone quite problematic, what I find more problematic is the philosophy of personal agency that Clark implies in this "My motto is simple" speech. On my reading, Clark commands his students not to look for any outside sources to understand the circumstances of their lives. To do so is to play with fire because such searches for causes may tempt one to attribute "blame," and for Clark, to "blame" is to fail in one's interpretation of one's life experiences. In a "fighting fire with fire" internal action, Clark implies that the way to ward off such a temptation to blame others is to internalize the impulse and blame ourselves. This is the supreme—and simple—form of agency for Clark. (In a chapter, I would develop an in-depth analysis of the problematic elements of this scene.)

To challenge Clark's philosophy of agency, I engaged in the critical pedagogical act of making a "videocollage," which I define as a video comprising strategically juxtaposed scenes from a variety of video sources. This videocollage became a counter-text to be read against the figure represented by Joe Clark in the film. One feature of this videocollage is that Clark's "My motto is simple" proclamations are juxtaposed with scenes from various sources, such as documentaries, news stories, other films, and television programs. Another feature is that Clark's "blame" speech is taken apart and reassembled in varying ways to highlight the problematic nature of what he says. Here is one example of such a reassemblage (the dashes signal when a "cut" has been made, and the italicization signifies emphasis placed on particular words):

CLARK: *My* motto is simple—
    I want you to blame *yourselves!*
    If you do not *succeed* in life—
    I want you to blame *yourselves!*—
    blame *yourselves!*
    My motto is—
    Blame *yourselves!*

Throughout the videocollage, about two dozen such reassemblages are tactically juxtaposed with clips from a variety of sources for the purpose of challenging Clark's "blame" message. The videocollage is far too long and multilayered to describe entirely (the transcript of the videocollage runs over 2,000 words). Instead, I will describe two representative (if rather short) sequences that capture the spirit, form, and content of the whole. The source material for these examples is the series *Eyes on the Prize*. The first jump cut of this segment occurs at the end of the scene from *Lean on Me* described above.

[1]

  CLARK: "*My* motto is simple. If you do not *succeed* in life, I don't
    want you to *blame* your parents! I don't want you to *blame*
    the *white* man! I *want* you to *blame yourselves!* The responsi-
    bility is *yours!*"

[2]

  Clip from *Eyes on the Prize*: The sequence of images includes a sign
on school grounds that reads **NO TRESPASSING/BY ORDER
OF THE SCHOOL BOARD,** rows of immobile school buses,
locks on the doors of a chain-link fence surrounding a school. We hear
the narrator's accompanying voice (uninflected in its tones) speaking
about the governor of Virginia at the time (1960): "Governor Almond
closed schools in Charlottesville, in Norfolk, and other towns, and he
called for unyielding rejection of integration."

  [The accompanying images of African American children and adults
  sitting in a courtroom, with white lawyers and spectators on one side
    and African Americans on the other.]

"The federal courts were also unyielding, ruling again and again that this resistance was unconstitutional. But while the court cases were fought, the schools stayed closed, and the children—especially the black children—paid the price."

[Image of a car pulling up to the entrance of a school. When it stops, two adult white males and a small black child get out of the car.]

"So the crisis in school desegregation continued. In the fall of 1960 in New Orleans, four little girls were sent to first grade in white schools."

[The men are on each side of the girl as they ascend the school steps. One man opens the door, and the girl enters the school first, followed by the men.]

"It caused a city-wide riot."

[3]

      CLARK: "If you do not *succeed* in life—
             I don't want you to *blame* the *white* man!—
             If you do not *succeed* in life—
             I *want* you to *blame yourselves*!"

[4]

Clip from *Eyes on the Prize*: The scene is a city street, and the images are of the tyrannical Police Chief Bull Connor barking directives at his white police officers and firemen amid a gathering of hundreds of peaceful black demonstrators on the sidewalk. The narrator's accompanying voice-over is: "The confrontation moved outside the park. Once again, Bull Connor summoned his firemen. With no place to run, no trees for protection, the demonstrators were hit with the full force of the water."

[Imagery of firemen blasting massive streams of water full-force from fire hoses as defenseless black men, women, and children are slammed into the sides of buildings or blown off their feet to the pavement.]

[5]

    CLARK: *"My* motto is simple.

               I *want* you to *blame yourselves!"*

As mentioned, the videocollage is much longer than what I have presented here, and after we viewed it in its entirety, the students and I discussed how the videocollage challenges Clark's "blame the victim" speech. In their emails about the workshop, many students discussed the effect that the videocollage had on them, and one student summarized what took place during the workshop after the class had viewed the videocollage. He wrote that the class,

> discussed in great detail the pros and cons of Joe Clark's choice of words as he attempts to bring about change in the school…The majority of the class felt that Joe Clark's speech was insensitive and strengthened the "blame the victim" mentality. Others felt Joe Clark was merely attempting to encourage and motivate his students to take ownership of their education. This conversation then transformed itself into a cultural awareness discussion. Many felt that in order to speak so frankly with the students and community, the leader must be from the same racial and cultural background.

Interestingly, this student's summary articulates perfectly with some of the critical strategies that Brown recommends that educational leadership professors can engage their students in for critically transformative purposes. For example, the student's references to "cultural awareness" and "cultural background" call to mind Brown's strategies of writing cultural autobiographies, participating in prejudice reduction workshops, doing cross-cultural interviews, taking educational plunges, and participating on diversity panels. I can imagine that the two activities/strategies that I have discussed thus far might serve as introductory strategies that could persuade students of the need for them to engage in the other strategies.

Negotiated Readings and *Boston Public*

The culminating two-part activity that I discuss here began during the seminar workshop and carried on afterward. The first part involved introducing the television series *Boston Public* to the students and reviewing the idea of "negotiated readings," and the second part entailed having students view an episode of the series and write an essay that articulates their experience of viewing the episode. The main purpose of the activity was to discover if the students would find "reading" this particular popular culture text interesting and pedagogically valuable, and if so, in what way?

I introduced the series *Boston Public* to the students by explaining that it was an hour-long television drama that was broadcast on the Fox Network (and lives on in reruns and on DVDs). The pilot for the program aired on October 23, 2000, and during the next four years eighty-one episodes of the program were aired, all of which I recorded on videotape. In a typical episode, much of the action takes place within Winslow High, an urban school in Boston, though the plot does occasionally situate teachers, administrators, and students outside of school. The main dramatic focus is on the principal, the vice principal, and a group of teachers, and though many students appear in each episode, most of the plots are concerned with the desires, thoughts, emotions, struggles, successes, failures, misjudgments, challenges, and disappointments of the administrators and teachers. During the four seasons of the program, many of the teacher characters were replaced with new characters, but the principal and vice principal characters remained constant. *Boston Public* won Black Entertainment Television Network's Image Award after its first season, and there was an almost equal casting of black and white main characters. The principal is black and the vice principal is white (both are males), and the staff of teachers comprises both blacks and whites.

I next explained that one main feature of *Boston Public* is that there are no slow, dull days at this television high school—slow, dull days don't translate into high ratings—and the program has at times necessarily been unrealistic, "over the top," and in some instances simply absurd. The main way this aspect of the program has played itself out is in how, during every episode, many crises of a violent, sexual, or life-and-death nature typically take place—more crises in one school day than typically visit a "real" school during an entire academic year. I also explained, however, that another main feature of *Boston Public* is that the series has dealt quite realistically with a plethora of important educational issues that have also been addressed in academic literature on education, as well as by the news media. For example, there have been episodes about budget cuts, standardized testing, teacher certification (or alternative routes into teaching), cheating on tests, gay-bashing among students, sexual relations between teachers and students, bullying, violence in school, the use of Ritalin, and literally dozens of other issues relevant to education.

I also explained, however, that another main feature of *Boston Public* is that the series has dealt quite realistically with a plethora of important educational issues that have also been addressed in academic literature on education, as well as by the news media. I then showed the students a videocompilation comprising pivotal scenes from many episodes (including scenes from the episodes mentioned above). Near the end of the workshop, I loaned each student a video from my collection of *Boston Public*. The students had different episodes of the program to view, and I asked them to write essays in response to the following prompt, which offers a range of interpretive/analytical strategies that would likely involve students in engaging in "negotiated readings":

> For your essay, you are to view the episode of *Boston Public* and then write a three-page (double-spaced) paper (longer is fine) in which you react to one or more of the various storylines or situations that involve either the principal or the vice principal. Some suggestions for what I mean by "react to" would include: relating some element of the episode to your own experiences; relating some element to issues discussed in your coursework (seminars, readings, discussions) in the Education Leadership program; focusing on the leadership styles of the principal and the vice principal; focusing on the relationships that the principal and vice principal have with one another, with teachers, with students, with parents, with school board members, with a superintendent, etc.; "agreeing" with how a situation was represented in the episode; "disagreeing" with how a situation was represented; and/or discussing both the realistic and the unrealistic elements in the episode. Of course, you will likely engage in a combination of the above interpretive strategies, thereby producing negotiated readings of the episode.

I also asked students to end their essays by writing an explanation about what the experience was like for them to have had a seminar about "popular culture" representations of educators, and what their experience had been in taking up an episode of *Boston Public* for analysis. I posed these suggestive questions: "Has it caused you to think about anything that you hadn't been thinking about? Has it added a new lens to your thinking? Has it been somewhat interesting but not really all that meaningful or relevant (it's certainly fine to say so, if this is what you think!)?" I ended the seminar by informing the students that I would read and respond to their essays within a week of receiving them.

A week after the workshop, I received the students' essays about the *Boston Public* episodes. One discovery that I made through analyzing and responding to the essays was that most of the students discussed many or all of the interrelated elements that I had incorporated into the essay prompt (see above), and they did so by discussing the elements in relation to one another, as in this passage (in brackets, I point out the element from the prompt that is addressed):

> Our various educational leadership classes have been guiding us in the development of our leadership styles [*refers to coursework and the particular issue of leadership style*]. As a prin-

cipal, Steven Harper has a very direct leadership style that is full of emotion and passion [*identifies major features of the principal's leadership style*]. His emotion and passion are what many admire in him [*grants that such a style is agreeable to some teachers*], but they are also a detriment [*begins developing a critique of the principal's leadership style*]. In a time of crisis, Steven isn't well known for maintaining a level head, and it directly influences his staff. His outward display of uncertainty over the budget and the future of teachers' jobs caused his staff to feel on the edge and tense. It also prevented him from being able to rationally mediate disagreements between his two vice principals, Ronnie and Scott [*identifies two situations in which the principal's decision-making process failed as a result of his leadership style, and the failure concerned his own relations with teachers as well as the relations between his two vice-principals*].

Another general discovery that I made through analyzing and responding to the essays was that, with a few exceptions, the students produced negotiated readings of their episodes. In other words, they agreed with the administrative style and decision making of an administrator in some instances but not in others; or they found some aspects of the episodes realistic, though they found other aspects unrealistic. For example, one student discussed a situation in his episode about a budget crisis. In the scenario, Principal Harper must drastically reduce the school budget, and as part of the process he informs his teachers that he will have to fire many of them. Here is a passage from the student's discussion of this scenario:

> The budget crisis in the episode was a likely occurrence. Budget deficiencies are commonplace today in schools and administrators receive inconsistent, untimely questions about money from the central office or even state officials. However, in this episode a few of the reactions to the budge crisis seemed unrealistic...If a teacher has a job in a system and is completely qualified for the job, it proves difficult to terminate employment simply to save money. They may be moved to another school or given another job, but they cannot be simply fired on the spot. The [principal's] suggestion then to fire teachers seemed outlandish.

Though I have given a few examples here of the ways students read their episodes of *Boston Public*, it is not possible—nor has it been my intention—to present a full discussion of the particularities of the students' readings (such a discussion will have to find another venue). What I am mainly interested in (as mentioned above) is whether the students found "reading" *Boston Public* to be enjoyable and pedagogically valuable. What I found was that nearly all of the students expressed having enjoyed the workshop seminar and finding the assignment of analyzing an episode of *Boston Public* quite worthwhile, which I can suggest through this representative passage:

> I thoroughly enjoyed the [workshop] seminar....The process of using video compilations as a springboard for discussion and personal reflection seems to be a very productive alternative to the read-summarize model often employed in education courses. Simply summarizing someone else's findings never gets to the core of the reader's belief systems or potential actions that may result from reading a text. I also think that the use of pop culture is appealing. Pop culture has helped us become a society that is bombarded with visual images designed to attract as well as distract us. Everywhere you look, messages are being thrown at us in the form of everything from magazine covers, billboards, commercials, tv shows, to book covers and movies. Learning to question those images rather than passively acknowledge their existence is critical to being more aware of the influence others really have on our beliefs and the beliefs of others.

Concluding Remarks

In a key passage from the introduction to this book, Carlson and Gause state that "the critique and deconstruction of dominant discourses, narratives, and images of educational leadership" is important for educators (p. ?). The activities in the workshop I have discussed here collectively had the very purposes that Carlson and Gause articulate. In each activity, a popular culture text that constructs a representation of an educator became the focus of students' deconstructive readings. In particular, the videocollage of *Lean on Me* served as an example of how a problematic cinematic narrative of educational leadership was reworked to become a counter-narrative with a more democratic promise about social agency. Also, the students' engagements with *Boston Public* offered them opportunities both to deconstruct problematic narratives and representations of educational leadership and to articulate their own visions of democratic decision making and leadership styles. Also, as I stated at the beginning, I conceptualize this workshop as being like the strategies that Brown (2004) has recommended, as well as like the method of film analysis that English and Steffy (1997) have articulated. My "preferred reading" of this chapter would be that it offers a strategy of engagement, grounded in theory, that preparers of future educational leaders can adopt in their own pedagogical contexts.

Notes

1. See Trier (2003c) for a discussion of videocollages, and Trier (2004) for a detailed discussion of how I have theorized this particular *Lean on Me* videocollage in terms of the critical artistic practice of "detournement" (Debord and Wolman, 1956), a theory/practice engaged in by an avant garde group known as "the Situationists," a group that formed in 1957 and dissolved in 1969 (see Plant, 1992).

References

Brown, K. (2004). Leadership for social justice and equity: Weaving a transformative framework and pedagogy. *Educational Administrative Quarterly*, 40(1): 79–110.

Burbach, H., and Figgins, M. (1991). Screen images of principals—A new vision is needed. *NASSP Bulletin*, 75(539): 52–58.

Dalton, M. (2004). *The Hollywood curriculum: Teachers in the movies*. New York: Peter Lang. [See chapter 7: "It's a control thing: The role of principals in the movies."]

Debord, G., and Wolman, G. (1956). Methods of detournement. In K. Knabb (Ed.), Situationist international anthology. Berkeley, CA: Bureau of Public Secrets, p. 8-14.

English, F., and Steffy, B. (1997). Using film to teach leadership in educational administration. *Educational Administration Quarterly*, 33(1): 107–115.

Fiske, J. (1987). *Television culture*. London: Methuen.

———. (1989). *Understanding popular culture*. New York: Routledge.

Foucault, M. (1977). *Discipline and punish: The birth of the prison*. New York: Random House.

Gause, C. P. (2005). Navigating stormy seas: Critical perspectives on the intersection of popular culture and educational leader-"ship." *Journal of School Leadership*, 15(3): 333–342.

Gee, J. (1996). *Social linguistics and literacies: Ideology in discourses*. Bristol, PA: Falmer Press.

Giroux, H. (2002). *Breaking in to the movies: Film and the culture of politics*. Malden, MA: Blackwell Publishers.

Glanz, J. (1997). Images of principals on television and in the movies. *Clearing House*, 70(6): 295–297.

Gore, J. (1998). Disciplining bodies: On the continuity of power relations in pedagogy. In T. Popkewitz and M. Brennan (Eds.), *Foucault's challenge: Discourse, knowledge, and power in education*. New York: Teachers College Press, p. 231–251.

Grossberg, L. (1992). *We gotta get out of this place: Popular conservatism and postmodern culture*. New York: Routledge.

Hall, S. (1980). Encoding/decoding. In S. Hall, D. Hobson, A. Lowe, and P. Willis (Eds.), *Culture, media, language*. London: Unwin Hyman, p. 128–138.

Horkheimer, M., and Adorno, T. (1972). *Dialectic of enlightenment*. New York: Seabury.

Joseph, P., and Burnaford, G. (1994). *Images of schoolteachers in twentieth-century America: Paragons, polarities, complexities*. New York: St. Martin's Press.

Kellner, D. (1995). *Media culture: Cultural studies, identity and politics between the modern and the postmodern.* London: Routledge.

Plant, S. (1992). *The most radical gesture: The Situationist International in a postmodern age.* London: Routledge.

Pristash, S. (2002). *What people think principals do.* Lanham, MD: Scarecrow Press.

Ryan, M., and Kellner, D. (1988). *Camera politica: The politics and ideology of contemporary Hollywood film.* Indianapolis: Indiana University Press.

Smith, P. (1999). Sex, lies, and Hollywood's administrators: The (de)construction of school leadership in contemporary films. *Journal of Educational Administration,* 37(1): 50–65.

Street, B. (1984). *Literacy in theory and practice.* Cambridge: Cambridge University Press.

Thomas, A. R. (1998). As they are portrayed: Principals in film. *International Journal of Educational Management,* 12(2): 90–100.

Trier, J. (2000). Using popular school films to engage student teachers in critical reflection. Paper presented at the Annual Meeting of the American Educational Research Association, New Orleans, LA (ERIC Document Reproduction Service No. ED 44499993).

———. (2001). Challenging the cinematic construction of "literacy" with preservice teachers. *Teaching Education,* 12(3): 301–314.

———. (2003a). School film "videocompilations" as pedagogical texts in preservice education. *Journal of Curriculum Theorizing,* 19(1): 125–147.

———. (2003b). Inquiring into "techniques of power" with preservice teachers through the "school film" *The Paper Chase. Teaching and Teacher Education,* 19(5): 543–557.

———. (2003c). Designing school film "videocollages" as pedagogical texts in preservice education. *Taboo: The Journal of Culture and Education,* 7(1): 31–46.

———. (2004). Detournement as pedagogical praxis. *Journal of Thought,* 39(4): 35–52.

———. (2005a). Pedagogy of the obsessed. *Journal of Adolescent and Adult Literacy,* 49(3): 238–241.

———. (2005b). "Sordid Fantasies": Reading popular culture "inner-city" school films as racialized texts with pre-service teachers. *Race, Ethnicity and Education,* 8(2): 171–189.

Contributors

Kathleen Knight Abowitz is an associate professor in the Department of Educational Leadership at Miami University. She teaches undergraduate social foundations and graduate philosophy of education courses, and her scholarship employs political theory and educational philosophy to address questions of community, citizenship, and the "public" of public education.

Michael W. Apple is the John Bascom Professor of Curriculum and Instruction and Educational Policy Studies at the University of Wisconsin, Madison. His recent books include: *Educating the "Right" Way: Markets, Standards, God, and Inequality* (second edition, 2006), *The Subaltern Speak: Curriculum, Power, and Educational Struggles* (editor, 2006), and *Democratic Schools* (co-authored with James Beane, second edition, 2007).

Jackie M. Blount is professor of Historical, Comparative, and Philosophical Studies in Education at Iowa State University. Her work has been published in the *Harvard Educational Review, Review of Educational Research*, and *Educational Administration Quarterly*. She also has written *Destined to Rule the Schools* (1998) and *Fit to Teach: Same-Sex Desire, Gender, and School Work in the Twentieth Century* (2004).

Dennis Carlson is a professor in the Department of Educational Leadership and the Center for Education and Cultural Studies at Miami University. He has published widely in educational journals and is the author of several books, including most recently *Leaving Safe Harbors: Toward a New Progressivism in American Education and Public Life* (2002). He also has co-edited a number of books, most recently (with Greg Dimitriadis) *Promises to Keep: Cultural Studies, Democratic Education, and Public Life* (2003). Currently, he is president of the American Educational Studies Association.

Lori Chajet is a doctoral student in the Urban Education program at the CUNY Graduate Center. Her research interests include public small school reform and race, class, and persistence in higher education. Formerly a public school teacher, she has continued to be involved with the development of small schools in New York City.

Joanne Chesley, is an assistant professor at the University of North Carolina at Greensboro. She received her Ed.D. in Educational Leadership from the University of North Carolina at Chapel Hill. Her research interests center around Culturally Relevant Leadership (with a focus on the role of the principal).

Camille Wilson Cooper is an assistant professor in the Department of Educational Leadership and Cultural Foundations at the University of North Carolina-Greensboro. Her scholarly interests relate to race, culture and equity in school reform, school-family partnerships, social justice education, and feminist theory.

Michael E. Dantley is a professor in the Department of Educational Leadership and the Interim Associate Dean of the School of Education and Allied Professions at Miami University, Oxford, Ohio. His research interests are in educational leadership, spirituality, and social justice. He is the past president of the University Council for Educational Administration and is the editor of the *Journal of Cases in Educational Leadership*.

Michelle Fine, distinguished professor of Social Psychology, Women's Studies and Urban Education at the Graduate Center, CUNY, has taught at CUNY since 1990. Her recent publications include, *Working Method: Social Research and Social Injustice* (with Lois Weis, 2004).

Stephanie A. Flores-Koulish is an assistant professor of Curriculum and Instruction. Her research centers on media literacy, critical literacy, and social justice education. She recently founded Loyola's "Putting Justice in Education" speaker series.

Rochelle Garner is an assistant professor of Organizational Leadership in the Department of Educational Leadership at Wright State University. She is the author of *Contesting the Terrain of the Ivory Tower: Spiritual Leadership of African-American Women in the Academy* (2004).

Charles P. Gause, a former elementary teacher and K-12 school administrator, is currently an assistant professor of educational administration in the Department of Educational Leadership and Cultural Foundations at the University of North Carolina-Greensboro. He recently was guest editor of a special issue of the

Journal of School Leadership on *"Edu-tainment,"* and has published articles on youth, identity, and popular culture.

Glenn M. Hudak, is a professor and program coordinator of the Cultural Foundations of Education Program, University of North Carolina-Greensboro. He has co-edited two books, the latest (with Paul Kihn) *Labeling: politics and pedagogy* (2001). Recently, he was guest editor for the *Journal of School Leadership* special issue: *School Leadership and Spirituality: A Critical Dialogue* (November 2005).

Lauri Johnson is an associate professor in the Department of Educational Leadership and Policy at the State University of New York at Buffalo. A former administrator with the New York City Public Schools, she is a co-editor of *Urban Education with an Attitude* (2005) and *Multicultural Education Policies in Canada and the United States* (2006).

Catherine A. Lugg is an associate professor of education, in the Department of Theory, Policy and Administration at the Graduate School of Education, Rutgers University. Her research interests include the politics of education and educational policy, history of education, queer theory, and queer legal theory.

Peter McLaren is professor of Urban Education, Graduate School of Education and Information Studies, University of California Los Angeles and a member of the Industrial Workers of the World. He is the author and editor of over forty books, and his writings have been translated into 17 languages. His latest book is *Rage and Hope* (2006).

Richard A. Quantz is a professor in the Department of Educational Leadership at Miami University. His area of scholarship is social theory and education with which he tackles many different areas in education including educational leadership.

Ulrich C. (Rick) Reitzug is professor and chair in the Department of Educational Leadership at the University of North Carolina at Greensboro. He has published numerous articles and book chapters, dealing primarily with topics of principal leadership, democratic schooling, and school renewal and has been involved with school improvement efforts in a number of states.

Kate Rousmaniere is a historian of education and professor in the Department of Educational Leadership at Miami University. She is the author of *City Teachers: Teaching and School Reform in Historical Perspective* (1997), and *Citizen Teacher: The Life and Leadership of Margaret Haley* (2005).

Valerie Scatamburlo-D' Annibale, an award-winning author and educator, is an associate professor in the Department of Communication Studies at the University of Windsor in Ontario, Canada. Her most recent publications include "The New P.C.: Patriotic Correctness and the Suppression of Dissent on American Campuses," in *Bound by Power: Intended Consequences* (Ed. J. Klaehn, 2006).

Juha Suoranta is a professor of Adult Education at the University of Tampere (Finland). His research interests include radical adult education and critical media education. Recently he has co-edited (with Olli-Pekka Moisio) *Education and the Spirit of Time* (Sense, 2006).

Linda C. Tillman is an associate professor in the Educational Leadership Program at the University of North Carolina at Chapel Hill. Her research interests include leadership theory, the education of *all* children, particularly African Americans in K-12 and post secondary education; mentoring African American teachers, administrators, and faculty; and, the use of racially and culturally sensitive qualitative research approaches. Dr. Tillman is vice president of Division A of the American Educational Research Association.

James Trier is an assistant professor at the Unversity of North Carolina at Chapel Hill, where he teaches cultural studies and English Education courses. His teaching and research interests involve investigating critical methods to engage preservice teachers in theoretical explorations of various important educational issues by considering—simultaneously, in juxtaposition—academic and popular culture texts.

Leila E. Villaverde is an associate professor of Cultural Foundations in the Department of Educational Leadership and Cultural Foundations and the director of Undergraduate Studies in Women's and Gender Studies at the University of North Carolina, Greensboro. Her research areas: curriculum studies, cultural studies, feminist theory, aesthetics, social foundations of art, and critical pedagogy. She has published numerous articles and book chapters.

Index

Studies in the Postmodern Theory of Education

General Editors
Joe L. Kincheloe & Shirley R. Steinberg

Counterpoints publishes the most compelling and imaginative books being written in education today. Grounded on the theoretical advances in criticalism, feminism, and postmodernism in the last two decades of the twentieth century, Counterpoints engages the meaning of these innovations in various forms of educational expression. Committed to the proposition that theoretical literature should be accessible to a variety of audiences, the series insists that its authors avoid esoteric and jargonistic languages that transform educational scholarship into an elite discourse for the initiated. Scholarly work matters only to the degree it affects consciousness and practice at multiple sites. Counterpoints' editorial policy is based on these principles and the ability of scholars to break new ground, to open new conversations, to go where educators have never gone before.

For additional information about this series or for the submission of manuscripts, please contact:

Joe L. Kincheloe & Shirley R. Steinberg
c/o Peter Lang Publishing, Inc.
29 Broadway, 18th floor
New York, New York 10006

To order other books in this series, please contact our Customer Service Department:

(800) 770-LANG (within the U.S.)
(212) 647-7706 (outside the U.S.)
(212) 647-7707 FAX

Or browse online by series:
www.peterlang.com